| READING |

| Basic | Intermediate | Advanced | Expert |

| LISTENING |

| Basic | Intermediate | Advanced | Expert |

Informative passages

HACKERS APEX LISTENING includes informative and interesting listening passages on a variety of academic topics and everyday situations in a university setting.

Useful online study materials

HACKERS APEX LISTENING provides access to quality online study materials at HackersBook.com. These include streaming audio recordings of all passages accessible through QR codes in the book.

HACKERS

APEX
LISTENING

for the
TOEFL iBT®

Expert

HACKERS

Preface

Preface

Thank you for purchasing *HACKERS APEX LISTENING for the TOEFL iBT Expert*. The TOEFL iBT is a highly challenging exam, so it is important to select an effective study guide. All of us at Hackers Language Research Institute are confident that this publication will be an invaluable resource as you prepare for the TOEFL iBT.

HACKERS APEX LISTENING for the TOEFL iBT is a series of comprehensive study guides for students planning to take the TOEFL iBT or for those wanting to improve their general English listening skills. This series includes four books that progress in difficulty. Students can begin at the level that matches their current abilities and then move on to the higher ones. All of the books in this series provide step-by-step question-solving strategies for every TOEFL question type. These are based on thorough research and years of instructional experience. Each book also includes informative and interesting listening passages that enable students to improve their English listening skills and familiarize them with academic topics and spoken English used in everyday university settings. Furthermore, students will receive access to quality online study materials that are designed to help them get the most out of the books in this series. Key features of *HACKERS APEX LISTENING for the TOEFL iBT* books include:

- Detailed explanations and question-solving strategies for all TOEFL Listening question types
- A large number of high-quality TOEFL Listening passages and questions
- Two full-length TOEFL Listening tests
- Dictation exercises to enhance listening comprehension ability
- Vocabulary exercises to review essential vocabulary that appeared in the passages
- An answer book with complete scripts, Korean translations, and lists of key vocabulary
- Access to streaming audio recordings of all passages through QR codes
- Access to supplementary study materials online (www.HackersBook.com)

Thank you again for choosing *HACKERS APEX LISTENING for the TOEFL iBT Expert*, and we wish you all the best whether you are preparing to take the TOEFL iBT in the near future or simply hoping to develop your English listening skills overall.

Table of Contents

How to Use This Book

1 Understand the Question Type

Each chapter includes an Overview page that provides essential information about the featured question type and key strategies for answering it. Make sure you fully understand the strategies before moving on to the Example section, where you can apply the key strategies to short conversation and lecture passages with one question each.

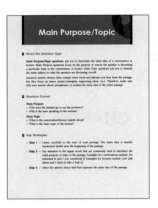

2 Improve Your Skills with Listening Practice Exercises

Each chapter includes four Listening Practice exercises, which consist of two conversation and two lecture passages. These will help you become more familiar with the featured question type, as well as other question types. Each exercise is accompanied by a dictation section so that you can enhance your listening comprehension ability.

3 Take the iBT Listening Tests

Each chapter includes two iBT Listening Tests, which consist of longer conversation and lecture passages with 5 to 6 questions each that are similar to those that appear on the TOEFL iBT. Taking these tests will enable you to improve your listening comprehension skills and prepare for the TOEFL iBT.

4 Review Essential Vocabulary

At the end of each chapter is a Vocabulary Review, which includes questions on essential vocabulary from the chapter. You will be able to easily memorize the vocabulary words through various types of questions.

5 Evaluate Your Progress with Actual Tests

The book includes two Actual Tests, which are full-length listening tests that include passages and questions that closely match what appears on the TOEFL iBT. They provide an excellent opportunity to apply the skills you have learned and evaluate your progress.

6 Check the Answer Book

The Answer Book specifies the correct answer choice for all questions and provides complete scripts and Korean translations of all passages and questions. It also includes a list of key vocabulary words from each passage with definitions.

About the TOEFL iBT

What Is the TOEFL iBT?

The TOEFL (Test of English as a Foreign Language) iBT (Internet-Based test) includes Reading, Listening, Speaking, and Writing sections to comprehensively assess English ability. Although most tasks require the application of only one of these skills, some require the use of two or more. The TOEFL iBT is designed to measure a student's capacity to use and understand English at a university level and is, therefore, much more difficult than many other English proficiency tests.

TOEFL iBT Structure

Section	No. of passages and questions	Time (min.)	Score	Notable Features
Reading	• 3-4 Passages • 10 Questions/Passage	54-72	30	• Each passage is approximately 700 words long.
Listening	• 2-3 Conversations • 5 Questions/Conversation • 3-4 Lectures • 6 Questions/Lecture	41-57	30	• Speakers have various accents, including American, British, Australian, etc.
10-minute break				
Speaking	• 1 Independent Task • 3 Integrated Tasks	17	30	• Independent Tasks ask you to state your opinion about a specific topic. • Integrated Tasks ask you to provide a response based on reading and listening content.
Writing	• 1 Integrated Task • 1 Independent Task	50	30	• Integrated Tasks ask you to provide a response based on reading and listening content. • Independent Tasks ask you to write about a specific topic.

Total Time: Approximately 3 hours 30 minutes / Total Score: 120

TOEFL iBT Listening Section

The TOEFL iBT Listening Section largely consists of conversations and lectures. Conversations mainly take place in university settings, and lectures discuss topics from different academic fields covered in university lectures. Note-taking is allowed while listening to conversations and lectures. Therefore, the ability to listen, understand, and organize information is more important than relying on memory. The test consists of 2 to 3 Parts with either 11 or 17 questions. Each Part has 1 conversation and 1 to 2 lectures.

TOEFL iBT Listening Question Types

Question Type	Description
Main Purpose/Topic	Choose the answer choice that best represents the main idea of the conversation or lecture.
Detail	Choose the answer choice that corresponds to specific information or important details introduced in the conversation or lecture.
Function	Choose the answer choice that best describes the underlying function or purpose of a speaker's specific statement.
Attitude	Choose the answer choice that best represents the speaker's attitude or opinion regarding a specific matter.
Organization	Choose the answer choice that best describes the overall organization of the passage or the relationship between ideas in the passage.
Connecting Contents	Choose the answer choices that correspond to related ideas clearly stated in the passage.
Inference	Choose the answer choice that can be inferred based on relevant information in the passage.

NOTE-TAKING

Strategies for Note-taking

1. Write down the main idea using key words.

Listen carefully to the beginning of the conversation or lecture. Write down the main idea in a short sentence or phrase using key words.

2. Organize information into subtopics and categories.

Identify the subtopics and organize the information into groups or categories. Listen for signal words (First of all, Secondly, Now, Later, Then, Another, etc.) used to introduce subtopics.

3. Write down the supporting details.

Write down the supporting details for each subtopic or category. Especially for lectures, it is good to take notes according to how the lecturer gives supporting details. For example, the lecturer may give the definition of a term, compare two or more ideas, or give a list of important items.

4. Do not try to write down everything.

Make your notes brief and do not try to write down every single word. Include only essential key words. It is also helpful to use symbols and abbreviations of your own.

Note-taking Example

Script

P: Today we are going to continue our discussion on the differences between mammals and reptiles. One of the key traits that distinguish these two types of animals is the way that they control their body temperatures. I'm sure you have all heard the expressions "hot-blooded" and "cold-blooded," right? Well, it's actually a bit more complicated than that. Basically, mammals rely on their ability to burn fats and sugars to generate heat as required. In contrast, reptiles depend on external factors, such as the sun, to warm their bodies, or cold water to cool them. OK... Let's look at these functions in a bit more detail.

Note

diffs. bet. mammals & reptiles: way they ctrl. body temp.	— *Main Topic*
1. mammals: burn fat & sugar → heat	— *Type 1*
2. reptiles: ext. factors	— *Type 2*
e.g. sun → warm	
e.g. cold water → cool	*Examples of Type 2*

Common Symbols and Abbreviations

The key to note-taking is writing down only the essential information of the conversation or lecture. Using symbols and abbreviations will allow you to make your notes brief and accurate. With symbols and abbreviations, you can write down more information in a quick and efficient way. Below are some commonly used symbols and abbreviations.

1. Symbols

Symbols can save you time and increase the amount of information you write down about a passage.

=	equals; to be	K	1,000	X	not, no
+	and; plus	&	and	/	per, each
>	more than	∴	therefore/so	/day	per day
<	less than	←	from	/h	per hour
↑	increase	@	at	/w	per week
↓	decrease	#	number (of)	∵	because

2. Abbreviations

There are several methods to make abbreviations, but make sure to keep your method consistent. Here are some ways to make abbreviations.

· Omit latter part: European → Eu
· Omit vowels: movement → mvmt
· Omit middle letters: government → govt

e.g.	for example	usu.	usually	info.	information
prob.	problem	w/	with	sum.	summary
ppl	people	cf.	compare	psych.	psychology
rsn.	reason	c.	century	Qs	questions
etc.	and so on	max.	maximum	pics	pictures
i.e.	that is; in other words	min.	minimum	w/o	without
intro.	introduction	fr.	from	vs	versus
concl.	conclusion	tech	technology	ea.	each
b.f.	before	reg	regular	btw	by the way

CHAPTER 01

Main Purpose/Topic

Main Purpose/Topic

About the Question Type

Main Purpose/Topic questions ask you to determine the main idea of a conversation or lecture. Main Purpose questions focus on the purpose or reason the speaker is discussing a particular topic in the conversation or lecture. Main Topic questions ask you to identify the main subject or what the speakers are discussing overall.

Incorrect answer choices often contain exact words and phrases you hear from the passage, but they focus on minor points (examples, supporting ideas, etc.). Therefore, make sure that your answer choice paraphrases or restates the main idea of the entire passage.

Question Format

Main Purpose
- Why does the student go to see the professor?
- Why is the man speaking to the woman?

Main Topic
- What is the conversation/lecture mainly about?
- What is the main topic of the lecture?

Key Strategies

- **Step 1** — Listen carefully to the start of each passage. The main idea is usually mentioned clearly near the beginning of the passage.

- **Step 2** — Pay attention to the signal words that are commonly used to introduce the main purpose or topic of the passage. Examples for conversations include: *I'm interested in* and *I was wondering if*. Examples for lectures include: *Let's talk about* and *I want to take a look at*.

- **Step 3** — Select the answer choice that best expresses the main idea of the passage.

Example

A. Listen to a conversation between a student and a professor.

Note-taking   C1_ExA

Why does the student go to see the professor?

(A) To find out how late the laboratory is open
(B) To get advice about possible future careers
(C) To ask about a job in the biology department
(D) To see if another student has graduated yet

B. Listen to part of a lecture in an environmental science class.

Note-taking   C1_ExB

What is the lecture mainly about?

(A) The impact of a scientific project
(B) The disadvantage of a mining method
(C) The development of a new technology
(D) The disappearance of a deep-sea species

Dictation

Answer Book p. 2

Listen again and fill in the blanks.

C1_ExA_D

A.

S: Hi, Professor Hoffman. Do you have a moment?

P: Sure, Ashley. How can I help you today?

S: I was wondering if the biology department has _____

_____ .

P: Actually, you came at the perfect time. How would you like to _____

_____? The previous assistant just graduated and _____

_____ .

S: That would be great! I want to apply to graduate school next year. So _____

_____ .

P: Excellent. You'll need to go to the student employment office to fill out a few forms. Once that's complete, you can get started.

C1_ExB_D

B.

P: OK... Let's talk about a recent research project, and _____ .
So, um, a robot was sent five kilometers below the surface of the Pacific Ocean.
_____, including worms and jellyfish. In total, scientists found 39 previously undiscovered species. These findings changed the way we think about the ocean. They showed that _____

_____ . In fact, it is home to many different organisms. The findings also have had an effect on companies that work in deep-sea mining... Um, this refers to the gathering of minerals from the bottom of the ocean. The companies now have to make sure that their activities _____ .

Listening Practice 1

Answer Book p. 3

Listen to a conversation between a student and a librarian.

Note-taking

C1_P1

---

1 What problem does the student have?

(A) He forgot the password to an account.

(B) The books that he needs are not in the library.

(C) He has to pay a fee to borrow more books.

(D) The books that he checked out are missing.

2 According to the librarian, why did the school lock the student's account?

(A) The student brought items back late.

(B) The student missed a return date.

(C) The student lost his student ID.

(D) The student let his friend use his account.

3 Why does the student need to check out books?

(A) To help a friend who forgot her library card

(B) To read while he is on vacation in Spain

(C) To write a research paper that is due soon

(D) To finish an assignment that is three weeks late

4 What does the librarian say about the payment office?

(A) They might unlock the student's account.

(B) They may not understand the situation.

(C) They are unlikely to be open during vacation.

(D) They can help the student on Tuesday.

5 What does the librarian suggest to the student?

(A) Go to a bank

(B) Work in the library

(C) Come back next week

(D) Contact his friend

Dictation

Listen again and fill in the blanks.

M: I'd like to check out these books, please. Here is my student ID.

W: Um... I'm sorry, but _____. It seems that you have unpaid fees. So you can't borrow more books _____.

M: I don't think I have any books checked out. And I usually return everything on time. Could you check what the problem is?

W: Well, _____ called *Literary Theory* on February 26. It's more than three weeks late, so _____.

M: Oh, now I remember. My friend needed to borrow that book, but she didn't have her library card. So _____, instead. She must have forgotten to bring it back... And now, she is on vacation in Spain.

W: When will she be back?

M: She'll be back sometime next week. But _____. It's due next Friday, so I can't wait that long. What if _____?

W: You can do that, but they are quite expensive. The book is more than three weeks late, so the fees are $55.

M: Did you say $55? You've got to be joking!

W: No, I'm afraid not. And that will increase by $2 each day until it's paid.

M: I don't have enough money to pay that right now.

W: Then... Maybe _____. They might be able to unlock your account. You should definitely try...

M: All right, I will. It was just a mistake. Maybe I'll get lucky and they'll help me. Do you know _____?

W: It usually takes one or two days. I think you would be able to use your account again by Tuesday.

M: Oh... That would be too late. Is there anything else I can do?

W: Well, why don't you just _____? There are plenty of quiet spaces you can use. The desks are comfortable, and you won't hear any noise from outside.

M: OK. _____. Oh, but, um, can I bring coffee and a snack with me?

W: Sure. You can have coffee and a small snack. But _____ or disturb the other library users. You can take any desk that's available.

M: All right, then. Thank you for being so helpful.

Listening Practice 2

Listen to part of a lecture in a physiology class.

Note-taking

C1_P2

_____

_____

1 What is the main topic of the lecture?

(A) The genetic diversity among humans

(B) Why some people cannot lose weight

(C) The role of genetics in body weight

(D) How lifestyle influences weight gain

2 What does the professor say about human DNA?

(A) It is different in parents and children.

(B) It is unrelated to weight loss.

(C) It is mostly the same in all people.

(D) It strongly influences human behavior.

3 According to the professor, what is a characteristic of the skinny gene?

(A) It is less active in certain types of people.

(B) It is found only in human beings.

(C) It causes people to get tired quickly.

(D) It makes people feel hungry more often.

4 According to the professor, what kind of species is better able to survive through changes in environmental conditions?

(A) A species that does not eat much

(B) A species with lots of body fat

(C) A species with various body types

(D) A species that is physically active

Listen again to part of the lecture. Then answer the question.

5 What does the professor mean when she says this: 🎧

(A) She thinks the students can give more examples.

(B) She does not want the students to get confused.

(C) She believes speed is not important in losing weight.

(D) She feels that people should diet and exercise more.

‖ Dictation ‖

Listen again and fill in the blanks.

C1_P2_D

P: Most people believe that they have the ability to control their weight. Um, they think that losing weight is simply about eating less food or exercising more often. However, recent research suggests that _____.
This is what I want to talk about today.
Let's start with an overview... As I'm sure you know, about 99.9 percent of human DNA in all humans is the same. What this means is that there isn't much difference between your genes and everyone else's genes. But, uh, even this small amount of genetic difference _____. In fact, it is responsible for everything that makes one person different from another. And this includes how easy it is to gain weight and _____.
S: Is this why some people can eat lots of food and never gain weight?
P: That's partly correct. However, _____... Anyway, researchers know that there are at least 52 individual genes that affect body weight. And _____ _____. So imagine that you make 50 people eat the same amount of calories and do the same amount of exercise. Each person will _____. Now, don't get me wrong... Obviously, diet and exercise are important for losing weight. But, because of genetic differences, some people must exercise more to burn the same number of calories as others. Studies of identical twins have also confirmed that _____. Identical twins have the same genes, and research has shown that _____.
This is true even when one of them exercises regularly and the other does not.
OK... Now, I want to look at a specific gene related to weight control. Um, it's called the "skinny gene." Uh, some people have this gene and others do not... Generally, _____. And, uh, the gene is also less active in obese people. Researchers have also discovered that individuals with active skinny genes are thinner than others, _____.
But why do some people have this gene and others do not? How does this make sense for human evolution? Well, it makes sense because a species with a variety of body types is better able to _____. When there is lots of food, thin people are generally healthier. However, when resources are limited, _____. Either way, the species will continue...

Listening Practice 3

Listen to a conversation between a student and a professor.

Note-taking

C1_P3

1 Why does the student go to see the professor?
(A) To get more information about a class
(B) To ask for advice about a research paper
(C) To find out which courses are available
(D) To learn what to do to change majors

2 How will the professor cover all of the topics during the semester?
(A) By teaching the class at a faster pace
(B) By introducing material before the semester starts
(C) By only going over the basic information
(D) By instructing the students to study more hours

3 What does the professor mention about textbooks?
(A) They can be borrowed from the library.
(B) They are not necessary for a class.
(C) They have not been purchased yet by the school.
(D) They are better than materials found online.

4 What is the student's attitude toward the group project?
(A) He hopes it will not take too much time.
(B) He wants to be the one to present it.
(C) He thinks he will enjoy working on it.
(D) He believes it should be a bigger part of the grade.

5 What concern does the student have about the class?
(A) He will have to work as a member of a team.
(B) The professor is known for being strict.
(C) The presentation will require lots of preparation.
(D) His poor writing skills could affect his grade.

Dictation

C1_P3_D

Listen again and fill in the blanks.

S: Hi, um... Professor Stone? Uh, I'll be taking your Psychology 101 class this semester. _____, so I was hoping you could tell me more about it.

P: Well, in the first week, there will be an overview of what psychology is and how people use it. Then, _____. Um, this will include the brain and behavior. Lastly, the course will end with a section about reasoning and decision-making.

S: That's quite a lot! Will we be able to _____?

P: Yes, of course. Since this is an introductory course, _____ _____. It's just a basic introduction.

S: I see. And will most of our assignments be reading from a textbook?

P: Actually, you won't be needing any textbooks for this class. We will mostly be _____ _____. So we will be using short academic articles and some videos. I will probably recommend some free online resources as well.

S: That's a relief. Uh, how many hours per week will _____?

P: Well, it depends on how quickly you read. In general, I would say two to three hours for each lecture.

S: OK. Um, I also heard most of the psychology courses have at least one group project. Are we going to have one as well? Or will we do all of the assignments by ourselves?

P: You'll _____. Then, each group will present their project to the class toward the end of the semester.

S: That sounds great. I've always loved working with a team. Will you _____ _____?

P: Yes, there will be two individual research papers. But they will only be about five pages each.

S: Oh, no. I'm not very good at writing papers, so _____.

P: Papers are 10 percent of your grade. The group project and midterm exam are 20 percent each. The final exam is 40 percent, and _____.

S: Wow, this is a lot to remember. I hope I don't forget anything. _____ _____, so this class is really important to me.

P: Don't worry. Everything you need to know will be in the course outline. If you come to each class on time and try your best, I'm sure you'll do well.

Listening Practice 4

Listen to part of a lecture in an economics class.

Note-taking

C1_P4

1 What is the main topic of the lecture?

(A) The problems with consumerism

(B) How economics affects activism

(C) A method for choosing products to buy

(D) Why countries regulate businesses

2 How does the professor explain ethical consumerism?

(A) By listing various types of businesses

(B) By emphasizing the importance of environmental issues

(C) By giving examples of different companies

(D) By comparing the results of several studies

3 According to the professor, what can people do to consume products ethically? *Choose 2 answers.*

(A) Spend less money on luxury products

(B) Look for products that are labeled organic

(C) Vote for leaders who support rights for workers

(D) Buy from companies that follow strict standards

4 Why does the professor encourage people to buy local products?

(A) Foreign products are often too expensive.

(B) Buying locally helps support small companies.

(C) Local products are less harmful to the environment.

(D) Buying locally helps to create jobs for local people.

Listen again to part of the lecture. Then answer the question.

5 Why does the professor say this: 🎧

(A) To show that ethical consumerism is hard to do

(B) To acknowledge the student's difficulty with an idea

(C) To say that ethical decisions are not always possible

(D) To agree that there are many ways to solve a problem

❚❚ Dictation ❚❚

C1_P4_D

Listen again and fill in the blanks.

P: Last week, I mentioned the idea of economic activism. Um, that is when people try to change a situation by choosing what to spend their money on. Well, today's topic is similar to that. It is called ethical consumerism.
Ethical consumerism is a way of selecting _____ _____. Um, we all have different reasons for buying products. Sometimes, we buy products because they are cheap. Other times, we buy products, uh, just because they make us feel better. Well, ethical consumerism is about _____ _____ or the environment. Um, let me give you an example... Imagine that there are two coffee companies that buy coffee beans from farmers. One company recognizes that growing coffee beans is hard work. So it pays farmers a fair amount of money. However, the other company wants to _____ _____. So it pays the coffee growers a low amount even if this hurts the farmers. An ethical consumer would _____ _____. And, through this, they are encouraging all coffee companies to _____.
Ethical consumerism can also work the other way. Ethical consumers can also _____ _____. For instance, if a company pollutes the environment, ethical consumers can choose to stop buying that company's products. That way, they can _____.
Um, so, as an ethical consumer, you have to think carefully about which products you buy... The money you spend can help the right kind of company succeed... It can help the wrong kind of company fail.
S: Uh, but there are so many different products these days. How can a consumer know _____? I mean, it seems impossible to know everything about all companies.
P: It does seem complex, doesn't it? But it's not as difficult as you might think... Um, perhaps the most familiar method of ethical consumerism is buying organic products. _____ because they are not made with harmful chemicals or in places that treat animals badly. Just look for the organic label on product packaging. An organic label tells us that _____ _____. Similarly, you can look for something called a "fair trade" label. The label shows that _____ _____. These standards include good working conditions and fair prices that help small businesses compete with large companies. And, lastly, you can also buy more local products. _____ because they don't have to be sent long distances. So less fuel is used and less pollution is released into the atmosphere.

Answer Book p. 8

TOEFL Listening

C1_T1

Note-taking

1 Why does the student go to the history department?

  (A) To put his name on a class waiting list

  (B) To speak with an employee about changing a class

  (C) To talk with a professor about joining a class

  (D) To ask about changing a class schedule

2 Why was the student unable to sign up online?

  (A) He did not have the necessary information.

  (B) A course is only open to graduating students.

  (C) He has not taken a required course.

  (D) A website was not working.

3 Why is the student unwilling to call the professor?

  (A) He does not want to bother her late at night.

  (B) He needs to speak to her in person.

  (C) He will be too busy because of work.

  (D) He cannot wait until an office opens.

4 What is an advantage of the student meeting the professor in the morning?

  (A) He can sign up for the class before it starts.

  (B) He can get to work on time after they speak.

  (C) He can register for a class in the afternoon.

  (D) He can turn in a form at the same time.

Listen again to part of the conversation. Then answer the question.

5 What does the student mean when he says this: 🎧

  (A) He is upset that the employee's advice is not helpful.

  (B) He does not want to follow the employee's suggestion.

  (C) He is uncertain about what the employee wants him to do.

  (D) He does not think the employee understands his problem.

Dictation

Listen again and fill in the blanks.

C1_T1_D

W: Good morning. How can I help you?

M: Um, this is the history department, right? I'm looking for Professor Hane's office.

W: Yes, this is where Professor Hane works. Unfortunately, _____.

M: Oh, OK. Do you know what time she'll be back? I have to talk to her about _____ _____. It starts tomorrow.

W: Actually, _____. She probably won't be in her office until this afternoon. You could come back then if you need to speak with her.

M: Well, _____, so I don't have time to meet with her this afternoon.

W: I see. Are you a history major?

M: No, but I'm studying environmental science, so I think _____ _____ And I'm also really interested in the subject.

W: OK. Did you already _____?

M: I tried to do it online yesterday, but I wasn't able to because _____ _____ called Introduction to History. So I went to the registrar's office. They told me that _____.

W: In that case, you will need to speak with her directly. Hmm… Have you thought about signing up for Introduction to History first? Most students take the courses in that order.

M: I don't know… The Introduction to History class is mostly about general history, _____. Plus, I have a friend who took Professor Hane's environmental history class last semester. He told me that he didn't have to take the Introduction to History class first.

W: OK. Why don't you try to call her later? I can give you her office number and you can speak with her on the phone. She should be back in the office by around 1 p.m.

M: I'm sorry, but I don't think I can do that. _____, so I will be too busy to call her until late at night. I'm sure she'll be gone by then.

W: OK… Then, how about this? Come back here tomorrow morning before your classes start. That way, _____ about getting permission.

M: I guess that could work. The class I want to register for isn't until tomorrow afternoon. So _____, then I will have enough time to register for the class.

W: Let me check her schedule. Hmm… You're in luck. She will be here at 8 a.m. tomorrow.

M: Oh, really? That's perfect. I'll stop by tomorrow. Thanks for your help!

Answer Book p. 10

TOEFL Listening

C1_T2

ART HISTORY

Note-taking

1 What does the professor mainly discuss?

  Ⓐ The main purposes of portrait painting

  Ⓑ How portrait painting has developed over time

  Ⓒ The way artists choose subjects for portraits

  Ⓓ How painters show the character of subjects

2 According to the professor, what can be known about Arnolfini from his portrait?

  Ⓐ He came from a very large family.

  Ⓑ He was a rich and important individual.

  Ⓒ He became famous as a furniture maker.

  Ⓓ He was a huge supporter of many artists.

3 What does the professor say about *Napoleon Crossing the Alps*?

  Ⓐ It is the most famous painting of Napoleon.

  Ⓑ It shows Napoleon standing next to a horse.

  Ⓒ It presents its subject as a powerful leader.

  Ⓓ It focuses on nature as an important subject.

4 According to the professor, how did Renaissance artists become skilled at painting facial expressions?

  Ⓐ By copying the work of older painters

  Ⓑ By analyzing the human body

  Ⓒ By studying drawings from books

  Ⓓ By painting themselves in the mirror

5 What is the professor's attitude toward portraits with facial expressions?

  Ⓐ She finds them less interesting than other portrait types.

  Ⓑ She thinks that they are easy for people to understand.

  Ⓒ She feels that other types of portraits require more skill.

  Ⓓ She believes those from the Renaissance are the best examples.

Listen again to part of the lecture. Then answer the question.

6 Why does the professor say this: 🎧

  Ⓐ To show that much research has been done about a style

  Ⓑ To suggest that some portraits require a lot of work

  Ⓒ To explain an advantage of a type of portrait

  Ⓓ To indicate that she has seen a portrait in person

Dictation

Listen again and fill in the blanks.

C1_T2_D

P: Portrait painting is one of the oldest forms of art. It has been around for thousands of years. Its main purpose is to _____.
But, of course, there is more to people than just their appearance. A good portrait also shows us something about a subject's character. So _____
_____? Well, today we will look at several methods.
So the first method uses clothing and objects. _____
_____ in order to tell us what the subjects are like. Um, think of the clothing and objects that you own. They probably help you express your personality, right? So portrait painters also carefully choose the clothing and objects shown in portraits to _____... Um, there are many examples of this in portrait art. For instance, take a look at this one called the *Arnolfini Portrait*. It was painted by the Dutch artist, Jan van Eyck, in 1434. It shows a wealthy Italian businessman named Arnolfini and his wife. You can see that they are wearing expensive clothes and there are some nice pieces of furniture around them. This shows that _____
_____.

Next, there is the method of using poses and actions. Although many portraits show only a subject's face, _____. This type of portrait can help us understand the subject's character better. The more we see, _____
_____. Um, look at this famous portrait of Napoleon called *Napoleon Crossing the Alps*, for example. It was done in 1801 by the French painter Jacques-Louis David. In the painting, we see Napoleon sitting on a horse. However, the horse is standing on its back legs as if it is preparing to attack. Napoleon is holding on to the horse with one hand and pointing toward the sky with the other. The entire image is exciting _____. It shows Napoleon as a strong and fearless leader _____.
Lastly, we have a method that uses facial expressions. Facial expressions don't have to be as dramatic as poses and actions. But they can still tell us a lot about a subject. Also, _____. In fact, many artists in the past did not have enough skill to paint facial expressions. Um, this all changed during the Renaissance. During the Renaissance, _____
_____, including the face. So they became very

skilled at painting facial expressions. One of the most famous examples, of course, is the *Mona Lisa* by Leonardo da Vinci. In the *Mona Lisa*, we see that the subject has a small and mysterious smile. It makes her look as if she knows something that the viewers do not. Portraits like this one are very effective for showing information about a subject. You know… _____.

Vocabulary Review

A. **Choose the correct word for each meaning.**

laboratory	lifeless	evolution	appearance

1 physical or outward characteristics: _____

2 without any living things: _____

3 a place to conduct experiments: _____

4 the process of development of an organism over time: _____

B. **Fill in the blanks with the appropriate words from the box.**

genetics	instructor	previous	reasoning	mysterious

5 The study of _____ could help us eliminate the diseases we are born with.

6 The name of the book's _____ author is still not known today.

7 We hired a golf _____ to teach us how to play the game.

8 Students must include in their essays the _____ behind their conclusions.

9 The house needs repairs because the _____ owner did not take care of it properly.

C. **Choose the closest meaning for each highlighted word.**

10 Soldiers must follow strict rules on how to behave at all times.
   (A) perfect   (B) rigid   (C) total   (D) steep

11 The general launched a fearless attack but ultimately lost the battle.
   (A) courageous   (B) nervous   (C) elegant   (D) lively

12 Eating too much unhealthy food has caused many people to become obese.
   (A) awkward   (B) muscular   (C) severe   (D) overweight

13 The article provides an overview of the problem and does not include many details.
   (A) list   (B) scan   (C) summary   (D) breakdown

14 Doctors have an ethical responsibility to be truthful to their patients.
   (A) ideal   (B) specific   (C) moral   (D) smooth

CHAPTER 02

Detail

Detail

About the Question Type

Detail questions ask you to identify specific details or facts that are mentioned in a conversation or lecture.

Correct answers restate specific information explicitly mentioned in the passage. Incorrect answers contain new, contradictory, or irrelevant information. Some questions may require you to select more than one correct answer choice.

Question Format

- According to the conversation, what is ~?

- What does the professor say about ~?

- According to the professor, what are the reasons for ~? *Choose 2 answers.*

- What are the two examples the man gives of ~? *Choose 2 answers.*

Key Strategies

- **Step 1** — Identify the main topic and focus on important information supporting the main idea. For example, listen carefully for definitions, examples, reasons, results, and features.

- **Step 2** — Listen carefully for signal words that are commonly used to introduce supporting ideas. Some examples include: *For instance, To illustrate, That's because, As a result, Similarly,* and *On the other hand.*

- **Step 3** — Select the answer choice that best presents the information from the conversation or lecture. Remember, the correct answer often paraphrases information, or repeats it using different words.

Example

Answer Book p. 11

A. Listen to a conversation between a student and a university housing office employee.

C2_ExA

Note-taking

What does the employee say about electric heaters?

(A) They waste a lot of electricity.

(B) They can get hot and cause a fire.

(C) They are commonly used by residents.

(D) They can break easily and need repairs.

Answer Book p. 11

B. Listen to part of a lecture in an architecture class.

C2_ExB

Note-taking

According to the professor, why is Venice sinking? *Choose 2 answers.*

(A) Sea levels are rising.

(B) The gates that control the water have failed.

(C) The ground is too weak to support the buildings.

(D) Groundwater is damaging the architecture.

Dictation

Listen again and fill in the blanks.

C2_ExA_D

A.

M: Hi, I live in one of the school dormitories. I received a letter saying that _____ _____.

W: I can help you with that... Uh, it looks like you received a fine because _____ _____.

M: Is there something wrong with that? It gets cold sometimes and my roommates don't like to turn on the main heater.

W: Yes, however, _____. If it reaches high temperatures, it can start a fire.

M: Oh, I never thought about that. _____.

W: Please read the list of rules that was given to all residents. They keep everyone safe and will _____.

C2_ExB_D

B.

P: Venice is known for its architecture. Around 20 million tourists visit it each year to enjoy the city and its famous waterways. However, _____. It's sinking at a rate of one to two millimeters a year. Uh, one factor is that _____ _____. The soil is so soft that it cannot hold the weight of the buildings above it. Another factor is climate change, _____. As the city continues to sink, water will rise above the foundations of the buildings and damage them. So _____. They have installed huge gates to try to control the water... Also, they are raising money to _____ _____.

Listening Practice 1

Answer Book p. 12

Listen to a conversation between a student and a students services office employee.

C2_P1

Note-taking

---

1 Why does the student visit the students services office?

(A) To pick up a graduation application

(B) To make a complaint about an advisor

(C) To find out how to register for a class

(D) To learn about the graduation procedure

2 According to the conversation, what are two requirements for students to graduate? *Choose 2 answers.*

(A) Complete the necessary classes

(B) Make payments to the university

(C) Submit a copy of their school transcript

(D) Review their graduation application

3 According to the employee, what must students do if there is a problem with their review?

(A) Take an additional exam

(B) Pay an added fee

(C) See an academic advisor

(D) Get a letter from a professor

4 What does the employee suggest that the student do after getting a diploma?

(A) Fill out a form at a registration desk

(B) Confirm that some information is correct

(C) Make copies to show to employers

(D) Request a record of any remaining fees

5 What does the employee say about school transcripts?

(A) They can be received through the mail.

(B) They must be collected on graduation day.

(C) They will take a few days to prepare.

(D) They must be signed by an academic advisor.

Dictation

C2_P1_D

Listen again and fill in the blanks.

M: Good morning! Welcome to the students services office.

W: Oh, good morning. Uh, _____?

M: Yes. I'm one of the graduate advisors and I would be happy to help you.

W: Well, I'm supposed to graduate this year. But I'm not sure what I have to do. Can you tell me about the process?

M: OK. First, you need to _____. You can do that here or online.

W: I see. But why do I have to apply? I got good grades in all of my classes. Isn't that enough?

M: No, not quite. There are other requirements. For instance, _____ _____. They also have to pay fees to the university. That's why graduate advisors _____.

W: OK. That makes sense. And what if there is a problem with my review?

M: Then, you will need to _____. Sometimes, students have to wait until the next semester to graduate.

W: Well, I don't think I'll have that problem, so I'm not worried. Uh, this may be a strange question to ask, but _____? I'm a little bit nervous about it.

M: I understand. It can be stressful. Well, on the day of the graduation, you have to go to the Main Hall when you arrive and register. Then, you need to _____ _____. There will be a person there to help you find the right place. The ceremony is mostly just people giving speeches. The only thing you have to do is wait for your name to be called. Then, you have to _____ _____.

W: Oh, I didn't know we would get our diplomas at the ceremony.

M: Yes, you'll get your diploma on stage. And when you get back to your seat, it's best to check your diploma to _____. If there are, and this does happen sometimes, then you should tell the staff at the registration desk near the entrance.

W: OK. _____?

M: No, I'm afraid not. You actually have to ask for one at the registrar's office, and it can take around three to four weeks to _____.

W: All right. Got it.

M: Great. If you need anything else, just give me a call or send an e-mail. Here's my contact information.

W: Thanks.

Listening Practice 2

Listen to part of a lecture in a history class.

Note-taking _____

C2_P2

1 What is the main topic of the lecture?

(A) Voting in different countries

(B) An important civil rights law

(C) A history of minority rights

(D) Immigration law in America

2 Why were many African Americans and immigrants not able to vote before the Voting Rights Act of 1965? *Choose 2 answers.*

(A) They did not own enough property.

(B) They were not able to pay the poll tax.

(C) They were not American citizens.

(D) They could not read and write English.

3 According to the professor, what got the attention of the government during the 1960s?

(A) The number of immigrants increased.

(B) Protestors refused to vote in elections.

(C) Some people were killed during protests.

(D) The president gave an inspiring speech.

4 According to the professor, what was one of the changes to the Voting Rights Act?

(A) Voting deadlines were extended.

(B) Language tests were no longer permitted.

(C) Voting instructions were simplified.

(D) States made their own voting laws.

Listen again to part of the lecture. Then answer the question.

5 What does the professor imply when he says this: 🎧

(A) A 1920 law also removed some rights.

(B) Some adult citizens still could not vote.

(C) Few women were allowed to vote.

(D) A 1920 law did not apply to black people.

‖ Dictation ‖

Listen again and fill in the blanks.

P: Today, I want to tell you about the civil rights movement in America. Uh, _____ _____. Specifically, I'm going to focus on the importance of the Voting Rights Act of 1965. This law made it easier for certain groups of people, like some minorities, to vote.

Uh, but first, let's review voting history briefly. Before 1869, only white men could vote in the United States. Then, a new law was passed in 1869. Because of this law, _____ _____. Similarly, women were allowed to vote after a 1920 law was passed. Therefore, it seemed that all adult citizens could vote at that time. But this was an illusion. Some states required people to _____. This tax was called a poll tax. Because many African Americans and immigrants were poor, _____. And if they did not pay the tax, they were not allowed to vote. Also, sometimes a language test was required. Voters had to be able to _____. However, many African Americans and immigrants were not able to read and write in English. So they failed the test.

Then, in the 1960s, civil rights became a big issue in America. Some people argued that _____. These people thought all adult citizens should be allowed to vote. There were many protests, and, uh, _____ _____. In fact, some people were even killed. This got the attention of the government. So, in 1965, President Lyndon Johnson made the Voting Rights Act a law. It gave voting rights to all American adults.

The initial effect of the act was that _____. This made America more democratic. But the law itself was not enough. _____ _____ to make sure that the law was applied. For instance, states had to get approval from the government to change any voting processes. Before making any changes, they had to _____. Also, government officials were sent to places where there had been voting issues in the past. The officials made sure that these places followed the new law.

Later, the significance of the Voting Rights Act became even greater through some changes. One of these was _____. Uh, states could no longer require people to take these tests. Similarly, _____ _____. Uh, for example, if areas had large minority populations, such as Mexican Americans or Chinese Americans, they had to provide voting instructions in those minority languages...

Listening Practice 3

Answer Book p. 15

Listen to a conversation between a student and a professor.

Note-taking

C2_P3

1 What is the conversation mainly about?

(A) The reasons for a late assignment

(B) The participants in an art competition

(C) The deadline for an upcoming project

(D) The feedback on some students' art

2 What does the professor say about the art competition?

(A) She has never heard of it before.

(B) She is excited to be a participant.

(C) She saw information about it on campus.

(D) She was told about it by some other professors.

3 What is the problem with submitting portfolios after the competition?

(A) The professor has to evaluate contest artworks.

(B) The contest is after the portfolio deadline.

(C) The students need to prepare for exams.

(D) The portfolio drawings are needed for an exhibit.

4 What does the professor offer to do?

(A) She will attend the student's show at a gallery.

(B) She will notify the other students of an event.

(C) She will help the student prepare for an art contest.

(D) She will allow more time for a class assignment.

5 What is the student going to do for the professor?

(A) Send a brochure by e-mail

(B) Prepare a schedule of activities

(C) Talk to other students in class

(D) Print out some invitations

▌▌ Dictation ▌▌

C2_P3_D

Listen again and fill in the blanks.

S: Hi, Professor Turner. Could I come in for a second?

P: Hello, Patrick. Of course... Have you been _____ _____?

S: Well, I've been busy with assignments for other classes, but the portfolio's going well. It's almost done...

P: Excellent. So what did you want to ask me about? I assume it's about your portfolio?

S: Yes, _____. Professor, do you know anything about the art competition? It's the one where _____ _____. A few other professors mentioned it, so I checked it out.

P: Hmm... I think it's called Ideas in Color, or something like that. It seems like many people are excited about it. I've seen a lot of posters around campus promoting it.

S: Yes, that's the one. Anyway, I'm almost done with a drawing that _____ _____. I have to turn it in on May 15.

P: OK, that's great. So what's your question?

S: I'd really like to _____. But the portfolio is due on May 13. So I can only add the drawing after the competition.

P: But _____, isn't it? That could be a problem.

S: Yes, that's why I wanted to check with you. I'm wondering if you could _____ _____. As you know, many of the students are participating in the competition, too.

P: Good point. Well, in that case, _____. I want to give everyone a chance to include their artwork from the contest. After all, I've always encouraged students to _____. It would be unfair if I didn't give everyone more time.

S: Thank you for understanding, Professor. And I'm sure _____ _____.

P: I certainly hope so. But I can't accept portfolios any later than May 15.

S: Sure. That sounds very reasonable. Um, do you want me to send you some more information about the contest? I don't know _____.

P: Oh, that would be great. Please give me a copy.

S: I'll do that. I'm going to my dormitory after this, so I'll send a copy to you by e-mail. Thanks again.

P: Thank you, too. If you hadn't told me about this, I wouldn't have thought about _____ _____.

Listening Practice 4

Answer Book p. 17

Listen to part of a lecture in a psychology class.

Note-taking _____

C2_P4

_____

1 What is the main purpose of the lecture?

(A) To discuss a psychological theory

(B) To explain a problem with memories

(C) To describe ways to reduce memory loss

(D) To compare two types of memories

2 What is the professor's opinion of false memories?

(A) They can show when a person is lying.

(B) They can indicate problems in the brain.

(C) They can cause severe problems for people.

(D) They can help us understand our lives better.

3 What does the professor say about wrong perceptions?

(A) They make people unsure about themselves.

(B) They cause false memories from the start.

(C) They are more common among elderly people.

(D) They can result from a childhood experience.

4 According to the professor, how are inference and interference similar?

(A) They add new information to memories.

(B) They are related to childhood memories.

(C) They help people improve their memories.

(D) They make people forget bad memories.

Listen again to part of the lecture. Then answer the question.

5 What does the professor mean when she says this: 🎧

(A) Science is more accurate than psychology.

(B) Science still cannot fully explain memory.

(C) Memory failure is not easy to overcome.

(D) Memory does not always work in an ideal way.

C2_P4_D

Listen again and fill in the blanks.

P: Most people believe their memories are true. But our memories might not be as reliable as we think. Today we're going to talk about an issue with memories called false memories. You see, memory is not an exact science. I mean, _____.
Um, there are several different ways that our memories can fail. For instance, we can forget something happened because we were not concentrating. Or, you know, we can forget details because something happened a long time ago... But _____
_____. False memories are a problem with remembering.
With false memories, _____. Or we remember something that never happened at all. For example, people can falsely remember that they were good at baseball in high school, _____.
Or they can falsely remember that they helped their team win a game, even if they were never on the team at all. Now, it's important to know that people with false memories honestly believe that they're true. So this is different from lying. Moreover, it's important to understand that false memories can cause serious problems. Um, _____
_____. For instance, if someone falsely remembers a crime, this could cause an innocent person to go to jail...
But why do false memories happen in the first place? Let's look at some of the ways...
Sometimes, _____. Um, perception is how we see, hear, or touch something, and so on. It helps us create new memories. But sometimes, _____. For instance, a person can remember a face incorrectly because it was dark when they saw it or because they have bad eyesight. So they create a false memory _____.
Or, um, another cause is related to inference. You see, people tend to _____
_____. So, sometimes, they will add new information to their memory of an experience based on an inference. The new information helps them understand the experience better. But it also creates a false memory. In one study, people were asked to read a list of words related to sleep. After, many of them remembered seeing the word sleep on the list, but _____.
They inferred it because the list had many words related to sleep. OK. And lastly, false memories can also be caused by interference. Like inference, _____. The difference is that the new information is added by someone else. This information interferes with, or changes, the original memory. One example is when you falsely remember events from your childhood because _____.

Answer Book p. 18

TOEFL Listening

C2_T1

Note-taking

1 Why does the student go to see the professor?

- Ⓐ To receive some advice about career plans
- Ⓑ To ask about submitting a report late
- Ⓒ To get ideas on how to improve a project
- Ⓓ To request help with preparing for an exam

2 What does the student say about the other students in a class?

- Ⓐ They made a lot of progress on an assignment.
- Ⓑ They chose a subject that is not very interesting.
- Ⓒ They are researching a wide variety of topics.
- Ⓓ They gave presentations that were very impressive.

3 What does the professor say about working mothers?

- Ⓐ They usually prefer the same kinds of products.
- Ⓑ They will be difficult to interview because they are busy.
- Ⓒ They are often careful about how they spend money.
- Ⓓ They are a large group with varied characteristics.

4 What does the professor expect the students to learn from a project?

- Ⓐ The importance of working together as a team
- Ⓑ What kinds of products a group of people like to buy
- Ⓒ Why different age groups prefer buying certain products
- Ⓓ The usefulness of having a strategy for selling to people

Listen again to part of the conversation. Then answer the question.

5 Why does the student say this: 🎧

- Ⓐ To remind the professor of something he said during class
- Ⓑ To explain how she has prepared for next week's exam
- Ⓒ To indicate that she expected the professor's response
- Ⓓ To correct what she said at the beginning of the conversation

Dictation

Listen again and fill in the blanks.

C2_T1_D

P: Hi, Sarah. Are you ready for the exam next week?

S: I think so. I've been reviewing my lecture notes every day, and I'm planning to study this weekend. Also, _____, so I feel pretty confident.

P: Great! Well, it sounds like you're going to do very well next week! So what can I help you with today?

S: I actually wanted to talk about the final project. Uh, you asked us to think of a product and some ways to _____. My project is going well, but I would like some advice on how to make it better.

P: Oh, that's right. _____?

S: Um, I'm not sure. I've noticed that almost everyone else in class is focusing on university students. I would like to _____. That idea just seems a bit boring...

P: I see what you mean. They probably chose to do that because it would be easy for them.

S: I think so, too. Anyway, I thought it would be interesting to _____
_____. There are many of them and they spend a lot of money.

P: That's a fine idea. However, _____.
That means that you will have to do a lot of research.

S: I was afraid you might say that... Um, _____?

P: Well, working mothers are a large group with a lot of variety. It would be good to get a lot of information about them. Do you know where they live and _____
_____? Do you know about their children or what kinds of activities they enjoy? The more you know, the easier it will be for you to _____
_____.

S: That sounds like a lot of work. I'm not sure that I'll have enough time. I already know some basic ideas about marketing. Couldn't I just use those to complete the project?

P: Yes, of course, you can do that. But you said that you wanted to make your project better. The goal of this project is for you to learn _____
when you're selling to a specific group of people.

S: You're right. The extra research should be helpful.

P: Yes, the experience will also help you if you plan to have a career in marketing.

S: That's true. I hope to _____... Well, I guess I'd better get started. I'm sure I can find lots of material at the library if I go now!

C2_T2

Note-taking

1 What does the professor mainly discuss?

- (A) The impact of electricity production on global warming
- (B) The difficulty of producing renewable energy
- (C) An alternative to the use of fossil fuels
- (D) The application of wind power throughout history

2 According to the professor, what creates wind?

- (A) Air that moves from areas of high to low pressure.
- (B) Powerful storms that form over the ocean
- (C) The movement of air with different temperatures
- (D) The movement of the Earth around the Sun

3 What does the professor say about Shepherds Flats Wind Farm?

- (A) It is the largest wind farm in the world.
- (B) It can produce electricity for many houses.
- (C) It was the first successful wind farm.
- (D) It produces 5 percent of a city's energy.

4 According to the professor, what are two challenges to the use of wind power?

Choose 2 answers.

- (A) Wind farms require lots of building material.
- (B) Wind turbines can kill some animals.
- (C) Wind does not always blow consistently.
- (D) Wind turbines are extremely noisy.

5 What is the professor's attitude toward the future of wind energy?

- (A) He thinks it will become as common as solar power.
- (B) He is worried that its challenges are too great.
- (C) He feels that people do not understand its advantages.
- (D) He believes that it will continue to develop.

Listen again to part of the lecture. Then answer the question.

6 Why does the professor say this: 🎧

- (A) To compare the heights of two common structures
- (B) To suggest that a problem is less serious than it seems
- (C) To emphasize that animals cause many problems
- (D) To indicate that there are other ways to help birds

Listen again and fill in the blanks.

P: Last class, we began talking about renewable forms of energy and how we will need them to produce electricity. As I mentioned, oil and natural gas supplies are getting smaller and smaller. Also, these fossil fuels cause global warming, so _____. Starting today, we are going to look at the various other energy options that are available. Let's begin with wind power... Um, it might be the best way to _____ _____. But first, how exactly is wind produced? Many people don't realize that _____. You see, the Sun heats Earth's atmosphere unevenly and _____. Warm air rises and cooler air falls. This movement of warm and cool air creates wind. And the energy of the wind can be used to make electricity.

So how do we make electricity from wind? Well, _____ _____. They are very tall and have massive blades that look like the blades on an airplane propeller. These blades are connected to a generator. So, _____, the generator produces electricity. Now, each wind turbine can only produce a certain amount of electricity. So, usually, large numbers of wind turbines are placed in one area called a wind farm. Together, _____. For example, the Shepherds Flats Wind Farm in Oregon has a total of 338 wind turbines. It can produce around 845 megawatts of electricity in all... Um, that's enough to supply over 200,000 homes with electricity. One day, wind farms like this one could produce more than 100 times _____. But, at present, wind power produces only around 5 percent of global electricity usage. This is because of a couple of challenges with this energy source...

First, _____. Uh, it is stronger at some times than at others. During long periods of low winds, _____. They can even stop completely. So, obviously, this creates problems for people who need electricity all of the time. Second, _____, bats, and other animals that fly. Many birds, for instance, often travel long distances every year during the summer and the fall. They pass through the same areas each time. However, when you build a wind farm in those areas, this causes some of the birds to _____ _____. And, uh, as a result, they die. Um, about a million birds are killed by wind turbines each year. Of course, even more birds are killed by tall buildings in our cities. That number is closer to a billion. Still, _____

_____.

Anyway, even with these and other challenges, I think wind energy still has a bright future. It offers more advantages than disadvantages. And I'm sure that scientists and engineers will eventually _____.

Vocabulary Review

A. Choose the correct word for each meaning.

> perception   transcript   immigrant   foundation

1 an observation made with the use of the senses: _____

2 someone who has moved permanently from a different country: _____

3 an official record of a student's grades: _____

4 the lowest part of a structure that gives it support: _____

B. Fill in the blanks with the appropriate words from the box.

> diploma   equal   minority   interference   democratic

5 As a _____ in Myanmar, the Rakhine people have been frequently persecuted.

6 A country that ignores the demands of its people is not very _____.

7 Companies must do more to fight wage discrimination and provide _____ pay for women.

8 The president of the university gave students their _____ and shook their hand.

9 He locked his door so he could work without _____.

C. Choose the closest meaning for each highlighted word.

10 We postponed the store opening so we could have more time to prepare.
   (A) announced   (B) delayed   (C) excluded   (D) opposed

11 The idea that money always brings happiness is an illusion.
   (A) image   (B) fault   (C) fantasy   (D) crime

12 Even small actions can have great significance over time.
   (A) importance   (B) priority   (C) concern   (D) fame

13 Since it can be edited by anyone, the online encyclopedia is not a reliable source.
   (A) powerful   (B) educational   (C) promotional   (D) dependable

14 Many of the town's residents have lived there for all of their lives.
   (A) homes   (B) inhabitants   (C) cultures   (D) subjects

CHAPTER 03

Function

Function

About the Question Type

Function questions ask you to determine the true meaning or intention behind a speaker's statement. This is usually different from what the speaker states directly.

These questions require you to listen again to part of a conversation or lecture. Some examples of the possible functions of a statement include: to explain a concept, to give an opinion, and to make a comparison.

Question Format

Listen again to part of the lecture. Then answer the question.

P: ⁑⁑⁑⁑⁑⁑⁑⁑⁑⁑⁑

Why does the professor say this: ⌒

Key Strategies

- **Step 1** — Listen carefully to the replay, and then identify the intention behind what the speaker has said within the context.

- **Step 2** — Focus on the words that the speaker emphasizes and the tone of voice that they use. They often indicate the true intention behind statements.

- **Step 3** — Select the answer choice that best represents the true meaning or intention of the speaker.

Example

Answer Book p. 21

A. Listen to a conversation between a student and a professor.

Note-taking

C3_ExA

Listen again to part of the conversation. Then answer the question.
What does the student mean when she says this: 🎧

(A) She doesn't know why the professor opened a book.
(B) She is uncertain if the professor understood her question.
(C) She doesn't know which part the professor is explaining.
(D) She thinks the professor is confused about a topic.

Answer Book p. 21

B. Listen to part of a lecture in an astronomy class.

Note-taking

C3_ExB

Listen again to part of the lecture. Then answer the question.
Why does the professor say this: 🎧

(A) To show how the telescope moves
(B) To illustrate the size of an object
(C) To emphasize the cost of a project
(D) To provide the reason for a special design

Dictation

Answer Book p. 21

Listen again and fill in the blanks.

A.

C3_ExA_D

S: Hi, Professor Ahmad. I have a question about today's lecture on the formation of stars.

P: Yes, what would you like to know?

S: Well, I got confused _____. I mean, it's really cold in space, right?

P: That's correct. You see, a star begins as a cold ball of gas and dust. Then, _____ _____, its gravity becomes stronger. _____ _____.

S: That's where you lost me...

P: Let's take a look at the textbook... Here, _____, it starts to heat up...

S: Hold on, Professor, where are we looking?

P: Oh, I'm right here on page 37. It's in the third paragraph.

B.

C3_ExB_D

P: I'm sure many of you have heard of the James Webb Space Telescope. It has produced incredible images of distant objects in space. Um, I'd like to take a bit of time this morning to explain _____.

Now, as the name suggests, the James Webb Space Telescope is, well, in space. In fact, it's moving around the Sun about 1.5 million kilometers from Earth. _____ _____. The side that faces the Sun is protected by a large shield. Um, think of a tennis court. That's how big it is. _____ _____. It also has a powerful camera on the other side to _____.

Listening Practice 1

Listen to a conversation between a student and a student fitness center employee.

Note-taking

C3_P1

1 Why does the student visit the student fitness center?

(A) To ask about joining a sports team

(B) To request that the gym extend its hours

(C) To find out about open job positions

(D) To share his opinion about closing the gym

2 Why is the gym unable to stay open past 5 p.m.?

(A) It requires hiring additional staff.

(B) There isn't enough time to set up the equipment.

(C) Exams are held in the space at the same time.

(D) Not many students want to exercise late in the day.

3 Why did the plan to put students in different rooms for exams fail?

(A) Cheating became more common.

(B) Too many staff members were in each room.

(C) Many students complained about the rooms.

(D) Distributing the tests took too much time.

4 What idea does the student have to solve a problem?

(A) Posting suggestions on the university website

(B) Placing exercise equipment in another building

(C) Letting students exercise for free on campus

(D) Allowing students to use a nearby private gym

Listen again to part of the conversation. Then answer the question.

5 Why does the employee say this: 🎧

(A) To clarify how the student can respond to a request

(B) To specify when the student should use a facility

(C) To show that anyone can post information on a site

(D) To explain that someone will hear about an idea

Dictation

C3_P1_D

Listen again and fill in the blanks.

W: Welcome to the student fitness center. How can I help you?

M: I wanted to ask about the opening hours of the gym next week...

W: Sure, as you know, next week is the beginning of the final exam period. So _____ _____ until exams are finished.

M: Right... That's why I'm here, actually. I don't think the university should close the gym during the exam period. That's when students have the most free time.

W: I understand that _____. But the university needs to use the gym as a place _____. And, when that happens, we have to take the gym equipment out and set up all the desks and chairs.

M: But all of the exams end by 5 p.m. every day. I'm sure _____ _____.

W: Well, I'm afraid that's not possible. It takes a lot of time to remove all the desks and chairs. Plus, _____. There wouldn't be any time for anyone to exercise by the time that's done.

M: Oh, I didn't think about how much time it would take to organize everything... Still, I think there are other ways to solve this problem. Maybe the university doesn't need to have an entire class take the exam in one room. They could _____ _____.

W: They've tried that in the past, but _____. Dividing students into different classrooms made it hard to watch them. Uh, there weren't enough staff for each room. So cheating happened often and _____. That's mainly why the university decided it wasn't a good idea. We also had other small problems. For instance, many students went to the wrong rooms by mistake.

M: Well, I guess there really is no way to _____.

W: Again, I apologize for the inconvenience.

M: I think the university should find another solution for people who want to exercise during the exam period. Um, for example, _____. Students could exercise there for free while the gym is closed.

W: That's a good suggestion. You should _____.

M: I could do that, but I'm not sure if anyone would actually see it.

W: Well, staff members check the website every day. And _____.

M: OK, then. I'll do that as soon as possible.

Listening Practice 2

Answer Book p. 24

Listen to part of a lecture in a history class.

Note-taking

C3_P2

_____

_____

_____

1 What is the lecture mainly about?

(A) The relationship between Rome and other regions

(B) The benefits of transporting goods by sea

(C) The reasons for the increase in Roman sea trade

(D) The link between Rome's military and economic power

2 According to the professor, why were many merchants unwilling to participate in sea trade?

(A) They were loyal to the government of Crete.

(B) They refused to pay taxes to the Romans.

(C) They were afraid of losing their products to pirates.

(D) They did not want to be attacked by Pompey's men.

3 According to the professor, why did Rome import large amounts of grain?

(A) The grain produced in Rome was of low quality.

(B) The country's farmlands could not feed all the locals.

(C) The population of the city had increased rapidly.

(D) The merchants were able to make high profits from it.

4 What does the professor say about the regions of the Roman Empire?

(A) They fought one another for control of the Mediterranean Sea.

(B) They depended on each other for necessary goods.

(C) They competed with Rome in producing goods.

(D) They learned farming methods from Rome.

Listen again to part of the lecture. Then answer the question.

5 Why does the professor say this: 🎧

(A) To suggest there was an obvious reason for Rome's demand

(B) To explain why Rome welcomed people from different cultures

(C) To emphasize that most goods were not expensive in the past

(D) To imply that many people in Rome were not Italian

Dictation

Listen again and fill in the blanks.

P: OK... You already know that ancient Rome had a strong military... However, did you know it also had a strong economy? Well, it did. And a lot of its wealth came from sea trade. Today, I'm going to discuss _____

_____.

Before the Roman Empire was established, _____.
Thus, many merchants did not want to participate in sea trade. It was too risky.
_____, pirates would attack the ships and steal the products. The situation got so bad that pirates took over the island of Crete. So, in 67 BC, _____. They gave him many ships, men, and money. Pompey attacked the pirates repeatedly. Within three years, the problem of pirates in the Mediterranean Sea was significantly reduced. This made _____.

At the same time, the city of Rome had a population of over a million residents. So _____. Rome had demand for all kinds of things. Think about it. It was a multicultural city even back then. _____

_____, and they were wealthy enough to afford exotic luxury goods. Most importantly, though, _____...

Italy's farms simply couldn't produce enough grain to feed the entire local population. The records show that over 400,000 tons of grain was brought into the city each year. That is about the same amount of grain that 1,200 ships could carry.

S: I guess the city of Rome must have had a very large port for all of those ships?

P: Absolutely. _____. It was at the opening of a river near Rome. Goods were sent there from around the Mediterranean Sea. However, _____, a larger port was built at Pozzuoli. Uh, this was a coastal city in the south of Rome. Merchant ships would drop off their goods there. Then, the goods would be delivered on smaller ships to Ostia.

Now, Rome wasn't the only center of sea trade in the region... A number of other regions became major ports as well. The reason is that _____

_____. For example, Egypt and Sardinia produced lots of grain. Meanwhile, other cities in Italy were famous for their wines, and Hispania was an important source of metals.

The different regions of the Roman Empire _____.
So ships constantly transported goods between them. As a result, the sea trade of Rome and its regions _____ in the Mediterranean Sea.

Listening Practice 3

Answer Book p. 25

Listen to a conversation between a student and a professor.

Note-taking

C3_P3

1 What is the main topic of the conversation?

(A) Requirements to pass a class

(B) Ideas for a group discussion

(C) Possible subjects for a report

(D) Details about an assignment topic

2 What led to the formation of the town of Calico?

(A) People identified minerals in the soil.

(B) People found silver in the mountains.

(C) People located oil beneath the ground.

(D) People discovered mines in the hills.

3 According to the professor, why did Calico grow rapidly?

(A) The town was located near a major city.

(B) Many people wanted to invest in the town.

(C) Miners came to the area looking for wealth.

(D) The price of silver suddenly increased.

4 What problem did Calico's new mining companies have?

(A) They could not sell silver for a high price.

(B) They could not find people to work in mines.

(C) They did not have enough mining equipment.

(D) They had to follow new laws about mining.

Listen again to part of the conversation. Then answer the question.

5 What does the professor mean when he says this: 🎧

(A) The student should complete the research herself.

(B) The professor thinks the student might be confused.

(C) The student should take her report to another professor.

(D) The professor wants the student to change her topic.

Listen again and fill in the blanks.

S: Excuse me, Professor Wilson, do you have time to talk?

P: Sure, Josie. What's on your mind?

S: Well, it's about the history assignment. I need some advice about my topic. _____
_____...

P: That's a great example of a ghost town. Uh, _____
_____...

S: Right. I read an article about it, but it didn't have a lot of details. Can you tell me a little
more about what happened there?

P: I can give you an introduction, but you should do more research at the library. Now, what
do you remember from the article?

S: Um, it said that _____.

P: That's right. So, in California in the 1880s, miners discovered silver in the Calico
mountains. They opened a mine to get the silver out of the mountain and, um, that's
_____.

S: But how did the place get so big? Didn't it _____?

P: That's a good question. The miners were the first ones there, but then people around
the world heard that Calico had a lot of silver. So _____
_____. There were even people from Europe and Asia. And
they all came to make money. That's why _____.

S: It seems like the place was really successful. I read that one of the mines there
_____.

P: Yes... For a while, the town was a huge success. The mines were producing more than
enough silver and everyone was making money. However, the good times didn't last very
long...

S: You mean _____? What happened, exactly?

P: It's complicated, but I'll give you the simple version of the story. The new mining
companies had a problem. They had taken so much silver out of the mountains that
_____. Eventually, the price of silver got so low
that they couldn't make enough money. So _____.

S: And that must be why everybody left the town. _____,
they had no reason to stay there.

P: Exactly. Well, that should be more than enough to get you started. I think you can take it
from here.

S: Thanks for the information. I'm going to the library right now to start working on my report.

Listening Practice 4

Answer Book p. 27

Listen to part of a lecture in an art history class.

Note-taking

C3_P4

1 What is the lecture mainly about?

(A) The role of women in Renaissance paintings

(B) The origin and development of art in Italy

(C) The first highly successful female artist

(D) The connection between philosophy and art

2 Why did Anguissola's father educate his daughters in music and art?

(A) He was encouraged by their obvious interest in art.

(B) He was a former musician and artist himself.

(C) He was following a philosophy popular at the time.

(D) He was inspired by a famous artist that he knew.

3 According to the professor, what are the characteristics of Anguissola's painting style? *Choose 2 answers.*

(A) She focused on accurately showing a person's body.

(B) She painted informal settings and relaxed poses.

(C) She showed people with serious facial expressions.

(D) She tried to capture the inner nature of her subjects.

4 What is the professor's opinion of the time Anguissola spent in Spain?

(A) He thinks it caused too many changes in Anguissola's painting style.

(B) He believes it created conflict between her Anguissola the queen.

(C) He feels it was when she produced Anguissola's best work.

(D) He views it as the main reason for Anguissola's success.

Listen again to part of the lecture. Then answer the question.

5 Why does the student say this: 🎧

(A) To show that she is familiar with an artist

(B) To confirm that her opinion is correct

(C) To imply that she is impressed by an artist's work

(D) To explain why she finds a detail confusing

▐▌ Dictation ▐▌

Listen again and fill in the blanks.

C3_P4_D

P: Let's continue our discussion of the Renaissance... Over the past few weeks, you may have noticed that all the painters we've talked about were men. However, there were a few female painters as well. Today, I'd like to discuss one in particular. Her name was Sofonisba Anguissola. She was _____ .
Now, Anguissola was born to a wealthy family in Italy. And back then, many wealthy families _____... Um, they did this because of a popular philosophy at the time. This philosophy encouraged the artistic and intellectual development of individuals... For wealthy families, this meant _____ . So that's why Anguissola's father educated his daughters in music and art...

S1: How did _____ ?

P: Well, Anguissola's father saw that she was talented. So he decided to continue her training in art. He even sent her to work with a well-known art teacher. That's when she met the famous artist, Michelangelo. She met him during a trip to Rome. _____ early in her career... Yes?

S2: Um, that seems odd. I mean, Michelangelo was one of the greatest painters of the time. Why would he care about an unknown artist?

P: Well, it was because _____... Here, take a look at the image on the screen. It's a drawing Anguissola produced for Michelangelo. It shows her younger brother as a child. He is screaming in pain because a crab is holding on to his finger... Now, it was the boy's expression that particularly impressed Michelangelo. _____ , and he recognized her special talent. Uh, this painting might seem normal today, but it was special during its time. You see, in those days, artists mostly painted people in formal poses and settings. However, Anguissola started a new style. _____ . And her subjects have lively expressions on their faces... Their personalities come alive. I guess you could say that Anguissola tried very hard to _____...
And, once Anguissola started working with oil paint, she was able to produce incredibly realistic works... Um, this one is *Portrait of the Artist's Family*. You can see it is a family portrait. Her father, sister, brother, and even the family dog, are in it. Again, this shows _____... However, this painting was never finished. Um, you see, at around the same time, Anguissola was invited to the palace of King Philip II of Spain. There, _____ . She was also the queen's personal painting instructor. It was a great honor to paint for the king's family. In my view, it was here in Spain that _____ .

Answer Book p. 28

TOEFL Listening

C3_T1

Note-taking

1 What problem does the student have?

   Ⓐ She could not find a job on campus.

   Ⓑ She cannot sign up for an event.

   Ⓒ She does not know how to use a website.

   Ⓓ She did not submit a form on time.

2 What does the employee say about companies at the fair?

   Ⓐ They will attend several different job fairs.

   Ⓑ They prefer students who are graduating soon.

   Ⓒ They plan to do some interviews online.

   Ⓓ They are all part of the same industry.

3 What has the student done in recent years?

   Ⓐ Improved her grades

   Ⓑ Joined campus programs

   Ⓒ Accepted jobs related to computers

   Ⓓ Organized activities for students

4 What does the employee suggest the student do before the job fair?

   Ⓐ Review a list of companies at the fair

   Ⓑ Prepare questions for company representatives

   Ⓒ Talk to students who have attended previous fairs

   Ⓓ Ask the school to change a policy

Listen again to part of the conversation. Then answer the question.

5 What does the employee mean when he says this: 🎧

   Ⓐ He is unable to do anything differently.

   Ⓑ He has misunderstood the student's request.

   Ⓒ He thinks the student has made a mistake.

   Ⓓ He disagrees with the rules for an event.

‖ Dictation ‖

Answer Book p. 28

Listen again and fill in the blanks.

C3_T1_D

W: Hi. I'm here to talk to someone about the job fair. Am I in the right place?

M: Sure. Do you want to sign up? There are still plenty of spaces available.

W: Well, that's actually why I came. _____,
but I couldn't register.

M: Oh, I think I know what the problem is. Are you graduating at the end of this year?

W: No, I'm a third-year student, so _____.

M: OK, so that's the issue. I'm afraid that _____.

W: Really? To be honest, _____. Students who aren't in their last
year might also be interested in going to the event.

M: I see your point. But my hands are tied. I tell students the rules and help them register.
That's it. _____, other students might hear about it and be upset.

W: I understand... I don't think I should get special treatment. But why can't the school just
_____?

M: Well, there is a reason why the fair is only for graduating students. The companies at the
fair are _____. Many of them will
even have interviews on the same day.

W: Right... I didn't think about that. But I'd like a chance to explain why I want to attend.

M: Sure. I'm willing to listen to what you have to say.

W: So, um... _____ after I graduate. In
recent years, I've even done part-time jobs that are related to my plan. So I really think it
would help my career _____.

M: Hmm... Then how about this? Talk to a professor or an advisor and get a note from them.
It should say that _____. If you bring me that note,
then I will let you sign up.

W: That's great! Thanks for understanding.

M: By the way, it might be a good idea to _____.
You know, questions you want to ask the company representatives that will be at the
event. That way _____.

W: I will definitely do that. Uh, what time does your office close?

M: I will be here until 5 p.m. That gives you about an hour and a half to get the note.

W: OK. I'll make sure to be back before you leave. Thanks so much!

Answer Book p. 30

TOEFL Listening

C3_T2

BIOLOGY

Note-taking

1 What is the main topic of the lecture?

Ⓐ Why certain insect species travel long distances

Ⓑ A navigation method used by some insects

Ⓒ How magnetic fields affect the bodies of insects

Ⓓ The role of the sun and the moon in insect navigation

2 According to the professor, what causes cryptochrome proteins to go through a chemical reaction?

Ⓐ They mix with other proteins in the brain.

Ⓑ They respond to chemicals in an insect's diet.

Ⓒ They are exposed to certain temperatures.

Ⓓ They are affected by a particular type of light.

3 Why does the professor mention an experiment with insects?

Ⓐ To explain how cryptochromes were discovered

Ⓑ To give a different explanation for a phenomenon

Ⓒ To show that only certain insects have cryptochromes

Ⓓ To introduce evidence that supports an idea

4 What do some scientists think about some groups of cryptochromes?

Ⓐ They probably do not affect an insect's vision.

Ⓑ Insects can see them as patterns.

Ⓒ Insects use them only during flight.

Ⓓ They are transferred from one insect to another.

5 What does the professor say about monarch butterflies?

Ⓐ They cannot navigate if one antenna is removed.

Ⓑ They lack cryptochrome proteins in their antennae.

Ⓒ They can also use their antennae for navigation.

Ⓓ They travel farther than any other insect.

Listen again to part of the lecture. Then answer the question.

6 Why does the professor say this: 🎧

Ⓐ To suggest that the student's question is unclear

Ⓑ To indicate that a question is not related to the topic

Ⓒ To point out that the student's guess is not correct

Ⓓ To imply that he cannot provide a clear answer

▌▌ Dictation ▌▌

Listen again and fill in the blanks.

P: As we've discussed, many insects use the sun and the moon to determine which way to travel. But in cloudy and rainy weather, _____. So some species have developed other methods of navigation. For example, _____. They use a special protein called cryptochrome to do this. But first, who can remind us about the magnetic field?

S1: Um, the earth is like _____. Its strongest points are at the North and South Poles. This is why the needle of a compass always points north.

P: Exactly. And _____. It allows them to always know which way is north or south. So how exactly does it work? Um, when cryptochrome proteins absorb light, uh, particularly blue light, _____. Scientists believe that this reaction allows the proteins to respond to Earth's magnetic field. And through this, _____. This theory is supported by an experiment with insects. In the experiment, scientists created an artificial magnetic field. Then, they exposed the insects to light at different times. _____, the insects were able to sense and follow the magnetic field. But when the light was removed... Well, they seemed to _____...

S2: Um, so what you're saying is that exposure to light causes the cryptochrome proteins to sense the magnetic field, right? But, uh, how exactly does this allow insects to find their way?

P: That's a good question. In fact, it's one that a lot of biologists are asking. Um, there are actually a few possibilities. For instance, we know that in many species, cryptochromes are found in the insect's eyes. So, naturally, this suggests that _____. Some scientists think that groups of cryptochromes appear as light and dark spots. The insect can actually _____. Now, the pattern may change as the insect moves around... But _____ _____. Uh, so if the insect is facing north, the spots caused by cryptochrome will always appear in one position. Then, if the insect faces south, the spots will always appear in another position. In this way, the insect always knows which way to go based on the pattern it sees.

Now, _____. They use other methods as well. For example, monarch butterflies have cryptochrome proteins in their eyes, but _____. So this gives the monarch butterflies additional information to help them navigate. Of course, this information probably doesn't look like an image since the cryptochrome proteins are found in the antennae and not in the eyes. And scientists still aren't sure how it all works. Still, regardless of how monarch butterflies use the information to navigate, _____. Every year, thousands of them fly from Canada to Mexico. This trip can take up to two months to complete.

Vocabulary Review

Answer Book p. 31

A. Choose the correct word for each meaning.

import	impress	multicultural	exotic

1 to bring in products from another country: _____

2 having people with different cultural backgrounds: _____

3 foreign, strange, or new: _____

4 to affect deeply or attract admiration: _____

B. Fill in the blanks with the appropriate words from the box.

pressure	cheating	apologize	formal	treatment

5 The low air _____ at the top of a mountain makes breathing more difficult.

6 Children have to be taught to _____ when they have hurt another person.

7 _____ on the test will automatically get you a failing grade.

8 A person's _____ of animals can reveal a lot about their character.

9 Some artists are self-taught, while others receive _____ training at an art school.

C. Choose the closest meaning for each highlighted word.

10 The speaker will respond to questions from the audience at the end of her talk.
(A) greet   (B) reply   (C) admit   (D) return

11 Tall waves and bad weather made crossing the ocean on ships extremely risky.
(A) unsafe   (B) durable   (C) expensive   (D) confident

12 Thanks to an artificial leg, Ron was able to walk again after his accident.
(A) pretentious   (B) abnormal   (C) supernatural   (D) synthetic

13 You can work out at home if going to a gym is too inconvenient.
(A) abrupt   (B) erratic   (C) bothersome   (D) uncertain

14 The fantasy movie was praised because the special effects were so realistic.
(A) unique   (B) obvious   (C) lifelike   (D) beautiful

CHAPTER 04

Attitude

Attitude

About the Question Type

Attitude questions ask you to identify the speaker's attitude or opinion regarding ideas mentioned in a conversation or lecture.

These questions require you to recognize the speaker's feelings, likes and dislikes, or reasons for particular feelings. These questions sometimes require you to listen again to part of the listening passage.

Question Format

- What does the man/woman mean/imply when he/she says this: 🎧
- What is the professor's attitude toward ~?
- What is the professor's opinion of ~?

Key Strategies

- **Step 1** — Pay close attention to parts of the talk where the speaker expresses personal opinions, suggestions, or feelings.

- **Step 2** — Listen to the speaker's tone of voice and way of talking. This can make it easier to identify the speaker's attitude towards a topic.

- **Step 3** — Select the answer choice that best illustrates the speaker's attitude or opinion.

Example

Answer Book p. 31

A. Listen to a conversation between a student and a professor.

C4_ExA

Note-taking

What is the professor's attitude toward the upcoming seminar?

(A) She thinks it was difficult to organize.

(B) She feels it will benefit the students.

(C) She worries it has an inconvenient schedule.

(D) She believes it should be a requirement.

Answer Book p. 31

B. Listen to part of a lecture in a history class.

C4_ExB

Note-taking

Listen again to part of the lecture. Then answer the question.

What does the professor mean when she says this: 🎧

(A) She thinks there is not enough news about an event.

(B) She wants the students to share what they have heard.

(C) She believes the students have some background knowledge.

(D) She expects the situation in Ukraine to keep changing.

▌▌ Dictation ▌▌

Answer Book p. 31

Listen again and fill in the blanks.

A.

C4_ExA_D

S: Professor Lewis, I have some bad news. _____
on Friday afternoon.

P: That's unfortunate. Do you have a problem with the schedule?

S: Yes... I'm a member of the university's basketball team, and _____
_____.

P: Well, as I mentioned in class, _____. However, I really
recommend that you participate. An opportunity like this doesn't come along often.

S: What do you mean?

P: The seminar will have several experts in the field of engineering. _____
_____ if you attended.

S: Hmm... That sounds interesting. Maybe I'll ask my coach _____
_____.

B.

C4_ExB_D

P: For most of its modern history, _____.
Uh, it was part of the Russian Empire. Then, it was a state in the Soviet Union.
But, um, when the Soviet Union fell apart in 1991, leaders in Ukraine declared that
_____. This was made official when over 90 percent
of Ukrainian citizens voted for independence. But there's a problem... Some regions of
Ukraine are home to _____.
These people voted to join Russia. The situation has led to conflicts. In 2014,
_____, a region in southern Ukraine. Additionally,
I'm sure you've all been following the news... Recent events now threaten the entire
country.

Listening Practice 1

Answer Book p. 32

Listen to a conversation between a student and an employee at a financial aid office.

C4_P1

Note-taking

1 What is the conversation mainly about?

(A) The questions that will be asked in an interview

(B) The application process to receive financial aid

(C) The status of the student's scholarship application

(D) The student's request to change an interview date

2 According to the employee, why was an application process delayed?

(A) There were difficulties finding a department head.

(B) There were issues contacting someone overseas.

(C) There was a conflict with the student's interview schedule.

(D) There was a problem receiving a reference letter.

3 What does the employee say about an application process?

(A) It takes a long time because of the students' schedules.

(B) It has to be completed within a specified number of weeks.

(C) It is challenging because only a few applicants are accepted.

(D) It gives an advantage to students with early applications.

4 What is the employee's attitude towards the student's situation?

(A) He is glad she will have additional time to prepare.

(B) He is hopeful that she will receive the results very soon.

(C) He is worried that she will be asked different questions.

(D) He is curious if it will affect the outcome of an application.

Listen again to part of the conversation. Then answer the question.

5 Why does the employee say this: 🎧

(A) To explain how the school reviews applications

(B) To say that the reference has a good personality

(C) To suggest that the student should look for other references

(D) To emphasize that an event is unlikely to happen

▌▌ Dictation ▌▌

C4_P1_D

Listen again and fill in the blanks.

W: Hi there, I was wondering if you could help me. I need to speak to someone about a scholarship.

M: I can help you with that. What exactly do you need to know?

W: Well, here's my situation. _____ about three weeks ago. And I heard that, um, some of the students who submitted applications _____ _____. But I haven't heard anything from the office. So, uh, does this mean _____?

M: Let me check on my computer... Um, it says that your application was reviewed and that _____. But the process could not continue because the school has not been able to _____.

W: I don't understand. I provided the name of my reference and his contact information. Do you know what caused the problem?

M: Well, _____. Didn't he tell you he would be traveling?

W: No, I don't think so. But it has been two months since I talked to him, so maybe he didn't know he'd be traveling at that time.

M: Or perhaps he just forgot to tell you. Anyway, we can't do the interview until we talk to him. So when he gets back and _____, then we'll schedule your interview.

W: I see. But what if the school doesn't like what he says?

M: That doesn't happen often. I mean, it's not like _____ _____, right?

W: I guess that's true. But I'm still worried because of the delay in the interview.

M: You don't need to worry about that. The timing of the interview has no impact on the outcome of your application.

W: That's good to know. _____, isn't it?

M: Oh, it definitely is. We get many applicants, but _____ _____.

W: Right. Well, I'm relieved that I still have a chance. Thanks for your help. By the way, _____?

M: You will get an e-mail that includes the interview date and time.

W: OK, thanks. I'll be waiting for the e-mail.

M: All right. And look on the bright side of your situation. Now, _____ _____ than the other applicants did.

W: That's true. Hmm... I'd better start practicing, then!

Listening Practice 2

Listen to part of a lecture in a music history class.

Note-taking

C4_P2

1 What is the main topic of the lecture?
- (A) Differences between Roman and Greek music
- (B) The use of Greek poetry in Renaissance music
- (C) Musical developments during a period of history
- (D) Common themes in European song lyrics

2 According to the professor, what inspired Renaissance musicians to make secular music?
- (A) The influence of church music
- (B) The decline of religion in Rome
- (C) The works of Greek humanists
- (D) The public demand for new music

3 What does the professor say about word painting?
- (A) A note was often repeated many times.
- (B) The notes of a song were very simple.
- (C) The music affected listeners' emotions.
- (D) A singer danced along with the music.

4 What is the professor's opinion of Renaissance music?
- (A) It is mostly very exciting music.
- (B) It is more important than older music.
- (C) It uses too many kinds of instruments.
- (D) It sounds less interesting today.

Listen again to part of the lecture. Then answer the question.

5 Why does the professor say this: 🎧
- (A) To warn students not to reach the wrong conclusion
- (B) To indicate that a topic is hard to understand
- (C) To point out that a previous statement was incorrect
- (D) To suggest that students often confuse two kinds of music

Dictation

C4_P2_D

Listen again and fill in the blanks.

P: Good afternoon, class. Last week, we talked about developments in European music during the Middle Ages. Today, we're going to move on to the Renaissance. This was another period _____. First, let's do a quick review of last week's material... Who had the most influence over music in Europe during the Middle Ages?

S: I think it was church leaders, right? I mean, _____ _____ at the time.

P: That's exactly right. And as a result, _____. But all of that started to change during the Renaissance. This is when secular music became more popular. Secular music is, of course, _____. Um, I think it'll help if I give you a little background here about the Renaissance. During the Renaissance period, many scholars from other parts of the world moved to Rome. When they did, they brought many examples of classical Greek works, such as poems. So Renaissance artists, including musicians, _____ _____. Now, many ancient Greek artists and writers were humanists. This means that they were more concerned about the lives of humans than gods. So, instead of making art that honored gods or religion, the Greek humanists focused on _____... This is why many Renaissance musicians started making music about people. In short, _____ _____. I'm not saying that church music stopped being made... I don't want to give you the wrong idea. It just means that other kinds of music became important as well.

In addition, the Greek writers also had an impact on _____.
The, uh, Greek philosopher Plato influenced this change... He believed that _____ _____. This led to a new focus on vocal music. Uh, vocal music simply means music with words and not just instruments. So Plato's writing inspired Renaissance composers to _____.
They did this through a technique known as word painting. Um, in word painting, _____ _____. For example, if someone sang about the stars, the musical notes would go up. Or, if the lyrics described an action like running, the notes would be played very fast. Word painting also _____... They could feel sad if both the lyrics and notes were sad, or feel happy if both the lyrics and notes were cheerful.
Of course, today, Renaissance music sounds a bit dull and boring. But, at the time, _____, especially compared to the music that was made before. This was because composers of the Middle Ages were not really interested in expressing emotions. Their main goal was to make religious music about God.

Listening Practice 3

Answer Book p. 35

Listen to a conversation between a student and a professor.

Note-taking

C4_P3

1 Why does the student go to see the professor?

(A) To ask about changing his major

(B) To get permission to attend an event

(C) To discuss an idea for a writing project

(D) To learn about an upcoming conference

2 What does the professor say about the biology conference?

(A) It will be bigger than previous events in the region.

(B) The school newspaper will write about the event.

(C) Biology majors are required to participate in it.

(D) It will receive money from universities in the state.

3 According to the professor, how can the student make sure he meets his deadline?

(A) By starting to write an outline early

(B) By choosing to interview fewer speakers

(C) By not including interviews in an article

(D) By asking professors fewer questions

Listen again to part of the conversation. Then answer the question.

4 Why does the student say this: 🎧

(A) To emphasize that doing a double major is very challenging

(B) To express disappointment that his studies are unrelated

(C) To indicate that he may change one of his majors

(D) To show that others have found his combination of majors unusual

Listen again to part of the conversation. Then answer the question.

5 What does the student mean when he says this: 🎧

(A) He is not sure how many professors there are.

(B) He has not decided how to do the interviews.

(C) He disagrees with the professor's opinion.

(D) He does not know when the deadline is.

‖ Dictation ‖

Answer Book p. 35

Listen again and fill in the blanks.

C4_P3_D

S: Good morning, Professor Murray. I know you are usually busy at this time. But I, uh, need to talk to you about something.

P: Sure. I have a meeting at 11 a.m., but I have some time now. What's on your mind?

S: Well, _____ and since you're in charge of the university paper, I would like to get your opinion.

P: Really? That's great to hear… You're in my journalism class, right?

S: That's right. You might not know this, but _____

_____.

P: I remember you mentioning that in class. I was a little surprised. Those subjects aren't really related.

S: Yeah, I get that a lot. But that's what I wanted to talk to you about. _____

_____, but I'm not sure how to write it, exactly.

P: All right. Why don't you tell me more?

S: Well, next weekend, _____.

I think it is going to be quite an event. Professors from, uh, 12 different universities will be

_____. So it should be exciting for all

of the students, especially for those majoring in biology.

P: Yes, I heard about the event. Apparently, it's going to be _____

_____.

S: Yes… That's why I thought of writing a story about it. I could interview all of the speakers and ask them about how their work will change people's lives. I mean, it'll basically be about _____.

P: Hmm… That's a good idea. I'm a little worried, though, that you're _____

_____. You would have to interview so many professors. Um, you might not have enough time to write the article before the deadline.

S: I don't know... _____, my article will be a little boring. It would just be a summary of the conference and presentations. I don't think anyone would be interested in reading that.

P: Um, I didn't mean to say that you shouldn't do any interviews. What I mean is that you should _____. That would save you a lot of time. So you'll find it easier to _____.

S: That makes sense. I guess I'll e-mail the professors I'm most interested in speaking with and _____.

P: Good plan. And if you need more help with the article, just call me. I'm really looking forward to reading it.

Listening Practice 4

Listen to part of a lecture in a physiology class.

Note-taking

C4_P4

1 What is the professor mainly discussing?

(A) Whether animals have thoughts

(B) How animal intelligence is determined

(C) The various brain sizes of different animals

(D) The intelligence of apes compared to other animals

2 According to the professor, why do people tend to think of apes as intelligent?

(A) They do well on intelligence tests.

(B) They act in similar ways to humans.

(C) They can be trained to follow instructions.

(D) They have similar brain structures as humans.

3 What does the professor say about chimpanzees?

(A) They are smarter than other apes.

(B) They can only distinguish certain colors.

(C) They have smaller brains than humans.

(D) They can recognize themselves in a mirror.

Listen again to part of the lecture. Then answer the question.

4 Why does the professor say this: 🎧

(A) To mention a difficulty with measuring brains

(B) To point out that large brains take longer to analyze

(C) To show that studying animals requires effort

(D) To say that an idea is complicated to understand

Listen again to part of the lecture. Then answer the question.

5 What does the professor mean when she says this: 🎧

(A) More studies of sperm whales need to be done.

(B) Sperm whales are probably not smarter than people.

(C) Some brains of sperm whales are even heavier than 18 pounds.

(D) Many people are wrong about the intelligence of sperm whales.

‖ Dictation ‖

Listen again and fill in the blanks.

C4_P4_D

P: I'm sure many of you have owned a pet before. And you probably thought they were intelligent because they followed your commands or, uh, did various tricks. But does that make these animals intelligent? How do scientists know _____? This is what I'd like to discuss today.

One of the challenges in studying animal intelligence is the way that we understand intelligence. Normally, um, _____. So, when we evaluate the intelligence of animals, we tend to see if they behave like humans... For instance, if you ask people to identify an intelligent animal, they will usually mention apes, like orangutans. This is because _____. However, animals can be intelligent in other ways. So we have to be careful not to consider animals intelligent just because they behave like humans.

Um, one thing scientists do when they study animal intelligence is look for certain characteristics. One of these is _____. You see, when some animals look in a mirror, they become confused and think that they are seeing a different animal. But other animals, like elephants and dolphins, _____. Um, in one famous experiment, researchers painted a red spot on a chimpanzee's forehead. Of course, the chimpanzee could only see the spot when it looked in a mirror. But when the chimpanzee saw the spot, it didn't reach out to the mirror. _____. This shows that it recognized itself in the mirror. For scientists, this is a sign of high intelligence. Previously, scientists believed that only humans had this kind of intelligence.

OK, now, _____... For example, dogs move their tails when they're happy. They can also appear sad when they lie on the ground and place their head on top of their paws. Some pet owners even believe that _____, like, uh, guilt. You've probably seen the sorry look on a dog's face after it's done something wrong, right? But, according to a recent experiment, dogs tend to look guilty _____... Um, this happens even when they've done nothing wrong. So dogs have emotions, but _____.

Anyway, another way scientists study animal intelligence is by analyzing their brains. One way to do this is to _____. The larger the brain, the smarter the animal. Sounds simple, right? Not so fast. Let's consider the animal with the largest brain, for instance: the sperm whale. The sperm whale's brain weighs 18 pounds on average. That's six times bigger than the human brain. But I don't think many people would agree that sperm whales are smarter than humans. Brain size is important for intelligence, but _____.

Answer Book p. 38

TOEFL Listening

C4_T1

Note-taking

_____

_____

1 What are the speakers mainly discussing?

(A) Applying to join a varsity sports team

(B) Promoting a club among students

(C) Starting a sports team at a school

(D) Renting a location for an activity

2 What is the woman's point of view regarding bowling organizations?

(A) They should be allowed to use a bowling alley.

(B) It is odd that the school doesn't have one.

(C) They need to hold events that will make money.

(D) It is possible that they will form varsity sports teams.

3 According to the man, what is a difference between varsity and club sports teams?

(A) Varsity teams have expensive equipment.

(B) Club teams do not receive school money.

(C) Club teams have to travel more often.

(D) Varsity teams do not play major sports.

4 What does the man say about collecting signatures?

(A) It is optional for all teams on campus.

(B) It is required to choose club members.

(C) It is necessary to get official recognition.

(D) It is needed to become a varsity sport.

Listen again to part of the conversation. Then answer the question.

5 What does the woman mean when she says this: 🎧

(A) She thinks many students are interested in a sport.

(B) She believes she has enough players to start a team.

(C) She does not expect students to cause any issues.

(D) She is sure that there is enough time to submit a form.

‖ Dictation ‖

Answer Book p. 39

Listen again and fill in the blanks.

C4_T1_D

W: Hi. I'm here because, uh, I want to start a new sports team here at school.

M: OK. _____?

W: Well, we have a bowling alley here at school... But, strangely, _____ _____, like a bowling team or a bowling club.

M: I've never thought about that before. But now that you mention it, you're right. First, are you familiar with the difference _____?

W: Not really, but, uh, I've heard of both before.

M: Well, _____. Players don't have to pay for travel, sports equipment, or anything else. All of our major sports teams, like the football team, are varsity sports teams. Then, there are teams for club sports like, um, chess. _____.

W: I don't think that bowling is going to become a varsity sport, which is fine. I'm sure the students who are interested won't mind _____ _____. We can also just take a bus or drive when we play at other schools. Also, renting a place for bowling events shouldn't be that expensive.

M: OK, then. It sounds like you've given this a lot of thought. Now, about becoming a club sport... The team first needs to _____. You'll need to choose a president for your group, and provide a written set of rules. Plus, _____ from at least 50 students on campus for the application.

W: Are you serious? But the team would only have five or six players, not 50!

M: Ha ha... Of course. Remember that anyone can put their signature on the document. They just have to be a student at this school. It's to show that _____ _____.

W: I see. Well, I don't think that will be a problem. I can probably get all the signatures in a couple of weeks.

M: Good... Oh, and lastly, I recommend that _____. The office will need time to review them.

W: OK, I'll do that... Um, do you think there's a good chance that _____ _____? I mean, I want to start looking for our uniforms and practice with the team. Maybe we can even find a coach and sign up for a competition.

M: I'd say your chances are pretty high, so you can probably start to do all those things... Um, but maybe _____.

Answer Book p. 40

C4_T2

ECOLOGY

Note-taking

1 What is the main topic of the lecture?

   Ⓐ Why the world's oceans have less fish

   Ⓑ The formation and impact of dead zones

   Ⓒ How humans can prevent dead zones

   Ⓓ The effects of air and water pollution

2 According to the professor, what is a consequence of excess nutrients in the water?

   Ⓐ Salt levels decrease.

   Ⓑ Blue-green algae develop.

   Ⓒ Oxygen levels increase.

   Ⓓ Large fish begin to die.

3 According to the professor, where can excess nutrients come from?

   Ⓐ Waste that is thrown into the ocean

   Ⓑ Plants that grow near the water

   Ⓒ Chemicals that are used on farms

   Ⓓ Gases from large factories

4 Why does the professor mention Jamaica and Lebanon?

   Ⓐ To highlight areas that rely on agriculture

   Ⓑ To illustrate the size of a certain dead zone

   Ⓒ To give examples of areas near dead zones

   Ⓓ To make a comparison of two regions

5 What is the professor's attitude toward the problem of dead zones?

   Ⓐ Its impact on commercial fishing is not significant.

   Ⓑ It will naturally disappear over time.

   Ⓒ Its negative effects are often exaggerated.

   Ⓓ It cannot be solved without human help.

Listen again to part of the lecture. Then answer the question.

6 Why does the professor say this: 🎧

   Ⓐ To suggest that large fish depend on smaller fish

   Ⓑ To show how a dead zone can grow very quickly

   Ⓒ To emphasize how difficult a process is

   Ⓓ To imply that one problem makes another worse

C4_T2_D

Listen again and fill in the blanks.

P: As everyone knows, it is important to understand environmental issues because we depend on the environment for our survival. Uh, one growing environmental problem is the increase in dead zones in the ocean. Dead zones are areas in the ocean that _____. So let's learn about how they form and their impact...

The main factor in the formation of dead zones is a process called eutrophication. Um, eutrophication is what happens _____.

Naturally, organisms need nutrients to survive. But, if there are too many nutrients, this is a problem for marine life... Uh, for example, excess nutrients like nitrogen and phosphorous can cause blue-green algae to grow. As the algae grow, _____

_____.

S: Uh, where do these excess nutrients come from?

P: Well, _____. Let's look at a common example of eutrophication in agriculture... _____.

Nitrogen, for instance, is an important chemical ingredient in fertilizers. It helps crops grow well. However, when it rains, some of this nitrogen enters streams and rivers. And, eventually, the water from these streams and rivers enters the ocean. When it does,

_____.

So what happens when nutrients enter the ocean? Well, remember the blue-green algae I mentioned? _____ and begin to grow out of control... When this happens, _____. Um, algae blooms are very large groups of algae that grow quickly. And the problem with algae blooms is that _____. This continues even after the algae die because most organisms remove oxygen when they break down... Anyway, after the algae remove oxygen from the water, _____.

And when small organisms die, they break down and remove more oxygen. Everything adds up. Even large fish are affected because they run out of food and have to leave. Eventually, the whole area becomes a dead zone. _____...

A famous example of a dead zone is in the Gulf of Mexico. Every summer, a large dead zone appears where the Mississippi River enters the Gulf. Um, _____. However, it can be greater than 10,000 square kilometers. That is similar to the size of the island of Jamaica or the country of Lebanon! Obviously, this large dead zone causes major changes to the local ecosystem. And it causes direct damage to humans as well. Commercial fishing is a big industry in the area. But _____.

Um, so what can be done about the problem of dead zones? Well, fortunately, _____. But this can only be done with human help. Communities must change farming practices. For instance, farmers can grow organic crops. This will reduce the amount of nutrients that enter the water. So _____ _____, and the wildlife can return.

Vocabulary Review

A. Choose the correct word for each meaning.

fertilizer	ingredient	instrument	guilt

1 a piece of equipment that produces musical sounds: _____

2 a substance added to plants to help them grow: _____

3 a material that is combined with other materials to make something: _____

4 a feeling of shame or of having done something wrong: _____

B. Fill in the blanks with the appropriate words from the box.

secular	cheerful	evaluate	commercial	humanists

5 In a modern _____ state, religion has little influence on politics.

6 Since ancient times, the marketplace has been a center of _____ activity.

7 Renaissance _____ believed in promoting human achievements.

8 IQ tests are not the only way to _____ a person's intelligence.

9 The room was painted in bright yellow to give it a _____ atmosphere.

C. Choose the closest meaning for each highlighted word.

10 World War II officially began when Germany invaded Poland.
   (A) dispersed   (B) expanded   (C) accessed   (D) attacked

11 My college application was rejected because my grades were not good enough.
   (A) reviewed   (B) denied   (C) weakened   (D) lowered

12 A special exhibit was held to honor the late artist's work.
   (A) attend   (B) boost   (C) celebrate   (D) inspect

13 Investigators have identified a suspect in last month's bank robbery.
   (A) named   (B) gathered   (C) studied   (D) arranged

14 Experts worry that competition for declining natural resources will lead to conflict.
   (A) contact   (B) confusion   (C) awareness   (D) fight

CHAPTER 05

Organization

Organization

About the Question Type

Organization questions ask you to identify how a speaker organizes a lecture or presents certain information. Alternatively, you may be asked the reason the speaker mentions a specific piece of information.

Sometimes, you may be asked to determine how specific information relates to the discussion as a whole. Common ways of organizing include: cause and effect, compare and contrast, and problem and solution.

Question Format

- How does the professor introduce/clarify/explain ~?

- How is the lecture organized?

- Why does the man/woman mention ~?

- Why does the man/woman talk about ~?

Key Strategies

- **Step 1** — While listening to the passage, identify the overall organization or structure of the discussion.

- **Step 2** — If the question asks about the organizational structure of the passage, identify how the main idea and its supporting details are organized. If the question asks about the reason why the speaker mentions a specific piece of information, identify how that information connects to the talk as a whole.

- **Step 3** — Select the answer choice that best describes the organizational structure of the passage or the purpose of a specific piece of information.

Example

Answer Book p. 42

A. Listen to a conversation between a student and an employee at the international students office.

C5_ExA

Note-taking

Why does the employee mention construction work?

(A) To indicate that a place cannot be visited
(B) To explain why a tour was canceled
(C) To suggest that a facility will be impressive
(D) To request that an event be postponed

Answer Book p. 42

B. Listen to part of a lecture in an anthropology class.

C5_ExB

Note-taking

How does the professor explain the evidence of an ancient civilization in Bolivia?

(A) By comparing it to a nearby society
(B) By discussing the structures people created
(C) By describing how advanced the technology was
(D) By providing the reason for a misunderstanding

‖ Dictation ‖

Answer Book p. 42

Listen again and fill in the blanks.

C5_ExA_D

A.

M: Welcome to the international students office. How can I help you today?

W: I was hoping you could give me some advice. _____

_____, but I'm not sure where to take them.

M: Well, I assume you're planning to show them the main facilities, like the library and so on.

W: Of course. But, um, I also wanted to show them _____

_____. Maybe we should stop by the sports stadium.

M: Actually, _____. What about the

arts center instead?

W: That's a great idea. The arts center is quite large and modern, so I'm sure they will like it.
Thanks for your help!

C5_ExB_D

B.

P: For years, anthropologists did not think large civilizations existed in the Amazon in ancient
times. However, we now know this isn't true... Um, in what is now Bolivia, _____

_____. And, uh, the people of this civilization

lived there between 500 and 1400 AD. _____, such

as pyramids. And, uh, they _____... Some of

these were built above the surrounding ground. So, uh, this allowed people to

use the roads during the rainy season, when the Amazon flooded. They also

_____. They, uh, used this water to grow rice.

Listening Practice 1

Answer Book p. 43

Listen to a conversation between a student and a professor.

C5_P1

Note-taking

1 What problem does the student have?

(A) He does not know what musicals to watch.

(B) He needs information about a performance.

(C) He has concerns about an assignment.

(D) He wants feedback on a report from class.

2 What does the professor say about live performances?

(A) They are more similar to books than movies.

(B) They cover a wide range of interesting topics.

(C) They have become less popular than before.

(D) They have a strong emotional effect on viewers.

3 What recommendation does the professor give the student?

(A) Choose a musical that is unfamiliar

(B) Select a play that is easy to write about

(C) Spend more time to finish a report

(D) Provide a short summary of a performance

4 What is the professor's opinion of musicals?

(A) They are more entertaining than plays.

(B) They take a long time to produce.

(C) They are harder to analyze than plays.

(D) They use words that are hard to understand.

5 Why does the professor mention drama criticism?

(A) To explain the reason for a requirement

(B) To show why a class is useful for students

(C) To give the student an example to follow

(D) To indicate that a report has to be longer

Dictation

C5_P1_D

Listen again and fill in the blanks.

S: Hello, Professor Shaw. I hope I'm not disturbing you.

P: Hi, Greg. No, not at all. Come in... What can I do for you?

S: Thanks. Um, it's about the report you asked us to write. I like the idea of writing about a play. But _____.

P: So when was the last time you watched one?

S: It was a long time ago... And I don't remember enough to write a report.

P: OK, well, it's important for this report that _____.
Seeing a live performance is very different from reading about it or watching it on video.
_____.

S: I understand. But what if I can't find a play to watch? I mean, the assignment is due next week. There might not be enough time.

P: All right. Well, if you really can't watch a live performance, then I'll allow you to _____. It should be easy to find one online.

S: Thank you, Professor. I can probably do that tonight... Um, _____
_____?

P: Any play will do. Um, but it would be best not to pick something that's too hard. So _____. Also, a modern play would be easier to understand because of the language.

S: All right. Can I ask one more question? Does it have to be a play? Or can it be a musical?

P: Either one will be fine. But I recommend you choose a play because _____
_____.

S: Oh? Why is that?

P: Well, besides analyzing the story, the characters, and so on, _____
_____.

S: Oh, right. OK. But, um, I didn't realize that _____.
I thought we just had to give a brief summary of the story and write our opinion about the performance.

P: Oh, there's more to it than that. Remember, _____.
It's not enough to simply state your opinion. You have to explain your reasons for it. That means _____, including the acting, the way the stage looks, and so on.

S: Umm… That sounds like a lot.

P: Yes, but each of those sections can be one or two paragraphs long. Then, _____
_____.

S: OK. I think I've got it now, Professor. Thank you so much!

Listening Practice 2

Answer Book p. 44

Listen to part of a lecture in a city planning class.

Note-taking

C5_P2

_____

_____

_____

_____

_____

1 What is the main topic of the lecture?

(A) The decline of cities in the Middle Ages

(B) The development of medieval cities

(C) The role of cities in Europe's growth

(D) The quality of life in medieval Europe

2 According to the professor, what were some factors that led to the growth of cities? *Choose 2 answers.*

(A) Better roads between cities

(B) Improved farming methods

(C) Large armies to protect cities

(D) More economic activity

3 According to the professor, what was an advantage of living outside the city walls?

(A) People could avoid paying taxes.

(B) People could live in quiet neighborhoods.

(C) People could buy cheaper products.

(D) People could trade more easily with farmers.

4 How does the professor organize the lecture?

(A) By contrasting the design of early and late medieval cities

(B) By listing the reasons people moved to cities in the Middle Ages

(C) By describing how medieval cities formed and changed over time

(D) By comparing how cities were built in medieval and modern times

Listen again to part of the lecture. Then answer the question.

5 What does the professor imply when she says this: 🎧

(A) Most people knew the cost of living in a city.

(B) Many people refused to pay their taxes.

(C) It is natural for people to pay for a benefit.

(D) It was common for cities to need protection.

▌▌ Dictation ▌▌

Listen again and fill in the blanks.

C5_P2_D

P: These days, many modern cities are carefully planned. But, uh, this wasn't the case hundreds of years ago. Most cities first developed as small towns, and then _____. This was true for European cities during the Middle Ages. Today, we're going to look at how these cities developed.

So, at the start of the Middle Ages, _____ in the countryside. However, advances in farming tools and methods allowed them to produce more food with less labor. This meant _____ _____. And, uh, not everyone had to grow crops to feed themselves. So some of them went to places with more people, such as castles, seaports, and rivers. There, they sold their crops. Over time, _____ _____ like merchants, builders, and so on. So, uh, around these areas, permanent cities and markets grew.

As the cities grew, _____. Walls made it easier to protect a city and to control who came in and out. Now, in exchange for the protection that cities provided, _____. No surprise there... I mean, you don't get something for nothing. In addition, outsiders who wanted to trade in a city had to _____. Gradually, that's how these walled cities became important trading centers.

_____, they attracted even more people. And, uh, eventually, the space inside the walls became too crowded. So _____. Uh, they built their homes and shops there. Also, there was an advantage to living outside the city walls... _____. Some merchants even did business outside the city walls just to avoid taxes.

These buildings outside the city walls became known as suburbs. City officials actively encouraged the growth of these suburbs because they, uh, _____ _____. Then, new suburbs would grow outside the old suburbs. And, like the old suburbs, these new ones later became part of the city as well. So, um, this process continued for many years... And, well, that's _____ _____. Over time, they grew far beyond their original walls. But, um, communities that were further away from the city's center were less organized. Um, _____. And they were less stable. People could easily move in and out, so illegal trade and other crimes became a problem. I think it's a shame. The original order of medieval walled cities was impressive before they grew bigger. Anyhow, the medieval walled city and its suburbs are considered _____.

Listening Practice 3

Answer Book p. 46

Listen to a conversation between a student and a professor.

Note-taking

C5_P3

1 Why does the student go to see the professor?

(A) To explain why she changed her major

(B) To discuss a school rule that she thinks is unfair

(C) To ask about which courses he is teaching

(D) To request his approval to take a class

2 Why does the student mention a window?

(A) To illustrate the importance of learning new things

(B) To suggest that art opens up opportunities

(C) To show the connection between psychology and art

(D) To identify the origins of an approach to art

3 What kind of job is the student interested in doing?

(A) Teaching art history

(B) Working in a museum

(C) Becoming a psychologist

(D) Creating professional art

4 What does the professor say about Professor Park's class?

(A) It is only for students with history majors.

(B) It covers some difficult course concepts.

(C) It focuses on a more specific topic.

(D) It includes discussions on reading materials.

Listen again to part of the conversation. Then answer the question.

5 Why does the professor say this:

(A) To emphasize that it is uncertain if there will be space

(B) To suggest that the student should not take a class

(C) To indicate that something he said earlier was wrong

(D) To introduce a new course for the student to consider

Dictation

Listen again and fill in the blanks.

S: Hi, Professor Bell. Do you have time to talk?

P: Sure, Lydia. Um, you were in my Introduction to Visual Arts class, right? Didn't you _____?

S: Yes, that's actually why I'm here. You see, I want to take the art history class that you're teaching this semester, but _____.

P: If you don't mind me asking, _____?

S: Well, I think psychology is present in every field, but especially art. Art is kind of like a window into the artist's mind. So, for me, _____.

P: That's a great point. So does this mean that you're changing your major back to art history?

S: No, _____. But I'm also thinking of getting a part-time job, and I want to do something related to art. A position as an assistant at a museum would be amazing, but _____...

P: That's very impressive... You know, when I was a student, I couldn't imagine getting a part-time job. My assignments and exams kept me busy... I mean, I had some free time, but I used it to relax, not to work. Unfortunately, _____ right now...

S: Oh, no. Did I forget a requirement? Do I need to get permission from someone else?

P: No, that's not the problem. Um, I'll just have to check _____ _____. Of course, you can register if the class is not full. But you never know...

S: Uh... _____? I really wanted to take your art history class...

P: Well, you could always wait and take it next semester. Or if you don't want to do that, _____.

S: I definitely don't want to wait. I want to get a job soon, so it's important that _____ _____. What is the other class?

P: It's taught by Professor Park. However, _____. It's specifically about African art... But you'll still learn a lot about general art history.

S: OK. It's good to know there is another option in case I can't get into your class. Thanks for all of your help.

Listening Practice 4

Answer Book p. 47

Listen to part of a lecture in a physics class.

Note-taking

C5_P4

1 What is the main topic of the lecture?

(A) The various types of sound waves

(B) Why sound waves have different speeds

(C) Why a sound changes as its source moves

(D) How sound waves and light waves are similar

2 Why does the professor mention a pool of water?

(A) To demonstrate how low sounds can become

(B) To show how sound waves change underwater

(C) To illustrate distances between sound waves

(D) To explain the sound of a dropping stone

3 How does the professor explain the importance of movement in the Doppler effect?

(A) By providing definitions from several sources

(B) By giving a familiar example from everyday life

(C) By illustrating how it was first discovered

(D) By comparing how it works in different places

4 According to the professor, what is true of the sound of an ambulance siren?

(A) It will be higher if the vehicle is fast.

(B) It will be louder if the sound is low.

(C) It will be faster as the vehicle moves away.

(D) It will be constant if the vehicle stops.

Listen again to part of the lecture. Then answer the question.

5 Why does the professor say this: 🎧

(A) To encourage the student to offer an opinion

(B) To acknowledge that the student understood a lesson

(C) To prevent confusion about a new concept

(D) To clarify the main point of the lecture

Dictation

C5_P4_D

Listen again and fill in the blanks.

P: Have you ever heard an ambulance go past you? Well, you may have noticed something strange. As the ambulance gets closer, the sound of the siren gets louder and faster. What explains this? Well, it's something called the Doppler effect.

So, uh, the Doppler effect is _____ from a moving object. And this change in sound is directly _____

_____. Um, as you know, sound moves through the air in waves. And when those waves reach our ears, we hear them as sound. Now, sound waves that are close together have a high sound, like a whistle. In contrast, sound waves that are far apart have a low sound, like thunder. Um, let me describe it another way... It's like _____. The stone creates a circle of waves around it. Near the middle, the waves are close together. The waves that are far away are farther apart. So, near the source of a noise, sound waves are close to each other and have a high sound. However, away from the source of a noise, sound waves are far apart and have a low sound. But, uh, surprisingly, _____

_____... Um, the speed of sound is around 1,200 kilometers per hour. So, again, why do we hear the sounds differently?

S: Uh, is it because _____?

P: Good. Someone was paying attention... But when we're talking about the Doppler effect, it isn't just the distance between sound waves that's important. _____

_____, too. Um, let's go back to our earlier example. You hear an ambulance coming. When the ambulance is moving toward you, you hear many sound waves near the source of the noise. So _____.

It will seem louder and faster than normal. But now, as the ambulance moves away, the sound waves you hear are getting farther and farther from their source. So _____. They seem lower and slower than normal. And what do you think happens if the ambulance stops in front of you? Well, _____. When the Doppler effect is not happening, _____. So you hear the siren at a constant speed and loudness.

And why is any of this important to know? Well, the Doppler effect is based on moving objects. So we can use it to _____

_____. For example, we can use it to detect thunderstorms, measure how fast a car is moving, and even see how blood moves through our bodies. So as you can see, it's a very useful concept.

CHAPTER 05

HACKERS APEX LISTENING for the TOEFL iBT Expert

Answer Book p. 48

TOEFL Listening

C5_T1

Note-taking

_____

_____

1 What are the speakers mainly discussing?

Ⓐ Whether the student should join a musical group

Ⓑ Why the student must officially register a school club

Ⓒ How the student can receive financial support for a group

Ⓓ Which events the student can hold on the campus

2 According to the student, why will the members of the club need to travel?

Ⓐ They hope to perform for other students.

Ⓑ They intend to promote a cappella at other schools.

Ⓒ They want to compete with other groups.

Ⓓ They plan to work with clubs at other universities.

3 How does the employee help the student?

Ⓐ By suggesting several ways to get funding

Ⓑ By showing the student some guidelines

Ⓒ By reviewing the student's request

Ⓓ By providing a list of multiple organizations

4 What will the student probably do next?

Ⓐ Visit another department

Ⓑ Fill out an application

Ⓒ Download a request form

Ⓓ View the university's website

Listen again to part of the conversation. Then answer the question.

5 Why does the employee say this: 🎧

Ⓐ To suggest that a process is not difficult

Ⓑ To ask that the student clarify a statement

Ⓒ To say he does not know which is the best choice

Ⓓ To express agreement with the student's opinion

Dictation

Listen again and fill in the blanks.

C5_T1_D

M: Good morning. Is there something I can help you with?

W: Yes, um, this the student activities office, right? Some students and I are forming an a cappella club. And, uh, I had some questions about this...

M: OK. Well, first, _____. I can give you one here or you can find one on our website. Once you've completed the form, we will review it. Uh, this usually takes a couple of weeks. If your club is approved, we will notify you by e-mail.

W: Um, actually, _____. I guess I should have mentioned it right away. What I wanted to find out was _____.

Um, for example, we're hoping to participate in singing competitions against other universities. Obviously, we will have to travel, and traveling can get expensive.

M: I see. Well, you have a couple of options... First, _____

_____. But, uh, it's not a lot of money.

W: Um, could you tell me how much we might get?

M: _____, the amount can be anything from $800 to $1,600 per semester. I can give you the application form to fill out now. It should only take a week or so to process...

W: Oh. _____... And, we only have seven members, so we might not even get the full amount.

M: That's right. Groups that have 10 members or less _____...

W: Well, that amount won't even cover the basics. But you mentioned another option?

M: That's right... _____. Um, these are funds offered by business or art groups outside the school. These organizations usually

_____.

W: Oh wow. That's great. But, um, could an a cappella club get one of these grants?

M: Possibly. There are a couple of grants for students who are studying music. The thing is, you would have to _____.

W: That sounds a little complicated.

M: You can say that again... It also takes time. But _____.

Um, it includes a list of these grants, with links to the organizations that offer them.

W: OK... Does the site also _____?

M: There are some general recommendations. But if you need more help, stop by the music department office. Um, they can give you some useful tips.

W: Great! Thank you so much. _____ now?

M: Oh, sure. Let me get the form for you...

C5_T2

CHEMISTRY

Note-taking

1 What is the lecture mainly about?

(A) The melting point of solid objects

(B) The effects of pressure and heat

(C) The process that turns water into ice

(D) The reason that ice is slippery

2 Why does the professor mention ice skating?

(A) To illustrate how ice is formed

(B) To show how a theory works

(C) To point out a flaw in an explanation

(D) To explain why an idea is incorrect

3 What does the professor mention as a problem with the pressure-melting theory?

(A) It only applies to ice in specific locations.

(B) It is wrong about the amount of melting.

(C) It does not explain differences in weight.

(D) It was introduced when temperatures were cooler.

4 How does the professor introduce the latest theory?

(A) By reminding students about a previous lesson

(B) By describing a famous experiment

(C) By explaining how water is structured

(D) By comparing different liquids

5 According to the professor, why does ice feel hard?

(A) Frozen water molecules form bonds.

(B) Water freezes in separate layers.

(C) The part exposed to air is very dry.

(D) Water molecules move slowly in ice.

Listen again to part of the lecture. Then answer the question.

6 What does the professor mean when she says this: 🎧

(A) Skating on ice slowly reduces its slipperiness.

(B) New ice skates can help people move faster.

(C) Moving air causes ice to melt more quickly.

(D) Heat is not enough to explain why ice is slippery.

Dictation

Listen again and fill in the blanks.

P: Yesterday, we learned how a solid object changes into a liquid. It has to reach its melting point. And, in order to do that, you have to increase the temperature or apply pressure to the object... Now, with this in mind, let's move on to our main topic for today... _____? Does anyone want to guess?

S1: Um, isn't it like you said? We apply pressure to ice when we walk on it. This causes _____... Then, the melted ice becomes slippery.

P: OK, that's a reasonable explanation. And since the 19th century, that is what scientists believed. They called it the pressure-melting theory because _____ _____. Let me give you the example that is commonly used. It's, uh, from ice skating... On the bottom of every pair of ice skates, there are very thin blades, right? Now, when you put the ice skates on, _____ _____. So, according to the pressure-melting theory, the blades create a lot of pressure on top of the ice and melt it. That's what makes the ice slippery. But there are problems with the pressure-melting theory. First, the ice is slippery _____. It's also slippery when you walk on it with regular shoes. And second, _____. Um, for instance, scientists have discovered that the pressure from a person's weight can only melt the ice a little. So, uh, you would need to be extremely heavy to melt the ice a lot... Are there any other guesses?

S2: What about heat? Doesn't the act of moving shoes or skates over ice create heat? Maybe it's the heat that melts the ice. Or maybe _____.

P: OK. Once again, that's a good guess based on what we know about pressure and heat. In fact, it's partly correct. Repeated movements create heat. So moving over ice can make skates hotter. Then, _____, which makes it slippery... However, we also know that ice becomes slippery as soon as you step on it. So _____. We need a better answer. All right. So the latest theory we have is that _____ _____. This happens due to the structure of water. Um, as you know, another name for water is H_2O. This is because each water molecule is made of two hydrogen atoms and one oxygen atom. Now, in liquid water, the molecules of water move around constantly. But _____, each frozen water molecule sticks to another molecule next to it. They form bonds and become fixed in place. This is why ice feels hard. But what happens on the top of the ice? There, _____. So some of the molecules in the ice are not able to form any bonds. As a result, these molecules do not stay fixed and continue to move around like liquid water. This movement is _____ _____. It is also what makes ice slippery.

Vocabulary Review

A. Choose the correct word for each meaning.

anthropologist	slippery	canal	criticism

1 not easy to stand or move on: _____

2 someone who studies human customs, beliefs, and traditions: _____

3 a manmade waterway used for transport: _____

4 a method of analyzing something closely: _____

B. Fill in the blanks with the appropriate words from the box.

fixed	suburbs	concept	funding	unplanned

5 Many student clubs rely on _____ from the university to pay for their activities.

6 Nearly 90 percent of Los Angeles residents live outside the city in _____.

7 The TV was _____ securely to the wall to ensure it would not fall off.

8 The bus was forced to make an _____ stop due to the heavy rain.

9 Isaac Newton is most famous for discovering the _____ of gravity.

C. Choose the closest meaning for each highlighted word.

10 The city government has decided to construct a large sports center.
 (A) build   (B) operate   (C) access   (D) open

11 Inequality is present in every country, but it is far worse in some than in others.
 (A) spreading   (B) excessive   (C) existing   (D) persuasive

12 Items from the museum's permanent collection are stored away when not in use.
 (A) perpetual   (B) remarkable   (C) visible   (D) contemporary

13 The labor of thousands of people was required to erect the Great Pyramid of Giza.
 (A) knowledge   (B) time   (C) work   (D) desire

14 The goods carried by the ship were transferred to the trucks by a crane.
 (A) moved   (B) secured   (C) displayed   (D) connected

CHAPTER 06

Connecting Contents

Connecting Contents

About the Question Type

Connecting Contents questions ask you to complete a table or chart that shows how the ideas directly mentioned in a conversation or lecture relate to one another.

List questions require you to identify whether the statements listed in a table are true or false. Matching questions ask you to classify the statements or identify which category they belong to, while Ordering questions require you to put the steps of a process or series of events in the correct order.

Question Format

List
- Indicate whether each of the following is mentioned/included/suggested/etc.
  Click in the correct box for each phrase.

	Yes/Included/Suggested	No/Not Included/Not Suggested
Statement A		
Statement B		
Statement C		

Matching
- Indicate for each example what type of ~.

Ordering
- The professor explains the steps ~. Put the steps listed below in the correct order.

Key Strategies

- **Step 1** — Pay attention to the important details and overall flow of the talk.
- **Step 2** — Identify the number of ideas being discussed, and predict which type of question will be asked. Types of questions include List, Matching, and Ordering.
- **Step 3** — Select the answer choices in the table or chart that best represent the information in the passage for each item.

Example

Answer Book p. 52

A. Listen to a conversation between a student and a professor.

Note-taking

C6_ExA

What does the professor suggest the student do for an interview? Indicate whether each of the following is a suggested option. *Click in the correct box for each phrase.*

	Suggested	Not Suggested
(A) Research a company online		
(B) Prepare for some questions		
(C) Speak with another professor		
(D) Arrive at a location early		

Answer Book p. 52

B. Listen to part of a lecture in a biology class.

Note-taking

C6_ExB

In the lecture, the professor discusses the teeth of carnivores, herbivores, and omnivores. Indicate whether each of the following describes the teeth of carnivores, herbivores, or omnivores. *Click in the correct box for each phrase.*

	Carnivores	Herbivores	Omnivores
(A) The back teeth are like knives.			
(B) The front and back teeth are similar to people's teeth.			
(C) The back teeth are broad and even.			
(D) The front teeth are long and pointy.			

Dictation

Answer Book p. 52

Listen again and fill in the blanks.

C6_ExA_D

A.

S: Hi, Professor Nelson. Do you have a minute?

P: Sure, Carl. What's on your mind?

S: I applied for a summer internship at a manufacturing company, and I have an interview on Thursday. I was wondering _____.

P: I'd be happy to. Let's see... First, go online and learn all you can about the company. And make sure to _____ with a friend.

S: Got it. Anything else?

P: I also recommend that you get to the interview location about 15 minutes _____ _____. That way, you will be less nervous and can _____ _____.

S: Great. Thanks for your suggestions, Professor Nelson.

C6_ExB_D

B.

P: So we've recently been discussing the diets of different animals. Well, _____ _____. Today, I'm going to talk about their teeth.

In carnivores, which are animals that eat only meat, the front teeth are long and pointed. This helps them to _____. Their back teeth are sharp and very thin. They are like knives that cut meat into smaller pieces. But, in herbivores, which only eat plants, _____. They also have very rough surfaces. This helps them chew leaves and nuts. Finally, there are omnivores, _____. Um, their teeth are quite similar to our own.

Listening Practice 1

Answer Book p. 53

Listen to a conversation between a student and a student activities office employee.

Note-taking   C6_P1

---

1 Why does the student visit the student activities office?

(A) To look for the head of an organization

(B) To ask for advice about a singing competition

(C) To inquire about how to start a new club

(D) To find out what happened to the old choir

2 Why does the employee mention the old school choir?

(A) To explain the steps for setting up a school club

(B) To suggest he is also surprised that there is no choir

(C) To remind the student that there is no need for a new club

(D) To recommend a school choir for the student to join

3 According to the student, what are some benefits of choir competitions? *Choose 2 answers.*

(A) Having the opportunity to travel the country performing

(B) Meeting other singers and learning from them

(C) Being able to sing in front of an audience

(D) Getting the chance to receive award money

4 In the conversation, the speakers make suggestions about how the choir can lower costs. Indicate whether each of the following was a suggestion. *Click in the correct box for each phrase.*

	Yes	No
(A) Create their own costumes		
(B) Get a discount on bus tickets		
(C) Participate only in local competitions		
(D) Print songbooks from a library		

Listen again to part of the conversation. Then answer the question.

5 Why does the student say this: 🎧

(A) To suggest that the employee has made a mistake

(B) To indicate that she did not hear the employee correctly

(C) To say that she does not know how to form a choir

(D) To show that she is disappointed in an amount of money

Dictation

Listen again and fill in the blanks.

C6_P1_D

M: Hi. What brings you to the office today?

W: Hello. Um, I'm here because I have an idea for a student club. But I'm not sure what to do. I'd like to know _____ .

M: OK... Could you tell me about what kind of club you want to form? We might already have one like it at the school.

W: Basically, _____ . Um, I was shocked to hear that the school doesn't have one already.

M: I know! Actually, _____ . But the students lost interest in it over time. It would be great to have a new one. So anyway, to start a club, first you're going to need to tell me _____ .

W: Well, obviously, I like to sing. But other than that, _____ , which is really important for young singers. _____ _____ . And they can also meet successful singers and get advice from them.

M: Hmm... I suppose competitions are very useful for students...

W: That's why I want to start an official school choir. Of course, _____ _____ to enter competitions.

M: Hmm... To be honest, new clubs receive just a hundred dollars at first.

W: A hundred dollars? _____ ... I mean, a choir needs money to pay for songbooks, costumes, bus tickets, and many other things...

M: Well, don't get discouraged. There are a few options that you can try. One of the quickest and simplest things you can do is to lower your costs. For example, you could have _____ instead of buying them from a store. And, um, another idea is to _____ . You can print out as many copies as you need and take them with you.

W: Yes, I guess we could do those things... And for a while, we could _____ _____ . Uh, that way, we can get there easily on local transportation.

M: That's a good idea.

W: Before I submit a new club registration form, though, I need to _____ _____ ...

M: Of course. Feel free to come back here anytime you have a question.

W: Thank you, I will.

Listening Practice 2

Listen to part of a lecture in an art history class.

Note-taking
_____

C6_P2

1 What is the main topic of the lecture?

(A) The different purposes of art

(B) How art led to a cultural revolution

(C) Why some artists choose murals as an art form

(D) The development and features of an art movement

2 Why does the professor mention the Mexican Revolution?

(A) To show that Mexico experienced many challenges

(B) To suggest that Mexican artists inspired many people

(C) To emphasize the importance of art in Mexican society

(D) To explain why the Mexican government started a project

3 According to the professor, why did the Mexican government choose murals as an art form? *Choose 2 answers.*

(A) They were not expensive to produce.

(B) They could easily be seen by the public.

(C) They used pictures instead of words.

(D) They wanted to cover up damaged buildings.

4 What is the professor's opinion of the government's guidelines for artists?

(A) They gave artists less freedom.

(B) They should have been explained better.

(C) They required much improvement.

(D) They were not strict enough.

5 Indicate whether each of the following describes the art of Rivera, Orozco, or Siqueiros. *Click in the correct box for each phrase.*

	Rivera	Orozco	Siqueiros
(A) Used dark and dramatic colors			
(B) Changed in style over time			
(C) Concerned with the future			
(D) Criticized the upper class			

Dictation

Listen again and fill in the blanks.

P: Last time, we learned about how art can be used for different purposes. Um, for instance, it can be used to communicate ideas and remember important events. Well, today, we will look at Mexican muralism, _____ in the early 20th century. Specifically, we will consider how muralism came about and discuss its characteristics.

So Mexican muralism started as a project of the Mexican government. Um, this happened after the Mexican Revolution of 1910 to 1920. You see, _____ _____. Mainly, it gave more power to the middle and lower classes of Mexican society. So the new Mexican government wanted to remember this important event. To do this, _____...

Um, murals are basically wall paintings. And, in Mexico, they were painted on the walls of public buildings.

Why murals? Well, there were several reasons... One reason is that _____ _____. Uh, many people in the lower classes couldn't read or write. But they could look at the pictures in a mural and quickly get its message. Also, anyone passing by could see the murals since _____.

They were often large and colorful...

Um, the murals covered many themes and ideas, too... As I said, they were intended to help people remember the Mexican Revolution, so _____.

But the government also wanted the murals to make Mexicans feel proud of their culture, and, um, to think positively about the future. So there were inspiring images of people working together on farms and in factories. Um, the government even tried to _____. But, uh, thankfully, these were later removed.

Artists work better when they have the freedom to choose their own styles and themes...

OK. Now, among the artists who painted murals, _____.

They were known as "The Three Great Ones." They were Diego Rivera, José Clemente Orozco, and David Siqueiros. Um, each one became _____ _____... For instance, Rivera's work was traditional and positive. He liked to show scenes of everyday life or images from Mexico's past. His murals were painted in a European style at first, but _____.

They, uh, frequently used earth colors and symbols of the land. Orozco's murals, however, were more negative. They were painted in dark, dramatic colors. They were also often _____. And, um, lastly, we have Siqueiros, who was the youngest. Siqueiros was involved in Communism and so _____. But he was also concerned about the future and painted scenes about science and technology with lots of bold lines.

Listening Practice 3

Listen to a conversation between a student and a university administrator.

Note-taking

C6_P3

1 What is the main topic of the conversation?

(A) Information about transferring to a new school

(B) The requirements for becoming an editor

(C) The possibility of joining an organization

(D) Advice for getting a job after graduation

2 Why does the man want to be a writer at the newspaper?

(A) He has previous experience with the job.

(B) He was offered the position by a professor.

(C) He wants to inform students about an issue.

(D) He missed the deadline for another position.

3 In the conversation, the woman explains the steps of an application process. Put the steps listed below in the correct order. *Drag each answer choice to the space where it belongs.*

Step 1	
Step 2	
Step 3	
Step 4	

(A) Receive a topic for a section

(B) Participate in an interview

(C) Allow qualifications to be reviewed

(D) Wait to be contacted about an article

4 Why does the woman mention the largest newspaper in the city?

(A) To introduce a volunteer opportunity for the man to consider

(B) To give an example of a benefit of working at the school paper

(C) To criticize companies that offer unpaid internships to students

(D) To compare newspapers in large cities with those in small towns

Listen again to part of the conversation. Then answer the question.

5 Why does the man say this: 🎧

(A) To confirm the date of a deadline

(B) To remind the woman of his original question

(C) To find out where to get more information

(D) To ask about something that was not explained

Dictation

C6_P3_D

Listen again and fill in the blanks.

M: Hi. Is this the office of *The College Times*?

W: That's correct. We produce the student newspaper for Boston College. How can I help you today?

M: I just transferred here from Texas. I used to work at a university newspaper there. So _____. Um, do you have any positions available?

W: Actually, we do. But what are you interested in doing, exactly? Most students work as writers.

M: Well, I was a writer at my old school's paper, so _____. Could you explain the application process to me?

W: First, _____ to make sure you have the right qualifications. So you'll need to submit one to us. Keep in mind that the deadline for applications is on September 15.

M: Got it. Um, just to check... _____?

W: Not when you apply. Once we have looked over your application, our editor will contact you to ask for one.

M: Could you tell me more about that? Would I need to write about a certain topic, or _____?

W: Just let us know which section you're interested in writing for in your application. Then, _____. Your article will have to be between 500 and 800 words long.

M: OK. And if the editor is satisfied with my article, will I be able to _____ _____?

W: Actually, there's one more step. _____. It gives us an opportunity to find out more about you and check if you'll get along well here.

M: I understand. Is there anything else I should be aware of _____?

W: Well, some of our students have become journalists at national newspapers after they graduated. Some of them even hold workshops for the students here.

M: That's wonderful. It seems like it'd also be a good opportunity for me to _____ _____.

W: Exactly. In addition, each summer, _____ at the *Boston Globe*. It's the city's largest newspaper.

M: Wow. How are they chosen?

W: _____ and then makes their selections.

M: OK, this all sounds amazing. I'm going to go back to my dormitory now and prepare my application.

Listening Practice 4

Listen to part of a lecture in a geology class.

Note-taking

C6_P4

1 What is the main purpose of the lecture?
- (A) To discuss the effects of glaciers
- (B) To describe the formation process of glaciers
- (C) To present a new theory about climate change
- (D) To explain a possible cause of a phenomenon

2 According to the professor, what evidence can be seen about glaciers? *Choose 2 answers.*
- (A) Large frozen lakes
- (B) Pieces of rock
- (C) Unusual types of plants
- (D) Marks in the ground

3 According to the professor, where does the name Snowball Earth come from?
- (A) The rolling movement of glaciers
- (B) The way a frozen Earth might look
- (C) The types of sediments found in glaciers
- (D) The effect of a climate event on the weather

4 In the lecture, the professor outlines the process by which the Snowball Earth might have happened. Put the steps listed below in the correct order. *Drag each answer choice to the space where it belongs.*

Step 1	
Step 2	
Step 3	
Step 4	

- (A) The oceans froze and ice spread.
- (B) Sunlight got reflected back into space.
- (C) Ice reached the middle of the planet.
- (D) High rainfall and low carbon dioxide caused a cooling effect.

Listen again to part of the lecture. Then answer the question.

5 Why does the professor say this: 🎧
- (A) To say that a theory is no longer accepted
- (B) To suggest that a theory will be discussed next time
- (C) To encourage the student to propose an idea
- (D) To indicate that a question has no clear answer

‖ Dictation ‖

C6_P4_D

Listen again and fill in the blanks.

P: Glaciers are thick layers of ice that move across the land. Uh, they are usually found in cold places like the North and South Pole, or high mountains like the Himalayas... However, _____ in parts of the world that are mostly warm today. Well, now, we'll discuss a theory that might explain this. It's called the Snowball Earth theory. It suggests that _____

_____.

So the Snowball Earth theory was developed to explain how glaciers could have existed all around the planet, _____. You see, as I said, glaciers usually form in extremely cold places. Um, they form when snow falls in one area over a long period of time. Eventually, _____.

These glaciers move because of gravity. When they move, _____

_____. They also leave marks in the ground beneath them. The sediments and marks have been found in countries such as India and Australia. This evidence is why scientists believe glaciers once existed in places that are now warm. So, um, we know for sure that _____. The question is, how did this happen?

Well, in general, _____: hot and cold. And, um, billions of years ago, these two types of climate lasted a very long time. So, for millions of years, Earth could be hot. Then, for millions of years, it could be cold... According to the Snowball Earth theory, _____, the ice that is normally found in the North and South Pole spread. And the ice continued to spread until it covered most of the planet. Um, this turned Earth into a frozen ball. So if you looked at Earth from outer space, _____... Obviously, that is where the name of the theory comes from.

S: Excuse me, but what caused the Snowball Earth to happen? Uh, do we know what it was?

P: Well, that's open for debate. A number of ideas have been given, such as a change in Earth's orbit or, uh, changes in the atmosphere... There's no way to know for certain. But there is a recent explanation for how the Snowball Earth could have happened. According to this explanation, high amounts of rain and low amounts of carbon dioxide in the atmosphere _____. This caused the water in the oceans to freeze. That's what _____. But then, as the ice spread, it reflected large amounts of sunlight back into space. Uh, _____ since sunlight is needed to warm the earth. This continued until the ice eventually spread all the way up to Earth's tropical regions, near the middle of the planet.

Answer Book p. 59

TOEFL Listening

C6_T1

Note-taking

1 What is the conversation mainly about?

(A) A report about the student's trip

(B) The details of a project for class

(C) A meeting with professional dancers

(D) The requirements for a summer program

2 How is the student going to gather more information about Flamenco?

(A) By visiting teachers of modern dance

(B) By interviewing family members in an area

(C) By talking to performers about the style

(D) By reading books about traditional folk music

3 Why does the professor mention summer break?

(A) To illustrate why she prefers to use e-mail

(B) To explain why it may be hard to meet some people

(C) To emphasize the deadline of a project

(D) To make a point about the best time to visit Seville

4 In the conversation, the professor explains the steps for completing a project. Put the steps listed below in the correct order.

Drag each answer choice to the space where it belongs.

Step 1	
Step 2	
Step 3	
Step 4	

(A) Arrange two more meetings with the professor

(B) Contact several dance schools in a city

(C) Write an outline of the research project

(D) Submit a form to the professor

Listen again to part of the conversation. Then answer the question.

5 Why does the student say this: 🎧

(A) To indicate that he is unfamiliar with a topic

(B) To remind the professor of why he is visiting Seville

(C) To suggest a different possible topic to use

(D) To explain the meaning of a term he just used

Dictation

Listen again and fill in the blanks.

C6_T1_D

S: Thank you for agreeing to meet with me, Professor Hayes.

P: No problem, Andrew. I got the e-mail that you sent. Um, you said that _____ _____, is that right?

S: Yes. I need to complete my research by this summer, and it's already April. So I'm rushing to get it organized.

P: OK. It's still possible to prepare everything in time. Do you have a topic yet?

S: Yes. _____... Uh, that's Spain's folk music and dance tradition. I'm already planning to visit my family in Seville for eight weeks in June and July. I want to _____ while I'm there, uh, to add to my research.

P: I see. That all sounds fine. However, I think it's important that we discuss a few more details before you get started. Um, first, you should _____ in the area that you're going to visit. That way, you can _____ _____ before you get there.

S: That's a great idea. It would save a lot of time. I was also going to send e-mails to some instructors _____. I'm hoping they can meet with me or answer questions over e-mail.

P: _____ since it will be summer break. Most of them will probably be away from campus. So if you're going to send them e-mails, you'd better do it soon. _____ yet?

S: Uh, no, I haven't, but I'm planning to make a list of 10 questions. And ideally, I'd like to interview 15 different dancers. I'm also planning on _____ _____ while I'm there.

P: I think that sounds reasonable. However, if you don't have enough time to interview 15 dancers, a smaller number will do. Second, I'd like you to _____ _____. It should be around a page long, but it should include a summary of your project, expected outcomes, and _____.

S: Sure, no problem. I can get started on the outline right away.

P: Third, you have to _____ before you leave. One to go over the outline and a second one to go over your interview questions. Is that all right?

S: Yeah, that would help me a lot. I'm sure I'll need more advice before I leave.

P: Finally, _____. You'll need to fill it out and I'll need to sign it before the end of the semester.

S: Perfect. I'll fill it out and leave it in your mailbox.

Answer Book p. 60

TOEFL Listening

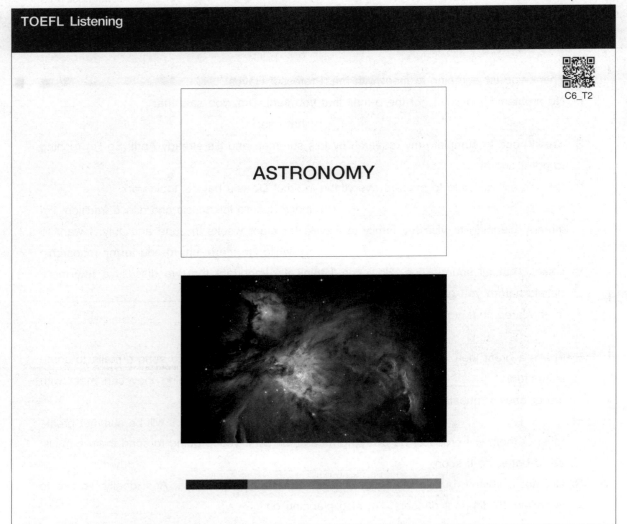

C6_T2

ASTRONOMY

Note-taking

1 What is the main topic of the lecture?

(A) The formation of stars inside nebulas

(B) How different nebulas form in the universe

(C) Where nebulas can be found in space

(D) The features of different types of nebulas

2 Why does the professor mention car pollution?

(A) To show how gas is released in space

(B) To illustrate how dust spreads in space

(C) To explain the name of an object

(D) To give an example of a common problem

3 According to the professor, what happens if a nebula mostly releases oxygen?

(A) The nebula will become smaller in size.

(B) The nebula will emit a variety of colors.

(C) The light from the nebula becomes brighter.

(D) The light of the nebula will appear green.

4 According to the professor, how are reflection nebulas measured?

(A) By estimating the number of stars they have

(B) By looking at the region of their brightness

(C) By comparing their light levels with other objects

(D) By checking the size of their gas and dust clouds

5 Indicate whether each of the following is related to an emission nebula or a reflection nebula.

Click in the correct box for each phrase.

	Emission Nebula	Reflection Nebula
(A) Usually appears blue		
(B) Releases many kinds of gases		
(C) Contains large amounts of heat		
(D) Does not produce light by itself		

Listen again to part of the lecture. Then answer the question.

6 What does the professor mean when he says this: 🎧

(A) He thinks that some nebulas look very similar.

(B) He believes that nebulas have accurate names.

(C) He agrees that the subject of nebulas is not too difficult.

(D) He knows that nebulas change in unexpected ways.

Dictation

Answer Book p. 60

Listen again and fill in the blanks.

C6_T2_D

P: So we've been talking about large objects in space... Um, if you remember, I told you that a nebula is a large cloud of gas and dust, and many stars are born in nebulas. Well, there are different kinds of nebulas. And today, I'll mainly discuss two types of nebulas according to their characteristics...

The first type is an emission nebula. So an emission is something that is emitted, right? Uh, _____. For example, cars emit pollution, which means they release emissions in the form of harmful gases. Well, emission nebulas are named for a similar reason. They emit light. Emission nebulas emit light because they have many stars. The stars are also extremely hot, so _____. Uh, now, the light of these nebulas can be almost any color. The color depends on the type of gas they emit. For instance, _____, the nebula's light will look green. However, if the nebula releases nitrogen, the light will be red. _____ _____, they sometimes look as colorful as a rainbow! This makes them very bright and beautiful. Now, _____ _____. You can easily find it in the sky because it is located just below Orion's Belt. I'm sure you all know Orion's Belt... It's one of the most familiar groups of stars in the night sky. It looks like three stars in a line.

Anyway, the next type is called a reflection nebula. Uh, like an emission nebula, _____ when we look at it with a telescope. However, there are some major differences. For one, the size of reflection nebulas is measured differently... They are not measured by the size of the cloud of dust and gas. Instead, _____. Also, a reflection nebula does not produce its own light. As its name suggests, _____.

The light of a reflection nebula actually comes from nearby stars. That is, uh, _____. As light from nearby stars meets the dust in a reflection nebula, all of the individual pieces of dust reflect that light outward. But how the light is reflected _____... For example, blue light waves are very short. And short light waves are reflected more easily. That's why reflection nebulas often look blue in color...

So, uh, _____. But not

all nebulas are bright. In fact, there is another kind of nebula that is not bright at all. Um, can anyone guess what it's called?

S: Uh, a dark nebula?

P: Correct! Emission nebulas emit light. Reflection nebulas reflect light. And dark nebulas are, well, dark. That makes sense, right? But why are they dark? Well, _____. This is because they are not near any stars. They are so cold that each piece of dust is covered in frozen gases. As a result, _____. But, uh, we'll talk more about this next time…

Vocabulary Review

A. Choose the correct word for each meaning.

carnivore	omnivore	sediment	mural

1 an animal that only eats meat: _____

2 loose rocks and soil that collect in one area: _____

3 an animal that eats both meat and plants: _____

4 a painting done on a wall: _____

B. Fill in the blanks with the appropriate words from the box.

political	symbol	exist	positively	orbit

5 The French Revolution changed France's _____ system from a monarchy to a republic.

6 The blue-and-red _____ in South Korea's national flag represents balance.

7 If you think _____ about a result, there is a greater chance that you will succeed.

8 Humans did not yet _____ during the time of the dinosaurs.

9 The moon takes 27 days to complete an _____ around the earth.

C. Choose the closest meaning for each highlighted word.

10 Because it lays eggs, the platypus is classified as a special kind of mammal.

(A) stored   (B) categorized   (C) preserved   (D) remembered

11 The device will emit a sound when its battery needs to be recharged.

(A) copy   (B) produce   (C) adjust   (D) exchange

12 Primitive humans used pointed rocks to cut animals into smaller pieces for food.

(A) rare   (B) sharp   (C) competent   (D) direct

13 Mark Zuckerberg left college to pursue his dream of starting a technology business.

(A) browse   (B) determine   (C) follow   (D) accompany

14 Painting a house white helps keep it cool because the color reflects sunlight.

(A) returns   (B) reveals   (C) displays   (D) considers

CHAPTER 07

Inference

Inference

About the Question Type

Inference questions ask you to infer the correct answer by using information that is implied, or not stated directly, in the conversation or lecture.

These questions require you to draw a conclusion based on a comprehensive understanding of the overall context and by connecting information mentioned in the conversation or lecture. Sometimes, questions may be about a speaker, an idea, or what a speaker will do next.

Question Format

- What can be inferred about ~?

- What does the professor imply about ~?

- What will the man/woman probably do next?

Key Strategies

- **Step 1** — Understand the overall context of the talk, and determine whether the question is about a speaker, an idea, or what a speaker will do next.

- **Step 2** — If the question is about a speaker or an idea, find information that is connected to the speaker or idea. If the question is about what a speaker will do next, listen to the statements that a speaker makes near the end of the conversation or lecture.

- **Step 3** — Select the answer choice that is best supported by information in the conversation or lecture.

Example

Answer Book p. 62

A. Listen to a conversation between a student and a librarian.

Note-taking

C7_ExA

What will the student most likely do next?

(A) Borrow a book from a library

(B) Download an article from a website

(C) Speak to a professor about an assignment

(D) Look for a book at a store near the campus

Answer Book p. 62

B. Listen to part of a lecture in a nutrition class.

Note-taking

C7_ExB

What does the professor imply about celiac disease?

(A) It mainly affects young children.

(B) It currently cannot be medically treated.

(C) It does not cause severe symptoms.

(D) It was discovered very recently.

Dictation

Answer Book p. 62

Listen again and fill in the blanks.

C7_ExA_D

A.

M: Excuse me. Um, I ordered a book two weeks ago for my architecture class. It's called *19th Century Bridges*. Do you know if it's arrived?

W: Let me see... Oh, it seems that _____. It's very old, you see.

M: Oh, but I need it for a paper I'm writing.

W: I'm sorry. Um, maybe you could try _____ near the campus. They might have a copy for sale.

M: All right. I'm just worried because _____.

W: Then, how about _____?

M: Do you think that will work? I've never done that before.

W: I think you should at least try.

M: OK. I'll do that right now.

C7_ExB_D

B.

P: Gluten is a protein found in grains like wheat and barley. Many people can eat it without a problem. However, some people cannot. These people _____ _____. Now, normally, they would not know they have the disease without a medical test. But _____. For example, they might feel sick in the stomach or have some kind of skin problem. And, in rare cases, the symptoms can be, uh, more serious. For instance, celiac disease can lead to bone loss. And it can also _____. Right now, there is only one solution for people with celiac disease... Um, _____ _____. This is why many food providers _____ _____...

Listening Practice 1

Answer Book p. 63

Listen to a conversation between a student and a professor.

Note-taking

C7_P1

1 What are the speakers mainly discussing?

(A) What the student should do as a candidate

(B) The application process for a school program

(C) How well the student is doing in a class

(D) The importance of joining school activities

2 What previous leadership experience does the student mention?

(A) She was the captain of a sports team.

(B) She has worked as a student activities organizer.

(C) She was the head of two student clubs.

(D) She played a big role in the last student election.

3 What advice does the professor include in his recommendations to the student? Indicate whether each of the following is included. *Click in the correct box for each phrase.*

	Included	Not Included
(A) Talk to various groups of students		
(B) Learn about the student loan process		
(C) Understand campaign rules and regulations		
(D) Become familiar with students' issues		

4 What does the professor imply about making speeches?

(A) It is easier than talking to students individually.

(B) It requires more than friendly conversation.

(C) It is the hardest part of running a campaign.

(D) It is easier for people who know about politics.

Listen again to part of the conversation. Then answer the question.

5 What does the professor mean when he says this: 🎧

(A) The student has a small chance of winning.

(B) The student needs to learn about other issues.

(C) The student should discuss an idea with students.

(D) The student already knows the important issues.

Dictation

Answer Book p. 63

C7_P1_D

Listen again and fill in the blanks.

S: Hello, Professor Green. Am I disturbing you? I can always come back another time if you're busy.

P: Hi, Julia. It's OK. Come on in.

S: Well, as you know, student elections are coming up. I submitted my application and _____.

P: That's fantastic! I hope you win.

S: Thanks. Actually, I was hoping you could _____ _____. I honestly don't have any idea how to prepare.

P: All right, then. Let's talk about it. So is this your first election?

S: Yes, it is. But _____. I was the leader of the math club in my freshman year. I've also been the leader of the political science club for the past two years.

P: Nice. Well, first, you'll need to _____ and the election process. You don't want to lose because you broke one of the rules.

S: Got it. The university gives all of the candidates _____ _____. I'm planning to read it this afternoon.

P: Good. Now, _____. It's essential that you know what the students care about. Uh, you do know _____, don't you?

S: Um, maybe school costs and student loans?

P: You're going to have to do better than that. Those are old issues, and they're too complex for a student representative to deal with.

S: Then... _____?

P: That's what you need to find out. You can do this by going around the campus and _____. The more students you talk to, the better. And I want to mention something that most student candidates overlook. That is _____.

S: What do you mean by that, Professor?

P: I mean that a visit to a classroom isn't just about saying "Hello" and "Vote for me." You need to explain _____. Students will vote for someone who can suggest good solutions to problems.

S: Well, I love talking to people and making speeches. I did that all the time as the leader of the political science club.

P: That's a big plus. But you have a lot to do. So if I were you, I'd sit down with my team and _____.

S: Thanks so much, Professor. I hope you'll let me visit you when I need more advice.

Listening Practice 2

Answer Book p. 64

Listen to part of a lecture in a geology class.

Note-taking

C7_P2

_____

_____

_____

1 What is the main topic of the lecture?
(A) The effects of the crust on the earth's surface
(B) A comparison of two types of geologic plates
(C) The discovery of new layers in the earth's structure
(D) A new development in the study of geologic plates

2 Why does the professor mention a boat floating on the water?
(A) To illustrate that the earth's crust is denser than the mantle
(B) To compare the density of water with a common object
(C) To explain why continental plates do not sink easily
(D) To highlight the thickness of the earth's crust

3 What does the professor imply about the Nazca Plate?
(A) It is moving faster than the South American Plate.
(B) It is larger than the South American Plate.
(C) It is denser than the South American Plate.
(D) It is rising above the South American Plate.

4 According to the professor, what is a result of the meeting of two plates?
(A) The creation of earthquakes
(B) The formation of new plates
(C) The mixture of old and new rocks
(D) The production of ocean waves

5 Indicate whether each of the following describes continental or oceanic plates. *Click in the correct box for each phrase.*

	Continental Plates	Oceanic Plates
(A) Mostly made up of volcanic rock		
(B) Considerably less dense		
(C) Generally younger in age		
(D) Around 40 kilometers thick		

Dictation

Answer Book p. 64

Listen again and fill in the blanks.

C7_P2_D

P: OK... Let's begin with a quick review. In the last lecture, we learned about the earth's structure. In the center of the earth is the core. Next is the mantle. And at the surface is the crust... Now, remember that the crust isn't just one solid layer of rock. Because it's on top of the mantle, _____, the crust is always moving. This, uh, causes _____...

These sections are called geologic plates. There are over a dozen of them... Um, some make up the land we live on, and others are found beneath the world's oceans... For today, we're going to focus on the two types of geologic plates. These are the continental plates and the oceanic plates.

Let's start with continental plates... As you know, we can divide the earth into continents, such as Asia, Africa, Europe, and so on... Well, _____ _____. They are composed of soil and rock. Uh, these rocks are quite light and not very dense... And _____ _____, they do not sink easily. It's kind of like a boat floating on water. The boat is less dense than the water, so it floats... The continental plates work in a similar way. _____... Also, the continental plates are usually very thick. On average, they are around 40 kilometers thick.

In contrast, oceanic plates are heavy and dense. They are _____ _____. Um, when volcanoes erupt under the sea, they increase the size of oceanic crust. Because oceanic plates are heavy and dense, they tend to sink into the earth's mantle... As they sink, _____... This is why oceans exist. The bottoms of these deep valleys are like giant swimming pools. They hold the ocean's water, so, uh, the water cannot escape... And, in contrast to continental plates, _____. Um, they are typically around 6 kilometers thick... They are also usually younger in age...

Now, what happens _____? Let's look at an example. In the Pacific Ocean, there is a huge oceanic plate. It's called the Nazca Plate. Well, the Nazca Plate is slowly moving east toward the South American Plate, which, of course, is a continental plate. So what happens where the two plates meet? Remember, _____... So the Nazca Plate goes under the South American plate. Then, as this happens, the continental plate breaks apart. _____... Um, at the same time, the continental plate is pushed backwards by the oceanic plate. So, uh, _____ _____... In fact, that is how South America's Andes mountains formed a long time ago.

Listening Practice 3

Answer Book p. 66

Listen to a conversation between a student and a career center employee.

Note-taking

C7_P3

1 Why does the student go to the career center?

(A) To advise other students about their career choices

(B) To find internships on campus she can apply for

(C) To ask about some job openings

(D) To get help preparing for an interview

2 Why is the student concerned about providing letters of recommendation?

(A) She has a limited amount of employment experience.

(B) She does not have the contact information of some companies.

(C) She does not want to bother her previous employer.

(D) She worries her last employer will not speak well of her.

3 What advice does the employee give to the student about interviews?

(A) Talk about personal career goals

(B) Pay attention to the questions asked

(C) Spend time preparing beforehand

(D) Answer as honestly as possible

4 What will the student probably do next?

(A) She will bring her résumé to the employer.

(B) She will make a list of things to say during an interview.

(C) She will collect all of her letters of recommendation.

(D) She will update a document for her application.

Listen again to part of the conversation. Then answer the question.

5 What does the student mean when she says this: 🎧

(A) She wants to know if the employee has more questions.

(B) She feels she did not do well in the job last year.

(C) She is not interested in the office job.

(D) She is unfamiliar with an organization.

Dictation

Listen again and fill in the blanks.

C7_P3_D

W: Hi. I'm looking for the career center. Am I in the right place?

M: Yes, absolutely. Do you have an appointment?

W: No. I just stopped by. _____?

M: I can let you know about some opportunities. Let me find your student information on the computer first... What's your name?

W: Oh, sure. It's, um, Lydia Lancaster.

M: OK... I see that you worked in the university administrative office as an assistant last year. It says you did a great job. Actually, _____ this summer. I think you'd have a good chance of being hired if you applied.

W: Hmm... Is there anything else? I'd rather work somewhere new. It would let me _____ _____.

M: OK. There's also a law firm downtown that's _____. It's mostly office work, but it'd still be a valuable experience.

W: Hmm... That sounds interesting. How can I apply?

M: To apply, you need to send a résumé and _____ _____. So you will need to ask two former employers to write letters for you.

W: Um, _____. I have a résumé, but my only previous job is the university job I had last year.

M: I see... You're not the first person to have this problem. There are other ways you can solve this. First, you can find other people _____ _____, like a professor.

W: I guess I could do that. But if the law firm asks about my previous experience, I won't know what to say.

M: If that happens, the best thing is to tell them that _____. But also tell them you're confident that you will do the job well.

W: Right, that's good advice. By any chance, _____ _____?

M: Well, one common mistake a lot of students make is, um, not preparing enough for an interview.

W: How can I prepare for an interview? I mean, it's just the interviewer asking questions, right?

M: That's true, but you can think about _____. That way, you can prepare some thoughts before you get there. You know, spend some time thinking about what you'd like to tell the employer about yourself. Ask yourself why you want the job, and _____.

W: Yeah, that does make a lot of sense. I'll do that, but first, my résumé. _____ _____ in a while, so I'll go work on that now... I want to make sure it's perfect.

Listening Practice 4

Listen to part of a lecture in a business class.

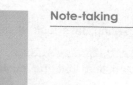

Note-taking

C7_P4

1 What is the lecture mainly about?

(A) Where businesses look for customers

(B) How companies categorize customers

(C) Why customers share their information

(D) Which customers should be avoided

2 How does the professor organize the lecture?

(A) By reviewing various topics from a textbook

(B) By comparing the strategies of two companies

(C) By describing the different ways a process is done

(D) By discussing the results of a survey

3 What example does the professor give about demographic segmentation?

(A) A company considers basic information like gender.

(B) A company collects information about lifestyles.

(C) A company identifies popular social media influencers.

(D) A company compares customers from different locations.

4 What can be inferred about psychographic segmentation?

(A) It is too expensive for small companies.

(B) It is useful for finding general information.

(C) It is only good for certain products.

(D) It is challenging for companies to do.

Listen again to part of the lecture. Then answer the question.

5 What does the professor mean when he says this: 🎧

(A) To see if the students understood a process

(B) To suggest that there are many examples

(C) To indicate that an idea was discussed earlier

(D) To encourage the students to provide more details

Dictation

C7_P4_D

Listen again and fill in the blanks.

P: So to continue our discussion of marketing, let's look at market segmentation. This is the process of categorizing customers _____.
These groups are based on characteristics that the customers share. Doing this helps companies focus on _____ instead of to everyone...

S: Sorry, um, isn't it better to sell products to as many people as possible?

P: Well, the goal is to sell many products, of course. But this has to be done efficiently. _____, you can end up wasting time and money with the wrong customers. Um, these are customers who are not going to buy your product. Segmentation lets _____. This makes their marketing more effective.
Anyway, to start the segmentation process, you have to _____ _____. You can do this by asking them questions in surveys. Or you can _____. This information can be about the customers' incomes, jobs, education... You name it. Once you have enough information, you can create groups.
Now, of course, there are many ways to create different groups. However, I will discuss the four main types of segmentation... First, there is geographic segmentation. This means that _____. So you can divide people by country, city, town, and so on. Um, you can even divide people based on climate. So, for example, a company can sell winter coats only to people who live in cold places.
OK, next, we have demographic segmentation. Here, _____ _____. So you look at people's ages, whether they are men or women, and so on. Um, so one example is a company that sells clothing. It can use demographic segmentation to make advertisements for customers who are men and _____.

Third, there is behavioral segmentation. This is where _____ _____. How do they like to shop? Do they shop through stores, websites, or smartphone apps? Do they read about products or follow social media influencers? Um, these are the kinds of questions to ask. They help _____.

And lastly, we have psychographic segmentation. With this type of segmentation, you are trying to _____. So, uh, this refers to characteristics like their interests, attitudes, opinions, and so on... This is complicated and time-consuming because companies have to gather information about individual people. And, of course, _____. However, it can be useful because it lets you focus your marketing on more specific groups. For example, if you want to sell furniture to certain young people, it helps to know _____.

Answer Book p. 69

TOEFL Listening

C7_T1

Note-taking

1 What is the main topic of the conversation?

   (A) Why the student did not complete an assignment

   (B) The reasons that an author is important

   (C) The differences between science and religion

   (D) What the professor talked about in a class

2 According to the professor, how was Bacon different from most people of his time?

   (A) He suggested that philosophers should explain science.

   (B) He thought that scientists could learn from religion.

   (C) He believed that scientists should use a new approach.

   (D) He argued that religious people should not study science.

3 Why does the professor mention triangles?

   (A) To describe an early scientific method

   (B) To compare mathematics with other sciences

   (C) To point out that Bacon was a religious person

   (D) To give an example of a relation of ideas

4 What will the student probably do next?

   (A) Review some reading material

   (B) Request a private tutoring session

   (C) Contact a friend for advice

   (D) Return a textbook to a library

Listen again to part of the conversation. Then answer the question.

5 What does the professor imply when she says this: 🎧

   (A) The professor would like the student to leave soon.

   (B) The student is already familiar with an idea.

   (C) The professor does not know the details of a topic.

   (D) The student should listen carefully during a class.

Dictation

Listen again and fill in the blanks.

C7_T1_D

S: Hello, Professor Miller. Um, unfortunately, I couldn't come to yesterday's class because I wasn't feeling well. Could you tell me _____?

P: Sure. In yesterday's class, we talked about Francis Bacon...

S: Oh, OK. _____, but I'm not sure who he is exactly.

P: Yes, well, he was an important 17th-century philosopher. At that time, _____ _____. So, um, it was normal for a scientist to use religious stories to explain how the world worked. Bacon had a better approach to science. He encouraged _____.

S: That doesn't sound like a big deal now, but I guess it was pretty shocking back then.

P: Yes, but that's not the only reason Bacon was important. He really wanted to make science better. He thought that _____ and then try to develop an idea that explains all of them.

S: You mean like _____?

P: Yes. This concept is part of what we usually call the scientific method. Um, I assume I don't have to go over that in detail.

S: Right, I studied this in one of my other classes. According to the scientific method, _____, right?

P: That's correct. Now, this seems obvious to us, but it wasn't the normal way of doing things when Bacon was alive. In those days, _____ in the world.

S: I think I remember this from one of your lectures. You said there are two kinds of knowledge. Um, you called them _____.

P: Yes, exactly. The first kind is the knowledge that we get from experiencing things in the world. And the second involves ideas that are simply true, like, uh, ideas from geometry. For example, _____ to find out that a triangle has three sides. This is a relation of ideas.

S: I see what you mean.

P: Bacon didn't think relations of ideas were very useful for discovering how things work in nature. That's why _____, make theories, and test those theories. And, well, he was pretty much correct.

S: I see. I'm glad I asked you about this. I can do some more reading on my own.

P: Yes. _____. So I suggest you do more reading. Um, there's a section on Bacon in Chapter 8 of your textbook.

S: Thanks, Professor. I'll work on that right away.

Answer Book p. 70

C7_T2

BIOLOGY

Note-taking

1 What is the main topic of the lecture?

   Ⓐ How wild animals are dangerous to human beings

   Ⓑ The impact of humans on the population growth of animals

   Ⓒ Why interactions between humans and animals are increasing

   Ⓓ The efforts of some organizations to protect wild animals

2 Why does the professor mention mining companies in the lecture?

   Ⓐ To point out an industry that is declining

   Ⓑ To give an example of why humans enter wild areas

   Ⓒ To illustrate how human activities lead to pollution

   Ⓓ To explain the importance of mining to certain communities

3 According to the professor, what is the main reason that cities are seeing more wildlife?

   Ⓐ Animals can longer find good food sources in nature.

   Ⓑ More people are interested in having wild animals as pets.

   Ⓒ People are using more of the land where animals live.

   Ⓓ The populations of some wild animals have been increasing.

4 What does the professor say about the presence of human food?

   Ⓐ It can cause conflicts between some animals.

   Ⓑ It can change what wild animals eat.

   Ⓒ It is harmful to the health of wild animals.

   Ⓓ It is necessary for the survival of some species.

5 What does the professor imply about the future of songbirds?

   Ⓐ Those that sing louder will increase in number.

   Ⓑ They will be able to find mates more easily.

   Ⓒ The sounds they make will become less noisy.

   Ⓓ They will grow smaller in size over time.

6 According to the professor, what are some solutions to the problems caused by wild animals in cities?

Choose 2 answers.

   Ⓐ Building better fences around busy roads

   Ⓑ Avoiding development in the areas they live

   Ⓒ Studying the diseases that they can cause

   Ⓓ Learning how to act differently around them

‖ Dictation ‖

Listen again and fill in the blanks.

C7_T2_D

P: Animals have always been a part of human communities. And as human communities

have grown, _____. Today, we are going to

discuss the reason why this has been happening.

The biggest factor is changes in land use. Uh, humans enter wild areas for a variety

of reasons. For example, mining companies go into the mountains to look for natural

resources like iron, coal, and copper. When they do this, _____

_____. The same thing happens when people enter forests to

cut wood. New human settlements are created in areas that were previously wild. So,

uh, _____… The same thing is

happening with cities. People are building more cities around the world. In addition, many

existing cities are becoming bigger. As this happens, _____

_____. Um, a good example is the city of Chicago. Chicago

has not had a large population increase in a long time. However, the amount of land used

for urban areas continues to increase. This is because _____

_____. Uh, they want to own houses in the suburbs. When this

happens, people move into land that was previously used by wild animals. That's why

people in these areas see many wild animals.

Now, because more people and wild animals are living in the same places, the behavior

of wild animals is changing, too. _____. Naturally,

most wild animals are afraid of humans. They will not go near people. However, as

interactions increase, _____. They

no longer fear them. And they learn that humans provide convenient sources of food.

Sometimes, _____ as a result. Researchers

have also found that animals in urban areas can change in other ways… For example,

some researchers studied songbirds that live in cities. Interestingly, they learned that

_____ than birds in the country. Can anyone guess why?

S: Uh, cities can be very noisy. Maybe the birds are _____.

P: That's what the researchers think too… And, uh, this can have real effects on future

genetics. Uh, birds that sing louder are easier to hear. So they are more likely to find

mates and continue growing…

And what else do you think happens? Well, the larger presence of wild animals in cities can also cause problems for people. For instance, wild animals carry diseases. _____. Uh, think of the coronavirus, for example, which probably came from a bat... And then, uh, there are other problems, too. Um, _____ when they try to cross busy roads... These are just a couple of examples... To reduce these problems, we have to find solutions. For instance, _____. Or we can also learn to act differently around wild animals... For example, we can change _____.

Vocabulary Review

A. Choose the correct word for each meaning.

candidate	grain	principle	observation

1 a crop such as corn and wheat that is grown for food: _____

2 someone trying to be elected to office: _____

3 a fundamental truth or assumption: _____

4 the act of being attentive to gather data: _____

B. Fill in the blanks with the appropriate words from the box.

dense	segmentation	potential	relation	geographic

5 Political campaigns use voter _____ to be more precise in their messaging.

6 Australia is a large _____ area that is both an island and a continent.

7 Several _____ treatments for cancer are currently being tested in the laboratory.

8 The _____ between time and space is of great interest to physicists.

9 Earth's core is believed to be made up of compressed and incredibly _____ metal.

C. Choose the closest meaning for each highlighted word.

10 Many students overlook the importance of taking clear notes during a lecture.
   (A) ignore   (B) forget   (C) consider   (D) respect

11 When a volcano erupts, hot lava and toxic gas can endanger nearby communities.
   (A) collapses   (B) explodes   (C) devastates   (D) forms

12 Interactions with parents are an important part of a child's emotional development.
   (A) sessions   (B) preparations   (C) dealings   (D) gatherings

13 The complaints of each individual customer will be addressed by the store manager.
   (A) identifiable   (B) significant   (C) particular   (D) exceptional

14 The tank of a scuba diver must be properly sealed so that none of the air escapes.
   (A) leaks   (B) changes   (C) moves   (D) appears

Actual Test

Actual Test 1
Actual Test 2

Actual Test 1

TOEFL Listening

PART 1. Passage 1

AT1_P1_1

Note-taking

1   Why does the student visit the university housing office?

   Ⓐ To find out when her dormitory fines are due

   Ⓑ To explain why her roommate has moved out

   Ⓒ To check if she needs to pay some fines

   Ⓓ To ask if she can pay for a bill in advance

2   What does the student imply about her roommate?

   Ⓐ She is not a careful person.

   Ⓑ She has already left the dormitory.

   Ⓒ She is refusing to speak with the student.

   Ⓓ She does not have money to pay the fines.

3   Why most likely was the student's closet door never fixed?

   Ⓐ The student forgot to inform the manager.

   Ⓑ The necessary form was not submitted.

   Ⓒ The student reported the problem too late.

   Ⓓ The request was not recorded in a system.

4   What does the employee offer to do for the student?

   Ⓐ He will help her move into a new dormitory.

   Ⓑ He will reduce the amount of the fines she must pay.

   Ⓒ He will instruct a technician to repair the door in her room.

   Ⓓ He will ask a manager about her situation.

Listen again to part of the conversation. Then answer the question.

5   Why does the employee say this: 🎧

   Ⓐ To remind the student to make a payment

   Ⓑ To encourage the student to provide details

   Ⓒ To indicate that he has forgotten about the fines

   Ⓓ To express surprise that the student received fines

AT1_P1_2

ART HISTORY

Note-taking

6 What is the main topic of the lecture?

- (A) A general history of early American art
- (B) A popular American art style from the 1800s
- (C) The reasons an artist is considered significant
- (D) The materials used by a famous landscape painter

7 According to the professor, why did Cole make landscape paintings?

- (A) He hoped to improve his painting skills.
- (B) He felt inspired by a place that he visited.
- (C) He was encouraged by one of his art teachers.
- (D) He wanted to be as successful as another artist.

8 What does the professor imply about Americans in the 1800s?

- (A) They were not interested in European ideas.
- (B) They did not often travel outside of the cities.
- (C) They liked artwork that was considered popular.
- (D) They bought more portraits than landscape paintings.

9 Why does the professor mention American Independence?

- (A) To give a reason that Cole moved to America
- (B) To explain why Cole tried to develop a personal art style
- (C) To show that Cole was a very independent person
- (D) To describe how Cole's art represented the story of America

Listen again to part of the lecture. Then answer the question.

10 Why does the professor say this:

- (A) To indicate that he intended to explain a topic
- (B) To acknowledge the student's interest in art
- (C) To encourage the student to listen more carefully
- (D) To show that he admires Cole's artwork

Listen again to part of the lecture. Then answer the question.

11 What does the professor mean when he says this:

- (A) He believes that American art developed very slowly.
- (B) He thinks people did not appreciate Cole's art for many years.
- (C) He is impressed that Cole's influence lasted so long.
- (D) He wants to show how the value of Cole's paintings increased.

Actual Test 1

HACKERS APEX LISTENING for the TOEFL iBT Expert

AT1_P2_1

Note-taking

1   Why does the student go to see the professor?

  (A) To give a reason for missing a class

  (B) To discuss an idea for an upcoming seminar

  (C) To get advice about an assignment

  (D) To submit a written report for a course

2   What does the professor say about some of the buildings on campus?

  (A) They use more resources due to their size and age.

  (B) They are too small for the number of students at the school.

  (C) There are more older buildings than new ones.

  (D) Their lights are often on even when no one is inside.

3   How does the professor help the student?

  (A) By explaining a task and then commenting on ideas

  (B) By showing a good report and then answering questions

  (C) By describing previous projects and then explaining methods

  (D) By recommending topics and then offering feedback

4   According to the professor, what must students do at the end of the semester?

  Choose 2 answers.

  (A) Give a presentation in class

  (B) Submit a written report

  (C) Apply their idea on campus

  (D) Collaborate with other students

Listen again to part of the conversation. Then answer the question.

5   What does the professor mean when she says this:

  (A) She is not familiar with the topic of a conversation.

  (B) She is uncertain if the student's information is correct.

  (C) She is not satisfied with the quality of a report.

  (D) She is doubtful that the student's idea would work.

Actual Test 1

HACKERS APEX LISTENING for the TOEFL iBT Expert

AT1_P2_2

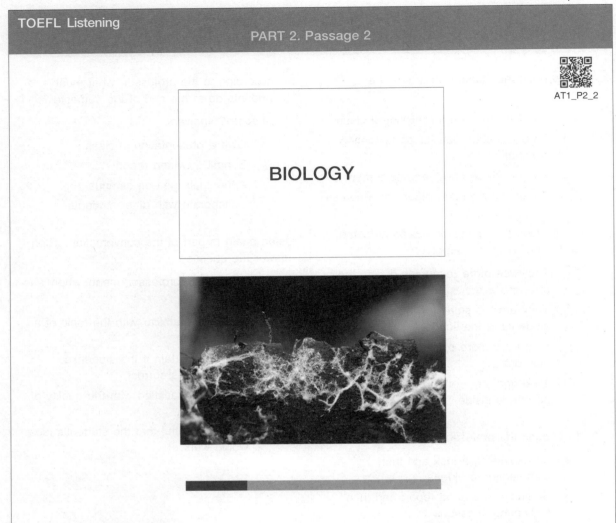

BIOLOGY

Note-taking

6 What does the professor mainly discuss?

Ⓐ The problems caused by soil pollution

Ⓑ How fungi can be used to clean soil

Ⓒ The different parts of fungi and their uses

Ⓓ How fungi get nutrients from the soil

7 What does the professor say about fungi?

Ⓐ They produce many mushrooms underground.

Ⓑ They add water and nutrients to soil.

Ⓒ They are often found near the roots of plants.

Ⓓ They change dead organisms into reusable materials.

8 According to the professor, what is the reason that fungi can break down pollutants from oil and chemicals used in farms?

Ⓐ The pollution enters the soil slowly.

Ⓑ Insects break down the pollution first.

Ⓒ Plant materials and pollution have similar chemicals.

Ⓓ Pollutants such as carbon naturally stick to fungi.

9 Why does the professor mention a magnet?

Ⓐ To highlight how long metals stay in the soil

Ⓑ To introduce a common type of metal

Ⓒ To illustrate how fungi branches attract metals

Ⓓ To explain how fungi are removed from the ground

10 According to the professor, what are some disadvantages of using fungi to remove metals from soil?

Choose 2 answers.

Ⓐ It costs more money than other methods.

Ⓑ It requires large amounts of fungi to work.

Ⓒ It does not allow the metals to be reused.

Ⓓ It takes too long to remove the metals.

Listen again to part of the lecture. Then answer the question.

11 What does the student mean when he says this: 🎧

Ⓐ He finds it hard to believe the professor's claim.

Ⓑ He wants to check the meaning of a term.

Ⓒ He would like the professor to repeat a statement.

Ⓓ He thinks that the professor made a mistake.

SOCIOLOGY

Note-taking

12 What is the main topic of the lecture?

- Ⓐ The history of politics in Afghanistan
- Ⓑ An ongoing border problem
- Ⓒ Military conflicts in Afghanistan
- Ⓓ International relations in Pakistan

13 According to the professor, why did the leader of Afghanistan want a clearer border?

- Ⓐ He felt Pakistan should be separate from India.
- Ⓑ He did not want any British influence in his country.
- Ⓒ He thought the previous border was confusing.
- Ⓓ He wanted part of the territory of Pakistan.

14 How does the professor explain the regional situation after Pakistan's independence?

- Ⓐ By emphasizing cultural similarities
- Ⓑ By giving a personal example
- Ⓒ By comparing two ethnic groups
- Ⓓ By discussing the latest research

15 In the lecture, the professor mentions some characteristics of the Durand Line. Indicate whether each of the following was mentioned as a characteristic.

Click in the correct box for each phrase.

	Yes	No
Ⓐ Separates Afghanistan and Pakistan		
Ⓑ Was originally created when India was a British colony		
Ⓒ Was rejected by a British secretary		
Ⓓ Has not been accepted in Afghanistan since 1947		

16 What does the professor imply about the Pashtuns?

- Ⓐ They have ruled Pakistan since the 1700s.
- Ⓑ They were political partners of the Punjabis.
- Ⓒ They are opposed to the government in Afghanistan.
- Ⓓ They were a minority ethnic group in Pakistan.

17 What is the professor's attitude toward America's recent war in Afghanistan?

- Ⓐ He is afraid it will happen again.
- Ⓑ He is convinced it was successful.
- Ⓒ He is certain it was significant.
- Ⓓ He is concerned it was unfair.

TOEFL Listening

PART 1. Passage 1

AT2_P1_1

Note-taking

1 Why does the student visit the registrar's office?

   Ⓐ To get a final copy of her schedule

   Ⓑ To explain that she has too many tests on one day

   Ⓒ To complain about problems with an online system

   Ⓓ To check on university policies

2 What does the employee imply about the school website?

   Ⓐ It requires a password to access.

   Ⓑ It needs to be updated more often.

   Ⓒ It contains a lot of useful information.

   Ⓓ It was recently redesigned by the school.

3 Why does the employee mention a serious illness?

   Ⓐ To provide an example of why students do poorly on exams

   Ⓑ To explain why it is impossible to change a schedule

   Ⓒ To give an acceptable reason for changing an exam date

   Ⓓ To remind the student of what to write on a form

4 What information will the student include in the application form? Indicate whether each of the following will be included or not.

Click in the correct box for each phrase.

	Included	Not Included
Ⓐ A note from the IT department		
Ⓑ Copy of the exam schedule		
Ⓒ IT employee's name and position		
Ⓓ Reasons for a requested change		

Listen again to part of the conversation. Then answer the question.

5 What does the student imply when she says this: 🎧

   Ⓐ The situation is no longer the same.

   Ⓑ The employee has misunderstood a problem.

   Ⓒ She has forgotten when exams will be held.

   Ⓓ The schedule has remained the same for a month.

AT2_P1_2

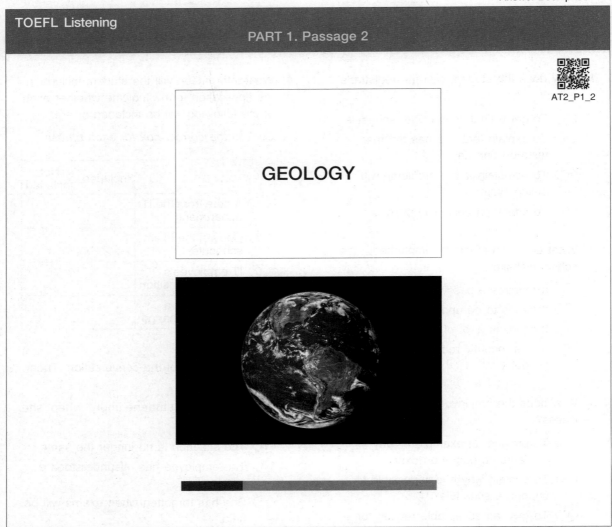

Note-taking

6 What is the main topic of the lecture?

Ⓐ How the study of Earth developed in the 17th century

Ⓑ A theory about the origin of the universe

Ⓒ Methods of measuring Earth's layers

Ⓓ How scientists have determined the age of Earth

7 What does the professor say about Lord Kelvin's view of Earth?

Ⓐ He believed its center was younger than its surface.

Ⓑ He thought it was older than other planets.

Ⓒ He believed it cooled at a constant rate.

Ⓓ He assumed it was made of hot liquid inside.

8 What is the professor's attitude toward Lord Kelvin's conclusion about Earth's age?

Ⓐ She is not sure why the range of dates is so large.

Ⓑ She is impressed because it was more accurate than others' at the time.

Ⓒ She is concerned that it was not based on scientific methods.

Ⓓ She is surprised that scientists quickly accepted it.

9 According to the professor, how did scientists learn that Earth was billions of years old?

Ⓐ They observed changes in plants and animals.

Ⓑ They exposed materials to radiation.

Ⓒ They studied layers of rocks.

Ⓓ They used mathematical formulas.

10 Why does the professor mention uranium?

Ⓐ To illustrate the first material used in radiometric dating

Ⓑ To provide an example of an element that breaks down slowly

Ⓒ To explain that some chemical elements are very rare

Ⓓ To demonstrate how carbon can combine with other materials

11 What does the professor imply about radiometric dating?

Ⓐ It can work only on objects that contain carbon.

Ⓑ It is very reliable according to most scientists.

Ⓒ It may never be able to predict Earth's exact age.

Ⓓ It cannot accurately measure age within 10,000 years.

Actual Test 2

HACKERS APEX LISTENING for the TOEFL iBT Expert

PART 2. Passage 1

AT2_P2_1

Note-taking

1 What is the student's problem?

  Ⓐ He is having difficulty finding some research articles.

  Ⓑ He is struggling to understand a topic discussed in class.

  Ⓒ He is unsure about how to prepare for an upcoming exam.

  Ⓓ He is thinking about changing his economics assignment.

2 How does the professor help the student?

  Ⓐ By mentioning a problem and then providing a solution

  Ⓑ By explaining an idea and then describing a situation

  Ⓒ By emphasizing the disadvantages of opportunity costs

  Ⓓ By comparing and contrasting factories and movie theaters

3 Why does the student mention going to the movies?

  Ⓐ To demonstrate that he is knowledgeable about a topic

  Ⓑ To clarify his understanding of a concept

  Ⓒ To give an example of a different economic idea

  Ⓓ To make a point about the rising cost of movie tickets

4 What will the student probably do next?

  Ⓐ Get the contact information of another professor

  Ⓑ Go to the campus bookstore to purchase a textbook

  Ⓒ Visit the library to read more about a topic

  Ⓓ Borrow an economics book from the professor

Listen again to part of the conversation. Then answer the question.

5 What does the student mean when he says this: 🎧

  Ⓐ He understands what the professor is trying to say.

  Ⓑ He is not sure what the professor will talk about next.

  Ⓒ He no longer needs to hear an explanation of a topic.

  Ⓓ He is thinking of another example of a concept.

AT2_P2_2

Note-taking

6 What is the main topic of the lecture?

  Ⓐ New methods of cleaning the ocean

  Ⓑ Recent advances in plastic technology

  Ⓒ Various types of ecosystems in the Pacific Ocean

  Ⓓ A specific example of pollution in the ocean

7 What does the professor say about the garbage of companies and individuals?

  Ⓐ It is highly controlled.

  Ⓑ It is mainly plastic.

  Ⓒ It is usually recycled.

  Ⓓ It is sometimes harmless.

8 What does the professor imply about ocean currents in the region?

  Ⓐ The patch would get bigger without them.

  Ⓑ They always move from east to west.

  Ⓒ The patch would break apart without them.

  Ⓓ They carry garbage from California to Hawaii.

9 How does the professor organize the information about the deadly effects of animals eating plastic?

  Ⓐ He mentions one theory and then discusses an opposing one.

  Ⓑ He lists the most dangerous types of plastic.

  Ⓒ He introduces the issue and then supports it with research.

  Ⓓ He compares the impact on various marine species.

10 What is the professor's opinion of the garbage problem in the Pacific?

  Ⓐ He hopes it will be reduced by ocean currents.

  Ⓑ He thinks technology is required to fix it.

  Ⓒ He believes it will be difficult to solve.

  Ⓓ He feels only a few nations are responsible for it.

11 In the lecture, the professor suggests steps that can be taken to protect the Pacific Ocean. Indicate whether the statements below are suggested steps.

Click in the correct box for each phrase.

	Yes	No
Ⓐ Encourage countries to work together		
Ⓑ Use ships to move garbage		
Ⓒ Produce new forms of plastic		
Ⓓ Increase the amount of recycling		

AT2_P2_3

PSYCHOLOGY

Note-taking

12 What is the main purpose of the lecture?

   Ⓐ To compare different experimental methods

   Ⓑ To discuss a famous idea in psychology

   Ⓒ To explain the origins of Russian psychology

   Ⓓ To examine the first psychological experiments

13 The professor describes the steps in Pavlov's first experiments. Put the steps listed below in correct order.

Drag each sentence to the space where it belongs.

Step 1	
Step 2	
Step 3	
Step 4	

   Ⓐ The dogs did not respond to a sound.

   Ⓑ The dogs responded with or without food.

   Ⓒ Pavlov introduced a sound.

   Ⓓ Pavlov gave the dogs food.

14 According to the professor, what happened when Pavlov repeated his experiment?

   Ⓐ The results remained the same.

   Ⓑ The dogs initially rejected the food.

   Ⓒ The dogs learned quicker than before.

   Ⓓ The conditioning did not last as long.

15 Why does the professor mention the color blue?

   Ⓐ To stress that any signal can be used in conditioning

   Ⓑ To show that people are conditioned to prefer certain colors

   Ⓒ To suggest that an experiment is less simple than it seems

   Ⓓ To test whether an experiment's conclusion is correct

16 What is the professor's attitude toward Pavlov's experiments?

   Ⓐ She thinks that they were done in a creative way.

   Ⓑ She believes they revealed something new about learning.

   Ⓒ She feels that they should be compared with other experiments.

   Ⓓ She is not sure that Pavlov was the first to perform them.

Listen again to part of the lecture. Then answer the question.

17 Why does the professor say this: 🎧

   Ⓐ To criticize the methods used by a psychologist

   Ⓑ To emphasize that a result of an experiment is logical

   Ⓒ To question the correctness of a conclusion

   Ⓓ To suggest that an experiment requires more research

Actual Test 2

HACKERS APEX LISTENING for the TOEFL iBT Expert

Photo Credits _____

MEMO

MEMO

|H|A|C|K|E|R|S|

APEX
LISTENING
for the
TOEFL iBT® Expert

COPYRIGHT © 2023, by Hackers Language Research Institute

January 13, 2023

All rights reserved. No part of this publication may be reproduced, stored in a retrieval system, or transmitted, in any form or by any means, electronic, mechanical, photocopying, recording, or otherwise, without the prior written permission of the author and the publisher.

Hackers Language Research Institute
23, Gangnam-daero 61-gil, Seocho-gu, Seoul, Korea
Inquiries publishing@hackers.com

ISBN 978-89-6542-545-8 (53740)

Printed in South Korea

1 2 3 4 5 6 7 8 9 10   29 28 27 26 25 24 23

The Most Preferred Education Brand in Korea,
HACKERS BOOK（www.HackersBook.com）
• Free supplementary study materials

No. 1 in Hankyung Business' Most Preferred Brand Rankings 2019, Education Group category

HACKERS

APEX
LISTENING
for the
TOEFL iBT®
Expert

Answer Book

HACKERS

APEX
LISTENING
for the
TOEFL iBT® Expert

Answer Book

CHAPTER 01
Main Purpose/Topic

Example   본문 p. 15

A. (C)   **B.** (A)

A.

Note-taking

S: Biology dept. has opening for part-time employee?
P: Work as lab assistant? ∵ previous assistant graduated
S: Want to graduate next yr. ∴ lab = good exp.
P: Go to employment office → fill out forms → start

Listen to a conversation between a student and a professor.

S: Hi, Professor Hoffman. Do you have a moment?

P: Sure, Ashley. How can I help you today?

S: I was wondering if the biology department has any openings for part-time student employees.

P: Actually, you came at the perfect time. How would you like to work as a laboratory assistant? The previous assistant just graduated and we need someone to replace him.

S: That would be great! I want to apply to graduate school next year. So working in a laboratory would be a good experience to have.

P: Excellent. You'll need to go to the student employment office to fill out a few forms. Once that's complete, you can get started.

학생과 교수 사이의 대화를 들으시오.

S: 안녕하세요, Hoffman 교수님. 잠시 시간 있으신가요?

P: 물론이지, Ashley. 오늘 어떻게 도와줄까?

S: 생물학과에 학생 아르바이트 직원을 위한 빈자리가 있는지 궁금해요.

P: 사실, 네가 완벽한 때에 왔단다. 실습실 조교로 일해보는 게 어떠니? 이전 조교가 막 졸업해서 우리는 그를 대신할 사람이 필요해.

S: 아주 좋겠네요! 저는 내년에 대학원에 지원하고 싶어요. 그래서 실습실에서 일하는 건 좋은 경험이 될 거예요.

P: 잘됐구나. 너는 몇 가지 양식을 작성하기 위해 학생 고용 사무실에 가야 할 거야. 그게 완료되면, 시작할 수 있어.

biology 몡 생물학   opening 몡 빈자리   laboratory 몡 실습실
previous 혱 이전의   replace 통 대신하다

학생은 왜 교수를 찾아가는가?

(A) 실습실이 얼마나 늦게까지 여는지 알아내기 위해

(B) 가능성이 있는 미래의 직업들에 관한 조언을 얻기 위해

(C) 생물학과 내의 일자리에 관해 문의하기 위해

(D) 다른 학생이 졸업했는지 알아보기 위해

B.

Note-taking

Impact of Research Project

- Robot was sent 5 km below surface of Pacific
- Collected creatures (e.g. worms & jellyfish)
- Showed that deepest ocean = lifeless place X
- Effect on companies work in deep-sea mining
  - Have to make sure activities harm X species

Listen to part of a lecture in an environmental science class.

P: OK... Let's talk about a recent research project, and why its findings are important. So, um, a robot was sent five kilometers below the surface of the Pacific Ocean. It collected a variety of creatures, including worms and jellyfish. In total, scientists found 39 previously undiscovered species. These findings changed the way we think about the ocean. They showed that the deepest part of the ocean is not a lifeless place. In fact, it is home to many different organisms. The findings also have had an effect on companies that work in deep-sea mining... Um, this refers to the gathering of minerals from the bottom of the ocean. The companies now have to make sure that their activities do not harm those species living in the ocean's depths.

환경 과학 강의의 일부를 들으시오.

P: 자... 최근의 한 연구 프로젝트에 관해, 그리고 그것의 연구 결과가 중요한 이유에 대해 얘기해 봅시다. 그러니까, 음, 로봇 한 대가 태평양 수면 5킬로미터 아래로 보내졌습니다. 그것은 벌레와 해파리를 포함한 다양한 생물들을 수집했어요. 모두 합해서, 과학자들은 이전에 발견되지 않았던 39개의 종을 발견했어요. 이 발견물들은 우리가 바다에 대해 생각하는 방식을 바꾸었어요. 그것들은 바다의 가장 깊은 곳이 생명체가 살지 않는 곳이 아니라는 걸 보여주었죠. 사실, 그것은 많은 서로 다른 유기체들의 서식지예요. 그 발견물들은 심해 채굴을 하는 회사들에도 영향을 미쳤습니다... 음, 이건 바다 맨 아래에서 광물을 채취하는 것을 가리켜요. 그 회사들은 이제 그들의 활동이 바다의 깊은 곳에 사는 종들에게 해를 끼치지 않도록 확실히 해야 해요.

finding 몡 연구 결과, 발견물   a variety of ~이 다양한
creature 몡 생물   jellyfish 몡 해파리   previously 뷔 이전에
lifeless 혱 생명체가 살지 않는   organism 몡 유기체, 생물체
mining 몡 채굴   mineral 몡 광물

강의는 주로 무엇에 관한 것인가?

(A) 과학 프로젝트의 영향

(B) 채굴 방법의 단점

(C) 새로운 기술의 개발

(D) 심해 종의 소멸

1 (C)   2 (B)   3 (C)   4 (A)   5 (B)

Note-taking

W: Account locked ∵ unpaid fees → borrow X until paid
More than 3 weeks late ∴ school locked account
M: Friend = library card X ∴ checked out for her
She is in Spain → back next week
Need books for research paper ∴ what if I pay?
W: Expensive = $55, increase by $2/day
Call payment office ∵ might unlock account
Take 1 or 2 days → use account by Tuesday
Read books in library?
Can have coffee and snack, leave a mess X

Listen to a conversation between a student and a librarian.

M: I'd like to check out these books, please. Here is my student ID.

W: Um… ¹I'm sorry, but your account has been locked. It seems that you have unpaid fees. So you can't borrow more books until the fees have been paid.

M: I don't think I have any books checked out. And I usually return everything on time. Could you check what the problem is?

W: ²Well, you were supposed to return a book called *Literary Theory* on February 26. It's more than three weeks late, so the school locked your account.

M: Oh, now I remember. My friend needed to borrow that book, but she didn't have her library card. So I checked it out for her, instead. She must have forgotten to bring it back… And now, she is on vacation in Spain.

W: When will she be back?

M: She'll be back sometime next week. ³But I need these books for my research paper. It's due next Friday, so I can't wait that long. What if I pay for the late fees?

W: You can do that, but they are quite expensive. The book is more than three weeks late, so the fees are $55.

M: Did you say $55? You've got to be joking!

W: No, I'm afraid not. And that will increase by $2 each day until it's paid.

M: I don't have enough money to pay that right now.

W: Then… ⁴Maybe you can call the payment office and explain your situation. They might be able to unlock your account. You should definitely try…

M: All right, I will. It was just a mistake. Maybe I'll get lucky and they'll help me. Do you know how long it would take to unlock my account?

W: It usually takes one or two days. I think you would be able to use your account again by Tuesday.

M: Oh… That would be too late. Is there anything else I can do?

W: ⁵Well, why don't you just read those books here in the library? There are plenty of quiet spaces you can use. The desks are comfortable, and you won't hear any noise from outside.

M: OK. That sounds like the best option. Oh, but, um, can I bring coffee and a snack with me?

W: Sure. You can have coffee and a small snack. But be careful not to leave a mess or disturb the other library users. You can take any desk that's available.

M: All right, then. Thank you for being so helpful.

학생과 사서 사이의 대화를 들으시오.

M: 이 책들을 대출하고 싶습니다. 여기 제 학생증이요.

W: 음… 죄송하지만, 학생의 계정이 잠겨 있어요. 미납된 요금이 있는 것 같네요. 그래서 요금이 지불될 때까지 책을 더 빌리실 수 없어요.

M: 제가 대출된 책들을 갖고 있는 것 같지 않은데요. 그리고 저는 보통 모든 걸 제시간에 반납해요. 문제가 무엇인지 확인해 주실 수 있나요?

W: 음, '문학 이론'이라는 책을 2월 26일에 반납하셨어야 해요. 3주 이상 연체되어서, 학교가 학생의 계정을 잠갔어요.

M: 오, 이제 기억나네요. 제 친구가 그 책을 빌렸어야 했는데, 그녀가 도서관 카드를 가지고 있지 않았어요. 그래서 제가 그녀를 위해 대신 대출해 줬어요. 그녀가 그걸 다시 가져오는 걸 까먹은 것 같네요… 그리고 지금, 그녀는 스페인에서 휴가를 보내고 있어요.

W: 그녀가 언제 돌아오나요?

M: 그녀는 다음 주 중에 돌아올 거예요. 그런데 저는 제 연구 보고서를 위해 이 책들이 필요해요. 다음 주 금요일이 마감 기한이라서, 저는 그렇게 오래 기다릴 수 없어요. 연체 요금을 제가 지불하면 어떨까요?

W: 그렇게 하셔도 되는데, 그게 꽤 비싸요. 그 책이 3주 이상 연체되어서, 요금이 55달러예요.

M: 55달러라고 하셨나요? 농담하시는 거죠!

W: 아니요, 유감스럽게도 아니에요. 그리고 그것이 지불될 때까지 하루에 2달러씩 늘어날 거예요.

M: 지금 당장은 그걸 지불할 충분한 돈이 없어요.

W: 그럼… 대학 청구 사무소에 연락해서 학생의 상황을 설명할 수도 있겠네요. 그들이 학생의 계정을 열어줄 수 있을지도 몰라요. 꼭 한번 해보세요…

M: 알겠어요, 그럴게요. 그냥 실수였어요. 제가 운이 좋아서 그들이 절 도와줄 수도 있겠네요. 제 계정을 여는 데 얼마나 걸릴지 아시나요?

W: 보통 하루나 이틀이 걸려요. 화요일쯤에는 학생의 계정을 다시 사용하실 수 있을 것 같네요.

M: 오… 그건 너무 늦은데요. 제가 할 수 있는 다른 게 있나요?

W: 음, 그 책들을 그냥 도서관 안에서 읽는 게 어때요? 이용하실 수 있는 조용한 공간들이 많아요. 책상은 편안하고, 밖에서 나는 소리도 들리지 않을 거예요.

M: 네. 그게 최선의 선택으로 들리네요. 오, 그런데, 음, 커피와 간식을 가져와도 되나요?

W: 물론이죠. 커피와 간단한 간식을 드셔도 돼요. 하지만 어질러 놓거나 다른 도서관 이용자들을 방해하지 않도록 주의하세요. 이용 가능한 아무 책상에나 앉으셔도 돼요.

M: 좋아요, 그럼. 큰 도움이 되어주셔서 감사합니다.

check out ~을 대출하다   unpaid 톙 미납된
research paper 연구 보고서   unlock 동 열다   plenty of ~이 많은
disturb 동 방해하다

1 학생의 문제는 무엇인가?

   (A) 그는 계정의 비밀번호를 잊어버렸다.

   (B) 그가 필요한 책들은 도서관에 없다.

   (C) 그는 책을 더 빌리기 위해서 요금을 지불해야 한다.

   (D) 그가 대출한 책들이 분실되었다.

2 사서에 따르면, 학교는 왜 학생의 계정을 잠갔는가?

   (A) 학생이 물품들을 늦게 돌려주었다.

   (B) 학생이 반납 일자를 놓쳤다.

   (C) 학생이 그의 학생증을 잃어버렸다.

   (D) 학생이 그의 친구에게 그의 계정을 사용하도록 해주었다.

3 학생은 왜 책들을 대출해야 하는가?

   (A) 그녀의 도서관 카드를 잃어버린 친구를 돕기 위해

   (B) 그가 스페인에서 휴가를 보내는 동안 읽기 위해

   (C) 곧 마감 기한이 되는 연구 보고서를 쓰기 위해

   (D) 3주 늦은 과제를 완료하기 위해

4 사서는 대학 청구 사무실에 관해 무엇이라고 말하는가?

   (A) 그들은 학생의 계정을 열어줄지도 모른다.

   (B) 그들은 상황을 이해하지 못할 수도 있다.

   (C) 그들은 방학 동안 열 것 같지 않다.

   (D) 그들은 화요일에 학생을 도와줄 수 있다.

5 사서는 학생에게 무엇을 제안하는가?

   (A) 은행에 가기

   (B) 도서관에서 작업하기

   (C) 다음 주에 다시 오기

   (D) 그의 친구에게 연락하기

Listening Practice 2

본문 p. 19

1 (C)   2 (C)   3 (A)   4 (C)   5 (B)

Note-taking

Role of Genetics in Body Weight

- Body weight influenced more by genetics > behavior
- Small genetic difference → a lot of physical diversity
- At least 52 genes affect body weight
  - Each person loses weight @ different speed
- Gene related to weight control = skinny gene
  - Individuals w/ active skinny gene = thinner
- Species w/ variety of body types = better survive
  - When lots of food → thin ppl. = healthier
  - When resources limited → store body fat = advantage

Listen to part of a lecture in a physiology class.

P: Most people believe that they have the ability to control their weight. Um, they think that losing weight is simply about eating less food or exercising more often. ¹However, recent research suggests that body weight is influenced more by genetics than by behavior. This is what I want to talk about today.

Let's start with an overview... ²As I'm sure you know, about 99.9 percent of human DNA in all humans is the same. What this means is that there isn't much difference between your genes and everyone else's genes. But, uh, even this small amount of genetic difference results in a lot of physical diversity. In fact, it is responsible for everything that makes one person different from another. And this includes how easy it is to gain weight and how difficult it is to lose it.

S: Is this why some people can eat lots of food and never gain weight?

P: That's partly correct. However, lifestyle also plays a key role... Anyway, researchers know that there are at least 52 individual genes that affect body weight. And each person has a different combination of these genes. ⁵So imagine that you make 50 people eat the same amount of calories and do the same amount of exercise. Each person will lose weight at a different speed. Now, don't get me wrong... Obviously, diet and exercise are important for losing weight. But, because of genetic differences, some people must exercise more to burn the same number of calories as others. Studies of identical twins have also confirmed that genes have a stronger role than behavior. Identical twins have the same genes, and research has shown that they will have similar body weights throughout their lives. This is true even when one of them exercises regularly and the other does not.

OK... Now, I want to look at a specific gene related to weight control. Um, it's called the "skinny gene." Uh, some people have this gene and others do not... Generally, people with the skinny gene do not gain weight easily. ³And, uh, the gene is also less active in obese people. Researchers have also discovered that individuals with active skinny genes are thinner than others, even if they consume the same amount of food.

But why do some people have this gene and others do not? How does this make sense for human evolution? ⁴Well, it makes sense because a species with a variety of body types is better able to survive through changes in environmental conditions. When there is lots of food, thin people are generally healthier. However, when resources are limited, those who can easily store body fat have an advantage. Either way, the species will continue...

생리학 강의의 일부를 들으시오.

P: 대부분의 사람들은 그들에게 체중을 조절하는 능력이 있다고 믿

습니다. 음, 그들은 살을 빼는 것이 단순히 음식을 덜 먹거나 더 자주 운동하는 것이라고 생각하죠. 하지만, 최근의 연구는 체중이 행동보다는 유전적 특징에 의해 더 많은 영향을 받는다는 것을 시사합니다. 이것이 오늘 얘기하고자 하는 거예요.

개요로 시작하죠... 여러분이 알고 있을 거라고 생각하는데, 사람 DNA의 약 99.9퍼센트는 모든 사람에서 동일합니다. 이게 의미하는 것은 여러분의 유전자와 다른 모든 사람들의 유전자 사이에 큰 차이가 없다는 거예요. 하지만, 어, 이렇게 적은 양의 유전적 차이조차도 많은 신체적 다양성을 야기한다는 거예요. 사실, 그것은 한 사람을 다른 사람과 차이가 나게 만드는 모든 것의 원인이 됩니다. 그리고 이것은 살이 찌는 것이 얼마나 쉬운지 그리고 살을 빼는 것이 얼마나 어려운지를 포함하죠.

S: 이게 어떤 사람들은 음식을 많이 먹어도 절대 살이 찌지 않는 이유인가요?

P: 부분적으로는 맞아요. 하지만, 생활 방식도 중요한 역할을 해요... 어쨌든, 연구자들은 체중에 영향을 미치는 개별 유전자가 적어도 52개라는 것을 알고 있어요. 그리고 각각의 사람은 이 유전자들의 서로 다른 조합을 가지고 있습니다. 자, 50명의 사람들에게 같은 양의 칼로리를 먹게 하고 같은 양의 운동을 하게 한다고 상상해 보세요. 각각의 사람은 서로 다른 속도로 살이 빠질 거예요. 자, 오해하지 마세요... 분명히, 식습관과 운동은 살을 빼는 데 있어 중요합니다. 하지만, 유전적 차이 때문에, 어떤 사람들은 다른 사람들과 똑같은 양의 칼로리를 태우기 위해 더 많이 운동해야만 합니다. 일란성 쌍둥이에 대한 연구도 유전자가 행동보다 더 강한 역할을 한다는 걸 확인했어요. 일란성 쌍둥이들은 동일한 유전자를 가지고 있고, 연구는 그들이 일생 동안 비슷한 체중을 가질 것이라는 걸 보여줬어요. 이것은 심지어 그들 중 한 명은 규칙적으로 운동하고 나머지 한 명은 그렇게 하지 않을 때조차 적용돼요.

자... 이제, 체중 조절과 관련된 특정 유전자를 살펴보려 합니다. 음, 그건 "스키니 진"이라 불려요. 어, 어떤 사람들은 이 유전자를 가지고 있고 다른 사람들은 가지고 있지 않아요... 일반적으로, 스키니 진을 가진 사람들은 쉽게 살이 찌지 않아요. 그리고, 어, 그 유전자는 또한 비만인 사람들에서 덜 활동적이에요. 연구자들은 또한 활동적인 스키니 진을 가진 사람들은 같은 양의 음식을 먹더라도 다른 사람들보다 더 말랐다는 것을 발견했어요.

그런데 왜 어떤 사람들은 이 유전자를 가지고 있고 다른 사람들은 그렇지 않을까요? 이게 어떻게 인간 진화의 이치에 맞을까요? 음, 다양한 체형을 가진 종이 환경적 조건의 변화에서 더 잘 살아남을 수 있기 때문에 그것은 이치에 맞습니다. 많은 음식이 있을 때는, 마른 사람들이 일반적으로 더 건강합니다. 하지만, 자원이 한정되어 있을 때는, 쉽게 체지방을 저장할 수 있는 사람들이 유리한 점을 가지고 있죠. 어느 쪽이든, 그 종은 존속할 거예요...

genetics 명 유전적 특징　behavior 명 행동　overview 명 개요
gene 명 유전자　diversity 명 다양성　combination 명 조합
obviously 부 분명히　diet 명 식습관　identical twins 일란성 쌍둥이
regularly 부 규칙적으로　obese 형 비만인
consume 동 먹다, 소비하다　evolution 명 진화　body fat 체지방

1 강의의 주된 주제는 무엇인가?

(A) 인간의 유전적 다양성

(B) 일부 사람들이 살을 뺄 수 없는 이유

(C) 체중에서 유전적 특징의 역할

(D) 생활 방식이 체중 증가에 영향을 미치는 방식

2 교수는 사람의 DNA에 관해 무엇이라고 말하는가?

(A) 그것은 부모와 자녀에서 다르다.

(B) 그것은 체중 감량과 무관하다.

(C) 그것은 모든 사람에서 대부분 동일하다.

(D) 그것은 사람의 행동에 강하게 영향을 미친다.

3 교수에 따르면, 스키니 진의 특징은 무엇인가?

(A) 그것은 특정 유형의 사람들에게서 덜 활동적이다.

(B) 그것은 인간에게서만 발견된다.

(C) 그것은 사람들이 빨리 지치게 한다.

(D) 그것은 사람들이 더 자주 배고프게 만든다.

4 교수에 따르면, 어떤 종이 환경적 조건의 변화에서 더 잘 살아남을 수 있는가?

(A) 많이 먹지 않는 종

(B) 체지방이 많은 종

(C) 다양한 체형을 가진 종

(D) 신체적으로 활동적인 종

강의의 일부를 다시 듣고 질문에 답하시오.

P: So imagine that you make 50 people eat the same amount of calories and do the same amount of exercise. Each person will lose weight at a different speed. Now, don't get me wrong... Obviously, diet and exercise are important for losing weight.

5 교수는 이렇게 말함으로써 무엇을 의미하는가?

P: Now, don't get me wrong...

(A) 그녀는 학생들이 더 많은 예시를 들 수 있다고 생각한다.

(B) 그녀는 학생들이 혼란스러워하기를 원하지 않는다.

(C) 그녀는 살을 빼는 데 있어 속도가 중요하지 않다고 생각한다.

(D) 그녀는 사람들이 다이어트와 운동을 더 많이 해야 한다고 생각한다.

Listening Practice 3　　본문 p. 21

1 (A)	2 (C)	3 (B)	4 (C)	5 (D)

Note-taking

S: This is my 1st psychology course → tell more about it
P: 1st week = overview of psychology & how ppl. use
　Different topics in psychology (e.g. brain & behavior)
　Lastly, section about reasoning & decision-making
　Introductory course ∴ topics in much detail X
　Work in groups on research project → present
S: Any individual research papers?
P: 2 individual research papers, five pages each
　Papers = 10%, group project & midterm = 20% each
　Final = 40%, attendance = rest of grade

Listen to a conversation between a student and a professor.

S: Hi, um... Professor Stone? ¹Uh, I'll be taking your Psychology 101 class this semester. This is my first psychology course, so I was hoping you could tell me more about it.

P: Well, in the first week, there will be an overview of what psychology is and how people use it. Then, we will look at different topics in psychology. Um, this will include the brain and behavior. Lastly, the course will end with a section about reasoning and decision-making.

S: That's quite a lot! ²Will we be able to cover everything in just four months?

P: Yes, of course. Since this is an introductory course, we won't study any of the topics in much detail. It's just a basic introduction.

S: I see. And will most of our assignments be reading from a textbook?

P: ³Actually, you won't be needing any textbooks for this class. We will mostly be discussing basic topics. So we will be using short academic articles and some videos. I will probably recommend some free online resources as well.

S: That's a relief. Uh, how many hours per week will we need to study for this class?

P: Well, it depends on how quickly you read. In general, I would say two to three hours for each lecture.

S: OK. Um, I also heard most of the psychology courses have at least one group project. Are we going to have one as well? Or will we do all of the assignments by ourselves?

P: ⁴You'll work in groups on a research project. Then, each group will present their project to the class toward the end of the semester.

S: That sounds great. I've always loved working with a team. Will you assign any individual research papers?

P: Yes, there will be two individual research papers. But they will only be about five pages each.

S: ⁵Oh, no. I'm not very good at writing papers, so I hope they aren't a big part of our grade.

P: Papers are 10 percent of your grade. The group project and midterm exam are 20 percent each. The final exam is 40 percent, and attendance makes up the rest of your grade.

S: Wow, this is a lot to remember. I hope I don't forget anything. I want to major in psychology, so this class is really important to me.

P: Don't worry. Everything you need to know will be in the course outline. If you come to each class on time and try your best, I'm sure you'll do well.

학생과 교수 사이의 대화를 들으시오.

S: 안녕하세요, 음... Stone 교수님? 어, 저는 이번 학기에 교수님의 심리학 101 수업을 수강할 예정입니다. 이게 저의 첫 심리학 강의라서, 교수님께서 그것에 대해 더 말씀해 주실 수 있으면 좋겠어요.

P: 음, 첫 주에는, 심리학이 무엇이고 사람들이 그것을 어떻게 사용하는지에 대한 개요가 있을 거야. 그러고 나서, 우리는 심리학의 다른 주제들을 살펴볼 거야. 음, 이것은 뇌와 행동을 포함할 거야. 마지막으로, 강의는 추론과 의사 결정에 관한 부분으로 끝날 거야.

S: 꽤 많네요! 저희가 4개월 만에 모든 것을 다룰 수 있을까요?

P: 그럼, 물론이지. 이것은 입문 강의이기 때문에, 우리는 어떤 주제도 아주 자세히 공부하지 않을 거야. 그냥 기본적인 소개일 뿐이야.

S: 그렇군요. 그리고 대부분의 과제는 교과서를 읽는 것이 될까요?

P: 사실, 너는 이 수업을 위한 어떤 교과서도 필요하지 않을 거야. 우리는 주로 기본적인 주제들에 대해 토론할 거야. 그러니까 우리는 짧은 학술 논문들과 몇몇 영상을 이용할 거야. 나는 아마 몇몇 무료 온라인 자료들도 추천할 거야.

S: 다행이네요. 어, 이 수업을 위해 일주일에 몇 시간씩 공부해야 할까요?

P: 글쎄, 그건 네가 얼마나 빨리 읽느냐에 달려있어. 일반적으로, 나는 각 강의 당 두세 시간이라고 말할 거야.

S: 네. 음, 저는 또 대부분의 심리학 강의들에 적어도 한 개의 그룹 프로젝트가 있다고 들었어요. 저희도 하나를 하게 될까요? 아니면 저희가 모든 과제를 스스로 하게 되나요?

P: 너희는 연구 프로젝트에서 그룹으로 작업하게 될 거야. 그런 다음, 각 그룹은 학기 말에 그들의 프로젝트를 반 학생들에게 발표할 거야.

S: 그거 좋네요. 저는 항상 팀과 함께 작업하는 것을 좋아했어요. 개인 연구 보고서를 과제로 내주실 건가요?

P: 맞아, 두 개의 개인 연구 보고서가 있을 거야. 하지만 그것들은 각각 겨우 5페이지 정도일 거야.

S: 오, 안 돼요. 저는 보고서 쓰는 것을 잘하지 못해요, 그래서 그것들이 저희 성적의 큰 부분이 아니었으면 좋겠어요.

P: 보고서는 네 성적의 10퍼센트야. 그룹 프로젝트와 중간고사는 각각 20퍼센트야. 기말고사는 40퍼센트이고, 출석이 성적의 나머지를 차지해.

S: 와, 기억해야 할 게 많네요. 아무것도 까먹지 않으면 좋겠네요. 저는 심리학을 전공하고 싶어요, 그래서 이 수업은 저에게 정말 중요해요.

P: 걱정하지 마. 네가 알아야 하는 모든 것은 강의 개요에 있을 거야. 각 수업에 제시간에 와서 최선을 다한다면, 네가 잘할 거라고 확신해.

psychology 몡 심리학   overview 몡 개요   behavior 몡 행동
lastly 튄 마지막으로   reasoning 몡 추론
decision-making 몡 의사 결정   introductory course 입문 강의
present 통 발표하다   attendance 몡 출석   outline 몡 개요

1 학생은 왜 교수를 찾아가는가?

(A) 수업에 대한 더 많은 정보를 얻기 위해

(B) 연구 보고서에 대한 조언을 구하기 위해

(C) 어떤 강의를 수강할 수 있는지 알아내기 위해

(D) 전공을 바꾸기 위해 무엇을 해야 하는지 알아내기 위해

2 교수는 어떻게 학기 동안 모든 주제를 다룰 것인가?

(A) 더 빠른 속도로 수업을 가르침으로써

(B) 학기가 시작하기 전에 자료를 소개함으로써

(C) 기본적인 정보만 살펴봄으로써

(D) 학생들에게 더 오랜 시간 동안 공부하도록 지시함으로써

3 교수는 교과서에 관해 무엇이라고 언급하는가?

(A) 그것들은 도서관에서 빌릴 수 있다.

(B) 그것들은 수업을 위해 필요하지 않다.

(C) 그것들은 아직 학교에 의해 구입되지 않았다.

(D) 그것들은 온라인에 있는 자료들보다 낫다.

4 그룹 프로젝트에 대한 학생의 태도는 무엇인가?

(A) 그는 그것에 너무 많은 시간이 걸리지 않기를 바란다.

(B) 그는 그것을 발표하는 사람이 되고 싶어 한다.

(C) 그는 그가 그것을 작업하는 것을 즐길 것이라고 생각한다.

(D) 그는 그것이 성적의 더 큰 부분이 되어야 한다고 생각한다.

5 학생은 수업에 관해 어떤 걱정을 하는가?

(A) 그가 팀의 구성원으로서 작업해야 한다.

(B) 교수가 엄격한 것으로 알려져 있다.

(C) 발표가 많은 준비를 필요로 할 것이다.

(D) 그의 부족한 글쓰기 실력이 그의 성적에 영향을 미칠 수도 있다.

Listening Practice 4 본문 p.23

1 (C) 2 (C) 3 (B), (D) 4 (C) 5 (B)

Note-taking

Ethical Consumerism

- Ethical Consumerism = buy based on ethical reasons
  - One company pays fair amount of money
  - The other company pays as little as possible
  - Ethical consumer = choose from 1st company
- Choose not to buy from companies behave unethically
- Most familiar method = buying organic products
  - Not made w/ harmful chemicals, organic label
- Look for "fair trade" label
- Buy more local products = environmentally friendly

Listen to part of a lecture in an economics class.

P: Last week, I mentioned the idea of economic activism. Um, that is when people try to change a situation by choosing what to spend their money on. ¹Well, today's topic is similar to that. It is called ethical consumerism.

Ethical consumerism is a way of selecting which products to buy based on ethical reasons. Um, we all have different reasons for buying products. Sometimes, we buy products because they are cheap. Other times, we buy products, uh, just because they make us feel better. ²Well, ethical consumerism is about buying products that do the smallest amount of harm to society or the environment. Um, let me give you an example... Imagine that there are two coffee companies that buy coffee beans from farmers. One company recognizes that growing coffee beans is hard work. So it pays farmers a fair amount of money. However, the other company wants to pay as little as possible to save on costs. So it pays the coffee growers a low amount even if this hurts the farmers. An ethical consumer would choose to buy coffee from the first company. And, through this, they are encouraging all coffee companies to pay farmers a fair amount of money.

Ethical consumerism can also work the other way. Ethical consumers can also choose not to buy from companies that behave unethically. For instance, if a company pollutes the environment, ethical consumers can choose to stop buying that company's products. That way, they can encourage companies to protect the environment. Um, so, as an ethical consumer, you have to think carefully about which products you buy... The money you spend can help the right kind of company succeed... It can help the wrong kind of company fail.

S: ⁵Uh, but there are so many different products these days. How can a consumer know which ones to support and which ones to avoid? I mean, it seems impossible to know everything about all companies.

P: It does seem complex, doesn't it? But it's not as difficult as you might think... Um, perhaps the most familiar method of ethical consumerism is buying organic products. Organic products are considered a type of ethical product because they are not made with harmful chemicals or in places that treat animals badly. ³BJust look for the organic label on product packaging. An organic label tells us that a product was made with ethical methods. ³DSimilarly, you can look for something called a "fair trade" label. The label shows that a company follows strict social and environmental standards. These standards include good working conditions and fair prices that help small businesses compete with large companies. ⁴And, lastly, you can also buy more local products. Local products are usually more environmentally friendly because they don't have to be sent long distances. So less fuel is used and less pollution is released into the atmosphere.

경제학 강의의 일부를 들으시오.

P: 지난주에, 저는 경제 행동주의의 개념을 언급했어요. 음, 그건 사람들이 그들의 돈을 무엇에 쓸지 선택함으로써 상황을 바꾸려고 하는 경우예요. 음, 오늘의 주제는 그것과 비슷해요. 그것은 윤리적 소비주의라고 불려요.

윤리적 소비주의는 윤리적인 이유를 기반으로 어떤 상품을 구입할 것인지를 선택하는 방식이에요. 음, 우리는 모두 상품을 구입하는 서로 다른 이유를 가지고 있죠. 때때로, 우리는 상품이 저렴하기 때문에 구입합니다. 다른 때에는, 우리는, 어, 단지 상품이 우리의 기분을 좋게 해주기 때문에 구입해요. 음, 윤리적 소비주의는 사회나 환경에 최소한의 해를 끼치는 상품을 구입하는 거예요. 음, 예를 하나 들어 볼게요... 농부들에게서 커피콩을 구입하는 두 개의 커피 회사가 있다고 상상해 보세요. 한 회사는 커피콩을 재배하는 것이 힘든 일이라는 걸 인정해요. 그래서 그것은 농부들에게 타당한 금액을 지불해요. 그런데, 다른 회사는 비용을 절약하기 위해 가능한 한 적은 돈을 지불하고 싶어 해요. 그래서 농부들에게 피해를 줌에도 불구하고 커피 재배자들에게 적은 금액을 지불하죠. 윤리적인 소비자는 첫 번째 회사에서 커피를 구입하는 것을 선택할 거예요. 그리고, 이를 통해, 그들은 모든 커피 회사들이 농부들에게 공정한 금액을 지불하도록 장려하고 있어요.

윤리적 소비주의는 반대로도 작용할 수 있어요. 윤리적인 소비자들은 비윤리적으로 행동하는 회사들로부터 구입하지 않는 것을 선택할 수도 있어요. 예를 들어, 어떤 회사가 환경을 오염시키면, 윤리적인 소비자들은 그 회사의 상품 구입을 중단할 것을 선택할 수 있죠. 그렇게 하면, 그들은 회사들이 환경을 보호하도록 장려할 수 있습니다. 음, 그러니까, 윤리적인 소비자로서, 여러분은 어떤 상품을 구입할지에 대해 신중히 생각해야 해요... 여러분이 쓰는 돈은 도덕적으로 옳은 종류의 회사가 성공하도록 도울 수 있어요... 그것은 도덕적으로 옳지 않은 종류의 회사가 실패하도록 도울 수 있죠.

S: 어, 하지만 요즘에는 여러 가지 상품들이 너무 많아요. 소비자가 어떻게 어떤 것을 후원하고 어떤 것을 피할지 알 수 있나요? 그러니까, 모든 회사들에 대해 모든 것을 아는 건 불가능해 보여요.

P: 정말 복잡해 보이죠, 그렇지 않나요? 하지만 생각하는 것만큼 어렵지 않아요. 음, 아마도 윤리적인 소비주의의 가장 친숙한 방법은 유기농 상품을 구입하는 거예요. 유기농 상품은 해로운 화학물질로 만들어지거나 동물을 학대하는 곳에서 만들어지지 않기 때문에 윤리적인 상품의 일종으로 여겨져요. 그저 상품 포장에서 유기농 라벨을 찾아보세요. 유기농 라벨은 우리에게 상품이 윤리적인 방법으로 만들어졌다는 것을 알려줘요. 비슷하게, "공정 무역" 라벨이라고 불리는 것을 찾아볼 수 있어요. 그 라벨은 회사가 엄격한 사회적 및 환경적 기준들을 따른다는 것을 보여줘요. 이 기준들은 좋은 근로 조건과 작은 회사가 큰 회사와 경쟁하는 것을 도와주는 공정 가격을 포함해요. 그리고, 마지막으로, 여러분은 또한 더 많은 지역 상품을 구입할 수 있어요. 지역 상품은 먼 거리로 운송될 필요가 없기 때문에 보통 더 환경친화적이에요. 그러니까 더 적은 연료가 사용되고 더 적은 오염 물질이 대기로 방출되는 거죠.

activism 명 행동주의   ethical 형 윤리적인   harm 명 해
recognize 동 인정하다   fair 형 적지 않은; 공정한
right 형 도덕적으로 옳은   avoid 동 피하다   complex 형 복잡한
method 명 방법   organic 형 유기농의   packaging 명 포장
strict 형 엄격한   pollution 명 오염 물질

1 강의의 주된 주제는 무엇인가?

(A) 소비주의의 문제
(B) 경제가 행동주의에 영향을 미치는 방식
(C) 구입할 상품을 선택하는 방식
(D) 국가가 회사를 규제하는 이유

2 교수는 윤리적 소비주의를 어떻게 설명하는가?

(A) 다양한 종류의 회사를 열거함으로써
(B) 환경적 문제의 중요성을 강조함으로써
(C) 다른 회사들의 예시를 제공함으로써
(D) 여러 연구의 결과를 비교함으로써

3 교수에 따르면, 사람들은 상품을 윤리적으로 소비하기 위해 무엇을 할 수 있는가? 2개의 답을 고르시오.

(A) 사치품에 돈을 덜 쓰기
(B) 유기농 라벨이 붙은 상품 찾기
(C) 노동자를 위한 권리를 지지하는 지도자에게 투표하기
(D) 엄격한 기준들을 따르는 회사들에서 구입하기

4 교수는 왜 사람들에게 지역 상품을 구입할 것을 권장하는가?

(A) 외국 상품은 종종 너무 비싸다.
(B) 지역에서 구입하는 것은 작은 회사들을 지원하는 데 도움이

된다.
(C) 지역 상품은 환경에 덜 해롭다.
(D) 지역에서 구입하는 것은 지역 사람들을 위한 일자리를 만드는 데 도움이 된다.

강의의 일부를 다시 듣고 질문에 답하시오.

S: Uh, but there are so many different products these days. How can a consumer know which ones to support and which ones to avoid? I mean, it seems impossible to know everything about all companies.

P: It does seem complex, doesn't it? But it's not as difficult as you might think...

5 교수는 왜 이렇게 말하는가:

P: It does seem complex, doesn't it?

(A) 윤리적 소비주의가 실천하기 어렵다는 것을 보여주기 위해
(B) 견해와 관련된 학생의 어려움을 인정하기 위해
(C) 윤리적인 결정이 항상 가능하지는 않다는 것을 말하기 위해
(D) 문제를 해결할 수 있는 많은 방법이 있다는 것에 동의하기 위해

iBT Listening Test 1

본문 p. 25

1 (C)   2 (C)   3 (C)   4 (A)   5 (B)

Note-taking

W: Prof. Hane not here right now
M: Have to talk about joining environmental history class
W: Won't be in office until afternoon
M: Have to go to work ∴ time X this afternoon
   Tried to do it online → haven't taken required class
   Went to registrar's office → need permission
   Intro. to history = little to do w/ environment
   Friend = didn't have to take Intro. to history
W: Call her later this afternoon?
M: Work part-time ∴ too busy
W: Come back tomorrow morning → speak w/ Prof.
M: Permission tomorrow morning → enough time

Listen to a conversation between a student and a university employee.

W: Good morning. How can I help you?

M: Um, this is the history department, right? I'm looking for Professor Hane's office.

W: Yes, this is where Professor Hane works. Unfortunately, she is not here right now.

M: Oh, OK. Do you know what time she'll be back? [1]I have to talk to her about whether I can join her environmental history class. It starts tomorrow.

W: Actually, she has meetings all morning. She probably won't be in her office until this afternoon. You could come back then if you need to speak with her.

M: Well, I have to go to work, so I don't have time to meet with her this afternoon.

W: I see. Are you a history major?

M: No, but I'm studying environmental science, so I think this class would be related to my studies. And I'm also really interested in the subject.

W: OK. Did you already try to sign up for the class on your own?

M: ²I tried to do it online yesterday, but I wasn't able to because I haven't taken a required class called Introduction to History. So I went to the registrar's office. They told me that I need permission from the instructor.

W: In that case, you will need to speak with her directly. ⁵Hmm… Have you thought about signing up for Introduction to History first? Most students take the courses in that order.

M: I don't know... The Introduction to History class is mostly about general history, which has little to do with the environment. Plus, I have a friend who took Professor Hane's environmental history class last semester. He told me that he didn't have to take the Introduction to History class first.

W: OK. ³Why don't you try to call her later? I can give you her office number and you can speak with her on the phone. She should be back in the office by around 1 p.m.

M: ³I'm sorry, but I don't think I can do that. I work part-time at a restaurant, so I will be too busy to call her until late at night. I'm sure she'll be gone by then.

W: OK... Then, how about this? Come back here tomorrow morning before your classes start. That way, you can speak directly with Professor Hane about getting permission.

M: I guess that could work. ⁴The class I want to register for isn't until tomorrow afternoon. So if she gives me permission tomorrow morning, then I will have enough time to register for the class.

W: Let me check her schedule. Hmm... You're in luck. She will be here at 8 a.m. tomorrow.

M: Oh, really? That's perfect. I'll stop by tomorrow. Thanks for your help!

학생과 교직원 사이의 대화를 들으시오.

W: 좋은 아침입니다. 어떻게 도와드릴까요?

M: 음, 여기가 역사학과죠, 그렇죠? Hane 교수님의 사무실을 찾고 있습니다.

W: 네, 여기가 Hane 교수님이 일하시는 곳이에요. 안타깝게도, 그녀는 지금 여기 안 계세요.

M: 오, 그렇군요. 그녀가 몇 시에 돌아오실지 아시나요? 그녀의 환경사 수업에 참여할 수 있는지에 대해 그녀와 이야기해야 해서요. 그것은 내일 시작해요.

W: 사실은, 그녀는 오전 내내 회의가 있으세요. 아마 오늘 오후에야 사무실에 계실 거예요. 그녀와 이야기해야 하시면 그때 돌아오셔도 돼요.

M: 음, 저는 일하러 가야 해서, 오늘 오후에는 그녀와 만날 시간이 없어요.

W: 그렇군요. 역사 전공 학생이신가요?

M: 아니요, 하지만 저는 환경 과학을 공부하고 있어요, 그래서 이 수

업이 제 학업과 관련이 있을 것 같아요. 그리고 저는 그 주제에 정말 관심이 많기도 해요.

W: 네. 혼자서 이미 수업 신청을 시도해 보셨나요?

M: 어제 온라인으로 하려고 시도해 봤는데, 제가 역사 개론이라는 필수 수업을 듣지 않아서 할 수 없었어요. 그래서 저는 학적과에 갔어요. 그들은 제가 강사의 허락이 필요하다고 했어요.

W: 그런 경우라면, 그녀에게 직접 이야기해야 할 거예요. 흠… 역사 개론을 먼저 신청하는 것에 대해서는 생각해 보셨나요? 대부분의 학생들은 그 순서로 강의를 들어요.

M: 잘 모르겠어요... 역사 개론 수업은 대부분 전반적인 역사에 관한 것이고, 그건 환경과 거의 관련이 없어요. 게다가, 저는 지난 학기에 Hane 교수님의 환경사 수업을 들은 친구가 있어요. 그가 저에게 역사 개론 수업을 먼저 들을 필요가 없었다고 말해줬어요.

W: 알았어요. 나중에 그녀에게 전화해 보는 게 어때요? 제가 그녀의 사무실 번호를 알려드릴 수 있고 학생은 그녀와 통화하실 수 있어요. 그녀는 오후 1시쯤에는 사무실로 돌아오실 거예요.

M: 죄송하지만, 그렇게 할 수 없을 것 같아요. 저는 식당에서 아르바이트를 해서, 그녀에게 전화하기에는 밤늦게까지 너무 바쁠 거예요. 그때쯤에는 그녀가 안 계실 거예요.

W: 네... 그럼, 이건 어때요? 내일 아침에 학생의 수업이 시작하기 전에 여기로 돌아오세요. 그렇게 하면, 허락을 받는 것에 관해 Hane 교수님과 직접 이야기할 수 있어요.

M: 그건 될 것 같네요. 제가 등록하기 원하는 수업은 내일 오후에야 있어요. 그러니까 만약 그녀가 내일 아침에 허락해 주시면, 수업에 등록할 충분한 시간이 있을 거예요.

W: 그녀의 일정을 확인해 볼게요. 흠... 운이 좋으시네요. 그녀는 내일 오전 8시에 여기에 계실 거예요.

M: 오, 정말요? 완벽하네요. 내일 들를게요. 도와주셔서 감사합니다!

---

unfortunately 🄫 안타깝게도   related to ~과 관련이 있는
permission 🄜 허락   instructor 🄜 강사   directly 🄫 직접
order 🄜 순서   in luck 운이 좋은

1 학생은 왜 역사학과를 찾아가는가?

(A) 그의 이름을 수업 대기자 명단에 올려두기 위해

(B) 수업을 변경하는 것에 관해 직원과 이야기하기 위해

(C) 수업에 참여하는 것에 관해 교수와 이야기하기 위해

(D) 수업 일정을 변경하는 것에 관해 문의하기 위해

2 학생은 왜 온라인으로 수강 신청할 수 없었는가?

(A) 그는 필요한 정보가 없었다.

(B) 수업은 졸업 예정자에게만 열려 있다.

(C) 그는 필수 과목을 듣지 않았다.

(D) 웹사이트가 작동하지 않았었다.

3 학생은 왜 교수에게 전화하기를 꺼리는가?

(A) 그는 밤늦게 그녀를 방해하고 싶지 않다.

(B) 그는 그녀에게 직접 이야기해야 한다.

(C) 그는 일 때문에 너무 바쁠 것이다.

(D) 그는 사무실이 열 때까지 기다릴 수 없다.

4 학생이 아침에 교수를 만나는 것의 장점은 무엇인가?

(A) 그는 수업이 시작하기 전에 수강 신청할 수 있다.

(B) 그는 그들이 이야기한 후에 제시간에 출근할 수 있다.

(C) 그는 오후에 수업에 등록할 수 있다.

(D) 그는 동시에 신청서를 제출할 수 있다.

대화의 일부를 다시 듣고 질문에 답하시오.

W: Hmm... Have you thought about signing up for Introduction to History first? Most students take the courses in that order.

M: I don't know... The Introduction to History class is mostly about general history, which has little to do with the environment.

5 학생은 이렇게 말함으로써 무엇을 의미하는가:

M: I don't know...

(A) 그는 직원의 조언이 도움이 되지 않아 속상하다.

(B) 그는 직원의 제안을 따르는 것을 원하지 않는다.

(C) 그는 직원이 그가 무엇을 하기를 원하는지 잘 모른다.

(D) 그는 직원이 그의 문제를 이해한다고 생각하지 않는다.

iBT Listening Test 2

1 (D) 2 (B) 3 (C) 4 (B) 5 (B) 6 (C)

Note-taking

How Artists Show Character of Subjects

- Good portrait = shows subject's character, how?
- 1st method = clothing & objects
  - Carefully choose to express subject's personality
  - E.g. *Arnolfini Portrait* = they are wealthy & important
- Next method = poses & actions
  - Some show entire body = help understand character
  - E.g. *Napoleon* ~ = strong & fearless leader
- Lastly = facial expressions
  - During Renaiss. artists study human body ∴ skilled
  - E.g. *Mona Lisa* = small & mysterious smile
  - Effective ∵ ppl. easily understand facial expressions

Listen to part of a lecture in an art history class.

P: Portrait painting is one of the oldest forms of art. It has been around for thousands of years. Its main purpose is to remember people by showing how they looked. But, of course, there is more to people than just their appearance. A good portrait also shows us something about a subject's character. [1]So how do artists show a subject's character or personality? Well, today we will look at several methods.

So the first method uses clothing and objects. Artists paint subjects with specific clothing and objects in order to tell us what the subjects are like. Um, think of the clothing and objects that you own. They probably help you express your personality, right? So portrait painters also carefully choose the clothing and objects shown in portraits to express their subject's personality... Um, there are many examples of this in portrait art. [2]For instance, take a look at this one called the *Arnolfini Portrait*. It was painted by the Dutch artist, Jan van Eyck, in 1434. It shows a wealthy Italian businessman named Arnolfini and his wife.

You can see that they are wearing expensive clothes and there are some nice pieces of furniture around them. This shows that they are a wealthy and important couple.

Next, there is the method of using poses and actions. [6]Although many portraits show only a subject's face, some show the entire body. This type of portrait can help us understand the subject's character better. The more we see, the more information we have. [3]Um, look at this famous portrait of Napoleon called *Napoleon Crossing the Alps*, for example. It was done in 1801 by the French painter Jacques-Louis David. In the painting, we see Napoleon sitting on a horse. However, the horse is standing on its back legs as if it is preparing to attack. Napoleon is holding on to the horse with one hand and pointing toward the sky with the other. The entire image is exciting with plenty of movement and action. It shows Napoleon as a strong and fearless leader who is in control of his actions.

Lastly, we have a method that uses facial expressions. Facial expressions don't have to be as dramatic as poses and actions. But they can still tell us a lot about a subject. Also, it takes a lot of skill to capture facial expressions in a painting. In fact, many artists in the past did not have enough skill to paint facial expressions. Um, this all changed during the Renaissance. [4]During the Renaissance, many artists focused on studying the human body closely, including the face. So they became very skilled at painting facial expressions. One of the most famous examples, of course, is the *Mona Lisa* by Leonardo da Vinci. In the *Mona Lisa*, we see that the subject has a small and mysterious smile. It makes her look as if she knows something that the viewers do not. [5]Portraits like this one are very effective for showing information about a subject. You know... People can easily understand facial expressions.

미술사학 강의의 일부를 들으시오.

P: 초상화는 미술의 가장 오래된 형태 중 하나입니다. 그것은 수천 년 동안 존재해 왔어요. 그것의 주된 목적은 사람들이 어떻게 생겼는지를 보여줌으로써 그들을 기억하는 것이에요. 하지만, 물론, 사람들에게는 단지 외모 이상의 것이 있습니다. 좋은 초상화는 우리에게 인물의 성격에 대한 무언가를 보여주기도 해요. 자, 화가는 어떻게 인물의 성격이나 개성을 보여줄까요? 음, 오늘 우리는 몇 가지 방법을 살펴볼 거예요.

자, 첫 번째 방법은 옷과 물건을 이용합니다. 화가는 우리에게 인물이 어땠는지 알려주기 위해 특정한 옷 그리고 물건과 함께 인물을 그려요. 음, 여러분이 가지고 있는 옷과 물건을 떠올려 보세요. 그것들은 아마 여러분의 개성을 표현하는 데 도움을 줄 거예요, 그렇죠? 그래서 초상화 화가들 또한 인물의 개성을 표현하기 위해 초상화에 보여지는 옷과 물건을 신중히 골라요... 음, 초상화 미술에는 이것의 예시가 많아요. 예를 들어, 이 '아르놀피니의 초상'을 한번 보세요. 그것은 1434년에 네덜란드 화가 얀 반 에이크에 의해 그려졌죠. 그것은 아르놀피니라는 부유한 이탈리아 사업가와 그의 아내를 보여줘요. 그들이 비싼 옷을 입고 있는 것을 볼 수 있고 그들 주위에는 멋진 가구 몇 점이 있죠. 이는 그들이 부유하고 영향력이 큰 부부라는 것을 보여줘요.

다음으로, 자세와 동작을 이용하는 방법이 있어요. 많은 초상화들이 인물의 얼굴만 보여주지만, 일부는 전신을 보여줍니다. 이런 유형의 초상화는 우리가 인물의 성격을 더 잘 이해하도록 도와줘요. 우리는 더 많이 볼수록, 더 많은 정보를 갖게 되죠. 음, 예를 들어, '알프스산맥을 넘는 나폴레옹'이라고 불리는 이 유명한 나폴레옹 초상화를 보세요. 그것은 1801년에 프랑스 화가 자크 루이 다비드에 의해 그려졌어요. 그림에서, 우리는 나폴레옹이 말 위에 앉아있는 걸 볼 수 있죠. 그런데, 말은 마치 공격을 준비하듯 뒷다리로 서 있어요. 나폴레옹은 한 손으로 말을 붙잡고 다른 손으로는 하늘을 가리키고 있어요. 많은 움직임과 동작으로 그림 전체가 흥미진진하죠. 그것은 나폴레옹을 자신의 동작을 통제하고 있는 강력하고 용감한 지도자로 나타내요.

마지막으로, 얼굴 표정을 이용하는 방법이 있습니다. 얼굴 표정은 자세와 동작만큼 극적일 필요가 없어요. 하지만 그것들은 여전히 우리에게 인물에 대해 많은 것을 알려줄 수 있죠. 또한, 그림에 얼굴 표정을 정확히 담아내는 것은 많은 기술을 요구해요. 사실, 많은 과거의 화가들은 표정을 그리기에 충분한 기술을 가지고 있지 않았어요. 음, 이 모든 것은 르네상스 시대에 바뀌었어요. 르네상스 시대 동안, 많은 화가들은 얼굴을 포함하여 인체를 면밀히 연구하는 데 집중했어요. 그래서 그들은 얼굴 표정을 그리는 것에 매우 능숙해졌어요. 물론, 가장 유명한 예시 중 하나는 레오나르도 다 빈치가 그린 '모나리자'입니다. '모나리자'에서, 우리는 인물이 엷고 신비로운 미소를 짓고 있는 걸 볼 수 있어요. 그것은 마치 그녀가 관람자는 모르는 무언가를 알고 있는 것처럼 보이게 해요. 이것과 같은 초상화들은 인물에 관한 정보를 보여주는 데 매우 효과적이죠. 그러니까... 사람들은 얼굴 표정을 쉽게 이해할 수 있어요.

appearance 명 외모, 생김새   character 명 성격
personality 명 개성   wealthy 형 부유한   fearless 형 용감한
facial expression 얼굴 표정   capture 동 정확히 담아내다, 포착하다
closely 부 면밀히   skilled at ~에 능숙한   mysterious 형 신비로운

1 교수는 주로 무엇에 관해 논하는가?

(A) 초상화의 주된 목적

(B) 초상화가 시간이 지나며 발전해온 방식

(C) 화가가 초상화를 위한 인물을 선택하는 방법

(D) 화가가 인물의 성격을 보여주는 방법

2 교수에 따르면, 아르놀피니의 초상화에서 그에 관해 무엇을 알 수 있는가?

(A) 그는 식구가 아주 많은 가족 출신이었다.

(B) 그는 부유하고 영향력이 큰 인물이었다.

(C) 그는 가구 제작자로 유명해졌다.

(D) 그는 많은 화가들의 열렬한 후원자였다.

3 교수는 '알프스산맥을 넘는 나폴레옹'에 관해 무엇이라고 말하는가?

(A) 그것은 가장 유명한 나폴레옹 그림이다.

(B) 그것은 말 옆에 서 있는 나폴레옹을 보여준다.

(C) 그것은 인물을 강력한 지도자로 나타낸다.

(D) 그것은 중요한 대상으로서 자연에 초점을 맞춘다.

4 교수에 따르면, 르네상스 시대의 화가들은 어떻게 얼굴 표정을 그리는 것에 능숙해졌는가?

(A) 옛날 화가들의 작품을 모방함으로써

(B) 인체를 분석함으로써

(C) 책으로 그림을 공부함으로써

(D) 거울 속의 자신을 그림으로써

5 얼굴 표정이 있는 초상화에 대한 교수의 태도는 무엇인가?

(A) 그녀는 그것들이 다른 초상화 유형들에 비해 덜 흥미롭다고 생각한다.

(B) 그녀는 그것들이 사람들이 이해하기에 쉽다고 생각한다.

(C) 그녀는 초상화의 다른 유형들이 더 많은 기술을 요한다고 생각한다.

(D) 그녀는 르네상스 시대의 것들이 최고의 예시라고 생각한다.

강의의 일부를 다시 듣고 질문에 답하시오.

P: Although many portraits show only a subject's face, some show the entire body. This type of portrait can help us understand the subject's character better. The more we see, the more information we have.

6 교수는 왜 이렇게 말하는가:
P: The more we see, the more information we have.

(A) 화풍에 대한 많은 연구가 이루어졌음을 보여주기 위해

(B) 일부 초상화는 많은 작업을 요한다는 것을 시사하기 위해

(C) 초상화 유형의 장점을 설명하기 위해

(D) 그녀가 초상화를 직접 봤다는 것을 나타내기 위해

Vocabulary Review

본문 p. 32

1 appearance	2 lifeless	3 laboratory
4 evolution	5 genetics	6 mysterious
7 instructor	8 reasoning	9 previous
10 (B)	11 (A)	12 (D)
13 (C)	14 (C)	

CHAPTER 02
Detail

Example

본문 p. 35

A. (B)   **B.** (A), (C)

A.

Note-taking

M: Live in school dorm, need to pay a fine?
W: Received fine ∵ used an electric heater
　Electric heater = unsafe → can start fire
　Read rules → keep everyone safe & help avoid fines

Listen to a conversation between a student and a university housing office employee.

M: Hi, I live in one of the school dormitories. I received a letter saying that I need to pay a fine.

W: I can help you with that... Uh, it looks like you received a fine because you used an electric heater in your room.

M: Is there something wrong with that? It gets cold sometimes and my roommates don't like to turn on the main heater.

W: Yes, however, an electric heater can be unsafe. If it reaches high temperatures, it can start a fire.

M: Oh, I never thought about that. I don't want to put anyone in danger.

W: Please read the list of rules that was given to all residents. They keep everyone safe and will help you avoid future fines.

학생과 대학 기숙사 사무실 직원 사이의 대화를 들으시오.

M: 안녕하세요, 저는 학교 기숙사 중 한 곳에 살고 있습니다. 제가 벌금을 내야 한다는 편지를 받았어요.

W: 제가 도와드릴 수 있어요... 어, 방에서 전기 난방기를 사용하셔서 벌금을 받으신 것 같네요.

M: 그것에 무슨 문제가 있나요? 때때로 날씨가 추워지고 제 룸메이트들은 중앙 난방기를 켜기 싫어해요.

W: 네, 하지만, 전기 난방기는 안전하지 않을 수 있어요. 높은 온도에 도달하면, 화재를 일으킬 수 있어요.

M: 오, 그건 생각해 본 적이 없네요. 저는 아무도 위험에 빠뜨리고 싶지 않아요.

W: 모든 거주자에게 제공된 규칙 목록을 읽어주세요. 그것들은 모두를 안전하게 지켜주고 미래의 벌금을 피할 수 있게 도와줄 거예요.

fine 명 벌금   electric 형 전기의, 전기를 이용하는   heater 명 난방기
unsafe 형 안전하지 않은   resident 명 거주자   avoid 동 피하다

직원은 전기 난방기에 관해 무엇이라고 말하는가?

(A) 그것들은 많은 전기를 낭비한다.
(B) 그것들은 뜨거워지고 화재를 일으킬 수 있다.
(C) 그것들은 거주자들에 의해 흔히 사용된다.
(D) 그것들은 쉽게 고장 나고 수리가 필요하다.

B.

Note-taking

Factors Why Venice is Sinking

- Venice = known for architecture, 20 mil. tourists/yr
- Problem = sinking @ 1 to 2 mm/yr
  - Built on weak ground ∴ hold weight of bldg. X
  - Climate change → sea levels rise
- Water will rise above foundation → damage bldg.
- Trying to save city → install gates & raising money

Listen to part of a lecture in an architecture class.

P: Venice is known for its architecture. Around 20 million tourists visit it each year to enjoy the city and its famous waterways. However, Venice has a serious problem. It's sinking at a rate of one to two millimeters a year. Uh, one factor is that the city was built on weak ground. The soil is so soft that it cannot hold the weight of the buildings above it. Another factor is climate change, which is causing sea levels to rise. As the city continues to sink, water will rise above the foundations of the buildings and damage them. So officials are trying to save the city. They have installed huge gates to try to control the water... Also, they are raising money to make the historic buildings waterproof.

건축학 강의의 일부를 들으시오.

P: 베니스는 건축으로 유명합니다. 매년 약 2천만 명의 관광객들이 도시와 그곳의 유명한 수로를 즐기기 위해 그곳을 방문해요. 하지만, 베니스에는 심각한 문제가 있어요. 그것은 1년에 1에서 2밀리미터의 속도로 가라앉고 있어요. 어, 한 가지 요인은 그 도시가 약한 지반 위에 세워졌다는 거예요. 토양이 너무 부드러워서 그것은 그 위에 있는 건물들의 무게를 지탱할 수 없죠. 또 다른 요인은 기후 변화인데, 이는 해수면 상승을 야기하고 있어요. 그 도시가 계속해서 가라앉으면서, 물이 건물의 토대 위로 상승하고 그것들을 손상시킬 거예요. 그래서 당국자들은 그 도시를 구하려 애쓰고 있어요. 그들은 물을 제어하려 노력하기 위해 거대한 수문을 설치했어요... 또한, 그들은 역사적으로 중요한 건물들을 방수로 만들기 위해 돈을 모금하고 있어요.

architecture 명 건축   waterway 명 수로   sink 동 가라앉다
sea level 해수면   foundation 명 토대   official 명 당국자, 공무원
install 동 설치하다   historic 형 역사적으로 중요한
waterproof 형 방수의

교수에 따르면, 베니스는 왜 가라앉고 있는가? 2개의 답을 고르시오.

(A) 해수면이 상승하고 있다.
(B) 물을 제어하는 수문이 고장 났다.
(C) 건물들을 지탱하기에 지반이 너무 약하다.
(D) 지하수가 건축물을 손상시키고 있다.

Listening Practice 1 본문 p.37

1 (D)   2 (A), (B)   3 (C)   4 (B)   5 (A)

Note-taking

W: Graduate this yr., tell me about process?
M: Apply for permission to graduate, here or online
   Must finish required classes & pay fees to university
   Problem → speak w/ academic advisor
   Day of graduation = go to Main Hall → register
   Find seat → name called → accept diploma
   Check diploma → error → tell staff @ registration desk
   Transcript = ask @ registrar's office → take 3~4 weeks

Listen to a conversation between a student and a students services office employee.

M: Good morning! Welcome to the students services office.

W: Oh, good morning. Uh, is this where I register for

graduation?

M: Yes. I'm one of the graduate advisors and I would be happy to help you.

W: [1]Well, I'm supposed to graduate this year. But I'm not sure what I have to do. Can you tell me about the process?

M: OK. First, you need to apply for permission to graduate. You can do that here or online.

W: I see. But why do I have to apply? I got good grades in all of my classes. Isn't that enough?

M: No, not quite. There are other requirements. [2A]For instance, students must finish all of their required classes. [2B]They also have to pay fees to the university. That's why graduate advisors review the records of everyone who wants to graduate.

W: OK. That makes sense. [3]And what if there is a problem with my review?

M: Then, you will need to speak with your academic advisor. Sometimes, students have to wait until the next semester to graduate.

W: Well, I don't think I'll have that problem, so I'm not worried. Uh, this may be a strange question to ask, but what is graduation day like? I'm a little bit nervous about it.

M: I understand. It can be stressful. Well, on the day of the graduation, you have to go to the Main Hall when you arrive and register. Then, you need to follow the signs to find your seat. There will be a person there to help you find the right place. The ceremony is mostly just people giving speeches. The only thing you have to do is wait for your name to be called. Then, you have to walk up to the stage and accept your graduation diploma.

W: Oh, I didn't know we would get our diplomas at the ceremony.

M: Yes, you'll get your diploma on stage. [4]And when you get back to your seat, it's best to check your diploma to make sure there aren't any errors. If there are, and this does happen sometimes, then you should tell the staff at the registration desk near the entrance.

W: OK. [5]Will I get a copy of my school transcript with the diploma?

M: No, I'm afraid not. You actually have to ask for one at the registrar's office, and it can take around three to four weeks to receive it in the mail.

W: All right. Got it.

M: Great. If you need anything else, just give me a call or send an e-mail. Here's my contact information.

W: Thanks.

학생과 학생 지원 사무실 직원 사이의 대화를 들으시오.

M: 좋은 아침입니다! 학생 지원 사무실에 오신 걸 환영합니다.

W: 오, 좋은 아침입니다. 어, 여기가 졸업을 신청하는 곳인가요?

M: 네. 저는 졸업지도 교수 중 한 명이고 제가 기꺼이 도와드릴게요.

W: 음, 저는 올해 졸업하기로 되어 있어요. 그런데 제가 무엇을 해야 할지 모르겠어요. 그 절차에 대해 말씀해주실 수 있나요?

M: 네. 먼저, 졸업 허가를 신청하셔야 해요. 여기에서나 온라인으로 하실 수 있어요.

W: 그렇군요. 그런데 제가 왜 신청해야 하죠? 저는 모든 수업에서 좋은 성적을 받았어요. 그러면 충분하지 않나요?

M: 아뇨, 그렇지 않아요. 다른 요건들이 있어요. 예를 들어, 학생들은 그들의 필수 수업들을 모두 완료해야 해요. 그들은 대학에 요금도 지불해야 해요. 그게 졸업지도 교수들이 졸업을 원하는 모든 사람들의 기록을 검토하는 이유예요.

W: 알겠습니다. 말이 되네요. 그리고 검토에 문제가 있으면 어떻게 되나요?

M: 그러면, 학생의 지도 교수와 이야기해야 할 거예요. 가끔, 학생들은 졸업하기 위해 다음 학기까지 기다려야 해요.

W: 음, 제게는 그 문제가 없을 것 같아요, 그러니까 걱정하지 않아요. 어, 이상한 질문일 수도 있는데, 졸업식 날은 어떤가요? 그게 약간 긴장되네요.

M: 이해해요. 많이 긴장될 수 있어요. 음, 졸업식 날에, 도착하면 본관에 가서 등록해야 해요. 그런 다음, 학생의 자리를 찾기 위해 표지판을 따라가야 해요. 올바른 자리를 찾는 걸 도와줄 사람이 있을 거예요. 졸업식은 대부분 그저 사람들이 연설하는 거예요. 학생이 해야 하는 유일한 건 학생의 이름이 불리기를 기다리는 거예요. 그 다음에, 단상 위로 걸어가서 졸업장을 받아야 해요.

W: 오, 졸업식에서 졸업장을 받는지는 몰랐네요.

M: 네, 학생은 단상 위에서 졸업장을 받을 거예요. 그리고 자리로 돌아오면, 오류가 없는지 졸업장을 확인하는 게 좋아요. 오류가 있으면, 그리고 이런 일은 가끔 일어나요, 입구 근처의 등록 데스크에 있는 직원에게 말해야 해요.

W: 알겠어요. 졸업장과 함께 제 학교 성적 증명서도 받게 되나요?

M: 유감스럽게도, 아니에요. 사실 그걸 학적과에 요청하셔야 하고, 그걸 우편으로 받는 데 3, 4주가 걸릴 수 있어요.

W: 좋아요. 알겠습니다.

M: 잘됐네요. 더 필요하신 게 있으면, 저에게 전화하시거나 이메일을 보내세요. 여기 제 연락처가 있어요.

W: 감사합니다.

---

graduate advisor 졸업지도 교수   process 명 절차, 과정
permission 명 허가   required 형 필수의
stressful 형 많이 긴장되는   diploma 명 졸업장
transcript 명 성적 증명서

1 학생은 왜 학생 지원 사무실을 방문하는가?

(A) 졸업 신청서를 찾아오기 위해

(B) 지도 교수에 관해 불평하기 위해

(C) 수업을 신청하는 방법을 알아내기 위해

(D) 졸업 절차에 관해 알아보기 위해

2 대화에 따르면, 학생들이 졸업하기 위한 두 가지 요건은 무엇인가? 2개의 답을 고르시오.

(A) 필요한 수업들 완료하기

(B) 대학에 지불하기

(C) 그들의 학교 성적 증명서 사본 제출하기

(D) 그들의 졸업 신청서 검토하기

3 직원에 따르면, 학생들은 그들의 검토에 문제가 있으면 어떻게 해야 하는가?

(A) 추가 시험 치르기

(B) 추가 요금 지불하기

(C) 지도 교수 만나기

(D) 교수에게 증서 받기

4 직원은 학생에게 졸업장을 받은 후에 무엇을 하라고 제안하는가?

(A) 등록 데스크에서 신청서 작성하기

(B) 정보가 올바른지 확인하기

(C) 고용주들에게 보여줄 사본 만들기

(D) 남아있는 요금에 대한 기록 요청하기

5 직원은 학교 성적 증명서에 관해 무엇이라고 말하는가?

(A) 그것들은 우편으로 받을 수 있다.

(B) 그것들은 반드시 졸업식 날에 받아야 한다.

(C) 그것들은 준비하는 데 며칠이 걸린다.

(D) 그것들은 반드시 지도 교수에 의해 서명되어야 한다.

Listening Practice 2
본문 p. 39

1 (B)　　2 (B), (D)　　3 (C)　　4 (B)　　5 (B)

Note-taking

Voting Rights Act of 1965

- Before 1869 = only white men could vote
- 1869 = Black men allowed, women = allowed aft. 1920
- Some states required tax to vote = poll tax
  - AA & immigrants = poor ∴ vote X
- Language test = AA & immigrants failed ∴ vote X
- 1960s, many protests → made Voting Rights Act law
  - Effect = more ppl. vote, required additional measures
- Significance of Voting Rights Act ↑ through changes
  - Ban language tests & instructions in minor languages

Listen to part of a lecture in a history class.

P: ¹Today, I want to tell you about the civil rights movement in America. Uh, this was a movement to give all Americans equal rights. Specifically, I'm going to focus on the importance of the Voting Rights Act of 1965. This law made it easier for certain groups of people, like some minorities, to vote.

Uh, but first, let's review voting history briefly. Before 1869, only white men could vote in the United States. Then, a new law was passed in 1869. ⁵Because of this law, black men were allowed to vote for the first time. Similarly, women were allowed to vote after a 1920 law was passed. Therefore, it seemed that all adult citizens could vote at that time. But this was an illusion. Some states required people to pay a tax to vote. This tax was called a poll tax. ²ᴮBecause many African Americans and immigrants were poor, they could not pay the poll tax. And if they did not pay the tax, they were not allowed to vote. ²ᴰAlso, sometimes a language test was

required. Voters had to be able to read and write in English. However, many African Americans and immigrants were not able to read and write in English. So they failed the test.

³Then, in the 1960s, civil rights became a big issue in America. Some people argued that the voting rules in some states were unfair. These people thought all adult citizens should be allowed to vote. There were many protests, and, uh, some of these were violent. In fact, some people were even killed. This got the attention of the government. So, in 1965, President Lyndon Johnson made the Voting Rights Act a law. It gave voting rights to all American adults.

The initial effect of the act was that more people could vote in elections. This made America more democratic. But the law itself was not enough. The Voting Rights Act also required additional measures to make sure that the law was applied. For instance, states had to get approval from the government to change any voting processes. Before making any changes, they had to prove the changes were fair. Also, government officials were sent to places where there had been voting issues in the past. The officials made sure that these places followed the new law.

⁴Later, the significance of the Voting Rights Act became even greater through some changes. One of these was a permanent ban on language tests. Uh, states could no longer require people to take these tests. Similarly, the changes protected the voting rights of minorities. Uh, for example, if areas had large minority populations, such as Mexican Americans or Chinese Americans, they had to provide voting instructions in those minority languages…

역사학 강의의 일부를 들으시오.

P: 오늘은, 미국의 민권 운동에 대해 얘기하려 합니다. 어, 이것은 모든 미국인들에게 동등한 권리를 주기 위한 운동이었어요. 구체적으로, 1965년 투표권법의 중요성에 초점을 맞추려고 합니다. 이 법은 일부 소수집단과 같은 특정 집단의 사람들이 투표하는 것을 더 쉽게 만들었어요.

어, 하지만 먼저, 투표의 역사를 간단히 복습해 봅시다. 1869년 이전에, 미국에서는 오직 백인 남성만 투표할 수 있었어요. 그 후, 1869년에 새로운 법이 통과되었어요. 이 법으로 인해, 흑인 남성들이 투표하는 것이 최초로 허용되었어요. 마찬가지로, 1920년의 법이 통과된 후에 여성들이 투표하는 것이 허용되었어요. 그래서, 당시에는 모든 성인 시민들이 투표할 수 있는 것처럼 보였어요. 하지만 이것은 착각이었죠. 어떤 주들은 사람들에게 투표를 하기 위해 세금을 내라고 요구했어요. 이 세금은 투표세라고 불렸어요. 많은 아프리카계 미국인들과 이민자들은 가난했기 때문에, 그들은 투표세를 낼 수 없었죠. 그리고 그들이 그 세금을 내지 않으면, 투표하는 것이 허용되지 않았어요. 또한, 때때로 언어 시험이 요구되었어요. 유권자들은 영어로 읽고 쓸 수 있어야 했어요. 하지만, 많은 아프리카계 미국인들과 이민자들은 영어로 읽고 쓸 수 없었죠. 그래서 그들은 시험에서 떨어졌어요.

그 후, 1960년대에, 민권은 미국에서 큰 쟁점이 되었어요. 몇몇 사람들은 일부 주의 투표 규칙이 불공평하다고 주장했죠. 이 사람들은 모든 성인 시민들이 투표하도록 허용되어야 한다고 생각했어요. 많은 시위가 있었고, 어, 이 중 일부는 폭력적이었어요. 사실,

몇몇 사람들은 심지어 죽임을 당하기까지 했어요. 이것이 정부의 관심을 끌었어요. 그래서, 1965년에, 린든 존슨 대통령은 투표권법을 법으로 만들었어요. 그것은 모든 미국 성인에게 투표권을 주었습니다.

그 법의 초기의 영향은 더 많은 사람들이 선거에서 투표할 수 있게 되었다는 것이었어요. 이는 미국을 더 민주적으로 만들었죠. 하지만 그 법 자체로는 충분하지 않았어요. 투표권법은 또한 법이 확실히 적용되도록 하기 위해 추가적인 조치를 요구했어요. 예를 들어, 주들은 어떠한 투표 절차라도 바꾸려면 정부로부터 승인을 받아야 했어요. 어떤 변화를 주기 전에, 그 변화가 공정하다는 것을 입증해야 했죠. 또한, 정부 당국자들은 과거에 투표 문제가 있었던 곳들로 파견되었어요. 당국자들은 이곳들이 새로운 법을 확실히 따르도록 했어요.

후에, 투표권법의 중요성은 몇몇 변화를 통해 더욱 커졌어요. 이것들 중 하나는 언어 시험의 영구적인 금지였어요. 어, 주들은 더 이상 사람들에게 이 시험들을 치르도록 요구할 수 없었어요. 마찬가지로, 그 변화들은 소수집단의 투표권을 보호했어요. 어, 예를 들어, 지역에 멕시코계 미국인이나 중국계 미국인 같은 소수집단의 인구가 많으면, 그들은 그 소수집단의 언어로 투표 지침을 제공해야 했죠...

civil rights movement 민권 운동   equal 형 동등한
specifically 부 구체적으로   minority 명 소수집단
briefly 부 간단히   similarly 부 마찬가지로   citizen 명 시민
illusion 명 착각, 환상   poll 명 투표   immigrant 명 이민자
unfair 형 불공평한   protest 명 시위   violent 형 폭력적인
election 명 선거   democratic 형 민주적인   apply 동 적용하다
approval 명 승인   significance 명 중요성
permanent 형 영구적인   ban 명 금지

1 강의의 주된 주제는 무엇인가?

(A) 여러 나라에서의 투표

(B) 중요한 민권법

(C) 소수집단 권리의 역사

(D) 미국의 이민법

2 많은 아프리카계 미국인들과 이민자들은 왜 1965년 투표권법 이전에 투표할 수 없었는가? 2개의 답을 고르시오.

(A) 그들은 충분한 재산을 소유하지 않았다.

(B) 그들은 투표세를 낼 수 없었다.

(C) 그들은 미국 시민이 아니었다.

(D) 그들은 영어를 읽고 쓸 수 없었다.

3 교수에 따르면, 1960년대에 무엇이 정부의 관심을 끌었는가?

(A) 이민자의 수가 증가했다.

(B) 시위자들이 선거에서 투표하기를 거부했다.

(C) 몇몇 사람들이 시위 중에 죽임을 당했다.

(D) 대통령이 고무적인 연설을 했다.

4 교수에 따르면, 투표권법에 대한 변화 중 하나는 무엇이었는가?

(A) 투표 기한이 연장되었다.

(B) 언어 시험이 더 이상 허용되지 않았다.

(C) 투표 지침이 간소화되었다.

(D) 주들이 그들 자신의 투표법을 만들었다.

강의의 일부를 다시 듣고 질문에 답하시오.

P: Because of this law, black men were allowed to vote for the first time. Similarly, women were allowed to vote after a 1920 law was passed. Therefore, it seemed that all adult citizens could vote at that time. But this was an illusion.

5 교수는 이렇게 말함으로써 무엇을 암시하는가:

P: But this was an illusion.

(A) 1920년의 법은 일부 권리를 없애기도 했다.

(B) 일부 성인 시민들은 여전히 투표할 수 없었다.

(C) 투표하도록 허용된 여성은 거의 없었다.

(D) 1920년의 법은 흑인들에게 적용되지 않았다.

Listening Practice 3   본문 p. 41

1 (C)   2 (C)   3 (B)   4 (D)   5 (A)

Note-taking

S: About portfolio deadline, know about art competition?
P: Have seen posters around campus
S: Almost done w/ drawing → turn in on May 15
   Want to include drawing in portfolio = due on May 13
   Give more time to submit? ∵ many participating
P: Postpone due date ∵ want to give everyone chance
   Can't accept later than May 15
S: Going to dorm. → send a brochure

Listen to a conversation between a student and a professor.

S: Hi, Professor Turner. Could I come in for a second?

P: Hello, Patrick. Of course... Have you been working on paintings to add to your portfolio project?

S: Well, I've been busy with assignments for other classes, but the portfolio's going well. It's almost done...

P: Excellent. So what did you want to ask me about? I assume it's about your portfolio?

S: ¹Yes, it's about the portfolio project deadline. Professor, do you know anything about the art competition? It's the one where the artists can only use black and white in their drawings. A few other professors mentioned it, so I checked it out.

P: Hmm... I think it's called Ideas in Color, or something like that. It seems like many people are excited about it. ²I've seen a lot of posters around campus promoting it.

S: Yes, that's the one. Anyway, I'm almost done with a drawing that I'm planning to submit. I have to turn it in on May 15.

P: OK, that's great. So what's your question?

S: I'd really like to include the drawing in my portfolio. ³But the portfolio is due on May 13. So I can only add the drawing after the competition.

P: But that's past the deadline, isn't it? That could be a problem.

S: Yes, that's why I wanted to check with you. I'm wondering if you could give everyone a little more time to submit their portfolios. As you know, many of the students are participating in the competition, too.

P: Good point. ⁴Well, in that case, I should postpone the due date of the portfolio. I want to give everyone a chance to include their artwork from the contest. After all, I've always encouraged students to participate in these kinds of competitions. It would be unfair if I didn't give everyone more time.

S: Thank you for understanding, Professor. And I'm sure this will motivate everyone to work even harder on their drawings.

P: I certainly hope so. But I can't accept portfolios any later than May 15.

S: Sure. That sounds very reasonable. Um, do you want me to send you some more information about the contest? ⁵I don't know if you have the brochure or not.

P: Oh, that would be great. Please give me a copy.

S: I'll do that. I'm going to my dormitory after this, so I'll send a copy to you by e-mail. Thanks again.

P: Thank you, too. If you hadn't told me about this, I wouldn't have thought about changing the deadline.

학생과 교수 사이의 대화를 들으시오.

S: 안녕하세요, Turner 교수님. 잠깐 들어가도 될까요?

P: 안녕, Patrick. 물론이지... 포트폴리오 과제에 추가할 그림을 작업하고 있니?

S: 음, 저는 다른 수업의 과제들로 바빴지만, 포트폴리오는 잘 되어가고 있어요. 거의 끝났어요...

P: 잘됐구나. 그래서 나에게 무엇에 대해 물어보고 싶었니? 네 포트폴리오에 관한 거겠지?

S: 네, 포트폴리오 과제의 기한에 관한 거예요. 교수님, 그 미술 경연 대회에 대해 아시는 게 있나요? 화가들이 그림에 검은색과 흰색만 사용할 수 있는 그거요. 다른 교수님 몇 분이 언급하셔서, 제가 조사해 봤어요.

P: 흠... 내 생각에는 그게 Ideas in Color나, 그와 비슷하게 불리는 것 같구나. 많은 사람들이 그것 때문에 들뜬 것 같구나. 캠퍼스 여기저기에서 그것을 홍보하는 포스터를 많이 봤단다.

S: 네, 바로 그거예요. 어쨌든, 저는 제출하려고 계획 중인 그림을 거의 끝냈어요. 저는 그걸 5월 15일에 제출해야 해요.

P: 그래, 잘됐구나. 그래서 네 질문이 무엇이니?

S: 저는 그 그림을 정말로 제 포트폴리오에 포함하고 싶어요. 그런데 포트폴리오는 5월 13일까지예요. 그래서 저는 경연 대회 이후에야 그 그림을 추가할 수 있어요.

P: 하지만 그건 기한이 지나야, 그렇지 않니? 그건 문제가 될 수 있겠구나.

S: 네, 그게 제가 교수님께 확인받고 싶었던 이유예요. 교수님께서 모두에게 포트폴리오를 제출할 시간을 조금 더 주실 수 있는지 궁금해요. 아시다시피, 많은 학생들이 이 경연 대회에 참가하고 있

기도 해요.

P: 좋은 지적이구나. 음, 그런 경우라면, 내가 포트폴리오의 기한을 연기해야겠구나. 나는 모두에게 그 대회에 낸 그림을 포함할 기회를 주고 싶어. 어쨌든, 나는 항상 학생들에게 이런 종류의 경연 대회에 참여할 것을 독려해 왔으니까. 내가 모두에게 더 많은 시간을 주지 않는다면 불공평할 거야.

S: 이해해 주셔서 감사합니다, 교수님. 그리고 이게 모두가 그림을 훨씬 더 열심히 작업하도록 동기를 부여할 거라고 확신해요.

P: 꼭 그러길 바란다. 하지만 5월 15일보다 더 늦게 포트폴리오를 받을 수는 없어.

S: 물론이죠. 그건 아주 합리적인 것 같아요. 음, 제가 그 대회에 대한 정보를 좀 더 보내드릴까요? 안내 책자를 가지고 계신지 아닌지 모르겠네요.

P: 오, 그러면 좋겠구나. 나에게 한 부 주렴.

S: 그럴게요. 저는 이게 끝나면 기숙사에 갈 거니까, 이메일로 한 부 보내드릴게요. 다시 한번 감사합니다.

P: 나도 고맙구나. 네가 말해주지 않았다면, 기한을 바꾸는 것에 대해 생각하지 못했을 거야.

---

deadline 뎽 기한   competition 뎽 경연 대회
promote 동 홍보하다   postpone 동 연기하다, 미루다
unfair 형 불공평한   reasonable 형 합리적인
brochure 뎽 안내 책자

1 대화는 주로 무엇에 관한 것인가?

(A) 과제가 늦은 이유

(B) 미술 경연 대회 참가자들

(C) 다가오는 과제의 기한

(D) 일부 학생들의 그림에 대한 의견

2 교수는 미술 경연 대회에 관해 무엇이라고 말하는가?

(A) 그녀는 전에 그것에 대해 들어본 적이 없다.

(B) 그녀는 참가자가 되는 것에 들떠있다.

(C) 그녀는 캠퍼스에서 그것에 대한 정보를 보았다.

(D) 그녀는 다른 몇 명의 교수들에게 그것에 대해 들었다.

3 경연 대회 이후에 포트폴리오를 제출하는 것의 문제는 무엇인가?

(A) 교수가 대회의 작품들을 평가해야 한다.

(B) 대회가 포트폴리오 기한 이후에 있다.

(C) 학생들이 시험을 준비해야 한다.

(D) 포트폴리오 그림들이 전시를 위해 필요하다.

4 교수는 무엇을 해주기로 하는가?

(A) 그녀는 미술관에서 열리는 학생의 전시회에 참석할 것이다.

(B) 그녀는 다른 학생들에게 행사에 관해 알릴 것이다.

(C) 그녀는 학생이 미술 대회를 준비하는 것을 도울 것이다.

(D) 그녀는 수업 과제를 위한 더 많은 시간을 허락할 것이다.

5 학생은 교수를 위해 무엇을 할 것인가?

(A) 이메일로 안내 책자 보내기

(B) 활동 일정 준비하기

(C) 수업의 다른 학생들에게 얘기하기

(D) 초대장 몇 부 출력하기

1 (B)　　**2** (C)　　**3** (B)　　**4** (A)　　**5** (D)

Note-taking
False Memories

- Several ways memories can fail
  - Forget ∵ not concentrating = issue about forgetting
- False memories = remember sth. diff. from reality
  - Ppl. w/ false memories believe they're true
  - Can cause serious prob. (e.g. falsely remember crime)
- Why false memories happen?
  - Wrong perception → create memory w/ wrong info.
  - Inference = look for meaning → add new info.
  - Interference = new info. added by someone else

Listen to part of a lecture in a psychology class.

P: Most people believe their memories are true. But our memories might not be as reliable as we think. ¹Today we're going to talk about an issue with memories called false memories.

⁵You see, memory is not an exact science. I mean, it doesn't always function accurately. Um, there are several different ways that our memories can fail. For instance, we can forget something happened because we were not concentrating. Or, you know, we can forget details because something happened a long time ago... But these issues are both about forgetting. False memories are a problem with remembering.

With false memories, we remember something different from reality. Or we remember something that never happened at all. For example, people can falsely remember that they were good at baseball in high school, even if this was never true. Or they can falsely remember that they helped their team win a game, even if they were never on the team at all. Now, it's important to know that people with false memories honestly believe that they're true. So this is different from lying. ²Moreover, it's important to understand that false memories can cause serious problems. Um, it can have a big effect on people's lives. For instance, if someone falsely remembers a crime, this could cause an innocent person to go to jail...

But why do false memories happen in the first place? Let's look at some of the ways... Sometimes, false memories are a result of wrong perception. Um, perception is how we see, hear, or touch something, and so on. It helps us create new memories. But sometimes, our perceptions can be wrong. For instance, a person can remember a face incorrectly because it was dark when they saw it or because they have bad eyesight. ³So they create a false memory using information that is wrong from the start. Or, um, another cause is related to inference. You see, people tend to look for meaning in their experiences. So, sometimes, they will add new information to their memory of an experience based on an inference. The new information

helps them understand the experience better. But it also creates a false memory. In one study, people were asked to read a list of words related to sleep. After, many of them remembered seeing the word sleep on the list, but the word was never there. They inferred it because the list had many words related to sleep. OK. And lastly, false memories can also be caused by interference. ⁴Like inference, interference happens when new information is added. The difference is that the new information is added by someone else. This information interferes with, or changes, the original memory. One example is when you falsely remember events from your childhood because someone else told you they happened.

심리학 강의의 일부를 들으시오.

P: 대부분의 사람들은 그들의 기억이 정확하다고 믿습니다. 하지만 우리의 기억은 생각하는 것만큼 믿을 만하지 않을 수도 있어요. 오늘 우리는 거짓 기억이라고 불리는 기억과 관련된 문제에 관해 이야기할 거예요.

그러니까, 기억은 정밀과학이 아닙니다. 제 말은, 그것이 항상 정확하게 기능하는 것은 아니라는 거예요. 음, 우리의 기억이 제대로 작동하지 않을 수 있는 여러 가지의 서로 다른 상황들이 있어요. 예를 들어, 우리는 집중하지 않고 있었기 때문에 일어난 일을 잊을 수 있죠. 혹은, 알다시피, 어떤 일이 오래전에 일어났기 때문에 세부 사항을 잊을 수 있어요... 하지만 이 문제들은 둘 다 망각과 관련된 것들입니다. 거짓 기억은 기억과 관련된 문제예요.

거짓 기억의 경우, 우리는 실제와 다른 어떤 일을 기억합니다. 혹은 전혀 일어나지 않았던 일을 기억하죠. 예를 들어, 사람들은 결코 사실이 아니라 할지라도, 그들이 고등학교에 다닐 때 야구를 잘했다고 거짓되게 기억할 수 있어요. 혹은 그들이 팀에 소속된 적이 없었다고 할지라도, 그들이 팀이 경기에서 승리하는 데 도움을 주었다고 거짓되게 기억할 수 있어요. 자, 거짓 기억을 가지고 있는 사람들이 정말로 그것들이 사실이라고 믿는다는 것을 아는 것이 중요합니다. 그러니까 이건 거짓말과는 달라요. 게다가, 거짓 기억이 심각한 문제를 일으킬 수 있다는 걸 이해하는 것이 중요해요. 음, 그것은 사람들의 삶에 큰 영향을 미칠 수 있어요. 예를 들어, 만약 누군가가 범죄를 거짓되게 기억한다면, 무고한 사람을 감옥에 가게 할 수도 있어요...

그런데 애초에 거짓 기억이 왜 발생할까요? 몇 가지 방식들을 봅시다... 때때로, 거짓 기억은 잘못된 인식의 결과예요. 음, 인식이란 우리가 무언가를 보고, 듣고, 혹은 만지는 등을 하는 방식이에요. 그것은 우리가 새로운 기억을 만드는 것을 도와주죠. 하지만 때때로, 우리의 인식은 잘못될 수 있어요. 예를 들어, 누군가는 얼굴을 봤을 때 주위가 어두웠거나 시력이 나쁘기 때문에 그것을 부정확하게 기억할 수 있어요. 그래서 그들은 처음부터 잘못된 정보를 이용하여 거짓 기억을 만들어냅니다. 혹은, 음, 또 다른 원인은 추론과 관련되어 있어요. 그러니까, 사람들은 그들의 경험에서 의미를 찾는 경향이 있습니다. 그래서, 때때로, 그들은 경험에 대한 기억에 새로운 정보를 추론에 근거하여 추가할 거예요. 새로운 정보는 그들이 그 경험을 더 잘 이해하도록 도와줘요. 하지만 그것은 거짓 기억을 만들어내기도 하죠. 한 연구에서, 사람들은 수면과 관련된 단어 목록을 읽도록 요청받았어요. 그 후, 그들 중 다수가 그 목록에서 수면이라는 단어를 봤다고 기억했지만, 그 단어는 거기에 없었죠. 그 목록에 수면과 관련된 단어가 많았기 때문에 그것을 추론했던 거예요. 자, 그리고 마지막으로, 거짓 기억은 간섭에 의해 초래될 수도 있어요. 추론처럼, 간섭은 새로운 정보가 추가될 때 발생해요. 차이점은 새로운 정보가 다른 사람에 의해 추가된다는 거예요. 이 정보는 원래의 기억에 간섭, 즉 그것을 바꾸어 놓아요. 한 가지 예는 누군가가 여러분에게 그런 일들이 일어났다고 얘기해 주었기 때문에 어린 시절의 일들을 거짓되게 기억하는 경우예요.

reliable (형) 믿을 만한   function (동) 기능하다
accurately (부) 정확하게   concentrate (동) 집중하다
forgetting (명) 망각(잊는 것)   reality (명) 실제, 현실
falsely (부) 거짓되게   innocent (형) 무고한, 정직한
in the first place 애초에   perception (명) 인식
incorrectly (부) 부정확하게   eyesight (명) 시력   inference (명) 추론
interference (명) 간섭, 방해

1 강의의 주된 목적은 무엇인가?

(A) 심리학 이론을 논의하기 위해

(B) 기억에 관련된 문제를 설명하기 위해

(C) 기억력 저하를 줄이는 방법을 설명하기 위해

(D) 두 가지 종류의 기억을 비교하기 위해

2 거짓 기억에 대한 교수의 의견은 무엇인가?

(A) 그것들은 사람이 거짓말을 하고 있을 때 나타날 수 있다.

(B) 그것들은 뇌의 문제를 나타낼 수 있다.

(C) 그것들은 사람들에게 심각한 문제를 일으킬 수 있다.

(D) 그것들은 우리가 우리의 삶을 더 잘 이해하도록 도와줄 수 있다.

3 교수는 잘못된 인식에 관해 무엇이라고 말하는가?

(A) 그것들은 사람들이 자신을 의심스러워하게 만든다.

(B) 그것들은 처음부터 거짓 기억을 유발한다.

(C) 그것들은 노인들 사이에서 더 흔하다.

(D) 그것들은 어린 시절의 경험에서 비롯될 수 있다.

4 교수에 따르면, 추론과 간섭은 어떻게 비슷한가?

(A) 그것들은 기억에 새로운 정보를 추가한다.

(B) 그것들은 어린 시절의 기억과 관련되어 있다.

(C) 그것들은 사람들이 그들의 기억력을 향상시키는 데 도움을 준다.

(D) 그것들은 사람들이 나쁜 기억을 잊게 만든다.

강의의 일부를 다시 듣고 질문에 답하시오.

P: You see, memory is not an exact science. I mean, it doesn't always function accurately. Um, there are several different ways that our memories can fail.

5 교수는 이렇게 말함으로써 무엇을 의미하는가:

P: You see, memory is not an exact science.

(A) 과학은 심리학보다 더 정확하다.

(B) 과학은 여전히 기억을 완전히 설명하지 못한다.

(C) 기억력 장애는 극복하기가 쉽지 않다.

(D) 기억이 항상 이상적인 방식으로 작동하는 것은 아니다.

Note-taking

S: About final project, want some advice to make it better
Almost everyone focusing on univ. students = bit boring
Create & sell product for working mothers

P: Need to understand the group = do a lot of research
Working mothers = large group w/ a lot of variety
E.g. where they live & how much money they make
Goal = learn importance of marketing strategy

Listen to a conversation between a student and a professor.

P: Hi, Sarah. Are you ready for the exam next week?

S: I think so. I've been reviewing my lecture notes every day, and I'm planning to study this weekend. Also, I took a marketing class last semester, so I feel pretty confident.

P: Great! Well, it sounds like you're going to do very well next week! So what can I help you with today?

S: ¹I actually wanted to talk about the final project. Uh, you asked us to think of a product and some ways to sell it to a specific group of people. My project is going well, but I would like some advice on how to make it better.

P: Oh, that's right. Which customer group are you planning to focus on?

S: Um, I'm not sure. ²I've noticed that almost everyone else in class is focusing on university students. I would like to do something different. That idea just seems a bit boring...

P: I see what you mean. They probably chose to do that because it would be easy for them.

S: I think so, too. Anyway, I thought it would be interesting to create and sell a product for working mothers. There are many of them and they spend a lot of money.

P: ⁵That's a fine idea. However, you need to understand the group that you're selling to. That means that you will have to do a lot of research.

S: I was afraid you might say that... Um, how detailed do I have to be?

P: ³Well, working mothers are a large group with a lot of variety. It would be good to get a lot of information about them. Do you know where they live and how much money they make? Do you know about their children or what kinds of activities they enjoy? The more you know, the easier it will be for you to develop a strategy to sell your products.

S: That sounds like a lot of work. I'm not sure that I'll have enough time. I already know some basic ideas about marketing. Couldn't I just use those to complete the project?

P: Yes, of course, you can do that. But you said that you wanted to make your project better. ⁴The goal of this project is for you to learn the importance of a marketing strategy when you're selling to a specific group of people.

S: You're right. The extra research should be helpful.

P: Yes, the experience will also help you if you plan to have a career in marketing.

S: That's true. I hope to <u>work in advertising after I graduate</u>... Well, I guess I'd better get started. I'm sure I can find lots of material at the library if I go now!

학생과 교수 사이의 대화를 들으시오.

P: 안녕, Sarah. 다음 주 시험을 위한 준비가 됐니?

S: 그런 것 같아요. 저는 매일 강의 노트를 복습하고 있고, 이번 주말에 공부할 계획이에요. 또, 지난 학기에 마케팅 수업을 들어서, 꽤 자신이 있어요.

P: 좋아! 음, 네가 다음 주에 아주 잘할 것 같구나! 그래서 오늘은 무엇을 도와줄까?

S: 저는 사실 기말 과제에 대해 이야기하고 싶었어요. 어, 교수님은 저희에게 하나의 상품과 그것을 특정 집단의 사람들에게 판매할 몇 가지 방법을 생각해 보라고 하셨죠. 제 과제는 잘 되어가고 있는데, 그것을 더 좋게 만들 방법에 관해 조언을 좀 듣고 싶어요.

P: 오, 그렇구나. 너는 어떤 고객 집단에 초점을 맞출 계획이니?

S: 음, 잘 모르겠어요. 수업의 거의 모든 사람들이 대학생들에게 초점을 맞추고 있다는 걸 알아챘어요. 저는 뭔가 다른 것을 하고 싶어요. 그 아이디어는 좀 지루해 보여요...

P: 무슨 말인지 알겠다. 아마 그게 그들에게 쉬울 것이라서 그렇게 하기로 했을 거야.

S: 저도 그렇게 생각해요. 어쨌든, 저는 직장에 다니는 어머니들을 위한 상품을 만들어 판매하는 게 흥미로울 거라고 생각했어요. 그들은 수가 많고 돈을 많이 쓰잖아요.

P: 좋은 아이디어구나. 하지만, 너는 네가 대상으로 판매하는 집단을 이해해야 해. 그건 네가 많은 조사를 해야 할 거라는 의미야.

S: 그렇게 말씀하실까 봐 걱정했어요... 음, 제가 얼마나 자세하게 해야 하나요?

P: 음, 직장에 다니는 어머니들은 많은 다양성을 가진 큰 집단이야. 그들에 대한 많은 정보를 얻는 게 좋을 거야. 그들이 어디에 살고 돈을 얼마나 버는지 아니? 그들의 아이들에 대해서나 그들이 어떤 종류의 활동을 즐겨 하는지 아니? 네가 더 많이 알수록, 네 상품을 판매할 전략을 개발하는 것이 더 쉬워질 거야.

S: 할 일이 많은 것 같네요. 제게 충분한 시간이 있을지 모르겠어요. 저는 이미 마케팅에 관한 몇몇 기본적인 개념들을 알고 있어요. 프로젝트를 완성하기 위해 그냥 그것들을 이용하면 안 될까요?

P: 그럼, 물론이지, 그렇게 해도 돼. 그런데 너는 네 프로젝트를 더 좋게 만들고 싶다고 했지. 이 프로젝트의 목표는 특정 집단의 사람들에게 판매할 때 마케팅 전략의 중요성을 배우는 거야.

S: 맞아요. 추가적인 조사가 도움이 될 거예요.

P: 맞아, 그 경험은 또한 네가 마케팅 분야에서 직업을 가질 계획이라면 도움이 될 거야.

S: 맞아요. 저는 졸업 후에 광고 분야에서 일하고 싶어요... 음, 이제 시작하는 게 좋을 것 같네요. 지금 가면 도서관에서 많은 자료를 찾을 수 있을 거예요!

---

review 동 복습하다, 검토하다   specific 형 특정한
customer 명 고객   variety 명 다양성   strategy 명 전략
extra 형 추가적인   advertising 명 광고 분야   material 명 자료

---

1 학생은 왜 교수를 찾아가는가?

(A) 진로 계획에 대한 조언을 받기 위해

(B) 보고서를 늦게 제출하는 것에 대해 문의하기 위해

(C) 과제를 개선할 방법에 대한 아이디어를 얻기 위해

(D) 시험 준비에 대한 도움을 요청하기 위해

2 학생은 수업의 다른 학생들에 대해 무엇이라고 말하는가?

(A) 그들은 과제에서 많은 진전을 이루었다.

(B) 그들은 별로 흥미롭지 않은 주제를 선택했다.

(C) 그들은 매우 다양한 주제를 조사하고 있다.

(D) 그들은 매우 인상적인 발표를 했다.

3 교수는 직장에 다니는 어머니들에 대해 무엇이라고 말하는가?

(A) 그들은 보통 같은 종류의 상품들을 선호한다.

(B) 그들은 바쁘기 때문에 인터뷰하기 어려울 것이다.

(C) 그들은 종종 돈을 어떻게 쓰는지에 관해 신중하다.

(D) 그들은 다양한 특징을 가진 큰 집단이다.

4 교수는 학생들이 과제에서 무엇을 배우기를 기대하는가?

(A) 팀으로 함께 작업하는 것의 중요성

(B) 사람들의 집단이 구매하기 좋아하는 상품의 종류

(C) 서로 다른 연령대의 사람들이 특정 상품 구매를 선호하는 이유

(D) 사람들에게 판매하기 위한 전략을 갖는 것의 유용성

대화의 일부를 다시 듣고 질문에 답하시오.

P: That's a fine idea. However, you need to understand the group that you're selling to. That means that you will have to do a lot of research.

S: I was afraid you might say that... Um, how detailed do I have to be?

5 학생은 왜 이렇게 말하는가:

S: I was afraid you might say that...

(A) 교수에게 그가 수업 중에 말한 것을 상기시키기 위해

(B) 그녀가 다음 주 시험을 위해 어떻게 준비했는지 설명하기 위해

(C) 그녀가 교수의 반응을 예상했다는 것을 나타내기 위해

(D) 그녀가 대화 초반에 말한 것을 바로잡기 위해

---

iBT Listening Test 2
본문 p. 48

1 (C)   2 (C)   3 (B)   4 (B), (C)   5 (D)   6 (B)

Note-taking
Wind Power

- Wind power = best way to prod. large amt. of electricity
- Wind = indirect form of solar energy
  - Sun heats → diff. in air temp. → mvmt. of air → wind
- How do we make electricity from wind? = wind turbines
  - Blades turn → generator prod. electricity
- Large # of turbines in 1 area = wind farm
  - E.g. wind farm in Oregon = 338 turbines
- Wind power prod. only 5% of global usage
  - Wind = constant X = prob. for ppl.

- Wind farm = threat to animals ∵ blades
• Has bright future ∵ adv. > disadv.

Listen to part of a lecture in an environmental science class.

P: Last class, we began talking about renewable forms of energy and how we will need them to produce electricity. As I mentioned, oil and natural gas supplies are getting smaller and smaller. Also, these fossil fuels cause global warming, so we need to replace them. [1]Starting today, we are going to look at the various other energy options that are available.

Let's begin with wind power... Um, it might be the best way to produce large amounts of electricity. But first, how exactly is wind produced? Many people don't realize that wind is actually an indirect form of solar energy. [2]You see, the Sun heats Earth's atmosphere unevenly and this causes differences in air temperature. Warm air rises and cooler air falls. This movement of warm and cool air creates wind. And the energy of the wind can be used to make electricity.

So how do we make electricity from wind? Well, we use very large structures called wind turbines. They are very tall and have massive blades that look like the blades on an airplane propeller. These blades are connected to a generator. So, every time the blades turn, the generator produces electricity. Now, each wind turbine can only produce a certain amount of electricity. So, usually, large numbers of wind turbines are placed in one area called a wind farm. Together, they produce more electricity. [3]For example, the Shepherds Flats Wind Farm in Oregon has a total of 338 wind turbines. It can produce around 845 megawatts of electricity in all... Um, that's enough to supply over 200,000 homes with electricity. One day, wind farms like this one could produce more than 100 times the amount of electricity currently consumed worldwide. But, at present, wind power produces only around 5 percent of global electricity usage. This is because of a couple of challenges with this energy source...

[4C]First, wind is not constant. Uh, it is stronger at some times than at others. During long periods of low winds, wind farms produce less electricity. They can even stop completely. So, obviously, this creates problems for people who need electricity all of the time. [4B]Second, wind farms are a threat to birds, bats, and other animals that fly. Many birds, for instance, often travel long distances every year during the summer and the fall. They pass through the same areas each time. [4B]However, when you build a wind farm in those areas, this causes some of the birds to fly into the blades of the wind turbines. And, uh, as a result, they die. [6]Um, about a million birds are killed by wind turbines each year. Of course, even more birds are killed by tall buildings in our cities. That number is closer to a billion. Still, the problem with wind turbines must be fixed.

[5]Anyway, even with these and other challenges, I think wind energy still has a bright future. It offers more advantages than disadvantages. And I'm sure that scientists and engineers will eventually develop solutions for the challenges that wind power has today.

환경 과학 강의의 일부를 들으시오.

P: 지난 시간에, 우리는 재생 가능한 형태의 에너지와 전기를 생산하기 위해 그것들이 어떻게 필요할지에 대해 이야기하기 시작했어요. 제가 언급했듯이, 석유와 천연가스 공급은 점점 줄어들고 있어요. 또한, 이 화석 연료들은 지구 온난화를 야기하기 때문에, 우리는 그것들을 대체할 필요가 있어요. 오늘부터, 우리는 이용 가능한 다양한 다른 에너지 선택지들을 살펴볼 거예요.

풍력으로 시작해 봅시다... 음, 그것은 많은 양의 전기를 생산하기에 가장 좋은 방법일지도 몰라요. 하지만 먼저, 바람은 정확히 어떻게 만들어질까요? 많은 사람들은 바람이 사실 태양 에너지의 간접적인 형태라는 것을 깨닫지 못해요. 그러니까, 태양은 지구의 대기를 고르지 않게 가열하고 이는 기온의 차이를 만들어내요. 따뜻한 공기는 상승하고 더 차가운 공기는 하강하죠. 따뜻하고 차가운 공기의 이러한 움직임은 바람을 만들어내요. 그리고 바람의 에너지는 전기를 만드는 데 이용될 수 있어요.

그래서 우리는 어떻게 바람으로 전기를 만들까요? 음, 우리는 풍력 터빈이라고 불리는 매우 거대한 구조물을 이용해요. 그것들은 매우 키가 크며 비행기 프로펠러의 날개처럼 생긴 거대한 날개들을 가지고 있어요. 이 날개들은 발전기에 연결되어 있죠. 그래서, 날개가 회전할 때마다, 발전기는 전기를 생산합니다. 자, 각 풍력 터빈은 일정량의 전기만을 생산할 수 있어요. 그래서, 보통, 풍력 발전 지대라고 불리는 한 지역에 많은 수의 풍력 터빈이 배치됩니다. 함께, 그것들은 더 많은 전기를 생산해요. 예를 들어, 오리건에 위치한 셰퍼드 플랫 풍력 발전 지대에는 총 338개의 풍력 터빈이 있어요. 그것은 총 약 845메가와트의 전기를 생산할 수 있죠... 음, 그건 20만 가구 이상에게 전기를 공급하기에 충분한 양이에요. 언젠가, 이와 같은 풍력 발전 지대들은 현재 전 세계에서 소비되는 전기 양의 100배 이상을 생산할 수 있을 거예요. 하지만, 현재, 풍력은 세계 전기 사용량의 약 5퍼센트만을 생산합니다. 이는 이 에너지원에 관련된 두 가지 난제 때문이에요...

첫째로, 바람은 일정하지 않아요. 어, 어떤 때는 다른 때보다 더 강하죠. 약한 바람이 부는 긴 기간 동안, 풍력 발전 지대는 더 적은 전기를 생산해요. 그것들은 심지어 완전히 멈출 수도 있어요. 그래서, 확실히, 이것은 항상 전기가 필요한 사람들에게 문제를 일으켜요. 둘째로, 풍력 발전 지대는 새, 박쥐, 그리고 날아다니는 다른 동물들에게 위협이 돼요. 예를 들어, 많은 새들은 매년 여름과 가을 동안 종종 먼 거리를 이동해요. 그것들은 매번 동일한 지역을 통과하죠. 하지만, 그 지역들에 풍력 발전 지대를 건설하면, 이는 일부 새들이 풍력 터빈의 날개로 날아들게 해요. 그리고, 어, 그 결과, 그것들은 죽죠. 음, 매년 약 100만 마리의 새들이 풍력 터빈에 의해 죽임을 당합니다. 물론, 훨씬 더 많은 새들이 도시의 높은 건물들에 의해 죽임을 당하죠. 그 숫자는 10억에 더 가까워요. 그럼에도 불구하고, 풍력 터빈의 문제는 반드시 고쳐져야 해요.

어쨌든, 이것들과 다른 난제들에도 불구하고, 저는 풍력 에너지가 여전히 밝은 미래를 가지고 있다고 생각해요. 그것은 단점보다 많은 이점을 제공해요. 그리고 과학자들과 공학자들이 결국 오늘날 풍력이 가지고 있는 난제들에 대한 해결책을 개발할 것이라고 확신해요.

---

renewable (형) 재생 가능한 electricity (명) 전기
fossil fuel 화석 연료 replace (동) 대체하다 indirect (형) 간접적인
solar energy 태양 에너지 unevenly (부) 고르지 않게

wind turbine 풍력 터빈, 풍력 발전기　massive 뒝 거대한
blade 뗑 날개, 날　wind farm 풍력 발전 지대　consume 뙝 소비하다
challenge 뗑 난제　constant 뒝 일정한

1 교수는 주로 무엇에 관해 논하는가?

(A) 전기 생산이 지구 온난화에 미치는 영향

(B) 재생 가능한 에너지를 생산하는 것의 어려움

(C) 화석 연료 사용에 대한 대안

(D) 역사 전반에 걸친 풍력 응용

2 교수에 따르면, 무엇이 바람을 만드는가?

(A) 기압이 높은 지역에서 기압이 낮은 지역으로 이동하는 공기.

(B) 바다 위에 형성되는 강력한 폭풍

(C) 온도가 다른 공기의 움직임

(D) 태양 주위를 도는 지구의 움직임

3 교수는 셰퍼드 플랫 풍력 발전 지대에 관해 무엇이라고 말하는가?

(A) 그것은 세계에서 가장 큰 풍력 발전 지대이다.

(B) 그것은 많은 가구를 위한 전기를 생산할 수 있다.

(C) 그것은 최초의 성공적인 풍력 발전 지대였다.

(D) 그것은 도시 에너지의 5퍼센트를 생산한다.

4 교수에 따르면, 풍력 사용의 두 가지 난제는 무엇인가?
2개의 답을 고르시오.

(A) 풍력 발전 지대가 많은 건축 자재를 필요로 한다.

(B) 풍력 터빈이 몇몇 동물들을 죽일 수 있다.

(C) 바람이 항상 지속적으로 불지 않는다.

(D) 풍력 터빈이 매우 시끄럽다.

5 풍력 에너지의 미래에 대한 교수의 태도는 무엇인가?

(A) 그는 그것이 태양열 발전만큼 흔해질 것이라고 생각한다.

(B) 그는 그것의 난제들이 너무 두드러진다고 걱정한다.

(C) 그는 사람들이 그것의 이점을 이해하지 못한다고 생각한다.

(D) 그는 그것이 계속 발전할 것이라고 생각한다.

강의의 일부를 다시 듣고 질문에 답하시오.

P: Um, about a million birds are killed by wind turbines each year. Of course, even more birds are killed by tall buildings in our cities. That number is closer to a billion. Still, the problem with wind turbines must be fixed.

6 교수는 왜 이렇게 말하는가:

P: Of course, even more birds are killed by tall buildings in our cities.

(A) 두 가지 흔한 구조물의 높이를 비교하기 위해

(B) 문제가 보이는 것보다 덜 심각하다는 것을 시사하기 위해

(C) 동물들이 많은 문제를 일으킨다는 것을 강조하기 위해

(D) 새들을 도울 다른 방법들이 있다는 것을 나타내기 위해

CHAPTER 03
Function

Example

본문 p. 55

A. (C)　　　**B.** (B)

A.

Note-taking

S: Have a question about formation of stars
　Confused when talking about temp.
P: Star = begins as cold ball of gas & dust
　Star grows → gravity stronger → pressure heats star
　Add pressure to gas → it starts to heat up

Listen to a conversation between a student and a professor.

S: Hi, Professor Ahmad. I have a question about today's lecture on the formation of stars.

P: Yes, what would you like to know?

S: Well, I got confused when you started talking about temperature. I mean, it's really cold in space, right?

P: That's correct. You see, a star begins as a cold ball of gas and dust. Then, as the star grows, its gravity becomes stronger. The pressure of gravity heats up the star.

S: That's where you lost me...

P: Let's take a look at the textbook... Here, it explains that when you add pressure to a gas, it starts to heat up...

S: Hold on, Professor, where are we looking?

P: Oh, I'm right here on page 37. It's in the third paragraph.

학생과 교수 사이의 대화를 들으시오.

S: 안녕하세요, Ahmad 교수님. 별의 생성에 대한 오늘 강의에 관해 질문이 있습니다.

P: 그래, 무엇을 알고 싶니?

S: 음, 교수님이 온도에 관해 말씀하기 시작하셨을 때 혼란스러웠어요. 그러니까, 우주는 매우 춥죠, 그렇죠?

P: 맞아. 그러니까, 별은 가스와 먼지의 차가운 공으로 시작해. 그 후

에, 별이 성장하면서, 그것의 중력은 더 강해져. 중력의 압력은 별을 뜨겁게 만들어.

S: 거기서 이해가 안 됐어요...

P: 교과서를 한번 보자... 여기, 가스에 압력을 더하면, 그것이 뜨거워지기 시작한다고 설명되어 있어...

S: 잠깐만요, 교수님, 저희가 어디를 보고 있는 거죠?

P: 오, 나는 여기 37페이지를 보고 있어. 그것은 세 번째 단락에 있단다.

formation (명) 생성 confuse (동) 혼란스럽게 만들다
space (명) 우주 dust (명) 먼지 gravity (명) 중력
pressure (명) 압력 paragraph (명) 단락

대화의 일부를 다시 듣고 질문에 답하시오.
P: Let's take a look at the textbook... Here, it explains that when you add pressure to a gas, it starts to heat up...
S: Hold on, Professor, where are we looking?
P: Oh, I'm right here on page 37. It's in the third paragraph.

학생은 이렇게 말함으로써 무엇을 의미하는가:
S: Hold on, Professor, where are we looking?

(A) 그녀는 교수가 왜 책을 펼쳤는지 모른다.
(B) 그녀는 교수가 그녀의 질문을 이해했는지 확실히 알지 못한다.
(C) 그녀는 교수가 어떤 부분을 설명하고 있는지 모른다.
(D) 그녀는 교수가 주제에 대해 혼란스러워한다고 생각한다.

B.
Note-taking
James Webb Space Telescope
- James Webb Space Telescope = images of distant obj.
- Moving around the Sun about 1.5 mil km from Earth
- Telescope = special design
  - Side that faces the Sun = protected by shield
  - Powerful camera on the other side = capture images

Listen to part of a lecture in an astronomy class.

P: I'm sure many of you have heard of the James Webb Space Telescope. It has produced incredible images of distant objects in space. Um, I'd like to take a bit of time this morning to explain why this telescope is so effective.

Now, as the name suggests, the James Webb Space Telescope is, well, in space. In fact, it's moving around the Sun about 1.5 million kilometers from Earth. The telescope has a special design. The side that faces the Sun is protected by a large shield. Um, think of a tennis court. That's how big it is. It protects the telescope from the Sun's radiation. It also has a powerful camera on the other side to capture highly detailed images of deep space.

천문학 강의의 일부를 들으시오.

P: 여러분 중 다수가 제임스 웹 우주망원경에 대해 들어봤을 거예요. 그것은 우주의 먼 곳에 있는 물체들의 믿을 수 없는 이미지들을 보여주어 왔죠. 음, 오늘 아침에는 시간을 좀 내서 이 망원경이 그렇게 효과적인 이유를 설명하려 해요.
자, 이름이 시사하듯이, 제임스 웹 우주망원경은, 음, 우주에 있어

요. 사실, 그것은 지구에서 약 150만 킬로미터 떨어져서 태양 주위를 돌고 있어요. 그 망원경은 특수한 디자인을 가지고 있습니다. 태양을 바라보는 측면은 큰 방패로 보호돼요. 음, 테니스 코트를 떠올려 보세요. 그게 그만큼 커요. 그것은 태양 복사로부터 그 망원경을 보호하죠. 그것의 다른 측면에는 먼 우주의 매우 상세한 이미지를 담아내기 위한 강력한 카메라도 있어요.

incredible (형) 믿을 수 없는 distant (형) 멀리 떨어진
shield (명) 방패 radiation (명) 복사(물체에서 방출되는 열)
highly (부) 매우

강의의 일부를 다시 듣고 질문에 답하시오.
P: The telescope has a special design. The side that faces the Sun is protected by a large shield. Um, think of a tennis court. That's how big it is. It protects the telescope from the Sun's radiation. It also has a powerful camera on the other side to capture highly detailed images of deep space.

교수는 왜 이렇게 말하는가:
P: Um, think of a tennis court.

(A) 망원경이 어떻게 움직이는지 보여주기 위해
(B) 물체의 크기를 설명하기 위해
(C) 프로젝트의 비용을 강조하기 위해
(D) 특수한 디자인에 대한 이유를 제공하기 위해

Listening Practice 1 본문 p. 57

1 (D) 2 (B) 3 (A) 4 (D) 5 (D)

Note-taking
W: Next week = final exam ∴ gym = close for 3 weeks
M: Univ. should close gym X ∵ students have free time
W: Gym = students take exam ∴ gym equipment out
M: Exams end by 5 p.m., open gym after that time
W: Take time to remove desks & chairs
   Have to bring equipment back → time for exercise X
M: Other ways = put students into diff. classrooms
W: Hard to watch → cheating happened → good idea X
M: Another solution = offer pass for private gym
W: Post idea on univ. website

Listen to a conversation between a student and a student fitness center employee.

W: Welcome to the student fitness center. How can I help you?

M: I wanted to ask about the opening hours of the gym next week...

W: Sure, as you know, next week is the beginning of the final exam period. So the gym is going to be closed for three weeks until exams are finished.

M: Right... That's why I'm here, actually. ¹I don't think the university should close the gym during the exam period. That's when students have the most free time.

W: I understand that it's quite inconvenient. But the university needs to use the gym as a place where

<u>students can take their exams</u>. And, when that happens, we have to take the gym equipment out and set up all the desks and chairs.

M: ²But all of the exams end by 5 p.m. every day. I'm sure <u>you can open the gym after that time</u>.

W: Well, I'm afraid that's not possible. It takes a lot of time to remove all the desks and chairs. Plus, <u>we would have to bring the gym equipment back in</u>. There wouldn't be any time for anyone to exercise by the time that's done.

M: Oh, I didn't think about how much time it would take to organize everything... Still, I think there are other ways to solve this problem. Maybe the university doesn't need to have an entire class take the exam in one room. They could <u>put the students into different classrooms</u>.

W: They've tried that in the past, but <u>it didn't work</u>. ³Dividing students into different classrooms made it hard to watch them. Uh, there weren't enough staff for each room. So cheating happened often and <u>became a bigger problem than before</u>. That's mainly why the university decided it wasn't a good idea. We also had other small problems. For instance, many students went to the wrong rooms by mistake.

M: Well, I guess there really is no way to <u>keep the university gym open during exams</u>.

W: Again, I apologize for the inconvenience.

M: I think the university should find another solution for people who want to exercise during the exam period. ⁴Um, for example, <u>it could offer passes for a private gym near campus</u>. Students could exercise there for free while the gym is closed.

W: ⁵That's a good suggestion. You should <u>post your idea on the university website</u>.

M: I could do that, but I'm not sure if anyone would actually see it.

W: Well, staff members check the website every day. And <u>they respond to every message</u>.

M: OK, then. I'll do that as soon as possible.

학생과 학생 헬스클럽 직원 사이의 대화를 들으시오.

W: 학생 헬스클럽에 오신 걸 환영합니다. 어떻게 도와드릴까요?

M: 다음 주 헬스클럽 영업시간에 관해 여쭤보고 싶었어요...

W: 물론이죠, 아시다시피, 다음 주는 기말고사 기간의 시작이에요. 그래서 헬스클럽은 시험이 끝날 때까지 3주 동안 문을 닫을 거예요.

M: 그렇군요... 사실, 그게 제가 여기 온 이유예요. 저는 대학이 시험 기간 동안 헬스클럽을 닫아야 한다고 생각하지 않아요. 그게 학생들이 자유 시간이 가장 많을 때예요.

W: 상당히 불편하다는 건 이해합니다. 하지만 대학은 헬스클럽을 학생들이 그들의 시험을 볼 수 있는 장소로 이용해야 해요. 그리고 그럴 때, 저희는 헬스클럽 기구를 치우고 모든 책상과 의자를 설치해야 해요.

M: 하지만 모든 시험은 매일 오후 5시쯤에 끝나요. 그 시간 이후에 헬스클럽을 개장하실 수 있다고 확신해요.

W: 음, 유감이지만 그건 가능하지 않아요. 모든 책상과 의자를 치우는 데는 많은 시간이 걸려요. 게다가, 저희는 헬스클럽 기구를 다시 안으로 가져와야 할 거예요. 그게 끝날 때쯤에는 아무도 운동할 시간이 없을 거예요.

M: 오, 모든 것을 정리하는 데 얼마나 많은 시간이 걸릴지에 대해서는 생각하지 못했네요... 그래도, 이 문제를 해결할 다른 방법들이 있을 것 같아요. 아마 대학은 반 전체가 한 방에서 시험을 보게 할 필요가 없을 거예요. 학생들을 서로 다른 교실에 들어가게 할 수 있을 거예요.

W: 그들은 과거에 그걸 시도해 봤는데, 효과가 없었어요. 학생들을 서로 다른 교실로 나누는 것은 그들을 감시하는 걸 어렵게 만들었어요. 어, 각 방에 충분한 직원이 없었거든요. 그래서 종종 부정행위가 일어났고 이전보다 더 큰 문제가 됐어요. 그게 대학이 그것이 좋은 생각이 아니라고 결정한 주된 이유예요. 다른 작은 문제들도 있었어요. 예를 들어, 많은 학생들이 실수로 잘못된 방으로 갔어요.

M: 음, 정말 시험 기간 동안 대학 헬스클럽을 열어 둘 방법이 없겠네요.

W: 다시 한번, 불편을 끼친 것에 대해 사과드려요.

M: 대학이 시험 기간 동안 운동하고 싶어 하는 사람들을 위해 다른 해결책을 찾아야 할 것 같아요. 음, 예를 들어, 캠퍼스 근처에 있는 사설 헬스클럽의 이용권을 제공할 수 있을 거예요. 학생들은 헬스클럽이 닫혀 있는 동안 거기에서 운동할 수 있을 거예요.

W: 좋은 제안이네요. 학생의 아이디어를 대학 웹사이트에 게시하셔야 해요.

M: 그렇게 할 수는 있는데, 실제로 누군가가 그걸 볼지 모르겠네요.

W: 음, 직원들이 그 웹사이트를 매일 확인해요. 그리고 그들은 모든 메시지에 응답해요.

M: 그럼, 알겠습니다. 가능한 한 빨리 그렇게 할게요.

---

fitness center 헬스클럽   inconvenient (형) 불편한
equipment (명) 기구, 장비   remove (동) 치우다, 제거하다
organize (동) 정리하다   divide (동) 나누다   cheating (명) 부정행위
by mistake 실수로   apologize (동) 사과하다   pass (명) 이용권
respond (동) 응답하다

1 학생은 왜 학생 헬스클럽을 방문하는가?

(A) 스포츠팀에 가입하는 것에 대해 문의하기 위해

(B) 헬스클럽이 영업시간을 연장할 것을 요청하기 위해

(C) 공석인 일자리에 대해 알아보기 위해

(D) 헬스클럽을 닫는 것에 대한 그의 의견을 공유하기 위해

2 헬스클럽은 왜 오후 5시 이후에 문을 열어 둘 수 없는가?

(A) 그것은 추가 직원 고용을 필요로 한다.

(B) 기구를 설치할 충분한 시간이 없다.

(C) 시험들이 그곳에서 동시에 치러진다.

(D) 늦은 시간에 운동하고 싶어 하는 학생들이 많지 않다.

3 학생들을 시험을 위해 서로 다른 방에 들어가게 하는 계획은 왜 실패했는가?

(A) 부정행위가 더 흔해졌다.

(B) 각 방에 너무 많은 직원들이 있었다.

(C) 많은 학생들이 방에 대해 불평했다.

(D) 시험을 나누어 주는 데 시간이 너무 오래 걸렸다.

4 학생은 문제를 해결하기 위한 어떤 아이디어를 가지고 있는가?

(A) 대학 웹사이트에 제안을 게시하는 것

(B) 운동 기구를 다른 건물에 놓는 것

(C) 학생들에게 캠퍼스에서 무료로 운동하게 해주는 것

(D) 학생들이 근처의 사설 헬스클럽을 이용하게 해주는 것

대화의 일부를 다시 듣고 질문에 답하시오.

W: That's a good suggestion. You should post your idea on the university website.

M: I could do that, but I'm not sure if anyone would actually see it.

W: Well, staff members check the website every day. And they respond to every message.

5 직원은 왜 이렇게 말하는가:

W: Well, staff members check the website every day. And they respond to every message.

(A) 학생이 요청에 응답할 수 있는 방법을 분명히 말하기 위해

(B) 학생이 언제 시설을 이용해야 하는지 구체적으로 말하기 위해

(C) 누구나 웹사이트에 정보를 게시할 수 있다는 것을 보여주기 위해

(D) 누군가가 아이디어에 대해 듣게 될 것이라는 것을 설명하기 위해

Listening Practice 2

본문 p. 59

1 (C) 2 (C) 3 (B) 4 (B) 5 (A)

Note-taking

Roman Sea Trade

- Before Roman Empire = pirates = huge problem
- 67 BC, Romans sent Pompey → problem reduced
- Rome = significant market for many products
  - Ppl. wanted diverse products & wealthy enough
  - Basic foods had to be imported ∵ enough grain X
- Port closest to Rome = Ostia
- Larger port built at Pozzuoli
- Regions → major ports ∵ responsible for specific items
- Ships transported goods between them

Listen to part of a lecture in a history class.

P: OK... You already know that ancient Rome had a strong military... However, did you know it also had a strong economy? Well, it did. And a lot of its wealth came from sea trade. [1]Today, I'm going to discuss why sea trade became more common during the Roman Empire.

[2]Before the Roman Empire was established, pirates were a huge problem. Thus, many merchants did not want to participate in sea trade. It was too risky. If merchant ships had valuable products, pirates would attack the ships and steal the products. The situation got so bad that pirates took over the island of Crete. So, in 67 BC, the Romans sent a man named Pompey to deal with the problem. They gave him many ships, men, and money. Pompey attacked the pirates repeatedly. Within three years, the problem of pirates in the Mediterranean Sea was significantly reduced. This made the sea much safer for merchant ships.

At the same time, the city of Rome had a population of over a million residents. So, it was a significant market for many products. [5]Rome had demand for all kinds of things. Think about it. It was a multicultural city even back then. People wanted diverse products, and they were wealthy enough to afford exotic luxury goods. [3]Most importantly, though, large amounts of basic foods had to be imported... Italy's farms simply couldn't produce enough grain to feed the entire local population. The records show that over 400,000 tons of grain was brought into the city each year. That is about the same amount of grain that 1,200 ships could carry.

S: I guess the city of Rome must have had a very large port for all of those ships?

P: Absolutely. The port closest to Rome was Ostia. It was at the opening of a river near Rome. Goods were sent there from around the Mediterranean Sea. However, as sea trade grew, a larger port was built at Pozzuoli. Uh, this was a coastal city in the south of Rome. Merchant ships would drop off their goods there. Then, the goods would be delivered on smaller ships to Ostia.

Now, Rome wasn't the only center of sea trade in the region... A number of other regions became major ports as well. The reason is that each region became responsible for producing specific items. For example, Egypt and Sardinia produced lots of grain. Meanwhile, other cities in Italy were famous for their wines, and Hispania was an important source of metals.

[4]The different regions of the Roman Empire relied on each other for these necessary goods. So ships constantly transported goods between them. As a result, the sea trade of Rome and its regions played a big role in overall sea trade in the Mediterranean Sea.

역사학 강의의 일부를 들으시오.

P: 자... 여러분은 고대 로마가 강력한 군대를 가지고 있었다는 걸 이미 알고 있을 거예요... 그런데, 그것이 또한 튼튼한 경제를 가지고 있었다는 걸 알고 있었나요? 음, 그랬어요. 그리고 그것의 부의 많은 부분은 해상 무역에서 비롯되었어요. 오늘은, 로마 제국 시기에 해상 무역이 더 흔해진 이유에 대해 논의해볼 거예요.

로마 제국이 세워지기 전에, 해적들은 큰 문제였어요. 그래서, 많은 상인들은 해상 무역에 참여하기를 원치 않았죠. 너무 위험했거든요. 상선들이 값진 상품을 가지고 있으면, 해적들은 그 배들을 공격하고 상품을 훔쳤어요. 상황이 너무 나빠져서 해적들은 크레타섬을 점령했어요. 그래서, 기원전 67년에, 로마인들은 그 문제를 처리하기 위해 폼페이라는 남자를 보냈어요. 그들은 그에게 많은 배, 부하, 돈을 주었죠. 폼페이는 반복해서 해적들을 공격했어요. 3년 이내에, 지중해의 해적 문제는 크게 줄어들었어요. 이는 상선들에 바다를 훨씬 더 안전하게 만들었습니다.

같은 시기에, 로마시에는 백만 이상의 주민 인구가 있었어요. 그래서 그곳은 많은 상품들에 중요한 시장이었죠. 로마에는 온갖 것들에 대한 수요가 있었어요. 생각해 보세요. 그곳은 심지어 그 당

시에도 다문화 도시였어요. 사람들은 다양한 상품들을 원했고, 그들은 이국적인 사치품을 살 수 있을 만큼 충분히 부유했어요. 하지만, 가장 중요한 것은, 많은 양의 기초식품들이 수입되어야 했어요... 이탈리아의 농장들은 결코 현지 주민 전부를 먹여 살리기에 충분한 곡물을 생산할 수 없었어요. 기록은 매년 40만 톤 이상의 곡물이 그 도시로 들여왔다는 것을 보여줍니다. 그건 1,200척의 배로 운반할 수 있는 곡물의 양과 거의 같아요.

S: 로마시는 그 모든 배들을 위한 매우 큰 항구를 가지고 있었겠죠?

P: 물론이죠. 로마에서 가장 가까운 항구는 오스티아였어요. 그것은 로마 근처의 강이 시작하는 곳에 있었죠. 상품들은 지중해 이곳저곳에서 그곳으로 보내졌어요. 하지만, 해상 무역이 성장하면서, 포츠올리에 더 큰 항구가 건설됐어요. 어, 이것은 로마 남쪽에 있는 해안 도시였어요. 상선들은 상품을 그곳에 내려놓았죠. 그런 다음, 상품들은 더 작은 배로 오스티아로 배달되었어요.

자, 로마가 그 지역 해상 무역의 유일한 중심지였던 것은 아니에요... 다른 많은 지역들 또한 주요 항구가 되었어요. 그 이유는 각 지역이 특정 품목의 생산을 담당하게 되었기 때문이에요. 예를 들어, 이집트와 사디니아는 많은 곡물을 생산했어요. 한편, 이탈리아에 있는 다른 도시들은 그들의 와인으로 유명했고, 히스파니아는 중요한 금속 공급원이었어요.

로마 제국의 서로 다른 지역들은 이 필수품들을 위해 서로에게 의존했습니다. 그래서 배들은 그것들 사이에서 끊임없이 상품을 수송했어요. 그 결과, 로마와 그것의 지역들의 해상 무역은 지중해의 전반적인 해상 무역에서 큰 역할을 했어요.

ancient 〔형〕고대의　wealth 〔명〕부　sea trade 해상 무역
pirate 〔명〕해적　participate in ~에 참여하다　risky 〔형〕위험한
merchant ship 상선　repeatedly 〔부〕반복해서
multicultural 〔형〕다문화의　exotic 〔형〕이국적인
import 〔동〕수입하다　coastal 〔형〕해안의　rely on ~에 의존하다
constantly 〔부〕끊임없이　transport 〔동〕수송하다

1 강의는 주로 무엇에 관한 것인가?

(A) 로마와 다른 지역들의 관계

(B) 바다로 상품을 수송하는 것의 이점

(C) 로마 해상 무역 증가의 이유

(D) 로마의 군대와 경제적 힘 사이의 연관성

2 교수에 따르면, 많은 상인들은 왜 해상 무역에 참여하기를 꺼렸는가?

(A) 그들은 크레타 정부에 충성했다.

(B) 그들은 로마인들에게 세금을 내는 것을 거부했다.

(C) 그들은 해적들에게 상품을 빼앗길까 봐 두려워했다.

(D) 그들은 폼페이의 부하들에게 공격받고 싶지 않았다.

3 교수에 따르면, 로마인들은 왜 많은 양의 곡물을 수입했는가?

(A) 로마에서 생산되는 곡물은 질이 나빴다.

(B) 그 국가의 농지는 모든 현지인을 먹여 살릴 수 없었다.

(C) 도시의 인구가 급격히 증가했다

(D) 상인들은 그것으로 큰 이익을 얻을 수 있었다.

4 교수는 로마 제국의 지역들에 관해 무엇이라고 말하는가?

(A) 그것들은 지중해의 지배권을 놓고 서로 싸웠다.

(B) 그것들은 필수품을 위해 서로에게 의지했다.

(C) 그것들은 상품 생산을 놓고 로마와 경쟁했다.

(D) 그것들은 로마로부터 농사짓는 방법을 배웠다.

강의의 일부를 다시 듣고 질문에 답하시오.

P: Rome had demand for all kinds of things. Think about it. It was a multicultural city even back then. People wanted diverse products, and they were wealthy enough to afford exotic luxury goods.

5 교수는 왜 이렇게 말하는가:

P: Think about it.

(A) 로마의 수요에 분명한 이유가 있었다는 것을 시사하기 위해

(B) 로마가 다른 문화에서 온 사람들을 환영했던 이유를 설명하기 위해

(C) 대부분의 상품들이 과거에는 비싸지 않았다는 것을 강조하기 위해

(D) 로마의 많은 사람들이 이탈리아인이 아니었다는 것을 암시하기 위해

Listening Practice 3　　　　본문 p.61

1 (D)　2 (B)　3 (C)　4 (A)　5 (A)

Note-taking

S: Need advice about topic = town of Calico

P: 1880s, discovered silver in Calico → opened mine
Miners came from all over the world ∴ grew quickly
Huge success = more than enough silver → last long X
Problem = taken so much silver ∴ value decreased
Make enough money X ∴ closed mines

Listen to a conversation between a student and a professor.

S: Excuse me, Professor Wilson, do you have time to talk?

P: Sure, Josie. What's on your mind?

S: [1]Well, it's about the history assignment. I need some advice about my topic. I'm writing about the town of Calico...

P: That's a great example of a ghost town. Uh, everyone left the town after a financial crisis...

S: Right. [1]I read an article about it, but it didn't have a lot of details. Can you tell me a little more about what happened there?

P: I can give you an introduction, but you should do more research at the library. Now, what do you remember from the article?

S: Um, it said that thousands of people lived in the town.

P: That's right. [2]So, in California in the 1880s, miners discovered silver in the Calico mountains. They opened a mine to get the silver out of the mountain and, um, that's how the town got started.

S: But how did the place get so big? Didn't it start with just small groups of miners?

P: That's a good question. The miners were the first ones there, but then people around the world heard that Calico had a lot of silver. ³So miners came from all over the world to work in Calico. There were even people from Europe and Asia. And they all came to make money. That's why the town grew so quickly.

S: It seems like the place was really successful. I read that one of the mines there produced the most silver in California at the time.

P: Yes... For a while, the town was a huge success. The mines were producing more than enough silver and everyone was making money. However, the good times didn't last very long...

S: You mean the town started to struggle? What happened, exactly?

P: It's complicated, but I'll give you the simple version of the story. ⁴The new mining companies had a problem. They had taken so much silver out of the mountains that the value of silver started to decrease. Eventually, the price of silver got so low that they couldn't make enough money. So they closed the mines.

S: And that must be why everybody left the town. ⁵Since there were no more mines, they had no reason to stay there.

P: Exactly. Well, that should be more than enough to get you started. I think you can take it from here.

S: Thanks for the information. I'm going to the library right now to start working on my report.

학생과 교수 사이의 대화를 들으시오.

S: 실례합니다, Wilson 교수님, 이야기할 시간 있으신가요?

P: 물론이지, Josie. 무슨 일이니?

S: 음, 역사 과제에 관한 거예요. 제 주제에 관해 조언이 좀 필요해서요. 저는 캘리코 마을에 관해 쓰고 있어요...

P: 유령 마을의 좋은 예구나. 어, 재정 위기 후에 모두가 마을을 떠났지...

S: 맞아요. 제가 그것에 관한 기사를 읽었는데, 자세한 내용은 많지 않았어요. 그곳에서 어떤 일이 일어났는지 좀 더 말씀해 주실 수 있나요?

P: 소개는 해줄 수 있지만, 너는 도서관에서 더 많은 조사를 해야 해. 자, 그 기사에서 기억나는 것이 뭐니?

S: 음, 그것은 수천 명의 사람들이 그 마을에 살았다고 했어요.

P: 맞아. 그러니까, 1880년대 캘리포니아에서, 광부들이 캘리코 산속에서 은을 발견했어. 그들은 산에서 은을 캐내기 위해 광산을 열었고, 음, 그게 그 마을이 시작된 방식이야.

S: 그런데 그곳은 어떻게 그렇게 커졌나요? 그저 소규모의 광부 집단들로 시작하지 않았나요?

P: 좋은 질문이야. 그 광부들은 처음 그곳에 있던 사람들이지만, 그 후에 세계 곳곳의 사람들이 캘리코에 많은 은이 있다는 것을 들었지. 그래서 전 세계의 광부들이 캘리코에서 일하기 위해 왔어. 심지어 유럽과 아시아에서 온 사람들도 있었지. 그리고 그들은 모두 돈을 벌러 왔어. 그게 그 마을이 매우 빠르게 성장한 이유야.

S: 그곳이 매우 성공적이었던 것 같네요. 그곳에 있는 광산 중 하나가 당시 캘리포니아에서 가장 많은 은을 생산했다는 걸 읽었어요.

P: 그래... 얼마 동안, 그 마을은 큰 성공을 거두었어. 광산들은 충분한 양 이상의 은을 생산하고 있었고 모두가 돈을 벌고 있었지. 그런데, 좋은 시절은 오래 가지 못했단다...

S: 마을이 어려움을 겪기 시작했다는 말씀이세요? 정확히, 무슨 일이 있었나요?

P: 그건 복잡하지만, 이야기의 간단한 버전을 알려줄게. 새로운 채광 회사들은 문제가 있었어. 그들이 산에서 너무나 많은 은을 캐내서 은의 가치가 하락하기 시작했어. 결국, 은의 가격이 너무 낮아져서 그들은 충분한 돈을 벌 수 없었지. 그래서 그들은 광산을 닫았어.

S: 그리고 그게 모두가 그 마을을 떠난 이유겠군요. 더 이상 광산이 없으니까, 거기에 머물러 있을 이유가 없었네요.

P: 정확해. 음, 네가 시작하기에 충분하고도 남을 것 같구나. 네가 거기에서부터 시작할 수 있겠어.

S: 정보 감사합니다. 지금 바로 도서관에 가서 보고서 작성을 시작할게요.

---

financial crisis 재정 위기   article 圆 (신문) 기사   miner 圆 광부   discover 동 발견하다   mine 圆 광산   produce 동 생산하다   complicated 圆 복잡한   mining 圆 채광

1 대화의 주된 주제는 무엇인가?

(A) 수업을 통과하기 위한 요건

(B) 그룹 토론을 위한 아이디어

(C) 보고서를 위한 가능한 주제

(D) 과제물 주제에 관한 자세한 내용

2 무엇이 캘리코 마을의 형성으로 이어졌는가?

(A) 사람들이 토양에서 광물을 발견했다.

(B) 사람들이 산속에서 은을 발견했다.

(C) 사람들이 땅 밑에서 석유를 찾았다.

(D) 사람들이 언덕에서 광산을 발견했다.

3 교수에 따르면 캘리코는 왜 빠르게 성장했는가?

(A) 마을이 주요 도시 근처에 있었다.

(B) 많은 사람들이 마을에 투자하고 싶어 했다.

(C) 광부들이 부를 찾아 그 지역에 왔다.

(D) 은의 가격이 갑자기 상승했다.

4 캘리코의 새로운 채광 회사들의 문제는 무엇이었는가?

(A) 그들은 비싼 값에 은을 팔 수 없었다.

(B) 그들은 광산에서 일할 사람들을 찾을 수 없었다.

(C) 그들은 충분한 채광 장비가 없었다.

(D) 그들은 채광에 관한 새로운 법을 따라야 했다.

대화의 일부를 다시 듣고 질문에 답하시오.

S: Since there were no more mines, they had no reason to stay there.

P: Exactly. Well, that should be more than enough to get you started. I think you can take it from here.

S: Thanks for the information. I'm going to the library right now to start working on my report.

5 교수는 이렇게 말함으로써 무엇을 의미하는가:

P: I think you can take it from here.

(A) 학생은 직접 조사를 완료해야 한다.

(B) 교수는 학생이 혼란스러울지도 모른다고 생각한다.

(C) 학생은 그녀의 보고서를 다른 교수에게 가져가야 한다.

(D) 교수는 학생이 그녀의 주제를 바꾸기를 원한다.

Listening Practice 4

1 (C)   2 (C)   3 (B), (D)   4 (C)   5 (D)

Note-taking

Sofonisba Anguissola

- Anguissola = 1st fem. painter to achieve great success
- Pop. philosophy → father educated music & art
- Michelangelo = provided advice early in career
  - Impressed by her talent & style (e.g. drawing for him)
- Painted subjects in casual settings w/ relaxed poses
  - Tried hard to capture inner natures
- Oil paint → produce realistic works
- Invited to palace of Spain → portraits of king's family
  - Produced her greatest work

Listen to part of a lecture in an art history class.

P: Let's continue our discussion of the Renaissance... Over the past few weeks, you may have noticed that all the painters we've talked about were men. ¹However, there were a few female painters as well. Today, I'd like to discuss one in particular. Her name is Sofonisba Anguissola. She was the first female painter to achieve great success.

Now, Anguissola was born to a wealthy family in Italy. ²And back then, many wealthy families tried to educate their daughters in subjects like music and art... Um, they did this because of a popular philosophy at the time. This philosophy encouraged the artistic and intellectual development of individuals... For wealthy families, this meant giving their children a good education in many subjects. So that's why Anguissola's father educated his daughters in music and art...

S1: How did Anguissola develop a career in art?

P: Well, Anguissola's father saw that she was talented. So he decided to continue her training in art. He even sent her to work with a well-known art teacher. ⁵That's when she met the famous artist, Michelangelo. She met him during a trip to Rome. He provided her with advice early in her career... Yes?

S2: Um, that seems odd. I mean, Michelangelo was one of the greatest painters of the time. Why would he care about an unknown artist?

P: Well, it was because he was impressed by her talent and style... Here, take a look at the image on the screen. It's a drawing Anguissola produced for Michelangelo. It shows her younger brother as a child. He is screaming in pain because a crab is holding on to his finger... Now, it was the boy's expression that particularly impressed Michelangelo. Human expression is hard to paint, and he recognized her special

talent. Uh, this painting might seem normal today, but it was special during its time. You see, in those days, artists mostly painted people in formal poses and settings. However, Anguissola started a new style. ³ᴮShe painted her subjects in casual settings and with relaxed poses. And her subjects have lively expressions on their faces... Their personalities come alive. ³ᴰI guess you could say that Anguissola tried very hard to capture their inner natures...

And, once Anguissola started working with oil paint, she was able to produce incredibly realistic works... Um, this one is *Portrait of the Artist's Family*. You can see it is a family portrait. Her father, sister, brother, and even the family dog, are in it. Again, this shows her preference for casual scenes... However, this painting was never finished. ⁴Um, you see, at around the same time, Anguissola was invited to the palace of King Philip II of Spain. There, she completed many formal portraits of the king's family. She was also the queen's personal painting instructor. It was a great honor to paint for the king's family. In my view, it was here in Spain that she produced her greatest work.

미술사학 강의의 일부를 들으시오.

P: 르네상스에 대한 논의를 계속해 보죠... 지난 몇 주 동안, 여러분은 우리가 얘기한 모든 화가들이 남성이었다는 걸 알아챘을지도 몰라요. 하지만, 여성 화가들도 몇 명 있었어요. 오늘은, 특히 한 명에 대해 논의해보려 합니다. 그녀의 이름은 소포니스바 안귀솔라였어요. 그녀는 큰 성공을 거둔 최초의 여성 화가였어요.

자, 안귀솔라는 이탈리아의 부유한 가정에서 태어났어요. 그리고 그 당시에, 많은 부유한 가족들은 딸들에게 음악과 미술 같은 과목을 교육하려 했어요... 음, 그들은 당시에 유행했던 철학 때문에 이렇게 했어요. 이 철학은 개인의 예술적 및 지적 발전을 장려했어요... 부유한 가족들에게, 이는 그들의 아이들에게 많은 과목의 좋은 교육을 제공하는 것을 의미했죠. 그러니까 그게 안귀솔라의 아버지가 그의 딸들에게 음악과 미술을 교육한 이유예요...

S1: 안귀솔라는 어떻게 미술 분야에서 경력을 쌓았나요?

P: 음, 안귀솔라의 아버지는 그녀에게 재능이 있다는 걸 알아봤어요. 그래서 그는 그녀의 미술 교육을 계속하기로 결정했어요. 그는 심지어 그녀를 유명한 미술 선생님과 함께 작업하도록 보냈어요. 그게 그녀가 유명한 화가인 미켈란젤로를 만난 때예요. 그녀는 로마로의 여행 중에 그를 만났어요. 그는 그녀의 경력 초기에 조언을 해주었어요... 네?

S2: 음, 이상해 보이는데요. 그러니까, 미켈란젤로는 당대의 가장 위대한 화가 중 한 명이었잖아요. 그가 왜 무명 화가를 신경 썼을까요?

P: 음, 그가 그녀의 재능과 화풍에 감명받았기 때문이에요... 여기, 화면의 이미지를 보세요. 그건 안귀솔라가 미켈란젤로를 위해 그린 그림이에요. 그녀의 남동생이 아이였을 때를 보여주죠. 게 한 마리가 그의 손가락을 집고 있어서 그는 고통스럽게 소리를 지르고 있어요... 자, 미켈란젤로에게 특히 감명을 준 것은 소년의 표정이었어요. 인간의 표정은 그리기 힘들고, 그는 그녀의 특별한 재능을 알아보았죠. 어, 오늘날에는 이 그림이 평범해 보일지도 모르지만, 그 시기에는 특별했어요. 그러니까, 그 당시에, 화가들은 대부분 형식적인 자세로 형식적인 배경에 있는 사람들을 그렸거든요. 하지만, 안귀솔라는 새로운 화풍을 시작했죠. 그녀는 일상적인 배경에 편안한 자세로 있는 인물들을 그렸어요. 그리고 그녀의

CHAPTER 03 | Function   **27**

인물들은 그들의 얼굴에 생동감 있는 표정을 짓고 있어요... 그들의 개성이 살아나죠. 안귀솔라가 그들의 내면을 담아내기 위해 매우 열심히 노력했다고 말할 수 있을 것 같네요...

그리고, 안귀솔라가 유화 물감으로 작업하기 시작하자, 그녀는 믿을 수 없을 정도로 사실적인 작품들을 그릴 수 있었어요. 음, 이건 '화가의 가족 초상화'에요. 그것이 가족 초상화라는 걸 알 수 있죠. 그녀의 아버지, 여동생, 남동생, 그리고 심지어 가족의 개도 그 안에 있어요. 다시 말하지만, 이것은 일상적인 장면에 대한 그녀의 선호를 보여줘요... 하지만, 이 그림은 결코 완성되지 못했어요. 음, 그러니까, 거의 같은 시기에, 안귀솔라는 스페인의 필립 2세 왕의 궁전으로 초대되었어요. 그곳에서, 그녀는 그 왕가의 많은 공식 초상화를 완성했어요. 그녀는 왕비의 개인 그림 강사이기도 했어요. 왕의 가족을 위해 그림을 그린다는 건 큰 영광이었죠. 제가 보기에, 그녀가 자신의 가장 위대한 작품을 그린 것은 여기 스페인에서였어요.

notice 동 알아채다　in particular 특히　wealthy 형 부유한
philosophy 명 철학　intellectual 형 지적인
talented 형 재능이 있는　unknown 형 무명의
impress 동 감명을 주다　formal 형 형식적인; 공식적인
lively 형 생동감 있는　capture 동 담아내다　realistic 형 사실적인
portrait 명 초상화　preference 명 선호

1 강의는 주로 무엇에 관한 것인가?

(A) 르네상스 그림에서 여성들의 역할

(B) 이탈리아 그림의 기원과 발달

(C) 매우 성공한 최초의 여성 화가

(D) 철학과 미술의 연관성

2 안귀솔라의 아버지는 왜 그의 딸들에게 음악과 미술을 교육했는가?

(A) 그는 미술에 대한 그들의 분명한 관심에 고무되었다.

(B) 그 자신이 전직 음악가이자 화가였다.

(C) 그는 당시에 유행하던 철학을 따르고 있었다.

(D) 그는 그가 알았던 유명한 화가에게 영감을 받았다.

3 교수에 따르면, 안귀솔라 화풍의 특징은 무엇인가? 2개의 답을 고르시오.

(A) 그녀는 사람의 몸을 정확히 보여주는 데 집중했다.

(B) 그녀는 격식을 차리지 않은 배경과 편안한 자세를 그렸다.

(C) 그녀는 심각한 얼굴 표정을 짓고 있는 사람들을 보여줬다.

(D) 그녀는 그녀의 인물들의 내면을 담아내려 노력했다.

4 안귀솔라가 스페인에서 보낸 시간에 대한 교수의 의견은 무엇인가?

(A) 그는 그것이 안귀솔라의 화풍에 너무 많은 변화를 일으켰다고 생각한다.

(B) 그는 그것이 안귀솔라와 왕비 사이에 갈등을 일으켰다고 생각한다.

(C) 그는 그것이 안귀솔라가 최고의 작품을 그린 때라고 생각한다.

(D) 그는 그것이 안귀솔라의 성공의 주된 이유라고 생각한다.

강의의 일부를 다시 듣고 질문에 답하시오.

P: That's when she met the famous artist, Michelangelo. She met him during a trip to Rome. He provided her with advice early in her career... Yes?

S2: Um, that seems odd. I mean, Michelangelo was one of the greatest painters of the time. Why would he care about an unknown artist?

5 학생은 왜 이렇게 말하는가:

S2: I mean, Michelangelo was one of the greatest painters of the time.

(A) 그녀가 화가를 익히 알고 있음을 보여주기 위해

(B) 그녀의 의견이 맞다는 것을 확인하기 위해

(C) 그녀가 화가의 작품에 감명받았다는 것을 암시하기 위해

(D) 그녀가 설명이 헷갈린다고 생각하는 이유를 설명하기 위해

iBT Listening　Test 1　본문 p.65

1 (B)　2 (B)　3 (C)　4 (B)　5 (A)

Note-taking

W: Sign up for job fair on website → couldn't register
M: Job fair = only for graduating students
W: Why can't let everyone attend?
M: Comp. = look for ppl. start working in near future
　Many will have interview on the same day
W: Plan = career in programming, done part-time jobs
　Help career if meet more ppl. in the biz.
M: Talk to prof. → get note = allowed to go to fair
　Prep. questions to ask comp. representatives

Listen to a conversation between a student and a career center employee.

W: Hi. I'm here to talk to someone about the job fair. Am I in the right place?

M: Sure. Do you want to sign up? There are still plenty of spaces available.

W: Well, that's actually why I came. ¹I tried to sign up for the job fair on the website, but I couldn't register.

M: Oh, I think I know what the problem is. Are you graduating at the end of this year?

W: No, I'm a third-year student, so I won't be graduating until next year.

M: OK, so that's the issue. I'm afraid that the job fair is only for graduating students.

W: Really? ⁵To be honest, that seems unfair. Students who aren't in their last year might also be interested in going to the event.

M: I see your point. But my hands are tied. I tell students the rules and help them register. That's it. If I make an exception for you, other students might hear about it and be upset.

W: I understand... I don't think I should get special treatment. But why can't the school just let everyone attend the fair?

M: ²Well, there is a reason why the fair is only for graduating students. The companies at the fair are looking for people who can start working in the near future. Many of them will even have interviews on the same day.

W: Right… I didn't think about that. But I'd like a chance to explain why I want to attend.

M: Sure. I'm willing to listen to what you have to say.

W: So, um… ³My plan is to have a career in computer programming after I graduate. In recent years, I've even done part-time jobs that are related to my plan. So I really think it would help my career if I could meet more people in the computer business.

M: Hmm… Then how about this? Talk to a professor or an advisor and get a note from them. It should say that you are allowed to go to the fair. If you bring me that note, then I will let you sign up.

W: That's great! Thanks for understanding.

M: ⁴By the way, it might be a good idea to prepare a list of questions before the job fair. You know, questions you want to ask the company representatives that will be at the event. That way you won't forget anything important on the day it happens.

W: I will definitely do that. Uh, what time does your office close?

M: I will be here until 5 p.m. That gives you about an hour and a half to get the note.

W: OK. I'll make sure to be back before you leave. Thanks so much!

학생과 직업 센터 직원 사이의 대화를 들으시오.

W: 안녕하세요. 취업 박람회에 대해 누군가와 이야기하러 왔습니다. 여기가 맞나요?

M: 물론이죠. 등록하시겠어요? 아직 이용 가능한 자리가 많아요.

W: 음, 사실 그게 제가 온 이유예요. 웹사이트에서 취업 박람회에 등록하려고 했는데, 등록할 수 없었어요.

M: 오, 문제가 무엇인지 알 것 같네요. 올해 말에 졸업하시나요?

W: 아뇨, 저는 3학년 학생이라서, 내년에야 졸업할 거예요.

M: 알겠습니다, 그러니까 그게 문제네요. 유감이지만 취업 박람회는 졸업하는 학생들만을 위한 거예요.

W: 정말요? 솔직히, 그건 불공평한 것 같아요. 마지막 학년이 아닌 학생들도 그 행사에 가는 것에 관심이 있을 수 있잖아요.

M: 무슨 말씀이신지 알겠어요. 하지만 어쩔 수가 없어요. 저는 학생들에게 규칙을 말해주고 그들이 등록하는 걸 도와요. 그게 다예요. 제가 학생을 예로 하면, 다른 학생들이 그것에 대해 듣고 마음이 상할지도 몰라요.

W: 이해해요… 제가 특별 대우를 받아야 한다고 생각하지 않아요. 하지만 학교는 왜 그냥 모두가 그 박람회에 참석하게 해줄 수 없나요?

M: 음, 그 박람회가 졸업하는 학생들만을 위한 것임에는 이유가 있어요. 박람회에 오는 회사들은 가까운 미래에 일을 시작할 수 있는 사람들을 찾고 있어요. 심지어 그들 중 다수는 같은 날에 면접을 보게 될 거예요.

W: 그렇군요… 그건 생각하지 못했어요. 하지만 제가 참석하고 싶은 이유를 설명할 기회를 갖고 싶어요.

M: 물론이죠. 하시고 싶은 말씀을 기꺼이 들어드릴게요.

W: 그러니까, 음… 제 계획은 졸업 후에 컴퓨터 프로그래밍 분야의 직업을 갖는 거예요. 최근 몇 년 동안, 저는 심지어 제 계획과 관련이 있는 아르바이트들을 했어요. 그래서 저는 컴퓨터 업계에 있는 더 많은 사람들을 만날 수 있다면 진로에 정말 도움이 될 거라고 생각해요.

M: 흠… 그럼 이건 어때요? 교수님이나 지도 교수님에게 말씀드리고 그들에게 문서를 받아오세요. 그것은 학생이 박람회에 가도록 허락받았다는 내용이어야 해요. 제게 그런 문서를 가져오시면, 학생이 등록하게 해드릴게요.

W: 좋네요! 이해해 주셔서 감사합니다.

M: 그런데, 취업 박람회 전에 질문 목록을 준비하시는 게 좋을 수도 있어요. 그러니까, 그 행사에서 학생이 회사 대표자들에게 묻고 싶은 질문들이요. 그렇게 하면 그것이 열리는 날 중요한 것을 아무것도 까먹지 않을 거예요.

W: 꼭 그렇게 할게요. 어, 사무실이 언제 닫죠?

M: 저는 오후 5시까지 여기 있을 거예요. 학생이 그 문서를 받아올 시간이 한 시간 반 정도 있네요.

W: 알겠어요. 떠나기 전에 꼭 돌아올게요. 정말 감사합니다!

---

job fair 취업 박람회   plenty of ~이 많은   register 동 등록하다
unfair 형 불공평한   exception 명 예외   treatment 명 대우
representative 명 대표자

1 학생의 문제는 무엇인가?
   (A) 그녀는 캠퍼스에서 일자리를 찾을 수 없었다.
   (B) 그녀는 행사에 등록할 수 없다.
   (C) 그녀는 웹사이트를 이용하는 방법을 모른다.
   (D) 그녀는 신청서를 제시간에 제출하지 않았다.

2 직원은 박람회에 참석하는 회사들에 관해 무엇이라고 말하는가?
   (A) 그것들은 여러 개의 서로 다른 취업 박람회에 참석할 것이다.
   (B) 그것들은 곧 졸업하는 학생들을 선호한다.
   (C) 그것들은 온라인으로 면접을 볼 계획이다.
   (D) 그것들은 모두 같은 업계의 일부이다.

3 학생은 최근 몇 년간 무엇을 했는가?
   (A) 그녀의 성적을 향상했다
   (B) 캠퍼스 프로그램들에 참가했다
   (C) 컴퓨터와 관련된 일자리들을 수락했다
   (D) 학생들을 위한 활동들을 조직했다

4 직원은 학생에게 취업 박람회 전에 무엇을 하라고 제안하는가?
   (A) 박람회에 참석하는 회사들 명단 검토하기
   (B) 회사 대표자들을 위한 질문 준비하기
   (C) 이전 박람회들에 참석했던 학생들에게 이야기하기
   (D) 학교에 정책 변경 요청하기

대화의 일부를 다시 듣고 질문에 답하시오.
W: To be honest, that seems unfair. Students who aren't in their last year might also be interested in going to the event.
M: I see your point. But my hands are tied. I tell students the rules and help them register. That's it.

5 직원은 이렇게 말함으로써 무엇을 의미하는가:
   M: That's it.

(A) 그는 달리 아무것도 할 수 없다.

(B) 그는 학생의 요청을 오해했다.

(C) 그는 학생이 실수를 했다고 생각한다.

(D) 그는 행사 규칙에 동의하지 않는다.

---

iBT Listening Test 2

본문 p. 68

1 (B)   2 (D)   3 (D)   4 (B)   5 (C)   6 (D)

Note-taking

How Insects Use Cryptochrome to Navigate

- Cryptochrome = functions like compass for insects
- Proteins absorb light → go through chemical reaction
  - Allow proteins to respond to magnetic field
  - Insects can determine direction & find way
- Exposure to light → sense magnetic field, how?
  - Crypto. = found in eyes → insect uses vision
  - Crypto. appear as spots → insects see as pattern
- Use other methods
  - Monarch butterfly = crypto. proteins in eyes
  - Scientists = not sure how it works

Listen to part of a lecture in a biology class.

P: As we've discussed, many insects use the sun and the moon to determine which way to travel. But in cloudy and rainy weather, this method isn't very effective. [1]So some species have developed other methods of navigation. For example, certain insects can sense and follow the earth's magnetic field. They use a special protein called cryptochrome to do this. But first, who can remind us about the magnetic field?

S1: Um, the earth is like a giant magnet that creates a magnetic field. Its strongest points are at the North and South Poles. This is why the needle of a compass always points north.

P: Exactly. And cryptochrome functions like a compass for insects. It allows them to always know which way is north or south. So how exactly does it work? [2]Um, when cryptochrome proteins absorb light, uh, particularly blue light, they go through a chemical reaction. [3]Scientists believe that this reaction allows the proteins to respond to Earth's magnetic field. And through this, insects can determine direction and find their way. This theory is supported by an experiment with insects. In the experiment, scientists created an artificial magnetic field. Then, they exposed the insects to light at different times. When there was light, the insects were able to sense and follow the magnetic field. But when the light was removed... Well, they seemed to lose their sense of direction...

S2: [6]Um, so what you're saying is that exposure to light causes the cryptochrome proteins to sense the magnetic field, right? But, uh, how exactly does this allow insects to find their way?

P: That's a good question. In fact, it's one that a lot of biologists are asking. Um, there are actually a few possibilities. For instance, we know that in many species, cryptochromes are found in the insect's eyes. So, naturally, this suggests that the insect uses its vision. [4]Some scientists think that groups of cryptochromes appear as light and dark spots. The insect can actually see these spots as a pattern. Now, the pattern may change as the insect moves around... But the spots caused by cryptochrome always appear in the same positions. Uh, so if the insect is facing north, the spots caused by cryptochrome will always appear in one position. Then, if the insect faces south, the spots will always appear in another position. In this way, the insect always knows which way to go based on the pattern it sees.

Now, some insects don't just use their eyes. They use other methods as well. [5]For example, monarch butterflies have cryptochrome proteins in their eyes, but they also have cryptochrome proteins in their antennae. So this gives the monarch butterflies additional information to help them navigate. Of course, this information probably doesn't look like an image since the cryptochrome proteins are found in the antennae and not in the eyes. And scientists still aren't sure how it all works. Still, regardless of how monarch butterflies use the information to navigate, they are very effective at doing it. Every year, thousands of them fly from Canada to Mexico. This trip can take up to two months to complete.

생물학 강의의 일부를 들으시오.

P: 우리가 논의했듯이, 많은 곤충들은 어떤 방향으로 이동할지 알아내기 위해 태양과 달을 이용합니다. 하지만 흐리고 비가 오는 날씨에는, 이 방법이 그다지 효과적이지 않아요. 그래서 어떤 종들은 다른 길 찾기 방법들을 발달시켰어요. 예를 들어, 특정 곤충들은 지구의 자기장을 감지하고 따라갈 수 있어요. 그것들은 이렇게 하기 위해 크립토크롬이라고 불리는 특수한 단백질을 이용해요. 하지만 먼저, 누가 자기장에 대해 다시 한번 말해볼래요?

S1: 음, 지구는 자기장을 만들어내는 거대한 자석과 비슷해요. 그것의 가장 강력한 지점들은 북극과 남극에 있죠. 이것이 나침반의 바늘이 항상 북쪽을 가리키는 이유예요.

P: 정확해요. 그리고 크립토크롬은 곤충을 위한 나침반처럼 기능해요. 그것들이 항상 어떤 방향이 북쪽인지 남쪽인지 알 수 있게 해주죠. 그래서 그것은 정확히 어떻게 작동할까요? 음, 크립토크롬 단백질이 빛을 흡수할 때, 어, 특히 푸른 빛을요, 그것들은 화학 반응을 거쳐요. 과학자들은 이 반응이 단백질이 지구의 자기장에 반응하게 해준다고 믿어요. 그리고 이를 통해, 곤충들은 방향을 알아내고 길을 찾을 수 있어요. 이 이론은 곤충을 이용한 실험에 의해 뒷받침돼요. 그 실험에서, 과학자들은 인공 자기장을 만들었어요. 그리고 나서, 그들은 곤충들을 서로 다른 시간에 빛에 노출시켰어요. 빛이 있었을 때, 곤충들은 자기장을 감지하고 따라갈 수 있었어요. 하지만 빛이 제거되었을 때는... 음, 그것들은 방향 감각을 잃는 것 같아 보였어요...

S2: 음, 그러니까 교수님 말씀은 빛에 대한 노출이 크립토크롬 단백질이 자기장을 감지하도록 했다는 거죠, 맞나요? 그런데, 어, 이게 정확히 어떻게 곤충들이 길을 찾도록 해주나요?

P: 좋은 질문이에요. 사실, 그건 많은 생물학자들이 묻고 있는 거예

요. 음, 실제로 몇 가지의 가능성이 있어요. 예를 들어, 우리는 많은 종들에서, 크립토크롬이 곤충의 눈에서 발견된다는 걸 알고 있어요. 그래서, 자연스럽게, 이는 곤충이 시각을 사용한다는 것을 시사해요. 일부 과학자들은 크립토크롬의 집단이 밝고 어두운 점으로 나타난다고 생각해요. 곤충은 실제로 이 점들을 패턴으로 볼 수 있죠. 자, 그 패턴은 곤충이 돌아다님에 따라 바뀔 수 있어요... 하지만 크립토크롬으로 인한 그 점들은 항상 같은 위치에 나타나요. 어, 그러니까 만약 곤충이 북쪽을 향하고 있다면, 크립토크롬으로 인한 점들은 항상 한 자리에 나타날 거예요. 그리고, 만약 곤충이 남쪽을 향하고 있다면, 그 점들은 항상 다른 자리에 나타날 거예요. 이런 식으로, 곤충은 그것이 보는 패턴에 따라 항상 어느 방향으로 갈지를 알고 있죠.

자, 어떤 곤충들은 그것들의 눈만을 사용하지 않아요. 다른 방법들도 사용하죠. 예를 들어, 왕나비는 눈 속에 크립토크롬 단백질을 가지고 있지만, 더듬이에도 크립토크롬 단백질을 가지고 있어요. 그래서 이것은 왕나비에게 그들이 길을 찾는 것을 도와주는 추가적인 정보를 줘요. 물론, 크립토크롬 단백질이 눈이 아니라 더듬이에서 발견되기 때문에 아마 이미지처럼 보이지는 않을 거예요. 그리고 과학자들은 여전히 그 모든 것이 어떻게 작동하는지에 대해 확신하지 못해요. 그럼에도 불구하고, 왕나비가 길을 찾기 위해 정보를 이용하는 방법과 관계없이, 그것들은 그것을 매우 효과적으로 해내요. 매년, 무수한 수가 캐나다에서 멕시코로 날아가요. 이 여행은 완료하는 데 최대 두 달이 걸릴 수 있어요.

determine (동) 알아내다 navigation (명) 길 찾기
magnetic field 자기장 protein (명) 단백질 magnet (명) 자석
function (동) 기능하다 absorb (동) 흡수하다 particularly (부) 특히
reaction (명) 반응 respond (동) 반응하다 artificial (형) 인공의
expose (동) 노출시키다 sense of direction 방향 감각
vision (명) 시각 antenna (명) 더듬이

1 강의의 주된 주제는 무엇인가?
   (A) 특정 곤충 종들이 먼 거리를 이동하는 이유
   (B) 일부 곤충들이 이용하는 길 찾기 방법
   (C) 자기장이 곤충의 몸에 영향을 미치는 방식
   (D) 곤충의 길 찾기에서 태양과 달의 역할

2 교수에 따르면, 무엇이 크립토크롬 단백질이 화학 반응을 거치게 하는가?
   (A) 그것들이 뇌에서 다른 단백질들과 섞인다.
   (B) 그것들이 곤충의 먹이에 있는 화학물질에 반응한다.
   (C) 그것들이 특정 온도에 노출된다.
   (D) 그것들이 특정 유형의 빛에 영향을 받는다.

3 교수는 왜 곤충을 이용한 실험을 언급하는가?
   (A) 크립토크롬이 발견된 방법을 설명하기 위해
   (B) 현상에 대한 다른 설명을 제공하기 위해
   (C) 오직 특정 곤충들만 크립토크롬을 가지고 있다는 것을 보여주기 위해
   (D) 견해를 뒷받침하는 증거를 소개하기 위해

4 일부 과학자들은 일부 크립토크롬 집단에 대해 어떻게 생각하는가?
   (A) 그것들은 아마 곤충의 시각에 영향을 미치지 않을 것이다.
   (B) 곤충들은 그것들을 패턴으로 볼 수 있다.
   (C) 곤충들은 비행 중에만 그것들을 이용한다.
   (D) 그것들은 한 곤충에서 다른 곤충으로 옮겨진다.

5 교수는 왕나비에 대해 무엇이라고 말하는가?
   (A) 그것들은 하나의 더듬이가 제거되면 길을 찾지 못한다.
   (B) 그것들은 더듬이에 크립토크롬 단백질이 없다.
   (C) 그것들은 길 찾기를 위해 더듬이도 이용할 수 있다.
   (D) 그것들은 다른 어떤 곤충보다 멀리 이동한다.

강의의 일부를 다시 듣고 질문에 답하시오.
S2: Um, so what you're saying is that exposure to light causes the cryptochrome proteins to sense the magnetic field, right? But, uh, how exactly does this allow insects to find their way?
P: That's a good question. In fact, it's one that a lot of biologists are asking. Um, there are actually a few possibilities.

6 교수는 왜 이렇게 말하는가:
   P: In fact, it's one that a lot of biologists are asking.
   (A) 학생의 질문이 명확하지 않다는 것을 시사하기 위해
   (B) 질문이 주제와 관련이 없다는 것을 나타내기 위해
   (C) 학생의 추측이 틀렸다는 것을 지적하기 위해
   (D) 그가 명확한 답을 줄 수 없다는 것을 암시하기 위해

Vocabulary Review
본문 p.72

1 import   2 multicultural   3 exotic
4 impress   5 pressure   6 apologize
7 Cheating   8 treatment   9 formal
10 (B)   11 (A)   12 (D)
13 (C)   14 (C)

Attitude

Example
본문 p.75

A. (B)   B. (C)

A.

Note-taking
S: Attend seminar on Friday X ∵ basketball practice
P: Attendance = required X, recommend participate
   Seminar will have experts in engineering
S: Ask coach if I can miss practice

Listen to a conversation between a student and a professor.

S: Professor Lewis, I have some bad news. I don't think I'll be able to attend the seminar on Friday afternoon.

P: That's unfortunate. Do you have a problem with the schedule?

S: Yes... I'm a member of the university's basketball team, and we have practice that day.

P: Well, as I mentioned in class, attendance isn't required. However, I really recommend that you participate. An opportunity like this doesn't come along often.

S: What do you mean?

P: The seminar will have several experts in the field of engineering. You would definitely learn a lot if you attended.

S: Hmm... That sounds interesting. Maybe I'll ask my coach if I can miss this Friday's practice.

학생과 교수 사이의 대화를 들으시오.

S: Lewis 교수님, 나쁜 소식이 있어요. 저는 금요일 오후 세미나에 참석하지 못할 것 같아요.

P: 그거 안됐구나. 일정에 문제가 있니?

S: 네... 저는 대학 농구팀의 멤버이고, 저희는 그날 연습이 있어요.

P: 음, 내가 수업에서 말했듯이, 출석이 필수는 아니야. 하지만, 나는 네가 꼭 참여하기를 추천한단다. 이런 기회는 자주 오지 않아.

S: 무슨 말씀이신가요?

P: 그 세미나에는 공학 분야의 여러 전문가들이 올 거야. 네가 참석한다면 분명히 많이 배울 거란다.

S: 흠... 흥미로워 보이네요. 감독님께 이번 금요일 연습에 참석하지 않아도 되는지 여쭤봐야겠어요.

attendance 명 출석   required 형 필수의   participate 동 참여하다
expert 명 전문가   engineering 명 공학   definitely 부 분명히

다가오는 세미나에 대한 교수의 태도는 무엇인가?

(A) 그녀는 그것이 준비하기 어려웠다고 생각한다.

(B) 그녀는 그것이 학생들에게 유익할 것이라고 생각한다.

(C) 그녀는 그것의 일정이 불편할까 봐 걱정한다.

(D) 그녀는 그것이 필수여야 한다고 생각한다.

B.

Note-taking

Relationship between Ukraine and Russia

- Ukraine = part of Russian Empire & state in Soviet
- 1991 = Ukraine declared that it was independent state
  - Official = 90% ↑ Ukrainian voted for independence
- Some regions = Russian speakers → vote to join Russia
- 2014 = Russia invaded Crimea
- Recent event = threaten entire country

Listen to part of a lecture in a history class.

P: For most of its modern history, Ukraine has been closely attached to Russia. Uh, it was part of the Russian Empire. Then, it was a state in the Soviet Union. But, um, when the Soviet Union fell apart in 1991, leaders in Ukraine declared that it was an independent state. This was made official

when over 90 percent of Ukrainian citizens voted for independence. But there's a problem... Some regions of Ukraine are home to many Russian speakers who consider themselves culturally Russian. These people voted to join Russia. The situation has led to conflicts. In 2014, the Russian military invaded Crimea, a region in southern Ukraine. Additionally, I'm sure you've all been following the news... Recent events now threaten the entire country.

역사학 강의의 일부를 들으시오.

P: 우크라이나 현대사의 대부분 동안, 그것은 러시아와 밀접하게 연관되어 왔습니다. 어, 그것은 러시아 제국의 일부였어요. 그 후, 그것은 소비에트 연방의 주가 되었어요. 하지만, 음, 1991년에 소비에트 연방이 무너져 내렸을 때, 우크라이나의 지도자들은 그것이 독립된 국가라고 선언했어요. 이는 90퍼센트 이상의 우크라이나 시민들이 독립을 위해 투표했을 때 공식화되었죠. 그런데 문제가 있어요... 우크라이나의 일부 지역들은 자신을 문화적으로 러시아인이라고 여기는 러시아어 구사자들의 고향이에요. 이 사람들은 러시아에 가입하기로 투표했어요. 그 상황은 갈등으로 이어졌습니다. 2014년에, 러시아 군대가 우크라이나 남부 지역인 크림반도를 침공했죠. 또한, 여러분 모두 뉴스를 보고 있었을 거라 생각해요... 최근의 사건들은 이제 그 나라 전체를 위협하고 있어요.

attach 동 연관 짓다   state 명 주; 국가   fall apart 무너져 내리다
declare 동 선언하다   independent 형 독립된   official 형 공식적인
culturally 부 문화적으로   conflict 명 갈등   invade 동 침공하다

강의의 일부를 다시 듣고 질문에 답하시오.
P: The situation has led to conflicts. In 2014, the Russian military invaded Crimea, a region in southern Ukraine. Additionally, I'm sure you've all been following the news... Recent events now threaten the entire country.

교수는 이렇게 말함으로써 무엇을 의미하는가:
P: Additionally, I'm sure you've all been following the news...

(A) 그녀는 사건에 대한 뉴스가 충분하지 않다고 생각한다.

(B) 그녀는 학생들이 그들이 들은 것을 공유하기를 원한다.

(C) 그녀는 학생들이 약간의 배경지식을 가지고 있다고 생각한다.

(D) 그녀는 우크라이나의 상황이 계속 변화할 것이라고 예상한다.

Listening Practice 1
본문 p.77

1 (C)   2 (B)   3 (C)   4 (A)   5 (D)

Note-taking

W: Applied for sch. → heard anything X → rejected?
M: Met qualifications, continue X ∵ contact reference X
  Reference = abroad & contact by phone X
  Have chance to speak w/ him → schedule interview
W: Worried because of delay
M: Worry X ∵ timing = no impact on outcome
  Many applicants → a few are chosen
  Will get e-mail = interview date & time
  Look on bright side ∵ have more time to prepare

Listen to a conversation between a student and an employee at a financial aid office.

W: Hi there, I was wondering if you could help me. I need to speak to someone about a scholarship.

M: I can help you with that. What exactly do you need to know?

W: Well, here's my situation. [1]I applied for a scholarship about three weeks ago. And I heard that, um, some of the students who submitted applications already had their interviews. But I haven't heard anything from the office. So, uh, does this mean my application got rejected?

M: Let me check on my computer… Um, it says that your application was reviewed and that you met all of the qualifications. [2]But the process could not continue because the school has not been able to contact your personal reference.

W: I don't understand. I provided the name of my reference and his contact information. Do you know what caused the problem?

M: [2]Well, it seems he's abroad and cannot be contacted by phone. Didn't he tell you he would be traveling?

W: No, I don't think so. But it has been two months since I talked to him, so maybe he didn't know he'd be traveling at that time.

M: Or perhaps he just forgot to tell you. Anyway, we can't do the interview until we talk to him. So when he gets back and we have a chance to speak with him, then we'll schedule your interview.

W: [5]I see. But what if the school doesn't like what he says?

M: That doesn't happen often. I mean, it's not like your reference is going to say anything bad about you, right?

W: I guess that's true. But I'm still worried because of the delay in the interview.

M: You don't need to worry about that. The timing of the interview has no impact on the outcome of your application.

W: That's good to know. [3]The application process is very competitive, isn't it?

M: Oh, it definitely is. We get many applicants, but only a few are chosen to receive scholarships.

W: Right. Well, I'm relieved that I still have a chance. Thanks for your help. By the way, how will I be contacted for the interview?

M: You will get an e-mail that includes the interview date and time.

W: OK, thanks. I'll be waiting for the e-mail.

M: All right. [4]And look on the bright side of your situation. Now, you will have more time to prepare for the interview than the other applicants did.

W: That's true. Hmm… I'd better start practicing, then!

재정 지원 사무소에서 학생과 직원 사이의 대화를 들으시오.

W: 저기 안녕하세요. 절 도와주실 수 있는지 궁금해요. 장학금에 관해 누군가와 얘기해야 해서요.

M: 제가 도와드릴 수 있어요. 정확히 무엇을 알고 싶으신가요?

W: 음, 제 상황은 이래요. 저는 3주 전쯤에 장학금을 신청했어요. 그리고 저는, 음, 신청서를 제출한 학생 중 일부가 이미 면접을 봤다고 들었어요. 그런데 저는 사무소에서 아무것도 듣지 못했어요. 그러니까, 어, 이건 제 신청서가 거절되었다는 뜻인가요?

M: 제 컴퓨터로 확인해 볼게요… 음, 학생의 신청서가 검토되었고 모든 자격 요건을 만족했다고 하네요. 그런데 학교가 학생의 개인 신원 보증인과 연락을 할 수 없어서 절차가 진행될 수 없었어요.

W: 이해가 안 돼요. 저는 제 신원 보증인의 이름과 그의 연락처를 제공했어요. 무엇이 문제를 일으켰는지 아시나요?

M: 음, 그가 해외에 있고 전화로 연락이 안 되는 것 같아요. 그가 학생에게 여행 중일 것이라고 얘기하지 않았나요?

W: 아뇨, 아닌 것 같아요. 그런데 제가 그와 이야기한 지 2달이 돼서, 아마 그는 그때 여행하고 있을 줄 몰랐을 거예요.

M: 아니면 아마 학생에게 말하는 걸 잊어버렸을 거예요. 어쨌든, 저희가 그와 얘기할 때까지 면접은 할 수 없어요. 그러니까 그가 돌아와서 저희가 그와 얘기할 기회가 생기면, 그 후에 학생의 면접 일정을 잡을게요.

W: 알겠습니다. 그런데 학교가 그가 말하는 것을 마음에 들어 하지 않으면 어떡하죠?

M: 그런 일은 자주 일어나지 않아요. 그러니까, 학생의 신원 보증인이 학생에 관해 나쁜 말을 할 건 아니잖아요, 그렇죠?

W: 그런 것 같아요. 그런데 면접이 지연되는 것 때문에 여전히 걱정되네요.

M: 그건 걱정할 필요 없어요. 면접의 시기는 신청 결과에 영향을 미치지 않아요.

W: 다행이네요. 신청 과정은 경쟁이 치열하죠, 그렇지 않나요?

M: 오, 확실히 그래요. 저희는 많은 신청자를 받지만, 몇 명만이 장학금을 받도록 선택돼요.

W: 그렇군요. 음, 제게 아직 기회가 있다니 마음이 놓이네요. 도와주셔서 감사해요. 그런데, 면접에 대해서는 어떻게 연락을 받게 되나요?

M: 면접 날짜와 시간이 포함된 이메일을 받으실 거예요.

W: 네, 감사합니다. 이메일을 기다리고 있을게요.

M: 네. 그리고 상황의 긍정적인 면을 보세요. 이제, 학생은 다른 신청자들이 그랬던 것보다 면접을 위해 준비할 시간이 더 많을 거예요.

W: 그렇네요. 흠… 그럼, 연습을 시작하는 게 좋겠어요!

---

scholarship 명 장학금   application 명 신청서, 신청
reject 동 거절하다   qualification 명 자격 요건
reference 명 신원 보증인   timing 명 시기   impact 명 영향
outcome 명 결과

1 대화는 주로 무엇에 관한 것인가?
   (A) 면접에서 받을 질문들
   (B) 재정 지원을 받기 위한 신청 절차
   (C) 학생의 장학금 신청 현황
   (D) 학생의 면접 날짜 변경 요청

2 직원에 따르면, 신청 절차는 왜 지연되었는가?

(A) 부서장을 찾는 데 어려움이 있었다.

(B) 해외에 있는 누군가에게 연락하는 데 문제가 있었다.

(C) 학생의 면접 일정에 충돌이 있었다.

(D) 신원 보증서를 받는 데 문제가 있었다.

3 직원은 신청 절차에 관해 무엇이라고 말하는가?

(A) 그것은 학생들의 일정 때문에 시간이 오래 걸린다.

(B) 그것은 지정된 수의 주 안에 완료되어야 한다.

(C) 그것은 몇 명의 신청자들만이 수락되기 때문에 도전적이다.

(D) 그것은 신청서를 일찍 낸 학생들에게 이점을 준다.

4 학생의 상황에 대한 직원의 태도는 무엇인가?

(A) 그는 그녀가 준비할 시간이 더 있을 것이라고 기뻐한다.

(B) 그는 그녀가 곧 결과를 받을 것이라고 기대한다.

(C) 그는 그녀가 다른 질문들을 받을까 봐 걱정한다.

(D) 그는 그것이 신청 결과에 영향을 미칠지 궁금해한다.

대화의 일부를 다시 듣고 질문에 답하시오.

W: I see. But what if the school doesn't like what he says?

M: That doesn't happen often. I mean, it's not like your reference is going to say anything bad about you, right?

5 직원은 왜 이렇게 말하는가:

M: I mean, it's not like your reference is going to say anything bad about you, right?

(A) 학교가 신청서를 검토하는 방법을 설명하기 위해

(B) 신원 보증인의 성격이 좋다는 것을 말하기 위해

(C) 학생이 다른 신원 보증인들을 찾아야 한다는 것을 시사하기 위해

(D) 일이 일어날 것 같지 않다는 것을 강조하기 위해

Listening Practice 2

1 (C)   2 (C)   3 (C)   4 (D)   5 (A)

Note-taking

Musical Development during the Renaissance

- Renaissance = important changes in music took place
- Medieval times = religious → Renaiss. = secular
  - Scholars brought Greek works → artists = inspired
  - Greek artists = humanists = making art about ppl.
  - Humanism → more secular music to be prod.
- Greek writers had impact on Renaiss. music
  - Plato = words > melody → focus on vocal music
  - Word painting = music matched meaning of words
- Renaiss. music = showed a lot of emotion > before

Listen to part of a lecture in a music history class.

P: Good afternoon, class. Last week, we talked about developments in European music during the Middle Ages. ¹Today, we're going to move on to the Renaissance. This was another period when important changes in music took place. First, let's do a quick review of last week's

material... Who had the most influence over music in Europe during the Middle Ages?

S: I think it was church leaders, right? I mean, the church was the most powerful institution at the time.

P: That's exactly right. And as a result, most music during medieval times was religious. But all of that started to change during the Renaissance. This is when secular music became more popular. Secular music is, of course, music that is not religious. Um, I think it'll help if I give you a little background here about the Renaissance. During the Renaissance period, many scholars from other parts of the world moved to Rome. When they did, they brought many examples of classical Greek works, such as poems. ²So Renaissance artists, including musicians, became inspired by these ancient Greek texts. Now, many ancient Greek artists and writers were humanists. This means that they were more concerned about the lives of humans than gods. So, instead of making art that honored gods or religion, the Greek humanists focused on making art that was about people... This is why many Renaissance musicians started making music about people. ⁵In short, the growth of humanism caused more secular music to be produced. I'm not saying that church music stopped being made... I don't want to give you the wrong idea. It just means that other kinds of music became important as well.

In addition, the Greek writers also had an impact on how Renaissance music sounded. The, uh, Greek philosopher Plato influenced this change... He believed that words were more important than melody. This led to a new focus on vocal music. Uh, vocal music simply means music with words and not just instruments. So Plato's writing inspired Renaissance composers to write music that worked well with song lyrics. They did this through a technique known as word painting. Um, in word painting, the music matched the meaning of the words being sung. For example, if someone sang about the stars, the musical notes would go up. Or, if the lyrics described an action like running, the notes would be played very fast. ³Word painting also had an effect on how listeners felt... They could feel sad if both the lyrics and notes were sad, or feel happy if both the lyrics and notes were cheerful.

⁴Of course, today, Renaissance music sounds a bit dull and boring. But, at the time, people thought it showed a lot of emotion, especially compared to the music that was made before. This was because composers of the Middle Ages were not really interested in expressing emotions. Their main goal was to make religious music about God.

음악사 강의의 일부를 들으시오.

P: 좋은 오후입니다, 여러분. 지난주에, 우리는 중세 시대 유럽 음악의 발전에 대해 얘기했습니다. 오늘, 우리는 르네상스로 넘어갈 거예요. 이것은 음악에 중요한 변화가 일어났던 또 다른 시기였어

요. 먼저, 지난주 자료를 간단히 복습해보죠... 누가 중세 시대 유럽의 음악에 대해 가장 큰 영향력을 가지고 있었죠?

S: 교회 지도자들이었던 것 같아요, 맞아요? 그러니까, 당시에 교회는 가장 강력한 기관이었잖아요.

P: 정확해요. 그리고 그 결과, 중세 시대 대부분의 음악은 종교적이었어요. 하지만 그 모든 건 르네상스 동안 바뀌기 시작했어요. 이것이 세속적인 음악이 더 인기를 끌게 된 때입니다. 물론, 세속적인 음악이란 종교적이지 않은 음악이에요. 음, 르네상스에 대한 약간의 배경지식을 드리면 도움이 될 것 같네요. 르네상스 기간 동안, 세계 다른 지역의 많은 학자들이 로마로 이주했어요. 그렇게 할 때, 그들은 시와 같은 그리스 고전 작품의 많은 예시를 들여왔어요. 그래서 음악가들을 포함한 르네상스 예술가들은 이 고대 그리스 원문들에 영감을 받게 되었죠. 자, 많은 고대 그리스 예술가들과 작가들은 인본주의자였어요. 이는 그들이 신보다는 인간의 삶에 더 관심을 가졌다는 것을 의미해요. 그래서, 신이나 종교를 찬미하는 예술 작품을 만드는 대신, 그리스 인본주의자들은 사람에 관한 예술 작품을 만드는 것에 집중했어요... 이것이 많은 르네상스 음악가들이 사람에 관한 음악을 만들기 시작한 이유예요. 요약하자면, 인본주의의 성장은 더 많은 세속적인 음악이 만들어지게 했어요. 교회 음악이 더 이상 만들어지지 않았다고 말하는 게 아니에요... 잘못된 생각을 알려주고 싶지 않아요. 그건 그냥 다른 종류의 음악도 중요해졌다는 말이에요.

게다가, 그리스의 작가들도 르네상스의 음악이 소리를 내는 방식에 영향을 미쳤어요. 그, 어, 그리스 철학자 플라톤이 이 변화에 영향을 미쳤어요... 그는 멜로디보다 가사가 더 중요하다고 생각했어요. 이는 성악에 대한 새로운 관심으로 이어졌어요. 어, 성악은 단지 악기뿐만 아니라 가사가 있는 음악을 의미해요. 그래서 플라톤의 글은 르네상스 작곡가들에게 노래 가사와 잘 어울리는 음악을 쓰도록 영감을 주었습니다. 그들은 가사그리기라고 알려진 기술을 통해 이것을 했어요. 음, 가사그리기에서, 음악은 노래되는 가사의 의미와 연결되었어요. 예를 들어, 만약 누군가가 별들에 대해 노래하면, 음이 위로 올라갔어요. 혹은, 만약 가사가 달리기 같은 동작을 묘사하면, 음은 매우 빠르게 연주되었죠. 가사그리기는 듣는 사람이 느끼는 방식에도 영향을 미쳤어요... 가사와 음이 둘 다 슬프면 슬픔을 느낄 수도 있었고, 가사와 음이 둘 다 경쾌하면 행복을 느낄 수도 있었죠.

물론, 오늘날, 르네상스 음악은 좀 따분하고 지루하게 들려요. 하지만, 당시에, 사람들은 특히 이전에 만들어진 음악에 비하면 그것이 많은 감정을 보여준다고 생각했어요. 이것은 중세 시대의 작곡가들이 감정을 표현하는 데 별로 관심이 없었기 때문이에요. 그들의 주된 목표는 신에 관한 종교적인 음악을 만드는 것이었죠.

the Middle Ages 중세 시대 take place (일 등이) 일어나다
influence 圀 영향력 institution 圀 기관 religious 혱 종교적인
secular 혱 세속적인 scholar 圀 학자 humanist 圀 인본주의자
honor 圐 찬미하다 philosopher 圀 철학자 word 圀 가사
vocal music 성악 instrument 圀 악기 composer 圀 작곡가
note 圀 (음악의) 음 cheerful 혱 경쾌한

1 강의의 주된 주제는 무엇인가?
  (A) 로마와 그리스 음악의 차이점
  (B) 르네상스 음악에서 그리스 시의 사용
  (C) 역사의 한 시기 동안의 음악적 발전
  (D) 유럽 노래 가사의 공통적인 주제

2 교수에 따르면, 무엇이 르네상스 음악가들에게 세속적인 음악을 만들도록 영감을 주었는가?
  (A) 교회 음악의 영향

  (B) 로마에서 종교의 쇠퇴
  (C) 그리스 인본주의자들의 작품
  (D) 새로운 음악에 대한 대중적 요구

3 교수는 가사그리기에 관해 무엇이라고 말하는가?
  (A) 음은 때때로 여러 번 반복되었다.
  (B) 노래의 음은 매우 단순했다.
  (C) 그 음악은 듣는 사람의 감정에 영향을 미쳤다.
  (D) 가수가 음악에 맞춰 춤을 추었다.

4 르네상스 음악에 대한 교수의 의견은 무엇인가?
  (A) 그것은 대부분 매우 신이 나는 음악이다.
  (B) 그것은 더 오래된 음악보다 중요하다.
  (C) 그것은 너무 많은 종류의 악기를 사용한다.
  (D) 그것은 오늘날 덜 흥미롭게 들린다.

강의의 일부를 다시 듣고 질문에 답하시오.

P: In short, the growth of humanism caused more secular music to be produced. I'm not saying that church music stopped being made... I don't want to give you the wrong idea. It just means that other kinds of music became important as well.

5 교수는 왜 이렇게 말하는가:
  P: I don't want to give you the wrong idea.
  (A) 학생들에게 잘못된 결론에 도달하지 말 것을 경고하기 위해
  (B) 주제가 이해하기 어렵다는 것을 나타내기 위해
  (C) 이전에 말한 것이 틀렸다는 것을 지적하기 위해
  (D) 학생들이 종종 두 종류의 음악을 헷갈린다는 것을 시사하기 위해

Listening Practice 3 본문 p. 81

1 (C) 2 (A) 3 (B) 4 (D) 5 (C)

Note-taking

S: Opp. to write news article, not sure how to write it
   Univ. holding conference → prof. give presentation
P: Going to be largest bio. conference held in state
S: Interview all speakers & ask about their work
P: Interview so many prof. → enough time to write X
S: Interview X → boring
P: Limit to 2 or 3 speakers → save time & meet deadline
S: E-mail prof. most interested in & arrange interview

Listen to a conversation between a student and a professor.

S: Good morning, Professor Murray. I know you are usually busy at this time. But I, uh, need to talk to you about something.

P: Sure. I have a meeting at 11 a.m., but I have some time now. What's on your mind?

S: [1]Well, I've got an opportunity to write a newspaper article and since you're in charge of the university paper, I would like to get your opinion.

P: Really? That's great to hear... You're in my journalism class, right?

S: [4]That's right. You might not know this, but I'm doing a double major in communications and biology.

P: I remember you mentioning that in class. I was a little surprised. Those subjects aren't really related.

S: Yeah, I get that a lot. But that's what I wanted to talk to you about. The article would allow me to use my knowledge of biology, but I'm not sure how to write it, exactly.

P: All right. Why don't you tell me more?

S: Well, next weekend, the university is holding an important biology conference. I think it is going to be quite an event. Professors from, uh, 12 different universities will be giving presentations on their newest research. So it should be exciting for all of the students, especially for those majoring in biology.

P: Yes, I heard about the event. [2]Apparently, it's going to be the largest biology conference ever held in the state.

S: Yes... That's why I thought of writing a story about it. I could interview all of the speakers and ask them about how their work will change people's lives. I mean, it'll basically be about how our future will change because of their work.

P: Hmm... That's a good idea. [5]I'm a little worried, though, that you're trying to include too much in one article. You would have to interview so many professors. Um, you might not have enough time to write the article before the deadline.

S: I don't know... If I don't do any interviews, my article will be a little boring. It would just be a summary of the conference and presentations. I don't think anyone would be interested in reading that.

P: [3]Um, I didn't mean to say that you shouldn't do any interviews. What I mean is that you should limit your interviews to two or three well-known speakers. That would save you a lot of time. So you'll find it easier to meet the deadline.

S: That makes sense. I guess I'll e-mail the professors I'm most interested in speaking with and arrange interviews with them.

P: Good plan. And if you need more help with the article, just call me. I'm really looking forward to reading it.

학생과 교수 사이의 대화를 들으시오.

S: 안녕하세요, Murray 교수님. 지금 시간에 보통 바쁘신 걸 알고 있어요. 그런데 저는, 어, 무언가에 대해 교수님께 말씀드려야 해요.

P: 물론이지. 나는 오전 11시에 회의가 있단다, 그런데 지금은 시간이 좀 있어. 무슨 일이니?

S: 음, 제가 신문 기사를 쓸 기회를 얻게 되었고 교수님께서 대학 신문을 담당하고 계시니까, 교수님의 의견을 듣고 싶어요.

P: 정말이니? 잘됐구나... 너는 내 저널리즘 수업을 듣고 있지, 그렇지?

S: 맞아요. 모르실 수도 있지만, 저는 정보통신학과 생물학을 복수 전공하고 있어요.

P: 수업에서 네가 그걸 언급한 게 기억나는구나. 나는 약간 놀랐어. 그 과목들은 서로 크게 관련이 없잖니.

S: 네, 그 말을 많이 들어요. 하지만 제가 교수님께 말씀드리고 싶었던 게 그거예요. 그 기사는 생물학에 대한 제 지식을 활용할 수 있게 해주겠지만, 정확히 어떻게 써야 할지 모르겠어요.

P: 좋아. 더 말해주겠니?

S: 음, 다음 주에, 대학은 중요한 생물학 학회를 개최해요. 저는 그게 꽤 큰 행사가 될 것 같아요. 어, 12개의 서로 다른 대학에서 온 교수님들이 그들의 최신 연구에 관한 발표를 할 거예요. 그러니까 모든 학생들, 특히 생물학을 전공하는 학생들에게 흥미로울 거예요.

P: 그래, 그 행사에 대해 들었단다. 듣자 하니, 지금까지 주에서 개최된 것 중 가장 큰 생물학 학회가 될 것 같구나.

S: 네... 그게 제가 그것에 관한 이야기를 쓰려고 생각했던 이유예요. 모든 연사들을 인터뷰하고 그들의 연구가 어떻게 사람들의 삶을 바꾸게 될 것인지에 관해 물어볼 수 있을 거예요. 그러니까, 그것은 기본적으로 그들의 연구 때문에 우리의 미래가 어떻게 바뀔지에 대한 것일 거예요.

P: 흠... 좋은 생각이구나. 그런데, 나는 네가 하나의 기사에 너무 많은 것을 포함하려는 것일까 봐 약간 걱정이란다. 너는 아주 많은 교수들을 인터뷰해야 할 거야. 음, 기한 전에 기사를 쓸 충분한 시간이 없을지도 몰라.

S: 잘 모르겠어요... 제가 인터뷰를 하지 않으면, 제 기사는 좀 지루해질 거예요. 그건 그냥 학회와 발표의 요약이 될 거예요. 아무도 그것을 읽는 데 관심이 있을 것 같지 않아요.

P: 음, 네가 인터뷰를 하지 말아야 한다는 말을 하려는 게 아니었어. 내 말은 네가 인터뷰를 두세 명의 유명한 연사들로 제한해야 한다는 거야. 그게 많은 시간을 아껴줄 거야. 그러면 너는 기한을 맞추기가 더 쉬워질 거야.

S: 말 되네요. 제가 가장 이야기하고 싶은 교수님들께 이메일을 보내서 그들과의 인터뷰 일정을 잡아야겠어요.

P: 좋은 계획이구나. 그리고 그 기사에 관해 도움이 더 필요하면, 나에게 연락하렴. 그것을 읽는 게 정말 기대되는구나.

---

opportunity 몡 기회   in charge of ~을 담당하는
double major 복수 전공   conference 몡 학회   newest 혱 최신의
deadline 몡 기한   summary 몡 요약   limit 동 제한하다
well-known 혱 유명한   arrange 동 일정을 잡다
look forward to ~을 기대하다

1 학생은 왜 교수를 찾아가는가?

   (A) 그의 전공을 바꾸는 것에 관해 문의하기 위해

   (B) 행사 참석 허락을 얻기 위해

   (C) 글쓰기 프로젝트를 위한 아이디어를 논의하기 위해

   (D) 다가오는 학회에 대해 알아보기 위해

2 교수는 생물학 학회에 관해 무엇이라고 말하는가?

   (A) 그 지역에서 있었던 이전의 행사들보다 클 것이다.

   (B) 학교 신문은 그 행사에 관해 쓸 것이다.

   (C) 생물학 전공자들은 그것에 참여해야 한다.

   (D) 그것은 그 주의 대학들로부터 돈을 받을 것이다.

3 교수에 따르면, 학생은 어떻게 확실히 그의 기한을 맞출 수 있는가?

   (A) 개요를 일찍 쓰기 시작함으로써

(B) 더 적은 연사들을 인터뷰하기로 선택함으로써

(C) 기사에 인터뷰를 포함하지 않음으로써

(D) 교수들에게 더 적은 질문을 함으로써

대화의 일부를 다시 듣고 질문에 답하시오.

S: That's right. You might not know this, but I'm doing a double major in communications and biology.

P: I remember you mentioning that in class. I was a little surprised. Those subjects aren't really related.

S: Yeah, I get that a lot.

4 학생은 왜 이렇게 말하는가:

S: Yeah, I get that a lot.

(A) 복수 전공을 하는 것이 매우 어렵다는 것을 강조하기 위해

(B) 그가 공부하는 것들이 관련이 없다는 것에 실망을 표현하기 위해

(C) 그가 그의 전공 중 하나를 바꿀 수도 있다는 것을 나타내기 위해

(D) 다른 사람들이 그의 전공 조합이 특이하다고 생각한다는 것을 보여주기 위해

대화의 일부를 다시 듣고 질문에 답하시오.

P: I'm a little worried, though, that you're trying to include too much in one article. You would have to interview so many professors. Um, you might not have enough time to write the article before the deadline.

S: I don't know... If I don't do any interviews, my article will be a little boring.

5 학생은 이렇게 말함으로써 무엇을 의미하는가:

S: I don't know...

(A) 그는 교수가 몇 명인지 잘 모른다.

(B) 그는 인터뷰를 어떻게 할지 결정하지 못했다.

(C) 그는 교수의 의견에 동의하지 않는다.

(D) 그는 기한이 언제인지 모른다.

Listening Practice 4
본문 p. 83

1 (B)   2 (B)   3 (D)   4 (D)   5 (B)

Note-taking

How Animal Intelligence is Determined

- Challenge = way we understand intelligence
  - Tend to see if they behave like humans
  - Animals = can be intelligent in other ways
- Animal's ability to recognize itself in mirror
  - Red spot on chimp's forehead → recognized itself
- Another sign = ability to exp. emotions
  - Dogs have emotions, what we think X
- Another way = analyzing brains
  - Brain size = important, only factor X

Listen to part of a lecture in a physiology class.

P: I'm sure many of you have owned a pet before. And you probably thought they were intelligent because they followed your commands or, uh, did various tricks. But does that make these animals intelligent? [1]How do scientists know when an animal is intelligent? This is what I'd like to discuss today.

One of the challenges in studying animal intelligence is the way that we understand intelligence. Normally, um, we think of intelligence as a human quality. So, when we evaluate the intelligence of animals, we tend to see if they behave like humans... [2]For instance, if you ask people to identify an intelligent animal, they will usually mention apes, like orangutans. This is because apes often show human-like behavior. However, animals can be intelligent in other ways. So we have to be careful not to consider animals intelligent just because they behave like humans.

Um, one thing scientists do when they study animal intelligence is look for certain characteristics. One of these is an animal's ability to recognize itself in a mirror. You see, when some animals look in a mirror, they become confused and think that they are seeing a different animal. But other animals, like elephants and dolphins, know that they are looking at themselves. Um, in one famous experiment, researchers painted a red spot on a chimpanzee's forehead. [3]Of course, the chimpanzee could only see the spot when it looked in a mirror. But when the chimpanzee saw the spot, it didn't reach out to the mirror. It touched its own forehead. This shows that it recognized itself in the mirror. For scientists, this is a sign of high intelligence. Previously, scientists believed that only humans had this kind of intelligence.

OK, now, another sign of intelligence is the ability to experience emotions... For example, dogs move their tails when they're happy. They can also appear sad when they lie on the ground and place their head on top of their paws. Some pet owners even believe that dogs have complex emotions, like, uh, guilt. You've probably seen the sorry look on a dog's face after it's done something wrong, right? But, according to a recent experiment, dogs tend to look guilty when they feel nervous or afraid... Um, this happens even when they've done nothing wrong. So dogs have emotions, but these emotions may not be what we think they are.

[4]Anyway, another way scientists study animal intelligence is by analyzing their brains. One way to do this is to measure the size of the brain. The larger the brain, the smarter the animal. Sounds simple, right? Not so fast. Let's consider the animal with the largest brain, for instance: the sperm whale. [5]The sperm whale's brain weighs 18 pounds on average. That's six times bigger than the human brain. But I don't think many people would agree that sperm whales are smarter than humans. Brain size is important for intelligence, but it is not the only factor.

생리학 강의의 일부를 들으시오.

P: 여러분들 중 다수가 전에 반려동물을 키워본 적이 있을 거예요. 그리고 그들이 여러분의 명령을 따르거나, 어, 다양한 재주를 부렸기 때문에 아마 그들이 똑똑하다고 생각했을 거예요. 그런데 그게 이 동물들을 똑똑한 것으로 만들까요? 과학자들은 어떻게 어떤 동물이 똑똑한지 알 수 있을까요? 이게 오늘 논의하고자 하는 것입니다.

동물의 지능을 연구하는 데 있어 난제들 중 하나는 우리가 지능을 이해하는 방식이에요. 보통, 음, 우리는 지능을 인간의 자질로 생각합니다. 그래서, 우리가 동물의 지능을 평가할 때, 우리는 그들이 인간처럼 행동하는지를 보는 경향이 있어요… 예를 들어, 사람들에게 똑똑한 동물을 식별해 보라고 하면, 그들은 보통 오랑우탄 같은 유인원을 언급할 거예요. 이것은 유인원들이 종종 인간과 비슷한 행동을 보여주기 때문이죠. 하지만, 동물들은 다른 방식들로 똑똑할 수도 있어요. 그래서 우리는 단지 인간과 비슷하게 행동한다는 이유만으로 동물들이 똑똑하다고 생각하지 않도록 주의해야 해요.

음, 동물의 지능을 연구할 때 과학자들이 하는 한 가지는 특정한 기질을 찾는 거예요. 이것들 중 하나는 거울 속에 있는 자신을 알아보는 동물의 능력입니다. 그러니까, 거울을 볼 때, 어떤 동물들은 혼란스러워하고 그들이 다른 동물을 보고 있다고 생각해요. 하지만 코끼리와 돌고래 같은 다른 동물들은 그들이 자신을 보고 있다는 것을 알아요. 음, 한 유명한 실험에서, 연구자들은 침팬지의 이마에 빨간 점을 칠했어요. 물론, 그 침팬지는 거울을 들여다볼 때만 그 점을 볼 수 있었죠. 하지만 침팬지가 그 점을 봤을 때, 그것은 거울로 손을 뻗지 않았어요. 자신의 이마를 만졌죠. 이것은 그것이 거울 속에 있는 자신을 알아봤다는 것을 보여줘요. 과학자들에게, 이것은 높은 지능의 표시예요. 이전에, 과학자들은 오직 인간만이 이런 종류의 지능을 가지고 있다고 믿었죠.

좋아요, 자, 지능의 또 다른 표시는 감정을 경험하는 능력이에요… 예를 들어, 개들은 기쁠 때 꼬리를 움직여요. 그들은 땅에 누워서 머리를 발 위에 올려놓을 때 슬퍼 보일 수도 있어요. 몇몇 반려동물 주인들은 심지어 개들이 마치, 어, 죄책감 같은 복잡한 감정을 가지고 있다고 믿어요. 여러분은 아마 개가 무언가를 잘못한 후에 그것의 얼굴에서 미안해하는 표정을 봤을 거예요, 그렇죠? 하지만, 최근 연구에 따르면, 개들은 긴장이나 두려움을 느낄 때 죄책감을 느끼는 것처럼 보이는 경향이 있어요… 음, 이것은 그들이 아무런 잘못을 하지 않았을 때도 일어납니다. 그러니까 개들은 감정을 가지고 있지만, 이 감정들은 우리가 생각하는 것 같지 않을 수도 있어요.

그건 그렇고, 과학자들이 동물의 지능을 연구하는 또 다른 방법은 그들의 뇌를 분석하는 것입니다. 이것을 하는 한 가지 방법은 뇌의 크기를 측정하는 거예요. 뇌가 더 클수록, 동물은 더 똑똑해집니다. 간단하게 들리죠, 그렇죠? 아직 아니에요. 예를 들어, 가장 큰 뇌를 가진 동물인 향유고래를 생각해 봅시다. 향유고래의 뇌는 평균적으로 18파운드입니다. 인간의 뇌보다 6배 더 크죠. 하지만 향유고래가 인간보다 더 똑똑하다는 데 많은 사람들이 동의하지는 않을 것 같네요. 뇌의 크기는 지능에 중요하지만, 그게 유일한 요소는 아니에요.

intelligent 형 똑똑한　various 형 다양한　trick 명 재주
quality 명 자질　evaluate 동 평가하다　behave 동 행동하다
identify 동 식별하다, 알아보다　ape 명 유인원
recognize 동 알아보다, 인식하다　forehead 명 이마
reach out to ~으로 손을 뻗다　complex 형 복잡한
guilt 명 죄책감　analyze 동 분석하다　measure 동 측정하다
on average 평균적으로　factor 명 요소

1 교수는 주로 무엇에 관해 논하는가?

(A) 동물들이 생각을 가지고 있는지 여부

(B) 동물의 지능을 알아내는 방법

(C) 서로 다른 동물들의 다양한 뇌 크기

(D) 다른 동물에 비한 유인원의 지능

2 교수에 따르면, 사람들은 왜 유인원이 똑똑하다고 생각하는 경향이 있는가?

(A) 그것들은 지능 시험을 잘 본다.

(B) 그것들은 인간과 비슷한 방식으로 행동한다.

(C) 그것들은 지시를 따르도록 훈련될 수 있다.

(D) 그것들은 인간과 비슷한 뇌 구조를 가지고 있다.

3 교수는 침팬지에 관해 무엇이라고 말하는가?

(A) 그것들은 다른 유인원보다 똑똑하다.

(B) 그것들은 특정한 색깔들만 구분할 수 있다.

(C) 그것들은 인간보다 더 작은 뇌를 가지고 있다.

(D) 그것들은 거울 속에 있는 자신을 알아볼 수 있다.

강의의 일부를 다시 듣고 질문에 답하시오.

P: Anyway, another way scientists study animal intelligence is by analyzing their brains. One way to do this is to measure the size of the brain. The larger the brain, the smarter the animal. Sounds simple, right? Not so fast.

4 교수는 왜 이렇게 말하는가:

P: Not so fast.

(A) 뇌를 측정하는 것과 관련된 어려움을 언급하기 위해

(B) 큰 뇌를 분석하는 데 더 오래 걸린다는 것을 지적하기 위해

(C) 동물을 연구하는 것에 노력이 필요하다는 것을 보여주기 위해

(D) 개념이 이해하기에 복잡하다는 것을 말하기 위해

강의의 일부를 다시 듣고 질문에 답하시오.

P: The sperm whale's brain weighs 18 pounds on average. That's six times bigger than the human brain. But I don't think many people would agree that sperm whales are smarter than humans. Brain size is important for intelligence, but it is not the only factor.

5 교수는 이렇게 말함으로써 무엇을 의미하는가:

P: But I don't think many people would agree that sperm whales are smarter than humans.

(A) 향유고래에 대한 더 많은 연구가 이루어져야 한다.

(B) 향유고래는 아마 사람보다 더 똑똑하지 않을 것이다.

(C) 향유고래의 어떤 뇌는 18파운드보다도 더 무겁다.

(D) 많은 사람들은 향유고래의 지능에 대해 잘못 알고 있다.

iBT Listening　Test 1　　　본문 p. 85

1 (C)　2 (B)　3 (B)　4 (C)　5 (A)

Note-taking

W: Want to start a new sports team @ school
M: Varsity teams = fully supported by univ.
　All major sports teams = varsity teams
　Club teams = pay for things themselves
W: Bowling = varsity sport X

Students won't mind paying & take bus or drive
M: Team needs to become officially recognized
Choose president & provide set of rules
Collect signatures fr. at least 50 students on campus
Submit documents as early as possible

Listen to a conversation between a student and the director of campus activities.

W: Hi. [1]I'm here because, uh, I want to start a new sports team here at school.

M: OK. What kind of team do you want to start?

W: Well, we have a bowling alley here at school… [2]But, strangely, we don't have any bowling organizations, like a bowling team or a bowling club.

M: I've never thought about that before. But now that you mention it, you're right. First, are you familiar with the difference between a varsity sports team and a club sports team?

W: Not really, but, uh, I've heard of both before.

M: [3]Well, varsity sports teams are fully supported by the university. Players don't have to pay for travel, sports equipment, or anything else. All of our major sports teams, like the football team, are varsity sports teams. Then, there are teams for club sports like, um, chess. [3]Club sports teams pay for things themselves.

W: I don't think that bowling is going to become a varsity sport, which is fine. I'm sure the students who are interested won't mind paying for their own uniforms and equipment. We can also just take a bus or drive when we play at other schools. Also, renting a place for bowling events shouldn't be that expensive.

M: OK, then. It sounds like you've given this a lot of thought. [4]Now, about becoming a club sport… The team first needs to become an officially recognized club on campus. You'll need to choose a president for your group, and provide a written set of rules. [4]Plus, you'll need to collect signatures from at least 50 students on campus for the application.

W: Are you serious? But the team would only have five or six players, not 50!

M: Ha ha… Of course. [5]Remember that anyone can put their signature on the document. They just have to be a student at this school. It's to show that there's enough interest in the sport to make a team.

W: I see. Well, I don't think that will be a problem. I can probably get all the signatures in a couple of weeks.

M: Good… Oh, and lastly, I recommend that you submit your documents as early as possible. The office will need time to review them.

W: OK, I'll do that… Um, do you think there's a good chance that the school will approve our application? I mean, I want to start looking for our uniforms and practice with the team. Maybe we can even find a coach and sign up for a competition.

M: I'd say your chances are pretty high, so you can probably start to do all those things… Um, but maybe don't spend too much money until you're sure.

학생과 캠퍼스 활동 책임자 사이의 대화를 들으시오.

W: 안녕하세요. 저는, 어, 학교에서 새로운 스포츠 팀을 시작하고 싶어서 여기 왔어요.

M: 네. 어떤 종류의 팀을 시작하고 싶으신가요?

W: 음, 여기 학교에는 볼링장이 있어요… 그런데, 이상하게도, 우리는 볼링 팀이나 볼링 동아리 같은 볼링 단체가 없어요.

M: 전에는 그런 생각을 해본 적이 없네요. 그런데 그렇게 말씀하시고 보니, 학생 말이 맞네요. 먼저, 바시티 스포츠 팀과 동아리 스포츠 팀의 차이점을 알고 계신가요?

W: 아뇨, 그런데, 어, 전에 둘 다 들어봤어요.

M: 음, 바시티 스포츠 팀은 대학에 의해 완전히 지원돼요. 선수들은 이동, 스포츠 장비, 그 외의 것들에 대해 돈을 지불할 필요가 없어요. 축구팀 같은 우리의 모든 주요 스포츠 팀들은 바시티 스포츠 팀들이에요. 그리고, 음, 체스 같은 동아리 스포츠를 위한 팀들이 있어요. 동아리 스포츠 팀들은 스스로 돈을 내요.

W: 볼링이 바시티 스포츠가 될 것 같지는 않은데, 그건 괜찮아요. 관심 있는 학생들은 그들 자신의 유니폼과 장비에 돈을 내는 것을 신경 쓰지 않을 거예요. 다른 학교에서 경기할 때 저희는 그냥 버스를 타거나 운전해서 갈 수도 있어요. 또, 볼링 행사를 위한 장소를 대여하는 것은 그렇게 비싸지 않을 거예요.

M: 그럼, 알겠습니다. 이것에 대해 많은 생각을 해보신 것 같네요. 이제, 동아리 스포츠가 되는 것에 관해서… 팀은 먼저 캠퍼스에서 공식적으로 인정받는 동아리가 되어야 해요. 학생의 그룹을 위한 회장을 선택하고, 서면으로 된 일련의 규정들을 제공해야 할 거예요. 또, 신청을 위해 캠퍼스에서 적어도 50명 이상의 학생들의 서명을 모아야 할 거예요.

W: 진심이신가요? 그런데 팀은 50명이 아니라 다섯이나 여섯 명의 선수만 있을 거예요!

M: 하하… 물론이죠. 누구든 그 문서에 서명을 할 수 있다는 걸 기억하세요. 그들은 그냥 이 학교의 학생이기만 하면 돼요. 팀을 만들 만큼 그 스포츠에 대한 충분한 관심이 있다는 걸 보여주기 위한 거예요.

W: 알겠어요. 음, 그건 문제가 되지 않을 것 같네요. 아마 두어 주 내에 모든 서명을 받을 수 있을 것 같아요.

M: 잘됐네요… 오, 그리고 마지막으로, 문서들을 가능한 한 일찍 제출하시는 것을 추천해요. 사무소는 그것들을 검토할 시간이 필요할 거예요.

W: 네, 그렇게 할게요… 음, 학교가 저희의 신청서를 승인할 가능성이 높다고 생각하세요? 그러니까, 저는 유니폼을 찾기 시작하고 팀과 함께 연습하고 싶어요. 아마 저희는 심지어 감독님을 찾고 대회에 참가할 수도 있어요.

M: 가능성은 꽤 높은 것 같아요, 그러니까 아마 그것들을 모두 시작하셔도 될 거예요… 음, 그런데 확실해질 때까지 너무 많은 돈을 쓰지는 마세요.

varsity sports team 바시티 스포츠 팀(학교를 대표하는 교내 스포츠 팀)
fully (부) 완전히 equipment (명) 장비 officially (부) 공식적으로
recognize (동) 인정하다 approve (동) 승인하다

- Small organisms die → remove more oxygen
• Famous example = Gulf of Mexico = damage to human
• Dead zone = can be brought back w/ human help

1 화자들은 주로 무엇을 논의하고 있는가?

　　(A) 바시티 스포츠 팀 입단에 지원하는 것

　　(B) 학생들에게 동아리를 홍보하는 것

　　(C) 학교에서 스포츠 팀을 시작하는 것

　　(D) 활동을 위한 장소를 대여하는 것

2 볼링 단체에 대한 여자의 관점은 무엇인가?

　　(A) 그것들은 볼링장을 이용하도록 허락되어야 한다.

　　(B) 학교에 그것이 없는 것이 이상하다.

　　(C) 그것들은 수익을 얻을 행사를 개최해야 한다.

　　(D) 그것들이 바시티 스포츠 팀을 구성할 가능성이 있다.

3 남자에 따르면, 바시티와 동아리 스포츠 팀의 차이점은 무엇인가?

　　(A) 바시티 팀은 비싼 장비를 가지고 있다.

　　(B) 동아리 팀은 학교의 돈을 받지 않는다.

　　(C) 동아리 팀은 더 자주 이동해야 한다.

　　(D) 바시티 팀은 주요 스포츠를 하지 않는다.

4 남자는 서명을 모으는 것에 관해 무엇이라고 말하는가?

　　(A) 그것은 캠퍼스의 모든 팀들에게 선택 사항이다.

　　(B) 그것은 동아리 회원을 선택하기 위해 요구된다.

　　(C) 그것은 공식 인정을 얻기 위해 필수적이다.

　　(D) 그것은 바시티 스포츠가 되기 위해 필요하다.

대화의 일부를 다시 듣고 질문에 답하시오.

M: Remember that anyone can put their signature on the document. They just have to be a student at this school. It's to show that there's enough interest in the sport to make a team.

W: I see. Well, I don't think that will be a problem. I can probably get all the signatures in a couple of weeks.

5 여자는 이렇게 말함으로써 무엇을 의미하는가:

　　W: Well, I don't think that will be a problem.

　　(A) 그녀는 많은 학생들이 스포츠에 관심이 있다고 생각한다.

　　(B) 그녀는 팀을 시작하기에 충분한 선수들을 보유하고 있다고 생각한다.

　　(C) 그녀는 학생들이 문제를 일으킬 것이라고 예상하지 않는다.

　　(D) 그녀는 신청서를 제출하기에 충분한 시간이 있다고 확신한다.

---

iBT Listening Test 2

본문 p. 88

1 (B)　　2 (B)　　3 (C)　　4 (B)　　5 (D)　　6 (D)

Note-taking

Dead Zones

• Dead zone = can't support much life ∵ oxygen ↓
• Main factor = eutrophication = too many nutrients
• Excess nutrients = come from human activity
　- Commercial farms use chemical (e.g. nitrogen)
　- Rain → nitrogen enters stream → enters ocean
• Algae = consume nutrients → grow = algae bloom
　- Consume oxygen → remove oxygen after they die

Listen to part of a lecture in an ecology class.

P: As everyone knows, it is important to understand environmental issues because we depend on the environment for our survival. [1]Uh, one growing environmental problem is the increase in dead zones in the ocean. Dead zones are areas in the ocean that cannot support much life because they have low amounts of oxygen. So let's learn about how they form and their impact…

The main factor in the formation of dead zones is a process called eutrophication. Um, eutrophication is what happens when there are too many nutrients in the water. Naturally, organisms need nutrients to survive. But, if there are too many nutrients, this is a problem for marine life… [2]Uh, for example, excess nutrients like nitrogen and phosphorous can cause blue-green algae to grow. As the algae grow, they take oxygen from the water.

S: [3]Uh, where do these excess nutrients come from?

P: Well, they mainly come from human activity. Let's look at a common example of eutrophication in agriculture… Modern commercial farms use a lot of chemicals. Nitrogen, for instance, is an important chemical ingredient in fertilizers. It helps crops grow well. However, when it rains, some of this nitrogen enters streams and rivers. And, eventually, the water from these streams and rivers enters the ocean. When it does, it carries the nitrogen with it.

So what happens when nutrients enter the ocean? Well, remember the blue-green algae I mentioned? They consume the excess nutrients and begin to grow out of control… When this happens, the algae become algae blooms. Um, algae blooms are very large groups of algae that grow quickly. And the problem with algae blooms is that they consume a lot of the oxygen in the water. This continues even after the algae die because most organisms remove oxygen when they break down… [6]Anyway, after the algae remove oxygen from the water, other small organisms start to die. And when small organisms die, they break down and remove more oxygen. Everything adds up. Even large fish are affected because they run out of food and have to leave. Eventually, the whole area becomes a dead zone. It can't support living organisms…

A famous example of a dead zone is in the Gulf of Mexico. [4]Every summer, a large dead zone appears where the Mississippi River enters the Gulf. Um, the size of this dead zone varies from year to year. However, it can be greater than 10,000 square kilometers. That is similar to the size of the island of Jamaica or the country of Lebanon! Obviously, this large dead zone causes major changes to the local ecosystem. And it causes direct damage to humans as well. Commercial fishing is a big industry in the area. But the dead zone threatens the jobs of fishermen.

[5]Um, so what can be done about the problem of dead zones? Well, fortunately, they can be brought back to life. But this can only be done with human help. Communities must change farming practices. For instance, farmers can grow organic crops. This will reduce the amount of nutrients that enter the water. So the nutrient balance in the ocean can be restored, and the wildlife can return.

생태학 강의의 일부를 들으시오.

P: 모두가 알다시피, 우리는 생존을 위해 환경에 의존하기 때문에 환경 문제를 이해하는 것은 중요합니다. 어, 커지고 있는 환경 문제 중 하나는 바다의 데드 존 증가예요. 데드 존은 낮은 산소량으로 인해 많은 생명체를 부양할 수 없는 바닷속의 지역이에요. 자, 그것들이 형성되는 방식과 영향을 알아봅시다...

데드 존 형성의 주요 요인은 부영양화라고 불리는 과정이에요. 음, 부영양화는 물속에 너무 많은 영양소가 있을 때 일어나는 일이에요. 당연히, 유기체는 생존하기 위해 영양소를 필요로 합니다. 하지만, 너무 많은 영양소가 있으면, 이것은 해양 생물에게 문제가 돼요... 어, 예를 들어, 질소와 인과 같은 과잉 영양소는 남조류가 자라게 할 수 있어요. 그 조류가 자라면서, 그것들은 물에서 산소를 앗아갑니다.

S: 어, 이 과잉 영양소들은 어디에서 비롯되는 건가요?

P: 음, 그것들은 주로 인간의 활동에서 비롯돼요. 농업에서 부영양화의 일반적인 예시를 살펴봅시다... 현대의 상업적 농장들은 많은 화학물질을 사용해요. 예를 들어, 질소는 비료의 중요한 화학 성분이에요. 그것은 작물들이 잘 자라도록 도와주죠. 하지만, 비가 내리면, 이 질소 중 일부는 개울과 강으로 들어가요. 그리고, 결국, 이 개울과 강에서 나온 물은 바다로 들어가죠. 그렇게 되면, 그것은 질소를 운반해 가요.

자, 영양소들이 바다로 들어가면 어떤 일이 일어날까요? 음, 제가 언급한 남조류를 기억하나요? 그것들은 과잉 영양소를 먹고 통제 불능으로 자라기 시작해요... 이런 일이 일어나면, 그 조류는 조류 대발생이 돼요. 음, 조류 대발생은 빠르게 자라는 조류의 매우 큰 집단이에요. 그리고 조류 대발생의 문제는 그것들이 물속에서 많은 산소를 소모한다는 거예요. 이것은 심지어 그 조류가 죽은 다음에도 계속되는데, 이는 대부분의 유기체들이 분해될 때 산소를 제거하기 때문이에요... 어쨌든, 그 조류가 물에서 산소를 제거한 후에, 다른 작은 유기체들이 죽기 시작해요. 그리고 작은 유기체들이 죽을 때, 그것들은 분해되고 더 많은 산소를 제거해요. 모든 것의 앞뒤가 맞죠. 심지어 큰 물고기들도 먹이가 떨어지고 떠나야 하기 때문에 영향을 받아요. 결국, 그 지역 전체가 데드 존이 돼요. 그것은 살아있는 유기체를 부양할 수 없어요...

데드 존의 유명한 예시는 멕시코만에 있어요. 매년 여름, 미시시피강이 그 만으로 들어가는 곳에 커다란 데드 존이 나타나요. 음, 이 데드 존의 크기는 매년 달라져요. 하지만, 그것은 1만 제곱킬로미터보다 커질 수도 있어요. 그건 자메이카 섬의 크기나 레바논의 크기와 비슷한 거예요! 분명히, 이 커다란 데드 존은 지역 생태계에 큰 변화를 일으켜요. 그리고 그것은 인간에게도 직접적인 피해를 줘요. 상업적 어업은 그 지역에서 큰 산업이에요. 하지만 데드 존은 어부들의 일자리를 위협하고 있죠.

음, 그러면 데드 존 문제에 관해 무엇을 할 수 있을까요? 음, 다행스럽게도, 그것들은 다시 살아날 수 있어요. 하지만 이것은 인간의 도움이 있어야만 해결될 수 있어요. 지역 사회는 농업 관행을

반드시 변화시켜야 해요. 예를 들어, 농부들은 유기농 작물을 재배할 수 있죠. 이는 물로 들어가는 영양소의 양을 줄일 거예요. 그래서 바다의 영양소 균형이 회복될 수 있고, 야생 생물이 돌아올 수 있죠.

---

depend on ~에 의존하다   form 동 형성되다
eutrophication 명 부영양화   nutrient 명 영양소
nitrogen 명 질소   phosphorous 명 인   algae 명 조류
agriculture 명 농업   commercial 형 상업적인
ingredient 명 성분   fertilizer 명 비료   stream 명 개울
add up 앞뒤가 맞다   ecosystem 명 생태계

1 강의의 주된 주제는 무엇인가?

　(A) 세계의 바다에 물고기가 적어진 이유

　(B) 데드 존의 형성과 영향

　(C) 인간이 데드 존을 예방할 수 있는 방법

　(D) 공기와 물 오염의 영향

2 교수에 따르면, 물속의 과잉 영양소의 결과는 무엇인가?

　(A) 염도가 낮아진다.

　(B) 남조류가 발달한다.

　(C) 산소 농도가 높아진다.

　(D) 큰 물고기가 죽기 시작한다.

3 교수에 따르면, 과잉 영양소는 어디에서 비롯될 수 있는가?

　(A) 바다에 버려지는 쓰레기

　(B) 물 근처에서 자라는 식물

　(C) 농장에서 사용되는 화학 물질

　(D) 대형 공장에서 나오는 가스

4 교수는 왜 자메이카와 레바논을 언급하는가?

　(A) 농업에 의존하는 지역들을 강조하기 위해

　(B) 특정 데드 존의 크기를 설명하기 위해

　(C) 데드 존 근처 지역들의 예시를 들기 위해

　(D) 두 지역을 비교하기 위해

5 데드 존 문제에 대한 교수의 태도는 무엇인가?

　(A) 상업적 어업에 미치는 그것의 영향은 크지 않다.

　(B) 그것은 시간이 지나면서 자연스럽게 사라질 것이다.

　(C) 그것의 부정적인 영향은 종종 과장된다.

　(D) 그것은 사람의 도움 없이는 해결될 수 없다.

강의의 일부를 다시 듣고 질문에 답하시오.

P: Anyway, after the algae remove oxygen from the water, other small organisms start to die. And when small organisms die, they break down and remove more oxygen. Everything adds up. Even large fish are affected because they run out of food and have to leave. Eventually, the whole area becomes a dead zone.

6 교수는 왜 이렇게 말하는가:
P: Everything adds up.

　(A) 큰 물고기가 더 작은 물고기에 의존한다는 것을 시사하기 위해

　(B) 데드 존이 어떻게 매우 빠르게 자랄 수 있는지를 보여주기 위해

(C) 과정이 얼마나 어려운지 강조하기 위해

(D) 하나의 문제가 다른 문제를 더 악화시킨다는 것을 암시하기 위해

Vocabulary Review

본문 p. 92

1 instrument	2 fertilizer	3 ingredient
4 guilt	5 secular	6 commercial
7 humanists	8 evaluate	9 cheerful
10 (D)	11 (B)	12 (C)
13 (A)	14 (D)	

CHAPTER 05
Organization

Example

본문 p. 95

A. (A)   **B.** (B)

A.

Note-taking

W: Volunteered to give exchange students campus tour
Wanted to show things that make univ. special
Maybe stop by sports stadium
M: Construction work being done there, arts center?
W: Great idea ∵ large & modern

Listen to a conversation between a student and an employee at the international students office.

M: Welcome to the international students office. How can I help you today?

W: I was hoping you could give me some advice. I volunteered to give several exchange students a campus tour, but I'm not sure where to take them.

M: Well, I assume you're planning to show them the main facilities, like the library and so on.

W: Of course. But, um, I also wanted to show them some of the things that make our university special. Maybe we should stop by the sports stadium.

M: Actually, some construction work is being done there this week. What about the arts center instead?

W: That's a great idea. The arts center is quite large and modern, so I'm sure they will like it. Thanks for your help!

국제 학생 사무소에서 학생과 직원 사이의 대화를 들으시오.

M: 국제 학생 사무소에 오신 것을 환영합니다. 오늘은 어떻게 도와드릴까요?

W: 저에게 조언을 좀 해주셨으면 해요. 교환학생 몇 명에게 캠퍼스 투어를 시켜주겠다고 자원했는데, 그들을 어디에 데려갈지 모르겠어요.

M: 음, 그들에게 도서관 등 주요 시설들을 보여줄 계획이시겠죠.

W: 물론이죠. 그런데, 음, 저는 그들에게 우리 대학을 특별하게 만드는 것들 중 일부도 보여주고 싶어요. 아마 저희는 스포츠 경기장에 들러야 할 것 같아요.

M: 사실은, 이번 주에 그곳에서 약간의 공사 작업이 진행되고 있어요. 대신 예술 센터는 어떤가요?

W: 좋은 생각이에요. 예술 센터는 꽤 크고 현대적이어서, 그들이 분명 좋아할 거예요. 도와주셔서 감사합니다!

international students office 국제 학생 사무소
volunteer 图 자원하다   exchange student 교환학생
facility 图 시설   stop by ~에 들르다   construction work 공사 작업
modern 图 현대적인

직원은 왜 공사 작업을 언급하는가?

(A) 장소에 방문할 수 없다는 것을 나타내기 위해

(B) 투어가 취소된 이유를 설명하기 위해

(C) 시설이 인상적일 것이라고 제안하기 위해

(D) 행사를 연기할 것을 요청하기 위해

B.

Note-taking

Evidence of Large Civilization in the Amazon

- Now Bolivia = evidence of large civilization
  - Ppl. lived between 500~1400 AD
  - Built many structures (e.g. pyramids)
  - Constructed roads → use during rainy season
  - Made canals & ponds to hold water → grow rice

Listen to part of a lecture in an anthropology class.

P: For years, anthropologists did not think large civilizations existed in the Amazon in ancient times. However, we now know this isn't true... Um, in what is now Bolivia, researchers discovered evidence of a large civilization. And, uh, the people of this civilization lived there between 500 and 1400 AD. They built many structures, such as pyramids. And, uh, they constructed a large network of roads... Some of these were built above the surrounding ground. So, uh, this allowed people to use the roads during the rainy season, when the Amazon flooded. They also made canals and ponds to hold water. They, uh, used this water to grow rice.

인류학 강의의 일부를 들으시오.

P: 수년간, 인류학자들은 고대 아마존에 거대한 문명이 존재했다고 생각하지 않았습니다. 하지만, 우리는 이제 이것이 사실이 아님을 알고 있죠... 음, 지금의 볼리비아인 곳에서, 연구자들은 거대한 문명의 증거를 발견했어요. 그리고, 어, 이 문명의 사람들은 서기 500년에서 1400년 사이에 그곳에서 살았어요. 그들은 피라미드 같은 많은 건축물을 건설했어요. 그리고, 어, 그들은 거대한 도로망을 건설했어요... 이것들 중 일부는 주위의 땅 위에 건설되었죠. 그래서, 어, 이는 사람들로 하여금 아마존이 범람했던 우기 동

안 그 도로들을 사용할 수 있게 해주었어요. 그들은 물을 담아두기 위해 운하와 연못을 만들기도 했어요. 그들은, 어, 벼를 재배하기 위해 이 물을 사용했습니다.

anthropologist 명 인류학자　civilization 명 문명
construct 동 건설하다　network 명 망　surrounding 형 주위의
rainy season 우기　flood 동 범람하다　canal 명 운하
pond 명 연못

교수는 볼리비아에 있었던 고대 문명의 증거를 어떻게 설명하는가?

(A) 그것을 인근에 있는 사회와 비교함으로써
(B) 사람들이 만들었던 건축물에 대해 논의함으로써
(C) 기술이 얼마나 진보했는지 설명함으로써
(D) 오해의 이유를 제공함으로써

Listening Practice 1

본문 p.97

1 (C)　　2 (D)　　3 (B)　　4 (C)　　5 (A)

Note-taking

S: Haven't been to many plays
P: Live performance = diff. from reading or watching video
S: Assignment due next week, enough time X
P: Allow to write about performance on video
　Try sth. not too long, modern play = easier ∵ language
S: Musical?
P: Recommend play ∵ musical = complicated ∵ music
　Simply state opinion X, have to analyze everything

Listen to a conversation between a student and a professor.

S: Hello, Professor Shaw. I hope I'm not disturbing you.

P: Hi, Greg. No, not at all. Come in... What can I do for you?

S: Thanks. ¹Um, it's about the report you asked us to write. I like the idea of writing about a play. But I actually haven't been to many plays.

P: So when was the last time you watched one?

S: It was a long time ago... And I don't remember enough to write a report.

P: OK, well, it's important for this report that you've seen a performance in person. ²Seeing a live performance is very different from reading about it or watching it on video. You tend to feel strong emotions.

S: I understand. But what if I can't find a play to watch? I mean, the assignment is due next week. There might not be enough time.

P: All right. Well, if you really can't watch a live performance, then I'll allow you to write your report about a performance on video. It should be easy to find one online.

S: Thank you, Professor. I can probably do that tonight... Um, do you have any recommendations?

P: Any play will do. ³Um, but it would be best not to pick something that's too hard. So try watching something that's not too long. Also, a modern play would be easier to understand because of the language.

S: All right. Can I ask one more question? Does it have to be a play? Or can it be a musical?

P: Either one will be fine. ⁴But I recommend you choose a play because a musical is more complicated.

S: Oh? Why is that?

P: Well, besides analyzing the story, the characters, and so on, you will also have to analyze the music.

S: Oh, right. OK. But, um, I didn't realize that we had to analyze all of those things. I thought we just had to give a brief summary of the story and write our opinion about the performance.

P: Oh, there's more to it than that. ⁵Remember, this is a class about drama criticism. It's not enough to simply state your opinion. You have to explain your reasons for it. That means you have to analyze everything about the play, including the acting, the way the stage looks, and so on.

S: Umm… That sounds like a lot.

P: Yes, but each of those sections can be one or two paragraphs long. Then, end the report with your opinion of the play.

S: OK. I think I've got it now, Professor. Thank you so much!

학생과 교수 사이의 대화를 들으시오.

S: 안녕하세요, Shaw 교수님. 제가 방해하는 게 아니었으면 해요.

P: 안녕, Greg. 전혀 아니야. 들어오렴... 무엇을 도와줄까?

S: 감사합니다. 음, 교수님께서 저희에게 쓰라고 하신 보고서에 관한 거예요. 연극에 대해 쓴다는 발상은 좋아요. 하지만 저는 사실 연극을 많이 보러 가보지 못했어요.

P: 그래서 마지막으로 본 게 언제니?

S: 오래전이에요... 그리고 보고서를 쓸 만큼 충분히 기억나지 않아요.

P: 그렇구나, 음, 이 보고서를 위해서는 네가 직접 공연을 봤다는 것이 중요해. 실황 공연을 보는 것은 그것에 대해 읽거나 비디오로 보는 것과는 매우 달라. 사람들은 강한 감정을 느끼는 경향이 있지.

S: 이해해요. 그런데 볼만한 연극을 찾을 수 없으면 어떡하나요? 그러니까, 과제는 다음 주까지잖아요. 충분한 시간이 없을지도 몰라요.

P: 그래. 음, 네가 정말 실황 공연을 볼 수 없으면, 비디오 공연에 관한 보고서를 쓰는 걸 허락하마. 온라인으로 쉽게 찾을 수 있을 거야.

S: 감사합니다, 교수님. 아마 오늘 밤에 할 수 있을 거예요... 음, 추천하실만한 게 있나요?

P: 어떤 연극이든 괜찮아. 음, 그런데 너무 어려운 것을 고르지 않는 게 좋을 거야. 그러니까 너무 길지 않은 걸 한번 봐보렴. 또, 언어 때문에 현대 연극이 이해하기에 더 쉬울 거야.

S: 네. 하나 더 여쭤봐도 되나요? 그게 꼭 연극이어야 하나요? 뮤지

컬이어도 괜찮을까요?

P: 둘 다 괜찮을 거야. 그런데 뮤지컬은 더 복잡하기 때문에 네가 연극을 고르는 걸 추천한다.

S: 오? 왜 그런가요?

P: 음, 줄거리와 인물 등을 분석하는 것 외에도, 너는 음악을 분석해야 할 거야.

S: 오, 그렇군요. 알겠습니다. 하지만, 음, 저희가 그 모든 것을 분석해야 하는지 몰랐어요. 저희가 그냥 줄거리의 짧은 개요를 제시하고 공연에 대한 의견을 쓰기만 하면 되는 줄 알았어요.

P: 오, 그게 다가 아니란다. 기억하렴, 이건 연극 비평에 관한 수업이야. 단지 네 의견을 말하는 것만으로는 부족해. 너는 그것에 대한 너의 이유를 설명해야 해. 그건 네가 연기, 무대가 보여지는 방식 등 연극에 대한 모든 것을 분석해야 한다는 의미야.

S: 음... 할 게 많은 것 같네요.

P: 그래, 하지만 그 부분들 각각은 한두 단락 길이어도 돼. 그런 다음, 연극에 대한 너의 의견으로 보고서를 마무리하렴.

S: 네. 이제 알겠어요, 교수님. 정말 감사합니다!

disturb 통 방해하다   play 명 연극   tend to ~하는 경향이 있다
emotion 명 감정   recommendation 명 추천
modern 형 현대의   complicated 형 복잡한
analyze 통 분석하다   realize 통 알다, 깨닫다   criticism 명 비평
simply 부 단지   state 통 말하다   acting 명 연기
paragraph 명 단락

1 학생의 문제는 무엇인가?

(A) 그는 어떤 뮤지컬들을 볼지 모른다.

(B) 그는 공연에 대한 정보가 필요하다.

(C) 그는 과제에 관해 걱정이 있다.

(D) 그는 수업 보고서에 대한 의견을 원한다.

2 교수는 실황 공연에 관해 무엇이라고 말하는가?

(A) 그것들은 영화보다는 책과 더 비슷하다.

(B) 그것들은 다양한 흥미로운 주제들을 다룬다.

(C) 그것들은 전보다 인기가 떨어졌다.

(D) 그것들은 관객들에게 강한 감정적 영향을 미친다.

3 교수는 학생에게 무엇을 추천하는가?

(A) 익숙하지 않은 뮤지컬 선택하기

(B) 관련한 내용을 쓰기 쉬운 연극 선택하기

(C) 보고서를 완료하기 위해 더 많은 시간 쓰기

(D) 공연에 대한 짧은 개요 제공하기

4 뮤지컬에 대한 교수의 의견은 무엇인가?

(A) 그것들은 연극보다 재미있다.

(B) 그것들은 제작하기에 오래 걸린다.

(C) 그것들은 연극보다 분석하기 어렵다.

(D) 그것들은 이해하기 어려운 단어들을 사용한다.

5 교수는 왜 연극 비평을 언급하는가?

(A) 요구 조건에 대한 이유를 설명하기 위해

(B) 수업이 학생들에게 유용한 이유를 설명하기 위해

(C) 학생이 따라야 할 예시를 제시하기 위해

(D) 보고서가 더 길어야 한다는 것을 나타내기 위해

Listening Practice 2
본문 p.99

1 (B)   2 (B), (D)   3 (A)   4 (C)   5 (C)

Note-taking
Development of Cities During the Middle Ages

- Start of Middle Ages = small farming communities
- Adv. in farming → prod. more food > needed
  - Ppl. went to places w/ more ppl. → sold crops
  - Increase in econ. activity → attracted more ppl.
- Leaders built walls = protect city & control in and out
- Inside walls = crowded ∴ some ppl. stayed outside
  - Advantage to living outside = pay tax X
  - Buildings outside city walls = suburbs
  - New suburbs outside old suburbs → city grew larger

Listen to part of a lecture in a city planning class.

P: These days, many modern cities are carefully planned. But, uh, this wasn't the case hundreds of years ago. Most cities first developed as small towns, and then grew larger in an unplanned way. ¹This was true for European cities during the Middle Ages. Today, we're going to look at how these cities developed.

⁴So, at the start of the Middle Ages, most people lived in small farming communities in the countryside. ²ᴮHowever, advances in farming tools and methods allowed them to produce more food with less labor. This meant they could produce more food than they needed. And, uh, not everyone had to grow crops to feed themselves. So some of them went to places with more people, such as castles, seaports, and rivers. There, they sold their crops. ²ᴰOver time, this increase in economic activity attracted more people like merchants, builders, and so on. So, uh, around these areas, permanent cities and markets grew.

⁴As the cities grew, local leaders built walls around them. Walls made it easier to protect a city and to control who came in and out. ⁵Now, in exchange for the protection that cities provided, residents had to pay taxes. No surprise there... I mean, you don't get something for nothing. In addition, outsiders who wanted to trade in a city had to pay fees to sell their goods. ⁴Gradually, that's how these walled cities became important trading centers.

Because they were important trading centers, they attracted even more people. And, uh, eventually, the space inside the walls became too crowded. So some people stayed outside the city walls. Uh, they built their homes and shops there. ³Also, there was an advantage to living outside the city walls... People didn't have to pay taxes. Some merchants even did business outside the city walls just to avoid taxes.

⁴These buildings outside the city walls became known as suburbs. City officials actively encouraged the growth of these suburbs because they, uh, added to the city's wealth. Then, new

suburbs would grow outside the old suburbs. And, like the old suburbs, these new ones later became part of the city as well. [4]So, um, this process continued for many years... And, well, that's how these old cities grew larger and larger. Over time, they grew far beyond their original walls. But, um, communities that were further away from the city's center were less organized. Um, they became difficult to manage and regulate. And they were less stable. People could easily move in and out, so illegal trade and other crimes became a problem. I think it's a shame. The original order of medieval walled cities was impressive before they grew bigger. Anyhow, the medieval walled city and its suburbs are considered the earliest versions of today's modern cities and suburbs.

도시 계획학 강의의 일부를 들으시오.

P: 요즘, 많은 현대적인 도시들은 면밀히 계획됩니다. 하지만, 어, 수백 년 전에는 그렇지 않았어요. 대부분의 도시들은 먼저 작은 마을로서 발달했고, 그 후 계획되지 않은 방식으로 더 커졌어요. 중세 유럽의 도시들이 이에 해당되었죠. 오늘, 우리는 이 도시들이 어떻게 발달했는지 살펴볼 거예요.

자, 중세가 시작되었을 때, 대부분의 사람들은 시골에 있는 작은 농경 공동체에서 살았어요. 하지만, 농기구와 농사 방법의 발전은 그들이 더 적은 노동으로 더 많은 음식을 생산할 수 있게 해주었어요. 이는 그들이 필요로 했던 것보다 더 많은 음식을 생산할 수 있었음을 의미했죠. 그리고, 어, 자급자족하기 위해 모든 사람이 농작물을 재배해야 했던 것은 아니에요. 그래서 그들 중 일부는 성, 항구, 강과 같이 더 많은 사람들이 있는 곳으로 갔어요. 그곳에서, 그들은 그들의 농작물을 판매했죠. 시간이 지나면서, 이러한 경제적 활동의 증가는 상인, 건설업자 등과 같은 더 많은 사람들을 끌어들였어요. 그래서, 어, 이 지역들을 중심으로, 영구적인 도시와 시장이 성장했어요.

도시들이 성장함에 따라, 지역 지도자들은 그것들 주위에 벽을 건설했습니다. 벽은 도시를 보호하고 누가 드나드는지 통제하는 것을 더 쉽게 만들어주었죠. 이제, 도시가 제공하는 보호의 대가로, 주민들은 세금을 내야 했어요. 놀랄 것도 없죠... 그러니까, 무엇도 공짜로 얻지는 못해요. 게다가, 도시에서 거래하기를 원하는 외부인들은 그들의 상품을 팔기 위해 요금을 내야 했어요. 차츰, 그것이 이 벽으로 둘러싸인 도시들이 중요한 무역 중심지가 된 방식이에요.

그것들은 중요한 무역 중심지였기 때문에, 훨씬 더 많은 사람들을 끌어들였습니다. 그리고, 어, 결국, 벽 안의 공간은 너무 혼잡해졌어요. 그래서 몇몇 사람들은 도시의 벽 바깥에 머물렀어요. 어, 그들은 그곳에 그들의 집과 상점을 건설했어요. 또한, 도시의 벽 바깥에 사는 것에는 이점이 있었어요... 사람들은 세금을 내지 않아도 됐거든요. 몇몇 상인들은 심지어 오로지 세금을 피하기 위해 도시의 벽 바깥에서 장사를 했어요.

도시의 벽 바깥에 있는 이러한 건물들은 교외라고 알려지게 되었어요. 교외가, 어, 도시의 부를 증가시켜 주었기 때문에 도시의 공무원들은 이것들의 성장을 적극적으로 장려했어요. 그리고, 새로운 교외가 오래된 교외의 바깥쪽에서 성장하곤 했어요. 그리고, 오래된 교외들처럼, 이 새로운 것들도 나중에는 도시의 일부가 되었어요. 그래서, 음, 이 과정은 여러 해 동안 계속되었어요... 그리고, 음, 그게 이 오래된 도시들이 점점 더 커지게 된 방식이에요. 시간이 지남에 따라, 그것들은 원래의 벽을 훨씬 넘어서까지 성장했어요. 하지만, 음, 도시의 중심에서 멀리 떨어진 공동체들은 덜 체계적이었어요. 음, 그것들은 관리하고 규제하기 어려워졌죠. 그

리고 그것들은 덜 안정적이었어요. 사람들이 쉽게 드나들 수 있었기 때문에, 불법 거래와 다른 범죄들이 문제가 되었죠. 아쉬운 일이라고 생각해요. 벽으로 둘러싸인 중세 도시들의 원래 체계는 그것들이 더 커지기 전에는 인상적이었어요. 어쨌든, 벽으로 둘러싸인 중세의 도시와 그것의 교외는 오늘날의 현대적인 도시와 교외의 최초의 형태로 여겨집니다.

carefully (부) 면밀히   unplanned (형) 계획되지 않은
countryside (명) 시골   advance (명) 발전   labor (명) 노동
feed oneself 자급자족하다   attract (동) 끌어들이다
merchant (명) 상인   permanent (형) 영구적인
in exchange for ~을 대가로   crowded (형) 혼잡한   avoid (동) 피하다
suburb (명) 교외   actively (부) 적극적으로   organized (형) 체계적인
regulate (동) 규제하다   stable (형) 안정적인

1 강의의 주된 주제는 무엇인가?

(A) 중세 도시의 쇠퇴
(B) 중세 도시의 발전
(C) 유럽의 성장에서 도시의 역할
(D) 중세 유럽의 삶의 질

2 교수에 따르면, 도시 성장을 이끈 일부 요소들은 무엇이었는가? 2개의 답을 고르시오.

(A) 도시들 사이의 더 나은 도로
(B) 개선된 농사 방법
(C) 도시를 지키는 큰 군대
(D) 더 많은 경제 활동

3 교수에 따르면, 도시의 벽 바깥에 사는 것의 이점은 무엇이었는가?

(A) 사람들은 세금을 내는 것을 피할 수 있었다.
(B) 사람들은 조용한 동네에서 살 수 있었다.
(C) 사람들은 더 저렴한 상품들을 살 수 있었다.
(D) 사람들은 농부들과 더 쉽게 거래할 수 있었다.

4 교수는 강의를 어떻게 구성하는가?

(A) 초기와 후기 중세 도시의 설계를 대조함으로써
(B) 중세에 사람들이 도시로 이주했던 이유를 나열함으로써
(C) 중세 도시가 시간이 지남에 따라 형성되고 변화한 방식을 설명함으로써
(D) 중세와 현대에 도시가 건설된 방식을 비교함으로써

강의의 일부를 다시 듣고 질문에 답하시오.

P: Now, in exchange for the protection that cities provided, residents had to pay taxes. No surprise there... I mean, you don't get something for nothing. In addition, outsiders who wanted to trade in a city had to pay fees to sell their goods.

5 교수는 이렇게 말함으로써 무엇을 암시하는가:
P: No surprise there...

(A) 대부분의 사람들은 도시에 거주하는 것의 비용을 알고 있었다.
(B) 많은 사람들은 세금 내기를 거부했다.
(C) 사람들이 혜택을 받기 위해 지불하는 것은 당연하다.
(D) 도시가 보호를 필요로 하는 것은 흔한 일이었다.

1 (D) 2 (C) 3 (B) 4 (C) 5 (A)

Note-taking

S: Want to take art history class, need permission
Psychology = in every field, art & psychology = related
Thinking part-time job related to art ∴ need knowledge
P: When student, part-time job X ∵ asgmt.
Decision X ∵ check how many signed up
If full, take it next semester, know another class
Prof. Park's subject = African art, learn general history

Listen to a conversation between a student and a professor.

S: Hi, Professor Bell. Do you have time to talk?

P: Sure, Lydia. Um, you were in my Introduction to Visual Arts class, right? Didn't you change your major to psychology?

S: Yes, that's actually why I'm here. ¹You see, I want to take the art history class that you're teaching this semester, but I need your permission.

P: If you don't mind me asking, why do you want to take an art history class?

S: ²Well, I think psychology is present in every field, but especially art. Art is kind of like a window into the artist's mind. So, for me, art and psychology are actually related to each other.

P: That's a great point. So does this mean that you're changing your major back to art history?

S: No, I'm going to continue studying psychology. ³But I'm also thinking of getting a part-time job, and I want to do something related to art. A position as an assistant at a museum would be amazing, but I will need some knowledge of art history...

P: That's very impressive... You know, when I was a student, I couldn't imagine getting a part-time job. My assignments and exams kept me busy... I mean, I had some free time, but I used it to relax, not to work. Unfortunately, I can't give you a decision right now...

S: Oh, no. Did I forget a requirement? Do I need to get permission from someone else?

P: No, that's not the problem. Um, I'll just have to check how many students have already signed up for the class. ⁵Of course, you can register if the class is not full. But you never know...

S: Uh... What if the class is full? I really wanted to take your art history class...

P: Well, you could always wait and take it next semester. Or if you don't want to do that, I know of another art history class.

S: I definitely don't want to wait. I want to get a job soon, so it's important that I take an art history class this semester. What is the other class?

P: ⁴It's taught by Professor Park. However, the subject is a little different. It's specifically about African art... But you'll still learn a lot about general art history.

S: OK. It's good to know there is another option in case I can't get into your class. Thanks for all of your help.

학생과 교수 사이의 대화를 들으시오.

S: 안녕하세요, Bell 교수님. 얘기할 시간 있으신가요?

P: 물론이지, Lydia. 음, 너는 내 시각 미술 입문 수업을 들었지, 그렇지? 네 전공을 심리학으로 바꾸지 않았니?

S: 네, 사실 그게 제가 여기에 온 이유예요. 있잖아요, 저는 이번 학기에 교수님께서 가르치시는 미술사 수업을 수강하고 싶은데, 교수님의 허락이 필요해요.

P: 내가 물어봐도 괜찮다면, 왜 미술사 수업을 수강하고 싶니?

S: 음, 저는 심리학이 모든 분야에 존재하지만, 특히 미술에 존재한다고 생각해요. 미술은 화가의 마음속으로 들어가는 창문과 같아요. 그러니까, 저에게는, 미술과 심리학은 사실 서로와 관련되어 있어요.

P: 좋은 의견이구나. 그래서 네가 전공을 다시 미술사학으로 바꾼다는 말이니?

S: 아뇨, 저는 계속해서 심리학을 공부할 거예요. 그런데 저는 아르바이트 일자리를 구하는 것도 생각하고 있고, 미술과 관련된 무언가를 하고 싶어요. 박물관의 조수 자리는 굉장하겠지만, 미술사에 대한 지식이 좀 필요할 거예요...

P: 아주 인상적이구나... 있잖아, 내가 학생이었을 때, 나는 아르바이트 일자리를 구하는 것을 상상할 수 없었단다. 과제물과 시험이 날 바쁘게 했어... 그러니까, 나는 약간의 자유시간이 있었지만, 그것을 일하는 데가 아니라 휴식을 취하는 데 사용했어. 안타깝게도, 지금 바로 네게 결정을 내려줄 수 없겠구나...

S: 오, 안 돼요. 제가 필요한 것을 잊었나요? 다른 사람에게 허락을 받아야 하나요?

P: 아니, 그건 문제가 아니야. 음, 나는 단지 얼마나 많은 학생들이 이미 수업에 등록했는지 확인해야 해. 물론, 수업이 만원이 아니라면 네가 등록할 수 있을 거야. 하지만 알 수 없는 일이지...

S: 어... 수업이 만원이면요? 저는 정말 교수님의 미술사 수업을 수강하고 싶었어요...

P: 음, 너는 언제나 기다렸다가 다음 학기에 그것을 수강할 수 있어. 아니면 네가 그렇게 하고 싶지 않으면, 내가 다른 미술사 수업을 알고 있어.

S: 확실히 저는 기다리고 싶지 않아요. 저는 곧 직장을 구하고 싶어요. 그래서 이번 학기에 미술사 수업을 듣는 게 중요해요. 다른 수업은 무엇인가요?

P: 그건 Park 교수님이 가르치셔. 하지만, 주제가 약간 달라. 그것은 특히 아프리카 미술에 관한 거야... 하지만 너는 여전히 일반적인 미술사에 대해 많이 배울 거야.

S: 네. 교수님의 수업에 들어가지 못할 경우에 다른 선택지가 있다는 걸 알게 되어 좋네요. 도와주셔서 감사합니다.

Visual Arts 시각 미술   psychology 몡 심리학
permission 몡 허락   present 혱 존재하는   assistant 몡 조수
impressive 혱 인상적인   requirement 몡 필요한 것, 요건
definitely 분 확실히   specifically 분 특히

1 학생은 왜 교수를 찾아가는가?

(A) 그녀가 그녀의 전공을 바꾼 이유를 설명하기 위해

(B) 그녀가 불공평하다고 생각하는 학교 규칙에 관해 논의하기 위해

(C) 그가 어떤 수업을 가르치고 있는지에 대해 문의하기 위해

(D) 수업 수강에 대한 그의 허락을 요청하기 위해

2 학생은 왜 창문을 언급하는가?

(A) 새로운 것을 배우는 것의 중요성을 설명하기 위해

(B) 예술이 기회를 열어준다는 것을 시사하기 위해

(C) 심리학과 미술의 연관성을 보여주기 위해

(D) 미술에 대한 접근 방식의 기원을 확인하기 위해

3 학생은 어떤 일을 하는 데 관심이 있는가?

(A) 미술사를 가르치는 것

(B) 박물관에서 일하는 것

(C) 심리학자가 되는 것

(D) 전문적인 미술품을 창작하는 것

4 교수는 Park 교수의 수업에 관해 무엇이라고 말하는가?

(A) 그것은 역사학을 전공하는 학생들만을 위한 것이다.

(B) 그것은 몇 개의 어려운 수업 개념을 다룬다.

(C) 그것은 더 구체적인 주제에 초점을 맞춘다.

(D) 그것은 읽기 자료에 대한 토론을 포함한다.

대화의 일부를 다시 듣고 질문에 답하시오.

P: Of course, you can register if the class is not full. But you never know...

S: Uh... What if the class is full? I really wanted to take your art history class...

5 교수는 왜 이렇게 말하는가:

P: But you never know...

(A) 자리가 있을지 불확실하다는 것을 강조하기 위해

(B) 학생이 수업을 수강하지 말아야 한다고 제안하기 위해

(C) 그가 전에 말했던 무언가가 틀렸다는 것을 나타내기 위해

(D) 학생이 고려할 만한 새로운 수업을 소개하기 위해

Listening Practice 4

본문 p. 103

1 (C)　　2 (C)　　3 (B)　　4 (D)　　5 (B)

Note-taking

The Doppler Effect

• Ambulance closer & siren louder = Doppler Effect
• Related to distance between each sound save
  - Close together = high sound, far apart = low sound
  - Drop stone into pool → middle = close
• Movement = important
  - Amb. coming → near source of noise = high sound
  - Amb. away → farther from source = low sound
  - Amb. stops → Doppler effect stops = constant
• Use to measure speed & direction (e.g. thunderstorm)

Listen to part of a lecture in a physics class.

P: Have you ever heard an ambulance go past you? Well, you may have noticed something strange. [1]As the ambulance gets closer, the sound of the siren gets louder and faster. What explains this? Well, it's something called the Doppler effect.

So, uh, the Doppler effect is a change in the way you hear sounds from a moving object. And this change in sound is directly related to the distance between each sound wave. Um, as you know, sound moves through the air in waves. And when those waves reach our ears, we hear them as sound. Now, sound waves that are close together have a high sound, like a whistle. In contrast, sound waves that are far apart have a low sound, like thunder. Um, let me describe it another way... [2]It's like dropping a stone into a pool of water. The stone creates a circle of waves around it. Near the middle, the waves are close together. The waves that are far away are farther apart. So, near the source of a noise, sound waves are close to each other and have a high sound. However, away from the source of a noise, sound waves are far apart and have a low sound. But, uh, surprisingly, all sound waves travel at the same speed... Um, the speed of sound is around 1,200 kilometers per hour. [5]So, again, why do we hear the sounds differently?

S: Uh, is it because the distance between the sound waves is different?

P: Good. Someone was paying attention... [3]But when we're talking about the Doppler effect, it isn't just the distance between sound waves that's important. Movement is important, too. Um, let's go back to our earlier example. You hear an ambulance coming. When the ambulance is moving toward you, you hear many sound waves near the source of the noise. So the siren will have a high sound. It will seem louder and faster than normal. But now, as the ambulance moves away, the sound waves you hear are getting farther and farther from their source. So they have a low sound. They seem lower and slower than normal. [4]And what do you think happens if the ambulance stops in front of you? Well, the Doppler effect also stops. When the Doppler effect is not happening, the distance between sound waves stays the same. So you hear the siren at a constant speed and loudness.

And why is any of this important to know? Well, the Doppler effect is based on moving objects. So we can use it to measure the speed and direction of any moving object that produces sound. For example, we can use it to detect thunderstorms, measure how fast a car is moving, and even see how blood moves through our bodies. So as you can see, it's a very useful concept.

물리학 강의의 일부를 들으시오.

P: 구급차가 여러분 옆을 지나가는 소리를 들어본 적이 있나요? 음, 아마 무언가 이상한 걸 눈치챘을 거예요. 구급차가 가까워질수록, 사이렌 소리는 점점 더 커지고 빨라지죠. 이걸 무엇으로 설명할까요? 음, 그건 도플러효과라고 불리는 거예요.

자, 어, 도플러효과는 움직이는 물체의 소리를 듣는 방식의 변화예요. 그리고 이 소리의 변화는 각 음파 사이의 거리와 직접적으로 관련이 있어요. 음, 알다시피, 소리는 음파의 형태로 공기를 통해 이동해요. 그리고 그 음파들이 우리의 귀에 닿을 때, 우리는 그것들을 소리로 듣죠. 자, 서로 가까운 음파들은 호루라기처럼 높은 소리를 가지고 있어요. 반대로, 멀리 떨어진 음파들은 천둥처럼 낮은 소리를 가지고 있어요. 음, 다른 방식으로 설명해 보죠... 그건 물웅덩이로 돌을 떨어뜨리는 것과 같아요. 돌은 그것의 주위에 물결의 원을 만들죠. 중앙 근처에서, 물결들은 서로 가깝죠. 먼 곳의 물결들은 더 멀리 떨어져 있어요. 그래서, 소음원의 근처에서, 음파들은 서로와 가깝고 높은 소리를 가지고 있어요. 하지만, 소음원과 멀리 떨어진 곳에서, 음파들은 멀리 떨어져 있고 낮은 소리를 가지고 있죠. 하지만, 어, 놀랍게도, 모든 음파는 동일한 속도로 이동해요. 음, 소리의 속도는 대략 시속 1,200킬로미터입니다. 자, 다시, 우리는 왜 소리를 다르게 들을까요?

S: 어, 음파들 사이의 거리가 다르기 때문인가요?

P: 좋아요. 누군가는 집중하고 있었네요... 하지만 우리가 도플러효과에 대해 이야기할 때, 중요한 것은 음파들 사이의 거리뿐만이 아니에요. 움직임 또한 중요합니다. 음, 이전의 예시로 돌아가 보죠. 여러분은 구급차가 오는 소리를 들어요. 구급차가 여러분을 향해 움직이고 있을 때, 여러분은 소음원 근처에서 많은 음파를 듣게 되죠. 그래서 사이렌은 높은 소리를 가지고 있을 거예요. 평소보다 더 크고 빠른 것처럼 보일 거예요. 하지만 이제, 구급차가 멀어짐에 따라, 여러분이 듣는 음파들은 그것들의 원천으로부터 점점 더 멀어지죠. 그래서 그것들은 낮은 소리를 가지고 있습니다. 평소보다 더 낮고 느린 것처럼 보일 거예요. 그럼 구급차가 여러분 앞에 멈추면 어떻게 될 것 같나요? 음, 도플러효과도 멈춰요. 도플러효과가 일어나지 않을 때, 음파들 사이의 거리는 동일하게 유지돼요. 그래서 여러분은 사이렌을 일정한 속도와 크기로 듣게 되죠.

그리고 이 모든 것이 왜 중요할까요? 음, 도플러효과는 움직이는 물체에 기초하고 있어요. 그래서 우리는 소리를 내며 움직이는 물체의 속도와 방향을 측정하는 데 그것을 사용할 수 있어요. 예를 들어, 우리는 뇌우를 감지하고, 차가 얼마나 빠르게 움직이고 있는지를 측정하고, 심지어는 우리의 피가 어떻게 우리 몸을 통해 움직이는지를 알아내기 위해 그것을 사용할 수 있어요. 그래서 보다시피, 그것은 매우 유용한 개념입니다.

notice 동 눈치채다   directly 부 직접적으로   sound wave 음파
whistle 명 호루라기   pool 명 웅덩이   differently 부 다르게
constant 형 일정한   detect 동 감지하다   thunderstorm 명 뇌우
concept 명 개념

1 강의의 주된 주제는 무엇인가?

(A) 음파의 다양한 종류
(B) 음파들이 서로 다른 속도를 가지고 있는 이유
(C) 원천이 움직임에 따라 소리가 변하는 이유
(D) 음파와 광파가 유사한 방식

2 교수는 왜 물웅덩이를 언급하는가?

(A) 소리가 얼마나 낮아질 수 있는지 보여주기 위해
(B) 음파가 물속에서 변화하는 방식을 보여주기 위해
(C) 음파들 사이의 거리를 설명하기 위해
(D) 떨어지는 돌의 소리를 설명하기 위해

3 교수는 도플러효과에서 움직임의 중요성을 어떻게 설명하는가?

(A) 여러 출처로부터의 정의를 제공함으로써

(B) 일상생활의 친숙한 예시를 듦으로써
(C) 그것이 처음 발견된 방법을 설명함으로써
(D) 그것이 서로 다른 장소들에서 작동하는 방식을 비교함으로써

4 교수에 따르면, 구급차의 사이렌 소리에 대한 설명으로 옳은 것은?

(A) 차량이 빠르면 그것은 더 높아질 것이다.
(B) 소리가 낮으면 그것은 더 커질 것이다.
(C) 차량이 멀어짐에 따라 그것은 더 빨라질 것이다.
(D) 차량이 멈추면 그것은 일정해질 것이다.

강의의 일부를 다시 듣고 질문에 답하시오.
P: So, again, why do we hear the sounds differently?
S: Uh, is it because the distance between the sound waves is different?
P: Good. Someone was paying attention...

5 교수는 왜 이렇게 말하는가:
P: Someone was paying attention...

(A) 학생에게 의견을 제시하도록 독려하기 위해
(B) 학생이 내용을 이해했다는 것을 인정하기 위해
(C) 새로운 개념에 대한 혼란을 방지하기 위해
(D) 강의의 요점을 명확히 하기 위해

iBT Listening Test 1   본문 p. 105

1 (C)   2 (C)   3 (A)   4 (B)   5 (D)

Note-taking

W: Forming a cappella club, had some questions
M: Fill out a club registration form = here or on website
   If approved, notify you by e-mail
W: Club already approved, how to get funding?
   Participate in competition → travel = expensive
M: Direct funding from univ. = $800 to $1,600/semester
   Apply for external grants = offered by biz. or art group
   Have to apply directly to org. that offer
   Website = list of grants & links to org.
   Need more help → stop by music dept.

Listen to a conversation between a student and a student activities office employee.

M: Good morning. Is there something I can help you with?

W: Yes, um, this the student activities office, right? Some students and I are forming an a cappella club. And, uh, I had some questions about this...

M: OK. Well, first, you need to fill out a club registration form. I can give you one here or you can find one on our website. Once you've completed the form, we will review it. Uh, this usually takes a couple of weeks. If your club is approved, we will notify you by e-mail.

W: Um, actually, our club was already approved last week. I guess I should have mentioned it right away. [1]What I wanted to find out was how to get funding for club activities. ²Um, for example, we're hoping to participate in singing competitions against other universities. Obviously, we will have to travel, and traveling can get expensive.

M: ³I see. Well, you have a couple of options... First, all student clubs can apply to get direct funding from the university. But, uh, it's not a lot of money.

W: Um, could you tell me how much we might get?

M: Depending on the number of members, the amount can be anything from $800 to $1,600 per semester. I can give you the application form to fill out now. It should only take a week or so to process...

W: Oh. That's much less money than I was hoping for... And, we only have seven members, so we might not even get the full amount.

M: That's right. Groups that have 10 members or less receive the lowest amount...

W: Well, that amount won't even cover the basics. ³But you mentioned another option?

M: That's right... Student clubs can also apply for external grants. Um, these are funds offered by business or art groups outside the school. These organizations usually provide money every year to support student groups.

W: Oh wow. That's great. But, um, could an a cappella club get one of these grants?

M: Possibly. There are a couple of grants for students who are studying music. ⁵The thing is, you would have to apply directly to the organizations that offer them.

W: That sounds a little complicated.

M: You can say that again... It also takes time. But visiting our website should help. Um, it includes a list of these grants, with links to the organizations that offer them.

W: OK... Does the site also provide advice about the application process?

M: There are some general recommendations. But if you need more help, stop by the music department office. Um, they can give you some useful tips.

W: Great! Thank you so much. ⁴Could I apply for direct funding from the university now?

M: Oh, sure. Let me get the form for you...

학생과 학생활동과 사무실 직원 사이의 대화를 들으시오.

M: 좋은 아침입니다. 제가 도와드릴 일이 있나요?

W: 네, 음, 여기가 학생활동과 사무실이죠, 그렇죠? 학생들 몇 명과 제가 아카펠라 동아리를 만들려고 해요. 그리고, 어, 이것에 대해 질문이 몇 개 있어요...

M: 네, 음, 먼저, 동아리 등록 신청서를 작성하셔야 해요. 제가 여기서 드릴 수도 있고 저희 웹사이트에서 찾으실 수도 있어요. 그 신청서 작성을 끝마치시면, 저희가 그걸 검토할 거예요. 어, 이건 보통 두어 주가 걸려요. 학생의 동아리가 승인되면, 저희가 이메일로 알려드릴 거예요.

W: 음, 사실, 저희 동아리는 지난주에 이미 승인되었어요. 제가 바로 말씀드렸어야 했던 것 같네요. 제가 알고 싶었던 건 동아리 활동을 위한 재정 지원을 받는 방법이에요. 음, 예를 들어, 저희는 다른 대학들에 맞서 노래 경연 대회에 참가하고 싶어요. 분명히, 저희는 여행을 해야 할 거고, 여행은 비싸질 수 있어요.

M: 그렇군요. 음, 두 개의 선택지가 있어요... 첫 번째로, 모든 학생 동아리는 대학으로부터 직접적인 재정 지원을 받기 위해 지원할 수 있어요. 하지만, 어, 많은 돈은 아니에요.

W: 음, 저희가 얼마를 받을 수 있는지 말씀해주실 수 있나요?

M: 회원의 수에 따라, 금액은 학기당 800달러에서 1,600달러까지 될 수 있어요. 지금 작성하실 수 있도록 지원서를 드릴 수 있어요. 처리하는 데 일주일 정도밖에 안 걸릴 거예요...

W: 오. 그건 제가 바랐던 것보다 훨씬 적은 돈이네요... 그리고 저희는 회원이 7명 밖에 없어서, 심지어 전액을 받지 못할 수도 있겠네요.

M: 맞아요. 10명 이하인 단체는 가장 적은 금액을 받아요...

W: 음, 그 금액은 기본적인 비용도 대지 못할 거예요. 그런데 다른 선택지도 언급하셨죠?

M: 맞아요... 학생 동아리는 외부 재정 보조금에도 지원할 수 있어요. 음, 이것들은 학교 외부의 기업이나 예술 단체들에 의해 제공되는 자금이에요. 이 단체들은 보통 매년 학생 단체들을 지원하기 위해 돈을 제공해요.

W: 와. 잘됐네요. 그런데, 음, 아카펠라 동아리도 이 보조금 중 하나를 받을 수 있을까요?

M: 아마도요. 음악을 공부하는 학생들을 위한 보조금이 두어 개 있어요. 중요한 것은, 학생이 그것들을 제공하는 단체에 직접 지원해야 한다는 거예요.

W: 약간 복잡하게 들리네요.

M: 정말 그래요... 게다가 시간도 걸려요. 하지만 저희 웹사이트를 방문하시는 게 도움이 될 거예요. 음, 그것은 이 보조금들의 목록과 그것들을 제공하는 단체들의 링크를 포함하고 있어요.

W: 네... 그 웹사이트가 지원 절차에 관한 조언도 제공하나요?

M: 몇 가지 일반적인 추천 사항들은 있어요. 하지만 더 많은 도움이 필요하시면, 음악학과 사무실에 들르세요. 음, 그들이 몇 가지 유용한 조언을 줄 수 있을 거예요.

W: 잘됐네요! 정말 감사해요. 지금 대학의 직접적인 재정 지원에 지원할 수 있을까요?

M: 오, 물론이죠. 지원서를 가져다 드릴게요...

---

student activities office 학생활동과 사무실 notify ⑧ 알리다
funding ⑲ 재정 지원 participate in ~에 참가하다
direct ⑱ 직접적인 external grant 외부 재정 보조금
general ⑱ 일반적인

1 화자들은 주로 무엇을 논의하고 있는가?

(A) 학생이 음악 단체에 가입해야 할지 여부

(B) 학생이 학교 동아리를 반드시 공식적으로 등록해야 하는 이유

(C) 학생이 단체를 위해 재정 지원을 받을 수 있는 방법

(D) 학생이 캠퍼스에서 어떤 행사들을 개최할 수 있는지

2 학생에 따르면, 동아리 회원들은 왜 여행해야 하는가?

(A) 그들은 다른 학생들을 위해 공연하고 싶어 한다.

(B) 그들은 다른 학교들에서 아카펠라를 홍보하려 한다.

(C) 그들은 다른 단체들과 경쟁하고 싶어 한다.

(D) 그들은 다른 대학의 동아리들과 함께 작업할 계획이다.

3 직원은 어떻게 학생을 돕는가?

(A) 재정 지원을 받을 수 있는 여러 방법을 제안함으로써

(B) 학생에게 몇 가지 지침을 보여줌으로써

(C) 학생의 요청을 검토함으로써

(D) 다수의 단체들의 목록을 제공함으로써

4 학생은 다음에 무엇을 할 것인가?

(A) 다른 과 방문하기

(B) 지원서 작성하기

(C) 신청서 다운로드하기

(D) 대학 웹사이트 보기

대화의 일부를 다시 듣고 질문에 답하시오.

M: The thing is, you would have to apply directly to the organizations that offer them.

W: That sounds a little complicated.

M: You can say that again... It also takes time. But visiting our website should help. Um, it includes a list of these grants, with links to the organizations that offer them.

5 직원은 왜 이렇게 말하는가:

M: You can say that again...

(A) 절차가 어렵지 않다는 것을 시사하기 위해

(B) 학생에게 언급된 내용을 명확하게 설명할 것을 요청하기 위해

(C) 그가 어떤 것이 가장 좋은 선택인지 모른다고 말하기 위해

(D) 학생의 의견에 동의를 표현하기 위해

---

iBT Listening Test 2　　　　　본문 p. 108

1 (D)　　2 (B)　　3 (B)　　4 (C)　　5 (A)　　6 (D)

Note-taking

What Makes Ice Slippery

- Pressure-melting theory = pressure cause ice to melt
  - Ice skates = weight transferred to blade → melt ice
  - Problem 1 = slippery w/o pressure
  - Problem 2 = pressure cause enough melting X
- Repeated mvmt. → heat → melt ice
  - Ice slippery w/o heat
- Latest theory = ice has small layer of liquid on top
  - Water = molecules move constantly
  - Frozen water = molecules form bond & fixed = hard
  - On top = exposed to air → bond X → fixed X

Listen to part of a lecture in a chemistry class.

P: Yesterday, we learned how a solid object changes into a liquid. It has to reach its melting point. And, in order to do that, you have to increase the temperature or apply pressure to the object... Now, with this in mind, let's move on to our main topic for today... ¹What makes ice slippery? Does anyone want to guess?

S1: Um, isn't it like you said? We apply pressure to ice when we walk on it. This causes the

surface of the ice to melt... Then, the melted ice becomes slippery.

P: OK, that's a reasonable explanation. And since the 19th century, that is what scientists believed. ²They called it the pressure-melting theory because pressure from a heavy object can cause ice to melt. Let me give you the example that is commonly used. It's, uh, from ice skating... On the bottom of every pair of ice skates, there are very thin blades, right? Now, when you put the ice skates on, all of your weight is transferred to the blades. So, according to the pressure-melting theory, the blades create a lot of pressure on top of the ice and melt it. That's what makes the ice slippery. ³But there are problems with the pressure-melting theory. First, the ice is slippery even without the pressure from ice skates. It's also slippery when you walk on it with regular shoes. ³And second, pressure doesn't cause enough melting. Um, for instance, scientists have discovered that the pressure from a person's weight can only melt the ice a little. So, uh, you would need to be extremely heavy to melt the ice a lot... Are there any other guesses?

S2: What about heat? Doesn't the act of moving shoes or skates over ice create heat? Maybe it's the heat that melts the ice. Or maybe it's both pressure and heat.

P: OK. Once again, that's a good guess based on what we know about pressure and heat. In fact, it's partly correct. ⁶Repeated movements create heat. So moving over ice can make skates hotter. Then, the increased heat helps to melt the ice, which makes it slippery... However, we also know that ice becomes slippery as soon as you step on it. So ice can be slippery even without heat. We need a better answer.

⁴All right. So the latest theory we have is that ice has a small layer of liquid water on top. This happens due to the structure of water. Um, as you know, another name for water is H_2O. This is because each water molecule is made of two hydrogen atoms and one oxygen atom. Now, in liquid water, the molecules of water move around constantly. ⁵But when you freeze liquid water to make ice, each frozen water molecule sticks to another molecule next to it. They form bonds and become fixed in place. This is why ice feels hard. But what happens on the top of the ice? There, the ice is exposed to air. So some of the molecules in the ice are not able to form any bonds. As a result, these molecules do not stay fixed and continue to move around like liquid water. This movement is what makes the top layer of ice stay partly liquid. It is also what makes ice slippery.

화학 강의의 일부를 들으시오.

P: 어제, 우리는 고체가 어떻게 액체로 변하는지에 대해 배웠어요. 그것이 용해점에 도달해야 하죠. 그리고, 그렇게 하기 위해서는, 온도를 높이거나 물체에 압력을 가해야 해요... 이제, 이를 염두에 두고, 오늘 우리의 주된 주제로 넘어갑시다... 무엇이 얼음을 미끄

럽게 만들까요? 추측해볼 사람 있나요?

S1: 음, 말씀하신 대로 아닌가요? 얼음 위를 걸어갈 때 우리는 얼음에 압력을 가하죠. 이것이 얼음의 표면이 녹게 만들어요... 그러면, 녹은 얼음은 미끄러워지죠.

P: 좋아요, 합리적인 설명이네요. 그리고 19세기 이래로, 그것이 과학자들이 믿었던 거예요. 무거운 물체로부터의 압력이 얼음을 녹게 할 수 있었기 때문에 그들은 그것을 압력 용해 이론이라고 불렀어요. 흔하게 사용되는 예시를 하나 들어 보죠. 그건, 어, 아이스 스케이팅에서 나온 거예요... 모든 아이스 스케이트의 바닥에는 매우 얇은 날이 있어요, 그렇죠? 자, 아이스 스케이트를 신을 때, 모든 체중은 날로 옮겨져요. 그러니까, 압력 용해 이론에 따르면, 그 날들은 얼음 위에 많은 압력을 만들어내고 그것을 녹여요. 그게 얼음을 미끄럽게 만드는 거죠. 하지만 압력 용해 이론에는 문제점이 있어요. 첫째로, 얼음은 아이스 스케이트로부터의 압력 없이도 미끄러워요. 보통 신발을 신고 그 위를 걸어도 역시 미끄럽죠. 그리고 둘째로, 압력은 충분한 용해를 만들어내지 않아요. 음, 예를 들어, 과학자들은 사람 체중으로부터의 압력이 얼음을 약간만 녹일 수 있다는 걸 발견했어요. 그래서, 어, 얼음을 많이 녹이려면 엄청나게 무거워야 할 거예요... 다른 추측 있나요?

S2: 열은 어떤가요? 얼음 위에서 신발이나 스케이트를 움직이는 행동이 열을 만들어내지 않나요? 얼음을 녹이는 것은 아마도 그 열일 거예요. 아니면 아마 압력과 열 둘 다이거나요.

P: 좋아요. 다시 한번, 그건 우리가 압력과 열에 대해 알고 있는 것에 기초한 좋은 추측이에요. 사실, 그건 부분적으로 맞아요. 반복된 움직임은 열을 만들어내요. 그래서 얼음 위에서 움직이는 것은 스케이트를 더 뜨겁게 만들 수 있어요. 그리고, 높아진 열은 얼음을 녹이는 것을 돕고, 이는 얼음을 미끄럽게 만들죠... 하지만, 우리는 얼음을 밟자마자 그것이 미끄러워진다는 것도 알고 있어요. 그러니까 얼음은 열 없이도 미끄러워질 수 있어요. 더 좋은 답이 필요해요.

좋습니다. 자, 우리가 가지고 있는 최신 이론은 얼음이 그 위에 액체 형태의 물의 작은 층을 가지고 있다는 거예요. 이것은 물의 구조 때문에 발생해요. 음, 알다시피, 물의 다른 이름은 H_2O입니다. 이는 각 물 분자가 두 개의 수소 원자와 한 개의 산소 원자로 이루어져 있기 때문이에요. 자, 액체 형태의 물에서, 물의 분자들은 끊임없이 움직여요. 하지만 얼음을 만들기 위해 액체 형태의 물을 얼리면, 각각의 얼린 물 분자는 그것의 옆에 있는 다른 분자에 달라붙어요. 그것들은 결합을 형성하고 제자리에 고정돼요. 이것이 얼음이 딱딱하게 느껴지는 이유예요. 그런데 얼음 위에서는 무슨 일이 일어날까요? 그곳에서, 얼음은 공기에 노출돼요. 그래서 얼음에 있는 분자들의 일부는 어떠한 결합도 형성할 수 없어요. 그 결과, 이 분자들은 고정되지 않고 액체 형태의 물처럼 계속해서 움직여요. 이 움직임이 얼음의 가장 위층이 부분적으로 액체 형태로 유지되도록 만드는 거예요. 그것이 얼음을 미끄럽게 만드는 것이기도 하죠.

solid object 고체   liquid 명 액체; 형 액체 형태의
melting point 용해점   pressure 명 압력   slippery 형 미끄러운
reasonable 형 합리적인   theory 명 이론   transfer 동 옮기다
partly 부 부분적으로   layer 명 층   molecule 명 분자
hydrogen 명 수소   atom 명 원자   bond 명 결합
fixed 형 고정된   in place 제자리에

1 강의는 주로 무엇에 관한 것인가?

(A) 고체의 용해점

(B) 압력과 열의 영향

(C) 물을 얼음으로 만드는 과정

(D) 얼음이 미끄러운 이유

2 교수는 왜 아이스 스케이팅을 언급하는가?

(A) 얼음이 형성되는 방법을 설명하기 위해

(B) 이론이 작동하는 방식을 보여주기 위해

(C) 설명에서의 결함을 지적하기 위해

(D) 견해가 틀린 이유를 설명하기 위해

3 교수는 압력 용해 이론의 문제로 무엇을 언급하는가?

(A) 그것은 특정한 장소에 있는 얼음에만 적용된다.

(B) 그것은 용해의 양에 대해 틀렸다.

(C) 그것은 무게의 차이를 설명하지 않는다.

(D) 그것은 기온이 더 시원할 때 발표되었다.

4 교수는 최신 이론을 어떻게 소개하는가?

(A) 학생들에게 이전 강의에 대해 상기시킴으로써

(B) 유명한 실험을 설명함으로써

(C) 물이 조직된 방식을 설명함으로써

(D) 서로 다른 액체들을 비교함으로써

5 교수에 따르면, 얼음은 왜 딱딱하게 느껴지는가?

(A) 얼린 물 분자들이 결합을 형성한다.

(B) 물이 서로 분리된 층으로 언다.

(C) 공기에 노출된 부분이 매우 건조하다.

(D) 물 분자가 얼음 속에서 느리게 움직인다.

강의의 일부를 다시 듣고 질문에 답하시오.

P: Repeated movements create heat. So moving over ice can make skates hotter. Then, the increased heat helps to melt the ice, which makes it slippery... However, we also know that ice becomes slippery as soon as you step on it. So ice can be slippery even without heat. We need a better answer.

6 교수는 이렇게 말함으로써 무엇을 의미하는가:

P: We need a better answer.

(A) 얼음 위에서 스케이트를 타면 미끄러움이 서서히 줄어든다.

(B) 새로운 아이스 스케이트는 사람들이 더 빠르게 움직이도록 도와줄 수 있다.

(C) 움직이는 공기는 얼음이 더 빠르게 녹게 한다.

(D) 열은 얼음이 미끄러운 이유를 설명하기에 충분하지 않다.

Vocabulary Review
본문 p. 112

1 slippery	2 anthropologist	3 canal
4 criticism	5 funding	6 suburbs
7 fixed	8 unplanned	9 concept
10 (A)	11 (C)	12 (A)
13 (C)	14 (A)	

Connecting Contents

Example
본문 p. 115

A. Suggested: (A), (B), (D) Not Suggested: (C)
B. Carnivores: (A), (D) Herbivores: (C) Omnivores: (B)

A.

Note-taking

S: Applied for internship → interview on Thursday
　Some tips?
P: Go online → learn about company
　Practice answering interview questions w/ friend
　Get to location b.f. interview → nervous ↓ & prepare

Listen to a conversation between a student and a professor.

S: Hi, Professor Nelson. Do you have a minute?

P: Sure, Carl. What's on your mind?

S: I applied for a summer internship at a manufacturing company, and I have an interview on Thursday. I was wondering if you could give me some tips.

P: I'd be happy to. Let's see... ^AFirst, go online and learn all you can about the company. ^B And make sure to practice answering common interview questions with a friend.

S: Got it. Anything else?

P: ^DI also recommend that you get to the interview location about 15 minutes before the interview starts. That way, you will be less nervous and can prepare for the interview.

S: Great. Thanks for your suggestions, Professor Nelson.

학생과 교수 사이의 대화를 들으시오.

S: 안녕하세요, Nelson 교수님. 잠깐 시간 있으신가요?

P: 물론이지, Carl. 무슨 일이니?

S: 저는 제조 회사에서의 여름 인턴직에 지원했고, 목요일에 면접이 있어요. 교수님께서 몇 가지 조언을 해주실 수 있는지 궁금해요

P: 기꺼이 그러마. 어디 보자... 먼저, 온라인에서 그 회사에 관해 네가 할 수 있는 모든 것을 알아보렴. 그리고 친구와 함께 일반적인 면접 질문들에 답변하는 것을 꼭 연습하렴.

S: 알겠습니다. 또 있나요?

P: 나는 네가 면접이 시작하기 15분쯤 전에 면접 장소에 가는 것을 추천해. 그렇게 하면, 너는 덜 긴장할 거고 면접에 대비할 수 있을 거야.

S: 좋네요. 의견 감사합니다, Nelson 교수님.

---

apply for ~에 지원하다　manufacturing company 제조 회사
tip 圆 조언, 팁　common 圆 일반적인, 흔한

B.

교수는 학생이 면접을 위해 무엇을 할 것을 제안하는가? 다음의 항목이 제안된 선택지인지를 표시하시오. 각 항목에 적절한 칸을 클릭하시오.

	제안됨	제안 안 됨
(A) 온라인으로 회사 조사하기	V	
(B) 몇 가지 질문에 대비하기	V	
(C) 다른 교수와 이야기하기		V
(D) 장소에 일찍 도착하기	V	

Note-taking
Teeth of Different Animals

- Carnivore = eat only meat
  - Front teeth = long & pointed ∴ catch & hold prey
  - Back teeth = sharp & thin like knives
- Herbivore = only eat plants
  - Back teeth = wide & flat ∴ help chew leaves & nuts
- Omnivore = eat both meat & plants
  - Teeth = similar to our own

Listen to part of a lecture in a biology class.

P: So we've recently been discussing the diets of different animals. Well, the diets of different animals have caused changes in their bodies. Today, I'm going to talk about their teeth.

^DIn carnivores, which are animals that eat only meat, the front teeth are long and pointed. This helps them to easily catch and hold prey. ^ATheir back teeth are sharp and very thin. They are like knives that cut meat into smaller pieces. ^CBut, in herbivores, which only eat plants, the back teeth are wide and flat. They also have very rough surfaces. This helps them chew leaves and nuts. ^BFinally, there are omnivores, which eat both meat and plants. Um, their teeth are quite similar to our own.

생물학 강의의 일부를 들으시오.

P: 자, 최근에 우리는 다양한 동물들의 식습관에 대해 논의해 왔어요. 음, 다양한 동물들의 식습관은 그것들의 몸에 변화를 일으켜 왔죠. 오늘은, 그것들의 치아에 대해 얘기할 거예요.
고기만을 먹는 동물인 육식동물의 경우, 앞니는 길고 뾰족해요. 이것은 그것들이 쉽게 먹이를 잡고 붙들고 있도록 도와줘요. 뒤쪽에 있는 치아들은 날카롭고 매우 얇아요. 그것들은 고기를 더 작은 조각들로 자르는 칼 같아요. 하지만, 식물만을 먹는 초식동물의 경우, 뒤쪽에 있는 치아들은 넓고 평평해요. 그것들은 또한 매우 거친 표면을 가지고 있어요. 이것은 그것들이 나뭇잎과 열매를 씹는 것을 도와줘요. 마지막으로, 고기와 식물을 둘 다 먹는 잡식동물이 있어요. 음, 그것들의 치아는 우리의 것과 꽤 비슷합니다.

---

carnivore 圆 육식동물　pointed 圆 뾰족한　herbivore 圆 초식동물
rough 圆 거친　omnivore 圆 잡식동물

강의에서, 교수는 육식동물, 초식동물, 잡식동물의 치아에 대해 논한다. 다음의 항목이 육식동물, 초식동물, 잡식동물의 치아 중 어떤 것에 대한 설명인지를 표시하시오. 각 항목에 적절한 칸을 클릭하시오.

	육식동물	초식동물	잡식동물
(A) 뒤쪽에 있는 치아들이 칼 같다.	V		
(B) 앞과 뒤에 있는 치아들이 사람의 치아와 비슷하다.			V
(C) 뒤쪽에 있는 치아가 넓고 평평하다.		V	
(D) 앞니가 길고 뾰족하다.	V		

Listening Practice 1

1 (C) 2 (B) 3 (B), (C) 4 Yes: (A), (C), (D) No: (B)
5 (D)

Note-taking

W: Want to know steps to form new org. = choir
M: Tell why you'd like to form a choir
W: Choirs compete = important for young singers
   Get exp. performing on stage
   Meet successful singers & get advice
M: New clubs receive $100
W: Choir needs money ∵ songbooks & costumes etc.
M: Lower costs = own costume & library for songbook
W: Perform only in competitions nearby
   Need to find out how much interest is on campus

Listen to a conversation between a student and a student activities office employee.

M: Hi. What brings you to the office today?

W: Hello. ¹Um, I'm here because I have an idea for a student club. But I'm not sure what to do. I'd like to know what the steps are to form a new organization.

M: OK... Could you tell me about what kind of club you want to form? We might already have one like it at the school.

W: Basically, I want to form a choir. ²Um, I was shocked to hear that the school doesn't have one already.

M: I know! Actually, there was an old school choir several years ago. But the students lost interest in it over time. It would be great to have a new one. So anyway, to start a club, first you're going to need to tell me why you'd like to form a choir.

W: Well, obviously, I like to sing. But other than that, choirs often compete, which is really important for young singers. ³CThe students can get experience performing on stage. ³BAnd they can also meet successful singers and get advice from them.

M: Hmm... I suppose competitions are very useful for students...

W: That's why I want to start an official school choir. Of course, we will need some money from the school to enter competitions.

M: ⁵Hmm... To be honest, new clubs receive just a hundred dollars at first.

W: A hundred dollars? That's not what I expected... I mean, a choir needs money to pay for songbooks, costumes, bus tickets, and many other things...

M: Well, don't get discouraged. There are a few options that you can try. One of the quickest and simplest things you can do is to lower your costs. ⁴AFor example, you could have the choir members make their own costumes instead of buying them from a store. ⁴DAnd, um, another idea is to go to the library for songbooks. You can print out as many copies as you need and take them with you.

W: Yes, I guess we could do those things... ⁴CAnd for a while, we could perform only in competitions that are being held nearby. Uh, that way, we can get there easily on local transportation.

M: That's a good idea.

W: Before I submit a new club registration form, though, I need to find out how much interest there is on campus...

M: Of course. Feel free to come back here anytime you have a question.

W: Thank you, I will.

학생과 학생활동과 사무실 직원 사이의 대화를 들으시오.

M: 안녕하세요. 어떤 일로 사무실에 오셨나요?

W: 안녕하세요. 음, 학생 동아리를 위한 구상이 있어서 왔어요. 그런데 무엇을 해야 할지 모르겠어요. 새로운 단체를 만들기 위한 단계들이 무엇인지 알고 싶어요.

M: 네... 어떤 종류의 동아리를 만들고 싶으신지 말씀해 주시겠어요? 학교에 이미 비슷한 것이 있을지도 몰라요.

W: 기본적으로, 저는 합창단을 만들고 싶어요. 음, 학교에 이미 합창단이 없다는 걸 듣고 깜짝 놀랐어요.

M: 맞아요! 사실, 몇 년 전에는 이전의 학교 합창단이 있었어요. 하지만 시간이 지나면서 학생들이 그것에 대한 관심을 잃었어요. 새로운 것이 생기면 정말 좋겠네요. 그러니까 어쨌든, 새로운 동아리를 시작하시려면, 먼저 합창단을 만들고 싶은 이유를 제게 설명해 주셔야 해요.

W: 음, 확실히, 저는 노래하는 걸 좋아해요. 하지만 그것 외에도, 합창단들은 자주 경쟁하는데, 이는 젊은 가수들에게 아주 중요해요. 학생들은 무대에서 공연하며 경험을 쌓을 수 있어요. 그리고 그들은 성공적인 가수들을 만나고 그들에게서 조언을 얻을 수도 있어요.

M: 흠... 대회가 학생들에게 매우 유용한 것 같네요...

W: 그게 제가 공식적인 학교 합창단을 시작하고 싶은 이유예요. 물론, 저희는 대회에 참가하기 위해 학교의 돈이 좀 필요할 거예요.

M: 흠... 솔직히 말씀드리자면, 새로운 동아리들은 처음에 100달러만 받아요.

W: 100달러요? 그건 제가 기대했던 게 아니에요... 제 말은, 합창단은 노래책, 의상, 버스표, 그리고 다른 많은 것들에 지불하기 위한 돈이 필요해요...

M: 음, 낙담하지 마세요. 시도해 보실 수 있는 몇 가지 선택지가 있어요. 하실 수 있는 가장 빠르고 간단한 방법 중 하나는 비용을 낮추는 거예요. 예를 들어, 상점에서 구매하는 대신 합창단원들에게

CHAPTER 06 | Connecting Contents **53**

자신의 의상을 만들게 할 수 있어요. 그리고, 음, 또 다른 방안은 노래책을 위해 도서관에 가는 거예요. 필요한 만큼의 부수를 인쇄해서 가지고 가실 수 있어요.

W: 네, 저희가 그런 것들을 할 수 있을 것 같네요... 그리고 얼마간, 저희는 근처에서 열리는 대회에서만 공연할 수 있겠네요. 어, 그렇게 하면, 저희는 지역 교통수단으로 그곳에 쉽게 갈 수 있어요.

M: 좋은 생각이에요.

W: 그런데, 새로운 동아리 등록 양식을 제출하기 전에, 저는 캠퍼스 내에 얼마나 많은 관심이 있는지 알아봐야 해요...

M: 물론이죠. 질문이 있으시면 언제든지 여기로 돌아오세요.

W: 감사합니다, 그럴게요.

form 동 만들다; 명 양식   choir 명 합창단
over time 시간이 지나면서   obviously 부 확실히, 분명히
official 형 공식적인   songbook 명 노래책   costume 명 의상
lower 동 낮추다   nearby 부 근처에서   transportation 명 교통수단

1 학생은 왜 학생활동과 사무실을 찾아가는가?

(A) 단체의 책임자를 찾기 위해

(B) 노래 대회에 관한 조언을 얻기 위해

(C) 새로운 동아리를 시작하는 방법에 관해 문의하기 위해

(D) 이전의 합창단에 무슨 일이 일어났는지 알아보기 위해

2 직원은 왜 이전의 학교 합창단을 언급하는가?

(A) 학교 동아리를 설립하기 위한 단계를 설명하기 위해

(B) 그 역시 합창단이 없는 게 놀랍다는 것을 시사하기 위해

(C) 새로운 동아리에 대한 필요성이 없다는 것을 상기시키기 위해

(D) 학생이 가입할 학교 합창단을 추천하기 위해

3 학생에 따르면, 합창 대회의 장점은 무엇인가? 2개의 답을 고르시오.

(A) 공연하며 나라를 여행할 기회를 갖는 것

(B) 다른 가수들을 만나고 그들로부터 배우는 것

(C) 관객 앞에서 노래할 수 있는 것

(D) 상금을 받을 기회를 얻는 것

4 대화에서, 화자들은 합창단이 비용을 낮출 수 있는 방법에 대해 제안한다. 다음의 항목이 제안사항이었는지를 표시하시오. 각 항목에 적절한 칸을 클릭하시오.

	예	아니오
(A) 자신의 의상 만들기	V	
(B) 버스표 할인받기		V
(C) 지역 대회에만 참가하기	V	
(D) 도서관에서 노래책 인쇄하기	V	

대화의 일부를 다시 듣고 질문에 답하시오.

M: Hmm... To be honest, new clubs receive just a hundred dollars at first.

W: A hundred dollars? That's not what I expected... I mean, a choir needs money to pay for songbooks, costumes, bus tickets, and many other things...

5 학생은 왜 이렇게 말하는가:

W: That's not what I expected...

(A) 직원이 실수했다는 것을 암시하기 위해

(B) 그녀가 직원의 말을 제대로 듣지 못했다는 것을 나타내기 위해

(C) 그녀가 합창단을 만드는 방법을 모른다는 것을 말하기 위해

(D) 그녀가 돈의 액수에 실망했다는 것을 보여주기 위해

Listening Practice 2
본문 p. 119

1 (D)   2 (D)   3 (B), (C)   4 (A)
5 Rivera: (B) Orozco: (A), (D) Siqueiros: (C)

Note-taking
Mexican Muralism

- Mexican muralism started as govt. project
- Why murals? easy to understand & anyone could see
- Rivera = traditional & positive, scenes of everyday life
  - European style at first → became more Mexican
  - Used earth colors & symbols of land
- Orozco = negative, painted in dark & dramatic colors
  - Often critical of upper class
- Siqueiros = themes related to lower class
  - Concerned about future, about science & technology

Listen to part of a lecture in an art history class.

P: Last time, we learned about how art can be used for different purposes. Um, for instance, it can be used to communicate ideas and remember important events. ¹Well, today, we will look at Mexican muralism, which was an art movement in Mexico in the early 20th century. Specifically, we will consider how muralism came about and discuss its characteristics.

²So Mexican muralism started as a project of the Mexican government. Um, this happened after the Mexican Revolution of 1910 to 1920. You see, the revolution changed Mexican society in many ways. Mainly, it gave more power to the middle and lower classes of Mexican society. So the new Mexican government wanted to remember this important event. To do this, it hired well-known Mexican artists to produce murals... Um, murals are basically wall paintings. And, in Mexico, they were painted on the walls of public buildings.

Why murals? Well, there were several reasons... ³ᶜOne reason is that the pictures on murals were easy to understand. Uh, many people in the lower classes couldn't read or write. But they could look at the pictures in a mural and quickly get its message. ³ᴮAlso, anyone passing by could see the murals since they were painted in public places. They were often large and colorful...

Um, the murals covered many themes and ideas, too... As I said, they were intended to help people remember the Mexican Revolution, so they were often political. But the government also wanted the murals to make Mexicans feel proud of their culture, and, um, to think positively about the future. So there were inspiring images of people working together on farms and in factories. ⁴Um, the government even tried to give artists guidelines on what to paint. But, uh, thankfully, these were later removed. Artists work better when they have the freedom to choose their own styles and themes...

OK. Now, among the artists who painted murals, three became very famous. They were known as "The Three Great Ones." They were Diego Rivera, José Clemente Orozco, and David Siqueiros. Um, each one became known for a particular style and theme of mural... For instance, Rivera's work was traditional and positive. He liked to show scenes of everyday life or images from Mexico's past. 5BHis murals were painted in a European style at first, but they gradually became more Mexican. They, uh, frequently used earth colors and symbols of the land. Orozco's murals, however, were more negative. 5AThey were painted in dark, dramatic colors. 5DThey were also often critical of Mexico's upper class. And, um, lastly, we have Siqueiros, who was the youngest. Siqueiros was involved in Communism and so his work often had themes related to Mexico's lower class. 5CBut he was also concerned about the future and painted scenes about science and technology with lots of bold lines.

미술사학 강의의 일부를 들으시오.

P: 지난 시간에, 우리는 미술이 어떻게 다양한 목적을 위해 사용될 수 있는지에 대해 배웠습니다. 음, 예를 들어, 그것은 생각을 전달하고 중요한 사건들을 기억하기 위해 사용될 수 있죠. 음, 오늘, 우리는 20세기 초반 멕시코의 미술 운동이었던 멕시코 벽화주의를 살펴볼 거예요. 특히, 벽화주의가 어떻게 생겨났는지를 살펴보고 그것의 특징에 대해 논의할 거예요.

자, 멕시코 벽화주의는 멕시코 정부의 프로젝트로 시작했어요. 음, 이것은 1910년부터 1920년까지의 멕시코 혁명 이후에 일어났어요. 그러니까, 그 혁명은 여러 방식으로 멕시코 사회를 변화시켰어요. 주로, 그것은 멕시코 사회의 중산층과 하층 계급에게 더 많은 권력을 주었죠. 자, 새로운 멕시코 정부는 이 중요한 사건을 기억하고 싶어했어요. 이렇게 하기 위해서, 유명한 멕시코 화가들을 고용하여 벽화를 제작하게 했죠... 음, 벽화는 기본적으로 벽에 그리는 그림이에요. 그리고, 멕시코에서, 그것들은 공공 건물의 벽에 그려졌어요.

왜 벽화일까요? 음, 몇 가지 이유가 있었어요... 한 가지 이유는 벽화의 그림이 이해하기 쉬웠기 때문이에요. 어, 하층 계급의 많은 사람들은 읽거나 쓸 수 없었어요. 하지만 그들은 벽화의 그림을 바라보고 그것의 메시지를 빠르게 이해할 수 있었죠. 또한, 그것들이 공공장소에 그려졌기 때문에 지나가는 누구든지 그 벽화들을 볼 수 있었어요. 그것들은 종종 크고 화려했어요...

음, 그 벽화들은 또한 많은 주제와 아이디어를 다루었어요... 제가 말했듯이, 그것들은 사람들이 멕시코 혁명을 기억하는 것을 돕기 위한 것이었기 때문에, 종종 정치적이었습니다. 하지만 정부는 또한 벽화가 멕시코인들로 하여금 그들의 문화에 자부심을 느끼고, 음, 미래에 대해 긍정적으로 생각하도록 해주기를 원했어요. 그래서 농장과 공장에서 사람들이 함께 일하는 것을 보여주는 고무적인 그림들이 있었어요. 음, 정부는 심지어 화가들에게 무엇을 그릴지에 대한 지침을 주려고 했어요. 하지만, 어, 고맙게도, 이것들은 나중에 없어졌어요. 화가들은 자신의 스타일과 주제를 선택할 자유가 있을 때 더 잘 작업하죠...

좋습니다. 자, 벽화를 그렸던 화가 중에서, 세 명이 매우 유명해졌어요. 그들은 "세 명의 위대한 사람들"로 알려졌어요. 그들은 디에고 리베라, 호세 클레멘테 오로스코, 다비드 시케이로스였어요. 음, 그들 각자는 독특한 스타일과 벽화의 주제로 알려지게 되었어요... 예를 들어, 리베라의 작품은 전통적이고 긍정적이었어요. 그는 일상생활이나 멕시코의 과거에 대한 그림을 보여주는 걸 좋아했어요. 그의 벽화는 처음에 유럽 스타일로 그려졌지만, 점차 더 멕시코식이 되었어요. 그것들은, 어, 자주 땅의 색과 대지의 상징을 사용했어요. 하지만, 오로스코의 벽화들은 더 부정적이었어요. 그것들은 어둡고, 극적인 색들로 그려졌죠. 그것들은 종종 멕시코의 상류층에 대해 비판적이기도 했어요. 그리고, 음, 마지막으로, 시케이로스가 있는데, 그는 가장 어렸어요. 시케이로스는 공산주의에 관여했고 그래서 그의 작품은 종종 멕시코의 하층 계급과 관련된 주제를 가지고 있었어요. 하지만 그 또한 미래에 관심이 있었으며 많은 굵은 선을 이용하여 과학과 기술에 대한 장면들을 그렸습니다.

---

purpose 명 목적   communicate 동 전달하다
muralism 명 벽화주의   specifically 부 특히   revolution 명 혁명
mural 명 벽화   cover 동 다루다   theme 명 주제
political 형 정치적인   positively 부 긍정적으로
inspiring 형 고무적인, 영감을 주는   guideline 명 지침
particular 형 독특한   traditional 형 전통적인
gradually 부 점차   frequently 부 자주   symbol 명 상징
negative 형 부정적인   critical 형 비판적인
Communism 명 공산주의

1 강의의 주된 주제는 무엇인가?

(A) 미술의 다양한 목적

(B) 미술이 문화적 혁명을 이끈 방식

(C) 일부 화가들이 미술 형식으로 벽화를 선택하는 이유

(D) 미술 운동의 발전과 특징

2 교수는 왜 멕시코 혁명을 언급하는가?

(A) 멕시코가 많은 도전을 겪었다는 것을 보여주기 위해

(B) 멕시코 화가들이 많은 사람들에게 영감을 주었다는 것을 시사하기 위해

(C) 멕시코 사회에서 미술의 중요성을 강조하기 위해

(D) 멕시코 정부가 프로젝트를 시작한 이유를 설명하기 위해

3 교수에 따르면, 멕시코 정부는 미술 형식으로 왜 벽화를 선택했는가? 2개의 답을 고르시오.

(A) 그것들은 제작하기에 비싸지 않았다.

(B) 그것들은 대중에 의해 쉽게 보여질 수 있었다.

(C) 그것들은 말 대신 그림을 이용했다.

(D) 그들은 손상된 건물을 가리기 원했다.

4 화가들에 대한 정부의 지침에 대한 교수의 의견은 무엇인가?

(A) 그것들은 화가들에게 더 적은 자유를 주었다.

(B) 그것들은 더 잘 설명되었어야 했다.

(C) 그것들은 많은 개선을 필요로 했다.

(D) 그것들은 충분히 엄격하지 않았다.

5 다음의 항목이 리베라, 오로스코, 시케이로스의 미술 중 어떤 것에 대한 설명인지를 표시하시오. 각 항목에 적절한 칸을 클릭하시오.

	리베라	오로스코	시케이로스
(A) 어둡고 극적인 색을 사용했다		V	
(B) 시간이 지나며 스타일이 변했다	V		
(C) 미래에 관심이 있었다			V
(D) 상류층을 비판했다		V	

Listening Practice 3

본문 p. 121

1 (C)   2 (A)   3 (C)-(D)-(A)-(B)   4 (B)   5 (D)

Note-taking

M: Just transferred, want to be involved in newspaper
    Writer at old school ∴ want that position again
W: Need to review application, deadline = Sept. 15
M: Require short article?
W: Not when apply, look over application → editor contact
M: Write about certain topic or choose topic?
W: Let us know section → get topic based on that
    Article = 500~800 words long
    All applicants = brief interview
    Each summer, 2 students = intern at *Boston Globe*

Listen to a conversation between a student and a university administrator.

M: Hi. Is this the office of *The College Times*?

W: That's correct. We produce the student newspaper for Boston College. How can I help you today?

M: I just transferred here from Texas. I used to work at a university newspaper there. ¹So I'd really like to be involved in the newspaper here. Um, do you have any positions available?

W: Actually, we do. But what are you interested in doing, exactly? Most students work as writers.

M: ²Well, I was a writer at my old school's paper, so I want to have that position again. Could you explain the application process to me?

W: ³ᶜFirst, we need to review your application to make sure you have the right qualifications. So you'll need to submit one to us. ⁵Keep in mind that the deadline for applications is on September 15.

M: Got it. Um, just to check... Do you require a short article as a sample?

W: Not when you apply. ³ᴰOnce we have looked over your application, our editor will contact you to ask for one.

M: Could you tell me more about that? Would I need to write about a certain topic, or can I choose any topic I want?

W: ³ᴬJust let us know which section you're interested in writing for in your application. Then, you'll get a topic based on that. Your article will have to be between 500 and 800 words long.

M: OK. And if the editor is satisfied with my article, will I be able to write for the newspaper after that?

W: ³ᴮActually, there's one more step. All applicants also have to go through a brief interview. It gives us an opportunity to find out more about you and check if you'll get along well here.

M: I understand. Is there anything else I should be aware of before I submit my application?

W: Well, some of our students have become journalists at national newspapers after they graduated. Some of them even hold workshops for the students here.

M: That's wonderful. It seems like it'd also be a good opportunity for me to pursue a career in journalism here.

W: Exactly. ⁴In addition, each summer, two of our students get a chance to work as interns at the *Boston Globe*. It's the city's largest newspaper.

M: Wow. How are they chosen?

W: The company reviews several articles from each student and then makes their selections.

M: OK, this all sounds amazing. I'm going to go back to my dormitory now and prepare my application.

학생과 대학 관리자 사이의 대화를 들으시오.

M: 안녕하세요. 여기가 'The College Times' 사무실인가요?

W: 맞아요. 저희는 보스턴 대학교를 위한 학생 신문을 만들어요. 오늘 어떻게 도와드릴까요?

M: 저는 이제 막 텍사스에서 여기로 편입했어요. 저는 그곳의 대학 신문에서 일했어요. 그래서 저는 정말로 이곳의 신문에 참여하고 싶어요. 음, 구할 수 있는 자리가 있나요?

W: 사실, 있어요. 그런데 정확히 무엇을 하는 데 관심이 있으시죠? 대부분의 학생들은 기자로 일해요.

M: 음, 저는 이전 학교 신문에서 기자였어서, 다시 그 자리를 갖고 싶어요. 제게 지원 절차를 설명해주실 수 있나요?

W: 먼저, 학생이 올바른 자격 요건을 갖고 계신지 확인하기 위해 저희가 학생의 지원서를 검토해야 해요. 그래서 학생은 저희에게 지원서를 제출해 주셔야 해요. 지원서의 기한이 9월 15일이라는 걸 기억해 주세요.

M: 알겠어요. 음, 확인하고 싶어서 그런데... 샘플로 짧은 기사가 필요하신가요?

W: 지원하실 때는 아니에요. 저희가 학생의 지원서를 살펴보고 나면, 저희 편집장이 기사를 요청하기 위해 학생에게 연락할 거예요.

M: 그것에 관해 더 말씀해주실 수 있나요? 제가 특정 주제에 대해 써야 하나요, 아니면 제가 원하는 주제를 선택할 수 있나요?

W: 그냥 학생의 지원서에 학생이 어떤 분야에 관해 쓰는 데 관심이 있는지 알려주세요. 그러면, 그것에 기반한 주제를 받게 될 거예요. 기사는 500에서 800단어 사이의 길이여야 할 거예요.

M: 알겠어요. 그리고 만약 편집장이 제 기사에 만족하면, 그 후에는 제가 신문을 위해 기사를 쓸 수 있게 되나요?

W: 사실, 한 단계가 더 있어요. 모든 지원자들은 짧은 면접을 거쳐야 해요. 그건 저희가 학생에 대해 더 많이 알고 여기서 잘 지내실지 확인할 기회를 주죠.

M: 이해해요. 지원서를 제출하기 전에 제가 알아야 할 다른 것이 있나요?

(D) 설명되지 않은 것에 대해 묻기 위해

W: 음, 저희 학생들 중 몇 명은 졸업 후에 전국지의 기자가 됐어요. 심지어 그들 중 몇 명은 이곳의 학생들을 위해 워크숍을 열어요.

M: 멋지네요. 제가 여기서 저널리즘 분야의 경력을 추구할 좋은 기회가 될 것 같아요.

W: 정확해요. 게다가, 매년 여름, 저희 학생들 중 두 명은 'Boston Globe'에서 인턴으로 일할 기회를 얻어요. 그건 시에서 가장 큰 신문이에요.

M: 와. 그들은 어떻게 선발되나요?

W: 그 회사가 각 학생의 기사 몇 개를 검토한 다음 선발을 해요.

M: 네, 모든 것이 놀랍게 들리네요. 이제 제 기숙사로 돌아가서 지원서를 준비할게요.

produce ⑧ 만들다 transfer ⑧ (대학을) 편입하다, 이동하다
involve ⑧ 참여하다 qualification ⑲ 자격 요건
look over 살펴보다 editor ⑲ 편집장, 편집자 satisfy ⑧ 만족시키다
brief ⑱ 짧은 journalist ⑲ 기자 pursue ⑧ 추구하다

1 대화의 주된 주제는 무엇인가?

(A) 새로운 학교로 편입하는 것에 관한 정보
(B) 편집장이 되기 위한 요건
(C) 단체에 참여할 가능성
(D) 졸업 후 취업을 위한 조언

2 남자는 왜 신문의 기자가 되고 싶어 하는가?

(A) 그는 그 일에 대한 과거 경험이 있다.
(B) 그는 교수로부터 그 자리를 제안받았다.
(C) 그는 문제에 관해 학생들에게 알리고 싶어 한다.
(D) 그는 다른 자리를 위한 기한을 놓쳤다.

3 대화에서, 여자는 지원 절차의 단계들을 설명한다. 아래의 단계들을 올바른 순서대로 나열하시오. 각 답변을 해당하는 곳으로 끌어다 놓으시오.

단계 1	(C) 자격 요건이 검토되게 하기
단계 2	(D) 기사에 관해 연락받기를 기다리기
단계 3	(A) 분야에 대한 주제 받기
단계 4	(B) 면접에 참여하기

4 여자는 왜 시에서 가장 큰 신문을 언급하는가?

(A) 남자가 고려할 만한 자원봉사 기회를 소개하기 위해
(B) 학교 신문에서 일하는 것의 이점의 예를 들기 위해
(C) 학생들에게 무급 인턴직을 제안하는 회사들을 비판하기 위해
(D) 큰 도시에 있는 신문을 작은 도시의 것들과 비교하기 위해

대화의 일부를 다시 듣고 질문에 답하시오.

W: Keep in mind that the deadline for applications is on September 15.

M: Got it. Um, just to check... Do you require a short article as a sample?

5 남자는 왜 이렇게 말하는가:

M: Um, just to check...

(A) 기한의 날짜를 확인하기 위해
(B) 여자에게 그의 원래 질문을 상기시키기 위해
(C) 어디서 더 많은 정보를 얻을 수 있는지 알아내기 위해

Listening Practice 4

본문 p. 123

1 (D) 2 (B), (D) 3 (B) 4 (D)-(A)-(B)-(C) 5 (D)

Note-taking

Snowball Earth Theory

- Glaciers = form in ext. cold place
  - Snow falls → turn into glaciers made of ice
  - Glaciers move → carry sediments & leave marks
  - Evidence in India & Australia = glaciers existed
- One of cold periods = ice spread → covered planet
  - Turned Earth into frozen ball ← name of the theory
- Recent explanation for Snowball Earth
  - High rain & low carbon dioxide → water to freeze
  - Ice spread → reflected sunlight → planet colder

Listen to part of a lecture in a geology class.

P: [1]Glaciers are thick layers of ice that move across the land. Uh, they are usually found in cold places like the North and South Pole, or high mountains like the Himalayas... However, scientists have also found evidence of glaciers in parts of the world that are mostly warm today. Well, now, we'll discuss a theory that might explain this. It's called the Snowball Earth theory. It suggests that almost the entire planet was covered in ice a long time ago.

So the Snowball Earth theory was developed to explain how glaciers could have existed all around the planet, including in places that are warm today. You see, as I said, glaciers usually form in extremely cold places. Um, they form when snow falls in one area over a long period of time. Eventually, the layers of snow turn into glaciers made of ice. These glaciers move because of gravity. [2B]When they move, they carry sediments or bits of rock. [2D]They also leave marks in the ground beneath them. The sediments and marks have been found in countries such as India and Australia. This evidence is why scientists believe glaciers once existed in places that are now warm. So, um, we know for sure that glaciers once existed in places around the world. The question is, how did this happen?

Well, in general, Earth experiences two kinds of climate: hot and cold. And, um, billions of years ago, these two types of climate lasted a very long time. So, for millions of years, Earth could be hot. Then, for millions of years, it could be cold... According to the Snowball Earth theory, during one of the cold periods, the ice that is normally found in the North and South Pole spread. And the ice continued to spread until it covered most of the planet. Um, this turned Earth into a frozen ball. [3]So if you looked at Earth from outer space, it would have looked like a giant snowball... Obviously, that is where the name of the theory comes from.

S: [5]Excuse me, but what caused the Snowball Earth to happen? Uh, do we know what it was?

P: Well, that's open for debate. A number of ideas have been given, such as a change in Earth's orbit or, uh, changes in the atmosphere... There's no way to know for certain. But there is a recent explanation for how the Snowball Earth could have happened. [4D]According to this explanation, high amounts of rain and low amounts of carbon dioxide in the atmosphere gradually cooled down the planet. [4A]This caused the water in the oceans to freeze. That's what allowed ice to spread outward from the poles. [4B]But then, as the ice spread, it reflected large amounts of sunlight back into space. Uh, this made the planet colder since sunlight is needed to warm the earth. [4C]This continued until the ice eventually spread all the way up to Earth's tropical regions, near the middle of the planet.

지질학 강의의 일부를 들으시오.

P: 빙하는 육지를 가로질러 이동하는 얼음의 두꺼운 층입니다. 어, 그것들은 보통 북극이나 남극처럼 추운 곳들이나, 혹은 히말라야 같은 높은 산들에서 발견됩니다... 하지만, 과학자들은 오늘날 대체로 따뜻한 세계의 일부 지역들에서도 빙하의 증거를 발견했어요. 음, 자, 우리는 이것의 원인을 설명할지도 모르는 이론에 대해 논의할 거예요. 그것은 눈덩이 지구 이론이라고 불려요. 그것은 오래전에 거의 지구 전체가 얼음으로 덮여 있었다고 말합니다.

자, 눈덩이 지구 이론은 빙하가 어떻게 오늘날 따뜻한 장소들을 포함하여 지구 전체에 존재할 수 있었는지를 설명하기 위해 개발되었습니다. 그러니까, 제가 말했듯이, 빙하는 보통 매우 추운 곳에서 형성돼요. 음, 그것들은 한 지역에 눈이 오랜 기간에 걸쳐 내릴 때 형성됩니다. 결국, 눈의 층은 얼음으로 만들어진 빙하로 변해요. 이 빙하는 중력 때문에 움직입니다. 그것들은 움직일 때 퇴적물이나 바위의 조각들을 운반해요. 그것들은 또한 그것들 아래에 있는 땅에 흔적을 남겨요. 퇴적물과 흔적들은 인도와 호주 같은 나라들에서 발견되어 왔어요. 이 증거가 과학자들이 빙하가 한때 지금은 따뜻한 장소들에 존재했다고 믿는 이유입니다. 그래서, 음, 우리는 빙하가 한때 세계 곳곳에 존재했다는 것을 확실히 알고 있어요. 문제는, 어떻게 이런 일이 일어났을까요?

음, 일반적으로, 지구는 두 종류의 기후를 경험하는데, 이는 더위와 추위예요. 그리고, 음, 수십억 년 전에, 이 두 종류의 기후는 매우 오래 지속되었어요. 그래서, 수백만 년 동안, 지구는 더웠을 수 있어요. 그 후, 수백만 년 동안, 그것은 추웠을 수 있어요... 눈덩이 지구 이론에 따르면, 그 추운 기간들 중 한 때, 일반적으로 북극과 남극에서 발견되는 얼음이 퍼져나갔어요. 그리고 그 얼음은 지구의 대부분을 덮을 때까지 계속해서 퍼져나갔죠. 음, 이것은 지구를 얼어붙은 공으로 만들었어요. 그래서 지구를 우주에서 봤다면, 거대한 눈덩이처럼 보였을 거예요... 명백하게도, 그게 그 이론의 이름이 유래한 곳이에요.

S: 실례지만, 무엇이 눈덩이 지구가 발생하게 했나요? 어, 그게 무엇이었는지 우리가 알고 있나요?

P: 음, 그건 논의의 여지가 있어요. 지구 궤도의 변화나, 어, 대기의 변화 같은 많은 의견들이 제시되어 왔어요... 확실히 알 방법은 없어요. 하지만 눈덩이 지구가 어떻게 발생할 수 있었을지에 대한 최근의 설명이 있어요. 이 설명에 따르면, 많은 양의 비와 적은 양의 대기 중 이산화탄소가 점차 지구를 식혔어요. 이것은 바다의 물이 얼어붙게 만들었죠. 그것이 얼음이 극지방에서 밖으로 퍼져 나갈

수 있게 한 거예요. 하지만 그 후, 얼음이 퍼져 나가면서, 그것은 많은 양의 햇빛을 우주로 반사했어요. 어, 지구를 따뜻하게 만들기 위해서는 햇빛이 필요하기 때문에 이것은 지구를 더 춥게 만들었어요. 이것은 얼음이 결국 지구의 중앙 부분 근처에 있는 열대 지역으로 퍼져 나갈 때까지 계속됐어요.

glacier 몡 빙하   exist 동 존재하다   extremely 뷔 매우, 극도로
gravity 몡 중력   sediment 몡 퇴적물   in general 일반적으로
debate 몡 논의   orbit 몡 궤도   cool down 식히다
outward 뷔 밖으로   reflect 동 반사하다   eventually 뷔 결국
tropical 톙 열대의

1 강의의 주된 목적은 무엇인가?
   (A) 빙하의 영향에 대해 논의하기 위해
   (B) 빙하의 형성 과정을 설명하기 위해
   (C) 기후 변화에 대한 새로운 이론을 보여주기 위해
   (D) 현상의 가능한 원인을 설명하기 위해

2 교수에 따르면, 빙하에 관해 어떤 증거를 볼 수 있는가? 2개의 답을 고르시오.
   (A) 얼어붙은 큰 호수들
   (B) 바위 조각
   (C) 특이한 종류의 식물
   (D) 땅에 있는 흔적

3 교수에 따르면, 눈덩이 지구라는 이름은 어디에서 유래하는가?
   (A) 빙하의 회전 운동
   (B) 얼어붙은 지구가 생긴 방식
   (C) 빙하에서 발견되는 퇴적물의 종류
   (D) 기후 사건이 날씨에 미치는 영향

4 강의에서, 교수는 눈덩이 지구가 발생했을지도 모르는 과정에 대한 개요를 서술한다. 아래의 단계들을 올바른 순서대로 나열하시오. 각 답변을 해당하는 곳으로 끌어다 놓으시오.

단계 1	(D) 높은 강우량과 낮은 이산화탄소가 냉각 효과를 일으켰다.
단계 2	(A) 바다가 얼어붙고 얼음이 퍼져 나갔다.
단계 3	(B) 햇빛이 우주로 반사되었다.
단계 4	(C) 얼음이 지구의 중앙 부분에 닿았다.

강의의 일부를 다시 듣고 질문에 답하시오.

S: Excuse me, but what caused the Snowball Earth to happen? Uh, do we know what it was?

P: Well, that's open for debate. A number of ideas have been given, such as a change in Earth's orbit or, uh, changes in the atmosphere... There's no way to know for certain.

5 교수는 왜 이렇게 말하는가:
   P: Well, that's open for debate.
   (A) 이론이 더 이상 받아들여지지 않는다는 것을 말하기 위해
   (B) 이론이 다음 시간에 논의될 것임을 시사하기 위해
   (C) 학생이 의견을 제시하도록 독려하기 위해
   (D) 질문이 명확한 답을 가지고 있지 않다는 것을 나타내기 위해

1 (B) 2 (C) 3 (B) 4 (B)-(C)-(A)-(D) 5 (D)

Note-taking

S: Study Flamenco = Spain's folk music & dance tradition
Visit family in Seville, interview dancers about Flamenco
P: Contact dance schools → set up interviews
S: E-mails to instructors → meet or answer over e-mail
P: Hard time meeting ∵ summer break ∴ do it soon
S: Make 10 questions, interview 15, attend performances
P: If enough time X → smaller number will do
Make outline = 1 p., summary, expected outcome, time
Two meetings = go over outline & interview questions
Bring approval form, I'll need to sign

Listen to a conversation between a student and a professor.

S: Thank you for agreeing to meet with me, Professor Hayes.

P: No problem, Andrew. I got the e-mail that you sent. ¹Um, you said that you wanted to discuss your research project, is that right?

S: Yes. I need to complete my research by this summer, and it's already April. So I'm rushing to get it organized.

P: ⁵OK. It's still possible to prepare everything in time. Do you have a topic yet?

S: Yes. I want to study Flamenco... Uh, that's Spain's folk music and dance tradition. I'm already planning to visit my family in Seville for eight weeks in June and July. ²I want to interview some dancers about Flamenco while I'm there, uh, to add to my research.

P: I see. That all sounds fine. However, I think it's important that we discuss a few more details before you get started. ⁴ᴮUm, first, you should contact several dance schools in the area that you're going to visit. That way, you can set up some interviews before you get there.

S: That's a great idea. It would save a lot of time. I was also going to send e-mails to some instructors who teach Flamenco at universities there. I'm hoping they can meet with me or answer questions over e-mail.

P: ³You might have a hard time meeting with instructors since it will be summer break. Most of them will probably be away from campus. So if you're going to send them e-mails, you'd better do it soon. Have you prepared your interview questions yet?

S: Uh, no, I haven't, but I'm planning to make a list of 10 questions. And ideally, I'd like to interview 15 different dancers. I'm also planning on attending some Flamenco performances while I'm there.

P: I think that sounds reasonable. However, if you don't have enough time to interview 15 dancers, a smaller number will do. ⁴ᶜSecond, I'd like you to make an outline for your research project.

It should be around a page long, but it should include a summary of your project, expected outcomes, and how much time it will take to complete.

S: Sure, no problem. I can get started on the outline right away.

P: ⁴ᴬThird, you have to schedule two more meetings with me before you leave. One to go over the outline and a second one to go over your interview questions. Is that all right?

S: Yeah, that would help me a lot. I'm sure I'll need more advice before I leave.

P: ⁴ᴰFinally, make sure you bring me an approval form. You'll need to fill it out and I'll need to sign it before the end of the semester.

S: Perfect. I'll fill it out and leave it in your mailbox.

학생과 교수 사이의 대화를 들으시오.

S: 만나 주셔서 감사합니다, Hayes 교수님.

P: 천만에, Andrew. 네가 보낸 이메일을 받았다. 음, 네 연구 과제에 관해 논의하고 싶다고 말했지, 맞니?

S: 네, 저는 이번 여름까지 제 연구를 완료해야 하고, 벌써 4월이에요. 그래서 저는 그것을 정리하려고 서두르고 있어요.

P: 그렇구나. 아직 제시간에 모든 것을 준비하는 게 가능하단다. 주제가 있니?

S: 네. 저는 플라멩코를 연구하고 싶어요... 어, 그건 스페인의 민속 음악과 무용 전통이에요. 저는 이미 6월과 7월에 8주 동안 세비야에 있는 제 가족을 방문할 계획이에요. 저는 제가 그곳에 있는 동안 플라멩코에 관해 몇 명의 무용가들을 인터뷰하고 싶어요, 어, 제 연구에 추가하기 위해서요.

P: 그렇구나. 전부 좋아 보이는구나. 하지만, 나는 네가 시작하기 전에 세부 사항 몇 개 더에 대해 논의하는 게 중요한 것 같구나. 음, 먼저, 너는 네가 방문할 지역의 무용 학교 몇 개에 연락해야 해. 그렇게 하면, 너는 그곳에 가기 전에 인터뷰 몇 개를 준비할 수 있어.

S: 좋은 생각이네요. 그건 시간을 많이 아껴줄 거예요. 저는 그곳에 있는 대학에서 플라멩코를 가르치는 강사들 몇 명에게 이메일을 보내려고 했어요. 저는 그들이 저와 만나주거나 이메일로 질문에 답해 주기를 바라고 있어요.

P: 여름 방학이 될 것이기 때문에 너는 강사들과 만나는 것에 어려움을 겪을지도 몰라. 그들 중 대부분은 아마 캠퍼스에서 떠나 있을 거야. 그러니까 네가 이메일을 보낼 거라면, 빨리하는 게 좋을 거야. 인터뷰 질문들은 준비했니?

S: 어, 아뇨, 아직이요. 그런데 저는 질문 10개의 목록을 만들 계획이에요. 그리고 이상적으로는, 15명의 무용가들을 인터뷰하고 싶어요. 저는 그곳에 있는 동안 플라멩코 공연 몇 개에도 참석할 계획이에요.

P: 합리적인 것처럼 들리는구나. 하지만, 네가 15명의 무용가들을 인터뷰할 충분한 시간이 없다면, 더 적은 수도 괜찮을 거야. 두 번째로, 나는 네가 연구 과제에 대한 개요를 만들었으면 해. 그건 한 페이지 정도의 길이여야 하지만, 네 과제의 요약, 예상되는 결과, 그것을 완료하는 데 시간이 얼마나 걸릴지를 포함해야 해.

S: 물론이죠, 문제없어요. 지금 바로 개요 만들기를 시작할 수 있어요.

P: 세 번째로, 너는 떠나기 전에 나와의 회의 일정을 두 번 더 잡아야 해. 한 번은 개요를 점검하기 위해서, 두 번째는 네 인터뷰 질문들을 점검하기 위해서. 괜찮겠니?

S: 네, 많은 도움이 될 것 같아요. 제가 떠나기 전에 분명 더 많은 조언이 필요할 거예요.

P: 마지막으로, 반드시 내게 승인 요청서를 가져오렴. 학기가 끝나기 전에 너는 그걸 작성해야 하고 내가 그것에 서명해야 해.

S: 완벽해요. 그걸 작성해서 교수님의 우편함에 넣어둘게요.

---

rush 통 서두르다 organize 통 정리하다 folk music 민속 음악
tradition 명 전통 set up ~을 준비하다 instructor 명 강사
ideally 부 이상적으로 reasonable 형 합리적인 outline 명 개요
outcome 명 결과

1 대화는 주로 무엇에 관한 것인가?

(A) 학생의 여행에 관한 보고서

(B) 수업을 위한 과제의 세부 사항

(C) 전문 무용가들과의 만남

(D) 여름 프로그램을 위한 요건들

2 학생은 플라멩코에 대한 더 많은 정보를 어떻게 수집할 것인가?

(A) 현대 무용 강사들을 방문함으로써

(B) 지역에 있는 가족 구성원들을 인터뷰함으로써

(C) 공연자들과 그 스타일에 관해 이야기함으로써

(D) 전통 민속 음악에 대한 책을 읽음으로써

3 교수는 왜 여름 방학을 언급하는가?

(A) 그녀가 이메일 사용을 선호하는 이유를 설명하기 위해

(B) 몇몇 사람들을 만나는 것이 어려울 수도 있는 이유를 설명하기 위해

(C) 과제의 기한을 강조하기 위해

(D) 세비야를 방문하기 가장 좋은 때에 대한 생각을 밝히기 위해

4 대화에서, 교수는 과제를 완료하기 위한 단계들을 설명한다. 아래의 단계들을 올바른 순서대로 나열하시오.
각 답변을 해당하는 곳으로 끌어다 놓으시오.

단계 1	(B) 도시에 있는 여러 무용 학교들에 연락하기
단계 2	(C) 연구 과제에 대한 개요 쓰기
단계 3	(A) 교수와의 회의를 두 번 더 잡기
단계 4	(D) 교수에게 신청서 제출하기

대화의 일부를 다시 듣고 질문에 답하시오.

P: OK. It's still possible to prepare everything in time. Do you have a topic yet?

S: Yes. I want to study Flamenco... Uh, that's Spain's folk music and dance tradition.

5 학생은 왜 이렇게 말하는가:

S: Uh, that's Spain's folk music and dance tradition.

(A) 그가 주제에 익숙하지 않음을 나타내기 위해

(B) 교수에게 그가 세비야에 방문하는 이유를 상기시키기 위해

(C) 사용 가능한 다른 주제를 제안하기 위해

(D) 그가 사용한 용어의 의미를 설명하기 위해

---

1 (D)　　2 (C)　　3 (D)　　4 (B)
5 Emission Nebula: (B), (C)　Reflection Nebula: (A), (D)
6 (B)

Note-taking

Bright Nebulas

- Emission nebula
  - Emit light ∵ have many stars = contain a lot of heat
  - Any color (e.g. oxygen → green, nitrogen → red)
- Reflection nebula = appear bright
  - Size = measured based on area of brightness
  - Produce own light X
  - Light from nearby stars meets dust → reflect light
- Dark nebula = ext. cold ∵ near any star X
  - Piece of dust = covered in frozen gas → reflect X

Listen to part of a lecture in an astronomy class.

P: So we've been talking about large objects in space... Um, if you remember, I told you that a nebula is a large cloud of gas and dust, and many stars are born in nebulas. [1]Well, there are different kinds of nebulas. And today, I'll mainly discuss two types of nebulas according to their characteristics...

[2]The first type is an emission nebula. So an emission is something that is emitted, right? Uh, it is something that is released in an outward direction. For example, cars emit pollution, which means they release emissions in the form of harmful gases. Well, emission nebulas are named for a similar reason. They emit light. [5C]Emission nebulas emit light because they have many stars. The stars are also extremely hot, so these nebulas also contain a lot of heat. Uh, now, the light of these nebulas can be almost any color. [3]The color depends on the type of gas they emit. For instance, if a nebula mostly releases oxygen, the nebula's light will look green. However, if the nebula releases nitrogen, the light will be red. [5B]Because emission nebulas can release different gases, they sometimes look as colorful as a rainbow! This makes them very bright and beautiful. Now, one of the most famous emission nebulas is the Orion Nebula. You can easily find it in the sky because it is located just below Orion's Belt. I'm sure you all know Orion's Belt... It's one of the most familiar groups of stars in the night sky. It looks like three stars in a line.

Anyway, the next type is called a reflection nebula. Uh, like an emission nebula, a reflection nebula can appear bright when we look at it with a telescope. However, there are some major differences. [4]For one, the size of reflection nebulas is measured differently... They are not measured by the size of the cloud of dust and gas. Instead, they are measured based on the area of their brightness. [5D]Also, a reflection nebula does not produce its own light. As its name suggests, it reflects light into space. The

---

light of a reflection nebula actually comes from nearby stars. That is, uh, these stars are not inside the nebula itself. As light from nearby stars meets the dust in a reflection nebula, all of the individual pieces of dust reflect that light outward. But how the light is reflected depends on the length of the wave of light… For example, blue light waves are very short. And short light waves are reflected more easily. [5A]That's why reflection nebulas often look blue in color…

So, uh, both emission and reflection nebulas are classified as bright nebulas. [6]But not all nebulas are bright. In fact, there is another kind of nebula that is not bright at all. Um, can anyone guess what it's called?

S: Uh, a dark nebula?

P: Correct! Emission nebulas emit light. Reflection nebulas reflect light. And dark nebulas are, well, dark. That makes sense, right? But why are they dark? Well, dark nebulas are extremely cold. This is because they are not near any stars. They are so cold that each piece of dust is covered in frozen gases. As a result, the dust has a dark color and does not reflect light. But, uh, we'll talk more about this next time…

천문학 강의의 일부를 들으시오.

P: 자, 우리는 우주에 있는 큰 개체들에 관해 얘기해 왔어요… 음, 기억한다면, 저는 성운이 가스와 먼지의 큰 구름이라고 말했고, 많은 별들이 성운에서 탄생하죠. 음, 다양한 종류의 성운이 있어요. 그리고 오늘, 저는 주로 두 종류의 성운을 그것들의 특징에 따라 논의할 거예요…

첫 번째 종류는 방출 성운이에요. 자, 방출이라는 건 내뿜어지는 무언가죠, 그렇죠? 어, 그건 바깥 방향으로 방출되는 무언가예요. 예를 들어, 자동차는 오염 물질을 내뿜는데, 이것은 그것들이 해로운 가스의 형태로 배출물을 방출하는 것을 의미해요.. 음, 방출 성운은 비슷한 이유로 이름이 붙여졌어요. 그것들은 빛을 내뿜어요. 방출 성운은 많은 별을 가지고 있기 때문에 빛을 내뿜어요. 그 별들이 극도로 뜨겁기 때문에, 이 성운들은 많은 열을 담고 있기도 해요. 어, 자, 이 성운들의 빛은 거의 모든 색이 될 수 있어요. 색은 그것들이 내뿜는 가스의 종류에 따라 달라져요. 예를 들어, 만약 성운이 대체로 산소를 방출하면, 성운의 빛은 녹색으로 보일 거예요. 하지만, 만약 성운이 질소를 방출하면, 그 빛은 빨간색이 될 거예요. 방출 성운이 다양한 가스를 방출할 수 있기 때문에, 그것들은 때때로 무지개만큼이나 다채로워 보여요! 이것은 그것들을 매우 밝고 아름답게 만들죠. 자, 가장 유명한 방출 성운 중 하나는 오리온 대성운이에요. 그것이 오리온자리의 세 별 바로 아래에 있기 때문에 하늘에서 쉽게 찾을 수 있어요. 여러분 모두 오리온자리의 세 별을 알 거라고 생각해요… 그건 밤하늘에서 가장 익숙한 별들의 무리 중 하나죠. 그것은 일렬로 늘어선 세 개의 별들처럼 보여요.

그건 그렇고, 다음 종류는 반사 성운이라고 불려요. 어, 방출 성운처럼, 반사 성운은 우리가 망원경으로 그것을 볼 때 밝게 보일 수 있어요. 하지만, 몇 가지의 주요 차이점들이 있습니다. 우선 한 가지는, 반사 성운의 크기는 다르게 측정돼요… 그것들은 먼지와 가스의 구름의 크기로 측정되지 않아요. 대신, 그것들은 밝기의 면적을 기반으로 측정돼요. 또한, 반사 성운은 자신의 빛을 내지 않아요. 이름이 시사하듯이, 그것은 빛을 우주로 반사하죠. 반사 성운의 빛은 사실 근처에 있는 별들에서 와요. 그러니까, 어, 이 별들

은 성운 자체의 안쪽에 있지 않아요. 근처에 있는 별들에서 오는 빛이 반사 성운 안에 있는 먼지와 만나면서, 모든 먼지 조각들이 그 빛을 바깥으로 반사해요. 하지만 빛이 반사되는 방식은 광파의 길이에 따라 달라져요. 예를 들어, 푸른 광파는 매우 짧아요. 그리고 짧은 광파는 더 쉽게 반사되죠. 그것이 반사 성운이 종종 파란색으로 보이는 이유예요…

그래서, 어, 방출 성운과 반사 성운은 둘 다 발광성운으로 분류됩니다. 하지만 모든 성운이 빛나는 건 아니에요. 사실, 또 다른 종류의 전혀 빛이 나지 않는 성운이 있어요. 음, 그게 뭐라고 불리는지 추측해볼 사람 있나요?

S: 어, 암흑 성운인가요?

P: 맞아요! 방출 성운은 빛을 내뿜어요. 반사 성운은 빛을 반사하죠. 그리고 암흑 성운은, 음, 어두워요. 말이 되죠, 그렇죠? 하지만 그것들이 왜 어두울까요? 음, 암흑 성운은 극도로 차가워요. 이는 그것들이 어떠한 별에도 가깝지 않기 때문이에요. 그것들이 너무 차가워서 각 먼지 조각은 얼어붙은 가스로 덮여 있어요. 그 결과, 먼지는 어두운색을 가지고 있고 빛을 반사하지 않죠. 하지만, 어, 다음 시간에 이것에 대해 더 얘기하죠…

nebula 명 성운 emission 명 방출, 배출물 emit 동 내뿜다
pollution 명 오염 물질 extremely 부 극도로
reflection 명 반사 telescope 명 망원경
brightness 명 밝기 length 명 길이 classify 동 분류하다
frozen 형 얼어붙은

1 강의의 주된 주제는 무엇인가?

(A) 성운 내부의 별 형성

(B) 우주에서 다양한 성운들이 형성되는 방식

(C) 우주에서 성운을 발견할 수 있는 곳

(D) 서로 다른 종류의 성운들의 특징

2 교수는 왜 자동차 오염을 언급하는가?

(A) 우주에서 가스가 방출되는 방식을 보여주기 위해

(B) 우주에서 먼지가 퍼지는 방식을 설명하기 위해

(C) 개체의 이름을 설명하기 위해

(D) 흔한 문제의 예시를 들기 위해

3 교수에 따르면, 성운이 대체로 산소를 방출하면 어떻게 되는가?

(A) 그 성운은 크기가 더 작아질 것이다.

(B) 그 성운은 다양한 색을 내뿜을 것이다.

(C) 그 성운에서 나오는 빛은 더 밝아질 것이다.

(D) 그 성운의 빛은 녹색으로 보일 것이다.

4 교수에 따르면, 반사 성운은 어떻게 측정되는가?

(A) 그것들이 가지고 있는 별들의 수를 추정함으로써

(B) 그것들이 밝히는 부분을 살펴봄으로써

(C) 그것들의 광도를 다른 개체들과 비교함으로써

(D) 그것들의 가스와 먼지구름의 크기를 확인함으로써

5 다음의 항목이 방출 성운 혹은 반사 성운과 관련 있는지를 표시하시오.
각각의 설명에 맞는 칸을 클릭하시오.

	방출 성운	반사 성운
(A) 주로 파란색으로 나타난다		V
(B) 많은 종류의 가스를 방출한다	V	
(C) 많은 양의 열을 담고 있다	V	
(D) 스스로 빛을 만들어내지 않는다		V

강의의 일부를 다시 듣고 질문에 답하시오.

P: But not all nebulas are bright. In fact, there is another kind of nebula that is not bright at all. Um, can anyone guess what it's called?

S: Uh, a dark nebula?

P: Correct! Emission nebulas emit light. Reflection nebulas reflect light. And dark nebulas are, well, dark. That makes sense, right?

6 교수는 이렇게 말함으로써 무엇을 의미하는가:

P: That makes sense, right?

(A) 그는 일부 성운들이 매우 비슷해 보인다고 생각한다.

(B) 그는 성운들이 정확한 이름을 가지고 있다고 생각한다.

(C) 그는 성운 주제가 그리 어렵지 않다는 데 동의한다.

(D) 그는 성운이 예기치 않은 방식으로 변한다는 것을 알고 있다.

Vocabulary Review
본문 p. 132

1 carnivore	2 sediment	3 omnivore
4 mural	5 political	6 symbol
7 positively	8 exist	9 orbit
10 (B)	11 (B)	12 (B)
13 (C)	14 (A)	

CHAPTER 07
Inference

Example
본문 p. 135

A. (C) **B.** (B)

A.

Note-taking

M: Ordered book 2 weeks ago, arrived?
W: Find copy X ∵ old → try used bookstore near campus
M: Paper due very soon
W: Asking professor for extension

Listen to a conversation between a student and a librarian.

M: Excuse me. Um, I ordered a book two weeks ago for my architecture class. It's called *19th Century Bridges*. Do you know if it's arrived?

W: Let me see… Oh, it seems that the library wasn't able to find a copy. It's very old, you see.

M: Oh, but I need it for a paper I'm writing.

W: I'm sorry. Um, maybe you could try going to one of the used bookstores near the campus. They might have a copy for sale.

M: All right. I'm just worried because my paper is due very soon.

W: Then, how about asking your professor for an extension?

M: Do you think that will work? I've never done that before.

W: I think you should at least try.

M: OK. I'll do that right now.

학생과 사서 사이의 대화를 들으시오.

M: 실례합니다. 음, 저는 2주 전에 제 건축학 수업을 위한 도서를 주문했어요. 제목은 '19세기의 다리들'이에요. 그게 도착했는지 아시나요?

W: 확인해 볼게요… 오, 도서관이 책을 찾을 수 없었던 것 같네요. 그러니까, 그건 아주 오래됐어요.

M: 오, 그런데 제가 쓰고 있는 보고서를 위해 그게 필요해요.

W: 죄송해요. 음, 아마 캠퍼스 근처에 있는 중고 서점들 중 한 곳에 가 보실 수 있을 것 같네요. 그들이 판매용 도서를 가지고 있을지도 몰라요.

M: 알겠어요. 제 보고서를 곧 제출해야 해서 그냥 좀 걱정되네요.

W: 그럼, 교수님께 기간 연장을 요청하는 건 어때요?

M: 그게 잘 될 거라고 생각하세요? 전에는 그렇게 해본 적이 없어서요.

W: 적어도 시도는 해보셔야 할 것 같아요.

M: 알겠습니다. 지금 바로 그렇게 할게요.

order 통 주문하다   architecture 명 건축학, 건축
for sale 판매용의   extension 명 기간 연장

학생은 다음에 무엇을 할 것인가?

(A) 도서관에서 책 빌리기

(B) 웹사이트에서 기사 다운로드하기

(C) 과제물에 관해 교수에게 이야기하기

(D) 캠퍼스 근처의 상점에서 책 찾기

B.

Note-taking

Celiac Disease

• Gluten = found in grains (e.g. wheat & barley)
• Some ppl. can't eat ∵ celiac disease
• Not know they have disease w/o medical test
• Others may experience symptoms
  - Feel sick in stomach or have skin problem
  - Can lead to bone loss & slow down growth of child
• Only 1 solution = avoid food w/ gluten
  - Food providers offer more gluten-free prod.

Listen to part of a lecture in a nutrition class.

P: Gluten is a protein found in grains like wheat and barley. Many people can eat it without a problem. However, some people cannot. These people have a disorder called celiac disease. Now, normally, they would not know they have the disease without a medical test. But others may experience symptoms. For example, they might feel sick in the stomach or have some kind of skin problem. And, in rare cases, the symptoms can be, uh, more serious. For instance, celiac disease can lead to bone loss. And it can also slow down the growth of children. Right now, there is only one solution for people with celiac disease... Um, they must avoid food with gluten. This is why many food providers offer more gluten-free products nowadays...

영양학 강의의 일부를 들으시오.

P: 글루텐은 밀과 보리 같은 곡물에서 발견되는 단백질입니다. 많은 사람들은 그것을 문제없이 먹을 수 있어요. 하지만, 어떤 사람들을 그럴 수 없죠. 이 사람들은 만성소화장애증이라고 불리는 장애를 가지고 있어요. 자, 보통, 그들은 건강 검진 없이는 그들이 그 병을 가지고 있다는 것을 알지 못할 거예요. 하지만 다른 사람들은 증상들을 경험할 수도 있어요. 예를 들어, 그들은 배가 아프거나 어떤 피부 질환을 갖게 될지도 몰라요. 그리고, 드문 경우에, 그 증상들은, 어, 더 심각해질 수 있어요. 예를 들어, 만성소화장애증은 골감소로 이어질 수 있어요. 그리고 그것은 아이들의 성장을 늦출 수도 있죠. 지금 당장은, 만성소화장애증을 가진 사람들을 위한 해결책이 하나밖에 없어요... 음, 그들은 글루텐이 들어간 음식을 피해야 해요. 이것이 요즘 많은 식품 공급자들이 글루텐이 없는 제품을 더 많이 제공하는 이유예요...

protein 명 단백질   grain 명 곡물   wheat 명 밀
barley 명 보리   disorder 명 장애   symptom 명 증상
rare 형 드문

교수는 만성소화장애증에 관해 무엇을 암시하는가?

(A) 그것은 주로 어린아이들에게 영향을 미친다.
(B) 그것은 현재 의학적으로 치료될 수 없다.
(C) 그것은 심각한 증상들을 초래하지 않는다.
(D) 그것은 매우 최근에 발견되었다.

Listening Practice 1

본문 p. 137

1 (A)   2 (C)   3 Included: (A), (C), (D) Not Included: (B)
4 (B)   5 (B)

Note-taking

S: Submitted application & became candidate
   Have leadership exp. = math & political science club
P: Become familiar w/ requirements & election process
S: Univ. give handbook → planning to read
P: Know what students care about
   Talking to diff. groups of students
   Sth. most overlook = importance of speeches
   Explain why students should vote for you

Listen to a conversation between a student and a professor.

S: Hello, Professor Green. Am I disturbing you? I can always come back another time if you're busy.

P: Hi, Julia. It's OK. Come on in.

S: ¹Well, as you know, student elections are coming up. I submitted my application and became an official candidate yesterday.

P: That's fantastic! I hope you win.

S: Thanks. ¹Actually, I was hoping you could give me some advice to improve my chances of winning. I honestly don't have any idea how to prepare.

P: All right, then. Let's talk about it. So is this your first election?

S: Yes, it is. ²But I do have some leadership experience. I was the leader of the math club in my freshman year. I've also been the leader of the political science club for the past two years.

P: Nice. ³ᶜWell, first, you'll need to become familiar with the campaign requirements and the election process. You don't want to lose because you broke one of the rules.

S: Got it. The university gives all of the candidates a handbook that explains everything. I'm planning to read it this afternoon.

P: Good. Now, let's talk about campaigning. ³ᴰ/⁵It's essential that you know what the students care about. Uh, you do know what their biggest issues are, don't you?

S: ⁵Um, maybe school costs and student loans?

P: You're going to have to do better than that. Those are old issues, and they're too complex for a student representative to deal with.

S: Then... What are the issues I should consider?

P: That's what you need to find out. ³ᴬYou can do this by going around the campus and talking to different groups of students. The more students you talk to, the better. ⁴And I want to mention something that most student candidates overlook. That is the importance of making effective speeches.

S: What do you mean by that, Professor?

P: ⁴I mean that a visit to a classroom isn't just about saying "Hello" and "Vote for me." You need to explain why the students should vote for you. Students will vote for someone who can suggest good solutions to problems.

S: Well, I love talking to people and making speeches. I did that all the time as the leader of the political science club.

P: That's a big plus. But you have a lot to do. So if I were you, I'd sit down with my team and write down a detailed plan.

S: Thanks so much, Professor. I hope you'll let me visit you when I need more advice.

학생과 교수 사이의 대화를 들으시오.

S: 안녕하세요, Green 교수님. 제가 교수님을 방해하고 있나요? 바쁘시면 언제든지 다른 시간에 다시 올 수 있어요.

P: 안녕, Julia. 괜찮단다. 들어오렴.

S: 음, 아시다시피, 학생 선거가 다가오고 있어요. 저는 지원서를 제출했고 어제 공식 후보자가 됐어요.

P: 멋지구나! 네가 이기길 바란다.

S: 감사합니다. 사실은, 교수님께서 제가 이길 가능성을 높이기 위한 조언을 좀 해주시기를 바랐어요. 저는 솔직히 어떻게 준비해야 할지 전혀 모르겠어요.

P: 좋아, 그럼. 얘기해 보자. 그래서 이게 네 첫 선거니?

S: 네, 맞아요. 그런데 저는 약간의 리더십 경험이 있어요. 저는 1학년 때 수학 동아리의 대표였어요. 저는 지난 2년 동안 정치학 동아리의 대표이기도 했어요.

P: 좋아. 음, 먼저, 너는 선거 운동 요건과 선거 과정을 잘 알아야 해. 규칙 중 하나를 어겨서 지고 싶지는 않잖니.

S: 알겠습니다. 대학은 모든 후보자에게 모든 것을 설명하는 안내서를 제공해요. 오늘 오후에 그걸 읽을 계획이에요.

P: 좋아. 이제, 선거 운동에 대해 얘기해보자. 학생들이 무엇을 중요하게 생각하는지 아는 건 필수야. 어, 그들이 가지고 있는 가장 큰 문제들이 무엇인지 알고 있지, 그렇지 않니?

S: 음, 아마 학비와 학자금 대출인가요?

P: 너는 그것보다는 잘해야 할 거야. 그것들은 오래된 문제들이고, 학생 대표가 다루기에는 너무 복잡하단다.

S: 그럼... 제가 고려해야 하는 문제들은 무엇인가요?

P: 그게 네가 알아내야 하는 거야. 너는 캠퍼스를 돌아다니고 다양한 그룹의 학생들과 이야기함으로써 이걸 할 수 있어. 더 많은 학생들과 얘기할수록 더 좋아. 그리고 대부분의 학생 후보자들이 간과하는 걸 언급하고 싶구나. 그건 효율적인 연설을 하는 것의 중요성이야.

S: 그게 무슨 말씀이신가요, 교수님?

P: 내 말은 교실에 방문하는 것이 단지 "안녕하세요"라고 말하고 "저에게 투표해 주세요"라고 말하는 것만이 아니라는 거야. 너는 학생들이 왜 너에게 투표해야 하는지를 설명해야 해. 학생들은 문제에 대한 좋은 해결책을 제안할 수 있는 사람에게 투표할 거야.

S: 음, 저는 사람들과 이야기하고 연설하는 것을 좋아해요. 정치학 동아리의 대표로서 항상 그렇게 했거든요.

P: 그건 큰 장점이야. 그런데 너는 해야 할 게 많아. 그러니까 내가 너라면, 팀과 함께 앉아서 자세한 계획을 적을 거야.

S: 정말 감사합니다, 교수님. 조언이 더 필요할 때 교수님을 찾아뵙게 해주셨으면 해요.

---

disturb 통 방해하다   election 명 선거   official 형 공식적인
candidate 명 후보자   chance 명 가능성
political science 정치학   campaign 명 선거 운동
student loan 학자금 대출   representative 명 대표(자)
overlook 통 간과하다

1 화자들은 주로 무엇을 논의하고 있는가?

(A) 후보자로서 학생이 해야 하는 것
(B) 학교 프로그램을 위한 지원 절차
(C) 학생이 수업에서 얼마나 잘하고 있는지
(D) 학교 활동에 참여하는 것의 중요성

2 학생은 어떤 과거 리더십 경험을 언급하는가?

(A) 그녀는 스포츠팀의 주장이었다.
(B) 그녀는 학생 활동 기획자로 일했다.
(C) 그녀는 학생 동아리 두 개의 대표였다.
(D) 그녀는 지난 학생 선거에서 큰 역할을 했다.

3 교수는 학생에 대한 그의 추천에 어떤 조언을 포함하는가? 다음의 항목이 포함되었는지를 표시하시오. 각 항목에 적절한 칸을 클릭하시오.

	포함됨	포함 안 됨
(A) 다양한 그룹의 학생들과 이야기하기	V	
(B) 학자금 대출 절차에 대해 알아보기		V
(C) 선거 운동 규칙과 규정 이해하기	V	
(D) 학생들의 문제에 친숙해지기	V	

4 교수는 연설하는 것에 관해 무엇을 암시하는가?

(A) 그것은 학생들에게 개별적으로 이야기하는 것보다 쉽다.
(B) 그것은 친근한 대화 이상의 것을 필요로 한다.
(C) 그것은 선거 운동 관리의 가장 어려운 부분이다.
(D) 그것은 정치에 대해 아는 사람들에게 더 쉽다.

대화의 일부를 다시 듣고 질문에 답하시오.

P: It's essential that you know what the students care about. Uh, you do know what their biggest issues are, don't you?

S: Um, maybe school costs and student loans?

P: You're going to have to do better than that. Those are old issues, and they're too complex for a student representative to deal with.

5 교수는 이렇게 말함으로써 무엇을 의미하는가:

P: You're going to have to do better than that.

(A) 학생은 이길 가능성이 작다.
(B) 학생은 다른 문제들에 관해 알아야 한다.
(C) 학생은 학생들과 아이디어에 관해 논의해야 한다.
(D) 학생은 이미 중요한 문제들을 알고 있다.

Listening Practice 2 본문 p. 139

1 (B)   2 (C)   3 (C)   4 (A)
5 Continental Plates: (B), (D) Oceanic Plates: (A), (C)

Note-taking
Two Types of Geologic Plates

- Continental plates
  - Light & dense X ∴ sink easily X ∴ float above mantle
- Oceanic plates
  - Heavy & dense, made up of volcanic rock
  - Tend to sink into earth's mantle → form huge valleys
  - Much thinner > continental plates, younger in age
- When oceanic & continental plates meet
  - Oceanic plate = heavier ∴ go under continental plate
  - Create earthquake, continental plate pushed backward

Listen to part of a lecture in a geology class.

P: OK... Let's begin with a quick review. In the last lecture, we learned about the earth's structure. In the center of the earth is the core. Next is the mantle. And at the surface is the crust... Now, remember that the crust isn't just one solid layer of rock. Because it's on top of the mantle, which is mostly hot and liquid, the crust is always moving. This, uh, causes the crust to break up into large sections separated by cracks... These sections are called geologic plates. There are over a dozen of them... Um, some make up the land we live on, and others are found beneath the world's oceans... ¹For today, we're going to focus on the two types of geologic plates. These are the continental plates and the oceanic plates.

Let's start with continental plates... As you know, we can divide the earth into continents, such as Asia, Africa, Europe, and so on... Well, under each of those continents are the continental plates. They are composed of soil and rock. ⁵ᴮUh, these rocks are quite light and not very dense... ²And because they are not heavy or dense, they do not sink easily. It's kind of like a boat floating on water. The boat is less dense than the water, so it floats... The continental plates work in a similar way. They float above the earth's liquid mantle... ⁵ᴰAlso, the continental plates are usually very thick. On average, they are around 40 kilometers thick.

In contrast, oceanic plates are heavy and dense. ⁵ᴬThey are mostly made up of volcanic rock. Um, when volcanoes erupt under the sea, they increase the size of oceanic crust. Because oceanic plates are heavy and dense, they tend to sink into the earth's mantle... As they sink, they form huge valleys... This is why oceans exist. The bottoms of these deep valleys are like giant swimming pools. They hold the ocean's water, so, uh, the water cannot escape... And, in contrast to continental plates, oceanic plates are much thinner. Um, they are typically around 6 kilometers thick... ⁵ᶜThey are also usually younger in age...

Now, what happens when an oceanic plate and a continental plate meet? Let's look at an example. ³In the Pacific Ocean, there is a huge oceanic plate. It's called the Nazca Plate. Well, the Nazca Plate is slowly moving east toward the South American Plate, which, of course, is a continental plate. ⁴So what happens where the two plates meet? ³Remember, oceanic plates are heavier and denser... So the Nazca Plate goes under the South American plate. Then, as this happens, the continental plate breaks apart. ⁴This creates earthquakes in the area... Um, at the same time, the continental plate is pushed backwards by the oceanic plate. So, uh, this results in the formation of mountains on land... In fact, that is how South America's Andes mountains formed a long time ago.

지질학 강의의 일부를 들으시오.

P: 자... 간단한 복습으로 시작해 보죠. 지난 강의에서, 우리는 지구의 구조에 대해 배웠어요. 지구의 중앙에는 중심핵이 있습니다. 다음은 맨틀이에요. 그리고 표면에는 지각이 있었죠. 자, 지각이 단지 하나의 단단한 암석층이 아니라는 걸 기억하세요. 대체로 뜨겁고 액체인 맨틀 위에 있기 때문에, 지각은 항상 움직입니다. 이것은, 어, 지각을 갈라진 틈으로 분리된 큰 부분들로 부서지게 합니다... 이 부분들은 지각판이라고 불려요. 십여 개가 넘는 지각판들이 있죠. 음, 일부는 우리가 살고 있는 땅을 구성하고, 다른 것들은 세계의 해양 아래에서 발견됩니다... 오늘, 우리는 두 가지 종류의 지각판에 초점을 맞출 거예요. 이것들은 대륙판과 해양판입니다.

대륙판으로 시작해 보죠... 알다시피, 우리는 지구를 아시아, 아프리카, 유럽 등의 대륙으로 나눌 수 있습니다... 음, 그 대륙들 각각의 아래에는 대륙판이 있어요. 그것들은 토양과 암석으로 구성되어 있어요. 어, 이 암석들은 꽤 가볍고 밀도가 그렇게 높지 않아요... 그리고 무겁거나 밀도가 높지 않기 때문에, 그것들은 쉽게 가라앉지 않죠. 그건 물 위에 떠 있는 배와 비슷합니다. 배는 물보다 밀도가 낮기 때문에, 떠오르죠. 대륙판들은 비슷한 방식으로 작동합니다. 그것들은 지구의 액체 맨틀 위를 떠다녀요... 또한, 대륙판은 보통 매우 두꺼워요. 평균적으로, 그것들의 두께는 약 40킬로미터입니다.

대조적으로, 해양판은 무겁고 밀도가 높아요. 그것들은 대부분 화산암으로 이루어져 있습니다. 음, 화산이 바다 밑에서 폭발할 때, 그것들은 해양 지각의 크기를 증가시켜요. 무겁고 밀도가 높기 때문에, 해양판은 지구의 맨틀 속으로 가라앉는 경향이 있어요... 가라앉으면서, 그것들은 거대한 골짜기를 형성하죠... 이것이 해양이 존재하는 이유예요. 이 깊은 골짜기들의 바닥은 거대한 수영장 같죠. 그것들은 해양의 물을 담고 있어서, 어, 그 물은 빠져나갈 수 없어요... 그리고, 대륙판과는 대조적으로, 해양판은 훨씬 더 얇아요. 음, 그것들의 두께는 보통 약 6킬로미터입니다... 그것들은 또한 보통 나이가 더 적어요...

자, 해양판과 대륙판이 만나면 무슨 일이 일어날까요? 예시를 살펴보죠. 태평양에는, 거대한 해양판이 있습니다. 그것은 나스카판이라고 불려요. 음, 나스카판은 남아메리카판을 향해 천천히 동쪽으로 이동하고 있는데, 물론, 남아메리카판은 대륙판입니다. 그래서 두 판이 만나면 무슨 일이 일어날까요? 기억하세요, 해양판은 더 무겁고 밀도가 더 높아요... 그래서 나스카판은 남아메리카판 아래로 들어가요. 그 후, 이런 일이 일어나면서, 대륙판은 쪼개져요. 이것은 그 지역에 지진을 발생시키죠... 음, 동시에, 대륙판은 해양판에 의해 뒤로 밀려나요. 그래서, 어, 이것은 땅에 산이 형성되는 결과를 낳죠... 사실, 그것은 오래전에 남아메리카의 안데스 산맥이 형성된 방법입니다.

core 명 (지구의) 중심핵　crust 명 지각　separate 동 분리하다
continental 형 대륙의　oceanic 형 해양의
composed of ~으로 구성된　dense 형 밀도가 높은
sink 동 가라앉다　float 동 (물 위에) 뜨다　erupt 동 폭발하다
valley 명 골짜기　escape 동 빠져나가다　formation 명 형성

1 강의의 주된 주제는 무엇인가?

(A) 지각이 지표면에 미치는 영향

(B) 두 가지 종류의 지각판 비교

(C) 지구의 구조 내에 있는 새로운 층들의 발견

(D) 지각판 연구에서의 새로운 발전

2 교수는 왜 물 위에 떠 있는 배를 언급하는가?

(A) 지구의 지각이 맨틀보다 밀도가 높다는 것을 설명하기 위해

(B) 물과 흔히 볼 수 있는 물체의 밀도를 비교하기 위해

(C) 대륙판이 쉽게 가라앉지 않는 이유를 설명하기 위해

(D) 지구의 지각의 두께를 강조하기 위해

3 교수는 나스카판에 관해 무엇을 암시하는가?

(A) 그것은 남아메리카판보다 더 빠르게 움직이고 있다.

(B) 그것은 남아메리카판보다 더 크다.

(C) 그것은 남아메리카판보다 밀도가 더 높다.

(D) 그것은 남아메리카판 위로 떠 오르고 있다.

4 교수에 따르면, 두 판이 만나는 것의 결과는 무엇인가?

(A) 지진의 발생

(B) 새로운 판의 형성

(C) 오래된 암석과 새로운 암석의 혼합

(D) 파도의 생성

5 다음의 항목이 대륙판과 해양판 중 어떤 것에 대한 설명인지를 표시하시오. 각 항목에 적절한 칸을 클릭하시오.

	대륙판	해양판
(A) 대부분 화산암으로 이루어져 있다		V
(B) 밀도가 훨씬 더 낮다	V	
(C) 일반적으로 나이가 더 적다		V
(D) 두께가 약 40킬로미터이다	V	

Listening Practice 3 본문 p. 141

1 (C)　　2 (A)　　3 (C)　　4 (D)　　5 (C)

Note-taking

W: Someone I can speak about summer jobs?
M: You worked in univ. admin. office last year
　 Same office posted opening for that position
W: Work somewhere new → new skills & diff. environ.
M: Law firm downtown for receptionist = valuable exp.
　 Send résumé & two letters of recommend. by e-mail
W: Issue = only previous job = univ. job last year
M: Find ppl. who can confirm abilities (e.g. professor)
　 1 common mistake = not preparing for interview
W: Résumé = haven't updated ∴ work on that now

Listen to a conversation between a student and a career center employee.

W: Hi. I'm looking for the career center. Am I in the right place?

M: Yes, absolutely. Do you have an appointment?

W: No. I just stopped by. [1]Is there someone I can speak to about summer jobs?

M: I can let you know about some opportunities. Let me find your student information on the computer first... What's your name?

W: Oh, sure. It's, um, Lydia Lancaster.

M: OK... I see that you worked in the university administrative office as an assistant last year. It says you did a great job. [5]Actually, the same office has posted an opening for that position this summer. I think you'd have a good chance of being hired if you applied.

W: Hmm... Is there anything else? I'd rather work somewhere new. It would let me learn new skills and be in a different environment.

M: OK. There's also a law firm downtown that's looking for a receptionist. It's mostly office work, but it'd still be a valuable experience.

W: Hmm... That sounds interesting. How can I apply?

M: To apply, you need to send a résumé and two letters of recommendation by e-mail. So you will need to ask two former employers to write letters for you.

W: [2]Um, that could be an issue. I have a résumé, but my only previous job is the university job I had last year.

M: I see... You're not the first person to have this problem. There are other ways you can solve this. First, you can find other people who can confirm your abilities and positive qualities, like a professor.

W: I guess I could do that. But if the law firm asks about my previous experience, I won't know what to say.

M: If that happens, the best thing is to tell them that you don't have much work experience. But also tell them you're confident that you will do the job well.

W: Right, that's good advice. By any chance, do you have any other tips you could give me?

M: Well, one common mistake a lot of students make is, um, not preparing enough for an interview.

W: [3]How can I prepare for an interview? I mean, it's just the interviewer asking questions, right?

M: That's true, but you can think about the kinds of questions they're likely to ask you. That way, you can prepare some thoughts before you get there. You know, spend some time thinking about what you'd like to tell the employer about yourself. Ask yourself why you want the job, and what some of your strengths are.

W: Yeah, that does make a lot of sense. [4]I'll do that, but first, my résumé. I haven't updated it in a while, so I'll go work on that now... I want to make sure it's perfect.

학생과 직업 센터 직원 사이의 대화를 들으시오.

W: 안녕하세요. 직업 센터를 찾고 있습니다. 제가 맞는 곳에 와있나요?

M: 네, 그럼요. 약속이 있으신가요?

W: 아뇨. 그냥 들렀어요. 제가 여름 일자리에 관해 얘기할 수 있는 분이 계신가요?

M: 제가 몇몇 기회들에 관해 알려드릴 수 있어요. 먼저 컴퓨터에서 학생의 정보를 찾아볼게요... 성함이 어떻게 되시죠?

W: 오, 물론이죠. 음, Lydia Lancaster에요.

M: 네... 작년에 대학 행정실에서 조교로 일하셨군요. 아주 잘하셨다고

되어있네요. 사실, 같은 사무실에서 이번 여름 그 자리를 위한 공고를 게시했어요. 지원하시면 채용되실 가능성이 높을 것 같네요.

W: 흠... 다른 게 있나요? 새로운 곳에서 일하는 게 낫겠어요. 그건 제가 새로운 기술을 배우고 다른 환경에 있게 해줄 거예요.

M: 네. 시내에 접수원을 찾고 있는 법률 회사도 있어요. 대부분 사무 업무지만, 그래도 가치 있는 경험이 될 거예요.

W: 흠... 흥미로워 보이네요. 어떻게 지원할 수 있나요?

M: 지원하시려면, 이메일로 이력서와 두 장의 추천서를 보내셔야 해요. 그러니까 두 명의 이전 고용주들에게 추천서를 써 달라고 요청하셔야 할 거예요.

W: 음, 그건 문제가 될 수 있겠네요. 이력서는 있지만, 제 유일한 이전 직장은 작년에 했던 대학교 일자리예요.

M: 그렇군요... 이런 문제를 가진 사람은 학생이 처음이 아니에요. 이걸 해결할 수 있는 다른 방법들이 있어요. 먼저, 교수님같이 학생의 능력과 긍정적인 자질들을 확인해줄 수 있는 다른 사람들을 찾으시면 돼요.

W: 그렇게 할 수 있을 것 같아요. 하지만 만약 그 법률 회사가 이전의 경험에 대해 물으면, 뭐라고 말해야 할지 모르겠네요.

M: 그런 일이 일어나면, 가장 좋은 것은 학생이 업무 경험이 많지 않다고 말하는 거예요. 하지만 일을 잘 해낼 자신이 있다고도 말씀하세요.

W: 그렇군요, 좋은 조언이네요. 혹시, 제게 해주실 수 있는 다른 조언이 있으신가요?

M: 음, 많은 학생들이 저지르는 흔한 실수 한 가지는, 음, 면접을 위해 충분히 준비하지 않는 거예요.

W: 제가 어떻게 면접을 위해 준비할 수 있나요? 그러니까, 그건 그냥 면접관이 질문을 하는 거잖아요, 그렇죠?

M: 맞아요, 그런데 그들이 물어볼 것 같은 질문들의 종류에 관해 생각해볼 수 있어요. 그렇게 하면, 그곳에 가시기 전에 몇몇 생각들을 준비할 수 있죠. 그러니까, 자신에 관해 고용주에게 얘기하고 싶은 것들에 대해 시간을 들여 생각해 보세요. 그 일자리를 원하는 이유와 학생의 강점들 중 몇몇이 무엇인지를 자신에게 물어보세요.

W: 네, 이해가 잘 되네요. 그렇게 할게요, 그런데 먼저, 제 이력서부터요. 한동안 그것을 업데이트하지 않아서, 이제 가서 그걸 할게요... 그게 완벽한지 확인하고 싶네요.

appointment 명 약속 stop by 들르다
administrative office 행정실 post 동 게시하다 law firm 법률 회사
receptionist 명 접수원 valuable 형 가치 있는
résumé 명 이력서 letter of recommendation 추천서
former 형 이전의 employer 명 고용주 previous 형 이전의
quality 명 자질 confident 형 자신이 있는

1 학생은 왜 직업 센터를 찾아가는가?

(A) 다른 학생들의 직업 선택에 관해 그들에게 조언하기 위해
(B) 그녀가 지원할 수 있는 캠퍼스 내의 인턴직을 찾기 위해
(C) 공석인 일자리에 관해 문의하기 위해
(D) 면접 준비에 도움을 받기 위해

2 학생은 왜 추천서를 제공하는 것에 대해 걱정하는가?

(A) 그녀는 제한된 양의 취업 경험이 있다.
(B) 그녀는 몇몇 회사의 연락처 정보가 없다.
(C) 그녀는 그녀의 이전 고용주를 귀찮게 하고 싶지 않다.
(D) 그녀는 전 고용주가 그녀에 대해 좋게 말하지 않을까 걱정한다.

3 직원은 면접에 관해 학생에게 어떤 조언을 하는가?

(A) 개인적인 직업 목표에 관해 얘기하기
(B) 질문에 주의 기울이기
(C) 사전에 시간을 들여 준비하기
(D) 가능한 한 정직하게 답변하기

4 학생은 다음에 무엇을 할 것인가?

(A) 그녀는 그녀의 이력서를 고용주에게 가져갈 것이다.
(B) 그녀는 면접 중에 말할 것들의 목록을 작성할 것이다.
(C) 그녀는 그녀의 모든 추천서들을 모을 것이다.
(D) 그녀는 그녀의 지원을 위한 서류를 업데이트할 것이다.

대화의 일부를 다시 듣고 질문에 답하시오.
M: Actually, the same office has posted an opening for that position this summer. I think you'd have a good chance of being hired if you applied.
W: Hmm... Is there anything else? I'd rather work somewhere new.

5 학생은 이렇게 말함으로써 무엇을 의미하는가:
W: Hmm... Is there anything else?

(A) 그녀는 직원에게 질문이 더 있는지 알고 싶어 한다.
(B) 그녀는 작년에 그 일자리에서 잘하지 못했다고 생각한다.
(C) 그녀는 그 사무실 일자리에 관심이 없다.
(D) 그녀는 단체에 익숙하지 않다.

Listening Practice 4

1 (B) 2 (C) 3 (A) 4 (D) 5 (B)

Note-taking
Market Segmentation
- Geographic segmentation
  - Divide by where they live or work (e.g. country, city)
- Demographic segmentation
  - Divide based on basic info. (e.g. ages, men or women)
- Behavioral segmentation
  - Divide based on behavior (e.g. how to shop?)
- Psychographic segmentation
  - Find based on psychology (e.g. interests, attitudes)
  - Complicated ∵ gather info. about individual ppl.

Listen to part of a lecture in a business class.

P: ¹So to continue our discussion of marketing, let's look at market segmentation. This is the process of categorizing customers by placing them into different segments or groups. These groups are based on characteristics that the customers share. Doing this helps companies focus on selling products to specific groups of people instead of to everyone...

S: Sorry, um, isn't it better to sell products to as many people as possible?

P: Well, the goal is to sell many products, of course.

CHAPTER 07 | Inference 67

But this has to be done efficiently. If you try to sell to everyone, you can end up wasting time and money with the wrong customers. Um, these are customers who are not going to buy your product. Segmentation lets companies sell products only to potential buyers. This makes their marketing more effective.

[5]Anyway, to start the segmentation process, you have to gather information about customers. You can do this by asking them questions in surveys. Or you can buy the information from companies that collect it. This information can be about the customers' incomes, jobs, education... You name it. Once you have enough information, you can create groups.

[2]Now, of course, there are many ways to create different groups. However, I will discuss the four main types of segmentation... First, there is geographic segmentation. This means that you divide customers based on where they live or work. So you can divide people by country, city, town, and so on. Um, you can even divide people based on climate. So, for example, a company can sell winter coats only to people who live in cold places.

OK, next, we have demographic segmentation. Here, you divide people based on their basic information. So you look at people's ages, whether they are men or women, and so on. [3]Um, so one example is a company that sells clothing. It can use demographic segmentation to make advertisements for customers who are men and other advertisements for customers who are women.

Third, there is behavioral segmentation. This is where you divide people based on their behavior as customers. How do they like to shop? Do they shop through stores, websites, or smartphone apps? Do they read about products or follow social media influencers? Um, these are the kinds of questions to ask. They help determine the best way to communicate with customers.

And lastly, we have psychographic segmentation. With this type of segmentation, you are trying to find customers based on their psychology. So, uh, this refers to characteristics like their interests, attitudes, opinions, and so on... [4]This is complicated and time-consuming because companies have to gather information about individual people. And, of course, every person is so different. However, it can be useful because it lets you focus your marketing on more specific groups. For example, if you want to sell furniture to certain young people, it helps to know how those specific groups of young people think.

경영학 강의의 일부를 들으시오.

P: 자, 마케팅에 대한 논의를 계속하기 위해, 시장 세분화를 살펴봅시다. 이것은 고객들을 서로 다른 부분이나 그룹에 놓음으로써 분류하는 과정이에요. 이 그룹들은 고객들이 공유하는 특징을 기반으로 합니다. 이것을 하는 것은 기업이 모두에게 그렇게 하는 대신 특정 그룹의 사람들에게 제품을 판매하는 것에 집중하도록 도

와줍니다...

S: 죄송하지만, 음, 가능한 한 많은 사람들에게 제품을 판매하는 게 더 낫지 않을까요?

P: 음, 물론, 목표는 많은 제품을 판매하는 거예요. 하지만 이것은 효율적으로 이루어져야 해요. 모두에게 판매하려고 하면, 결국 잘못된 고객들에게 시간과 돈을 낭비하게 될 수도 있어요. 음, 이들은 여러분의 제품을 구입하지 않을 고객들이죠. 세분화는 기업들이 잠재 구매자들에게만 제품을 판매하도록 해줘요. 이것은 그들의 마케팅을 더 효과적이게 만들죠.

그건 그렇고, 세분화 과정을 시작하기 위해서는, 고객들에 대한 정보를 수집해야 해요. 설문조사에서 그들에게 질문을 함으로써 이것을 할 수 있어요. 혹은 정보를 수집하는 기업들로부터 그것을 구입할 수 있어요. 이 정보는 고객의 수입, 직업, 교육에 대한 것일 수 있죠... 그 밖에 무엇이든지요. 충분한 정보를 얻으면, 그룹을 만들 수 있어요.

자, 물론, 서로 다른 그룹을 만드는 많은 방법들이 있어요. 하지만, 세분화의 네 가지 주요 유형에 대해 논의해 볼게요... 첫째로, 지리적 세분화가 있어요. 이는 고객들을 그들이 살거나 일하는 곳에 따라 나누는 것을 말해요. 그래서 사람들을 국가, 도시, 마을 등으로 나눌 수 있죠. 음, 심지어 사람들을 기후에 따라 나눌 수도 있어요. 그러니까, 예를 들어, 기업은 겨울 코트를 추운 곳에 사는 사람들에게만 판매할 수도 있죠.

자, 다음으로, 인구통계학적 세분화가 있어요. 여기에서는, 사람들을 그들의 기본적인 정보에 따라 나눠요. 그래서 사람들의 나이, 남성인지 여성인지 등을 살펴보죠. 음, 그래서 한 가지 예시는 옷을 판매하는 기업이에요. 그것은 남성인 고객들을 위한 광고를 만들고 여성인 고객들을 위해서는 다른 광고를 만들기 위해 인구통계학적 세분화를 이용할 수 있어요.

세 번째로, 행동적 세분화가 있습니다. 이것은 사람들을 고객으로서의 행동에 따라 나누는 경우예요. 그들이 어떻게 쇼핑하는 걸 좋아하나요? 그들이 상점, 웹사이트, 혹은 스마트폰 앱을 통해 쇼핑하나요? 그들이 제품에 대해 읽거나 소셜 미디어의 인플루언서를 팔로우하나요? 음, 이런 것들이 묻는 질문의 종류들이에요. 그것들은 고객과 소통하는 최선의 방법을 결정하는 데 도움을 줘요.

그리고 마지막으로, 심리묘사적 세분화가 있어요. 이 유형의 세분화에서, 여러분은 그들의 심리에 기반하여 고객을 찾으려 합니다. 그러니까, 어, 이것은 그들의 관심사, 태도, 의견 등과 같은 특징을 가리켜요... 기업이 개개인의 사람들에 대한 정보를 수집해야 하기 때문에 이것은 복잡하고 시간이 많이 걸립니다. 그리고, 물론, 모든 사람은 서로 너무 달라요. 하지만, 그것은 마케팅이 더 특정한 그룹에 집중하도록 해주기 때문에 유용할 수 있어요. 예를 들어, 여러분이 특정한 젊은 사람들에게 가구를 판매하고 싶다면, 그 특정한 그룹의 젊은 사람들이 어떻게 생각하는지를 아는 것은 도움이 돼요.

---

segmentation 몝 세분화   categorize 통 분류하다
efficiently 뷔 효율적으로   potential 혭 잠재적인
income 몝 수입   geographic 혭 지리적인
demographic 혭 인구통계학적인   advertisement 몝 광고
behavioral 혭 행동적   psychology 몝 심리

1 강의는 주로 무엇에 관한 것인가?

  (A) 기업이 어디에서 고객들을 찾는지

  (B) 기업이 고객들을 분류하는 방법

  (C) 고객들이 그들의 정보를 공유하는 이유

  (D) 어떤 고객들을 피해야 하는지

2 교수는 강의를 어떻게 구성하는가?

(A) 교과서의 다양한 주제를 복습함으로써

(B) 두 기업의 전략을 비교함으로써

(C) 과정이 수행되는 다양한 방법들을 설명함으로써

(D) 설문조사의 결과에 대해 논의함으로써

3 교수는 인구통계학적 세분화에 대해 어떤 예시를 드는가?

(A) 기업은 성별과 같은 기본적인 정보를 고려한다.

(B) 기업은 생활방식에 대한 정보를 수집한다.

(C) 기업은 인기 있는 소셜 미디어 인플루언서들을 찾는다.

(D) 기업은 다양한 지역의 고객들을 비교한다.

4 심리묘사적 세분화에 관해 추론할 수 있는 것은 무엇인가?

(A) 그것은 작은 기업들에게 너무 비싸다.

(B) 그것은 일반적인 정보를 찾는 데 유용하다.

(C) 그것은 특정 제품에만 좋다.

(D) 그것은 기업들이 하기에 도전적이다.

강의의 일부를 다시 듣고 질문에 답하시오.

P: Anyway, to start the segmentation process, you have to gather information about customers. You can do this by asking them questions in surveys. Or you can buy the information from companies that collect it. This information can be about the customers' incomes, jobs, education... You name it.

5 교수는 이렇게 말함으로써 무엇을 의미하는가:

P: You name it.

(A) 학생들이 과정을 이해했는지 확인하기 위해

(B) 많은 예시가 있다는 것을 시사하기 위해

(C) 아이디어가 이전에 논의되었음을 나타내기 위해

(D) 학생들에게 더 많은 세부 사항을 제공하도록 독려하기 위해

---

iBT Listening Test 1

1 (D) 2 (C) 3 (D) 4 (A) 5 (B)

Note-taking

P: Yesterday's class, talked about Francis Bacon
  17c. = scientists used religious stories to explain world
  Bacon = better approach = learn through observation
  Science should look at indiv. events → develop idea
  Ppl. would start w/ general principle & look for proof
S: 2 kinds of knwl. = matters of fact & relations of ideas
P: 1st = knwl. from experiencing things
  2nd = ideas that are simply true (e.g. geometry)
  Bacon = relations of ideas = useful X

Listen to a conversation between a student and a professor.

S: Hello, Professor Miller. Um, unfortunately, I couldn't come to yesterday's class because I wasn't feeling well. [1]Could you tell me what you discussed in class?

P: Sure. In yesterday's class, we talked about Francis Bacon...

S: Oh, OK. I've heard the name before, but I'm not sure who he is exactly.

P: Yes, well, he was an important 17th-century philosopher. At that time, most people thought that science and religion were the same. [2]So, um, it was normal for a scientist to use religious stories to explain how the world worked. Bacon had a better approach to science. He encouraged people to learn about the world through observation.

S: That doesn't sound like a big deal now, but I guess it was pretty shocking back then.

P: Yes, but that's not the only reason Bacon was important. He really wanted to make science better. He thought that science should look at lots of individual events separately and then try to develop an idea that explains all of them.

S: [5]You mean like developing a theory for why something happened?

P: Yes. This concept is part of what we usually call the scientific method. Um, I assume I don't have to go over that in detail.

S: Right, I studied this in one of my other classes. According to the scientific method, you do experiments to test your ideas about how something works, right?

P: That's correct. Now, this seems obvious to us, but it wasn't the normal way of doing things when Bacon was alive. In those days, people would start with a general principle and look for proof of it in the world.

S: I think I remember this from one of your lectures. You said there are two kinds of knowledge. Um, you called them matters of fact and relations of ideas.

P: Yes, exactly. The first kind is the knowledge that we get from experiencing things in the world. And the second involves ideas that are simply true, like, uh, ideas from geometry. [3]For example, we don't have to do experiments to find out that a triangle has three sides. This is a relation of ideas.

S: I see what you mean.

P: Bacon didn't think relations of ideas were very useful for discovering how things work in nature. That's why he encouraged scientists to observe events, make theories, and test those theories. And, well, he was pretty much correct.

S: I see. I'm glad I asked you about this. I can do some more reading on my own.

P: Yes. This was just a basic overview. [4]So I suggest you do more reading. Um, there's a section on Bacon in Chapter 8 of your textbook.

S: Thanks, Professor. [4]I'll work on that right away.

학생과 교수 사이의 대화를 들으시오.

S: 안녕하세요, Miller 교수님. 음, 안타깝게도, 저는 몸이 안 좋아서 어

제 수업에 갈 수 없었어요. 수업에서 논의하신 걸 말씀해주실 수 있나요?

P: 물론이지. 어제 수업에서, 우리는 프랜시스 베이컨에 대해 이야기했단다...

S: 오, 알겠습니다. 전에 그 이름을 들어본 적이 있는데, 그가 정확히 누군지는 모르겠네요.

P: 그래, 음, 그는 중요한 17세기 철학자였어. 그 당시에, 대부분의 사람들은 과학과 종교가 같다고 생각했어. 그래서, 음, 세상이 작동하는 방식을 설명하기 위해 과학자가 종교적인 이야기를 사용하는 건 평범한 것이었어. 베이컨은 과학에 대한 더 나은 접근법을 가지고 있었지. 그는 사람들에게 관찰을 통해 세상에 관해 배울 것을 독려했어.

S: 지금은 그게 별일이 아닌 것처럼 들리지만, 당시에는 꽤 충격적이었겠네요.

P: 맞아, 하지만 그게 베이컨이 중요했던 유일한 이유는 아니야. 그는 정말로 과학을 더 낫게 만들고 싶어 했어. 그는 과학이 많은 개별 사건들을 따로따로 살펴본 다음 그것들 모두를 설명하는 관념을 개발하려 노력해야 한다고 생각했어.

S: 어떤 일이 일어난 이유를 위한 이론의 개발 같은 걸 말씀하시는 건가요?

P: 그래. 이 개념은 우리가 보통 과학적 방법론이라고 부르는 것의 일부야. 음, 그것을 자세히 살펴볼 필요는 없을 것 같구나.

S: 맞아요, 저는 이걸 다른 수업들 중 하나에서 공부했어요. 과학적 방법론에 따르면, 사람들은 어떤 것이 작동하는 방식에 관한 관념을 시험하기 위해 실험을 해요, 그렇죠?

P: 맞아. 지금은, 이게 우리에게 명백해 보이지만, 베이컨이 살아있을 때는 그게 무언가를 하는 일반적인 방식이 아니었어. 그 당시에, 사람들은 일반적인 원칙에서 출발해서 세상에서 그것의 증거를 찾곤 했지.

S: 교수님의 강의 중 하나에서 이걸 들은 기억이 나는 것 같아요. 두 종류의 지식이 있다고 말씀하셨죠. 음, 교수님은 그것들을 사실의 문제들과 관념들의 관계라고 부르셨어요.

P: 맞아, 정확해. 첫 번째 종류는 우리가 세상에 있는 것들을 경험함으로써 얻는 지식이야. 그리고 두 번째는 그저 사실인 관념들을 포함해, 마치, 어, 기하학의 관념들처럼 말이야. 예를 들어, 우리는 삼각형이 세 개의 변을 가지고 있다는 것을 알아내기 위해 실험을 할 필요가 없어. 이것이 관념들의 관계야.

S: 무슨 말씀인지 알겠어요.

P: 베이컨은 관념들의 관계가 자연에서 사물이 작동하는 방식을 밝혀내기에 그다지 유용하지 않다고 생각했어. 그것이 그가 과학자들에게 사건을 관찰하고, 이론을 만들고, 그 이론들을 시험해 보라고 독려한 이유야. 그리고, 음, 그는 거의 정확했어.

S: 알겠어요. 제가 이것에 대해 여쭤봐서 기뻐요. 혼자서 좀 더 읽어볼 수 있겠어요.

P: 그래. 이건 그냥 기본적인 개요였어. 그러니까 네가 더 읽어볼 것을 추천한다. 음, 교과서 8장에 베이컨에 관한 부분이 있어.

S: 감사합니다, 교수님. 지금 바로 그걸 할게요.

philosopher 명 철학자   religion 명 종교
approach 명 접근법, 접근   observation 명 관찰
individual 형 개별적인   separately 부 따로따로   in detail 자세히
obvious 형 명백한   principle 명 원칙   proof 명 증거
knowledge 명 지식   relation 명 관계   geometry 명 기하학

1 대화의 주된 주제는 무엇인가?

(A) 학생이 과제물을 완료하지 않은 이유

(B) 저자가 중요한 이유

(C) 과학과 종교의 차이점

(D) 교수가 수업에서 이야기한 것

2 교수에 따르면, 베이컨은 그의 시대의 대부분의 사람들과 어떻게 달랐는가?

(A) 그는 철학자들이 과학을 설명해야 한다고 제안했다.

(B) 그는 과학자들이 종교로부터 배울 수 있다고 생각했다.

(C) 그는 과학자들이 새로운 접근법을 사용해야 한다고 생각했다.

(D) 그는 종교인들이 과학을 공부하면 안 된다고 주장했다.

3 교수는 왜 삼각형을 언급하는가?

(A) 초기의 과학적 방법론을 설명하기 위해

(B) 수학과 다른 과학들을 비교하기 위해

(C) 베이컨이 종교적인 사람이었다는 것을 지적하기 위해

(D) 관념들의 관계의 예를 들기 위해

4 학생은 다음에 무엇을 할 것인가?

(A) 읽기 자료 검토하기

(B) 개인 과외 요청하기

(C) 조언을 위해 친구에게 연락하기

(D) 도서관에 교과서 반납하기

대화의 일부를 다시 듣고 질문에 답하시오.

S: You mean like developing a theory for why something happened?

P: Yes. This concept is part of what we usually call the scientific method. Um, I assume I don't have to go over that in detail.

S: Right, I studied this in one of my other classes.

5 교수는 이렇게 말함으로써 무엇을 암시하는가:

P: Um, I assume I don't have to go over that in detail.

(A) 교수는 학생이 곧 떠나길 바란다.

(B) 학생은 이미 견해에 익숙하다.

(C) 교수는 주제의 세부 사항을 모른다.

(D) 학생은 수업 중에 주의 깊게 들어야 한다.

iBT Listening Test 2
본문 p. 148

1 (C)	2 (B)	3 (C)	4 (B)	5 (A)	6 (B), (D)

Note-taking

Increased Interactions between Humans and Animals

- Interactions w/ animals have increased → discuss why
- Biggest factor = changes in land use
  - Humans enter wild areas (e.g. mining companies)
  - Chicago = ppl. moving from main city to suburbs
- Behavior of wild animals changing
  - Get used to humans → fear X → diets can change
  - Birds in city sing louder > birds in country
  - Effect on genetics = find mate & continue growing
- Problems for ppl. = carry diseases & cause accidents
  - Solutions = limit development, act differently

Listen to part of a lecture in a biology class.

P: [1]Animals have always been a part of human communities. And as human communities have grown, interactions with animals have also increased. Today, we are going to discuss the reason why this has been happening.

The biggest factor is changes in land use. [2]Uh, humans enter wild areas for a variety of reasons. For example, mining companies go into the mountains to look for natural resources like iron, coal, and copper. When they do this, they build mining communities for their workers. The same thing happens when people enter forests to cut wood. New human settlements are created in areas that were previously wild. So, uh, contact between humans and wild animals increases... The same thing is happening with cities. People are building more cities around the world. In addition, many existing cities are becoming bigger. As this happens, the amount of land used for urban areas grows. Um, a good example is the city of Chicago. Chicago has not had a large population increase in a long time. However, the amount of land used for urban areas continues to increase. This is because people are moving away from the main city. Uh, they want to own houses in the suburbs. [3]When this happens, people move into land that was previously used by wild animals. That's why people in these areas see many wild animals.

Now, because more people and wild animals are living in the same places, the behavior of wild animals is changing, too. They are adapting to urban environments. Naturally, most wild animals are afraid of humans. They will not go near people. However, as interactions increase, the animals get used to the presence of humans. They no longer fear them. [4]And they learn that humans provide convenient sources of food. Sometimes, the diets of these wild animals can change as a result. Researchers have also found that animals in urban areas can change in other ways... [5]For example, some researchers studied songbirds that live in cities. Interestingly, they learned that birds in the city sing louder than birds in the country. Can anyone guess why?

S: Uh, cities can be very noisy. Maybe the birds are trying to sing louder than the city noise.

P: That's what the researchers think too... And, uh, this can have real effects on future genetics. Uh, birds that sing louder are easier to hear. So they are more likely to find mates and continue growing...

And what else do you think happens? Well, the larger presence of wild animals in cities can also cause problems for people. For instance, wild animals carry diseases. Diseases that come from animals can be deadly to people. Uh, think of the coronavirus, for example, which probably came from a bat... And then, uh, there are other problems, too. Um, wild animals can cause traffic accidents when they try to cross busy roads.

These are just a couple of examples... To reduce these problems, we have to find solutions. [6B]For instance, we can limit new development in wild areas. [6D]Or we can also learn to act differently around wild animals... For example, we can change how we throw away food waste.

생물학 강의의 일부를 들으시오.

P: 동물들은 항상 인간 공동체의 일부여 왔습니다. 그리고 인간 공동체가 성장해옴에 따라, 동물들과의 상호작용도 증가했죠. 오늘, 우리는 이런 일이 일어나고 있는 이유에 대해 논의할 거예요.

가장 큰 요인은 토지 이용의 변화입니다. 어, 인간들은 다양한 이유로 야생 지역에 들어가요. 예를 들어, 광산 회사들은 철, 석탄, 구리와 같은 천연자원들을 찾기 위해 산으로 들어가죠. 이렇게 할 때, 그들은 그들의 노동자들을 위한 광산 공동체를 건설해요. 사람들이 나무를 베기 위해 숲으로 들어갈 때도 같은 일이 일어나죠. 이전에 야생이었던 지역에 새로운 인간 정착지가 만들어져요. 그래서, 어, 인간들과 야생 동물들의 접촉이 증가합니다... 도시에서도 같은 일이 일어나고 있어요. 사람들은 전 세계에 더 많은 도시를 건설하고 있어요. 게다가, 이미 존재하는 많은 도시들은 더 커지고 있죠. 이런 일이 일어나면서, 도시 지역을 위해 사용되는 토지의 양이 늘어나요. 음, 좋은 예시는 시카고에요. 시카고는 오랫동안 큰 인구 증가를 겪지 않았어요. 하지만, 도시 지역을 위해 사용되는 토지의 양은 계속해서 증가하고 있어요. 이는 사람들이 중심 도시에서 멀어지고 있기 때문이에요. 어, 그들은 교외에 집을 소유하고 싶어 하죠. 이런 일이 일어날 때, 사람들은 이전에 야생 동물들에 의해 이용되었던 땅으로 이주해 들어가요. 그게 이 지역에 있는 사람들이 많은 야생 동물들을 보게 되는 이유예요.

자, 더 많은 사람들과 야생 동물들이 같은 장소에 살고 있기 때문에, 야생 동물들의 행동 또한 변하고 있어요. 그것들은 도시 환경에 적응하고 있죠. 당연히, 대부분의 야생 동물들은 인간들을 두려워해요. 그것들은 사람들에게 가까이 가지 않을 거예요. 하지만, 상호작용이 증가하면서, 동물들은 인간들의 존재에 익숙해져요. 그것들은 더 이상 그들을 두려워하지 않죠. 그리고 그것들은 인간들이 먹이의 편리한 공급원을 제공한다는 걸 학습해요. 때때로, 그 결과 이 야생 동물들의 식습관이 바뀔 수 있어요. 연구자들은 도시 지역의 동물들이 다른 방식으로 변할 수 있다는 것도 알아냈어요... 예를 들어, 일부 연구자들은 도시에 사는 명금들을 연구했어요. 흥미롭게도, 그들은 도시에 사는 새들이 시골에 사는 새들보다 더 크게 노래한다는 것을 알게 됐어요. 이유를 추측해볼 사람 있나요?

S: 어, 도시는 매우 시끄러울 수 있잖아요. 아마도 새들이 도시의 소음보다 더 크게 노래하려고 하는 것 같아요.

P: 그게 연구자들이 생각하는 것이기도 해요... 그리고, 어, 이는 미래의 유전적 특징에 실질적인 영향을 미칠 수 있어요. 어, 더 크게 노래하는 새들은 더 듣기 쉬워요. 그래서 그것들은 짝을 찾고 계속해서 성장할 가능성이 더 크죠...

그리고 또 어떤 일이 일어날 것 같나요? 음, 도시에 야생 동물들이 더 많이 존재하는 것은 사람들에게 문제를 일으킬 수도 있어요. 예를 들어, 야생 동물들은 질병을 옮겨요. 동물에서 비롯되는 질병은 사람들에게 치명적일 수 있어요. 어, 예를 들어, 아마도 박쥐에서 비롯되었을 코로나바이러스를 생각해 보세요... 그리고, 어, 다른 문제들도 있어요. 음, 야생 동물들은 붐비는 도로를 건너려 할 때 교통사고를 일으킬 수 있어요. 이것들은 단지 몇 가지의 예시예요... 이 문제들을 줄이기 위해, 우리는 해결책을 찾아야 해요. 예를 들어, 우리는 야생 지역에서의 새로운 개발을 제한할 수 있어요. 혹은 우리는 또한 야생 동물들 주변에서 다르게 행동하는 법을 배울 수도 있어요... 예를 들어, 우리는 음식물 쓰레기를 버리는 방식을 바꿀 수 있죠.

community 명 공동체　interaction 명 상호작용
natural resource 천연자원　coal 명 석탄　copper 명 구리
settlement 명 정착지　suburb 명 교외　adapt to ~에 적응하다
presence 명 존재　convenient 형 편리한
genetics 명 유전적 특징　deadly 형 치명적인
differently 부 다르게

1 강의의 주된 주제는 무엇인가?

　(A) 야생 동물들이 인간들에게 어떻게 위험한지

　(B) 동물들의 개체수 증가에 대한 인간들의 영향

　(C) 인간들과 동물들의 상호작용이 증가하고 있는 이유

　(D) 야생 동물들을 보호하기 위한 일부 단체들의 노력

2 강의에서 교수는 왜 광산 회사들을 언급하는가?

　(A) 쇠퇴하는 산업을 언급하기 위해

　(B) 인간들이 야생 지역에 들어가는 이유의 예시를 들기 위해

　(C) 인간의 행동이 오염을 초래하는 방식을 설명하기 위해

　(D) 특정 공동체에 대한 광산업의 중요성을 설명하기 위해

3 교수에 따르면, 도시에서 더 많은 야생 동물이 보이는 주된 이유는
무엇인가?

　(A) 동물들이 더 이상 자연에서 좋은 먹이 공급원을 찾을 수 없다.

　(B) 더 많은 사람들이 야생 동물을 반려동물로 갖는 데 관심이 있다.

　(C) 사람들이 동물들이 사는 땅의 더 많은 부분을 이용하고 있다.

　(D) 일부 야생 동물들의 개체수가 증가해오고 있다.

4 교수는 인간 음식의 존재에 관해 무엇이라고 말하는가?

　(A) 그것은 몇몇 동물들 사이에 갈등을 초래할 수 있다.

　(B) 그것은 야생 동물들이 먹는 것을 바꿀 수 있다.

　(C) 그것은 야생 동물들의 건강에 해롭다.

　(D) 그것은 일부 종들의 생존을 위해 필수적이다.

5 교수는 명금의 미래에 관해 무엇을 암시하는가?

　(A) 더 크게 노래하는 것들은 수가 증가할 것이다.

　(B) 그것들은 짝을 더 쉽게 찾을 수 있을 것이다.

　(C) 그것들이 내는 소리는 덜 시끄러워질 것이다.

　(D) 그것들은 시간이 지나며 크기가 더 작아질 것이다.

6 교수에 따르면, 도시에서 야생 동물들에 의해 초래되는 문제들에
대한 해결책은 무엇인가?
2개의 답을 고르시오.

　(A) 붐비는 도로 주위에 더 나은 울타리를 건설하는 것

　(B) 그것들이 사는 지역에서의 개발을 피하는 것

　(C) 그것들이 초래할 수 있는 질병을 연구하는 것

　(D) 그것들 주변에서 다르게 행동하는 법을 배우는 것

Vocabulary Review　　　본문 p. 152

1 grain	**2** candidate	**3** principle
4 observation	**5** segmentation	**6** geographic
7 potential	**8** relation	**9** dense
10 (A)	**11** (B)	**12** (C)
13 (C)	**14** (A)	

Actual Test 1

PART 1. Passage 1　　　본문 p. 154

1 (C)　　2 (A)　　3 (B)　　4 (D)　　5 (B)

Note-taking

W: Received 2 room fines, have to pay them?
　1st = stain on carpet = my fault X, roommate spilled
M: Each roommate has to pay part
　Tried talking to roommate?
W: She doesn't remember, no choice but accept decision
　Closet door broken = already broken when first came
　Asked maint. manager to fix → never fixed
M: Repair X w/o form, she can confirm → cancel fine
W: Hard to contact her ∵ busy ∵ end of semester
M: I'll talk → save time

Listen to a conversation between a student and a
university housing office employee.

W: Hi. I was wondering if you could explain
something to me... Um, but just to check, this is
the housing office, isn't it?

M: Yes, it is. Tell me what the problem is, and I'll see
if I can help you.

W: [1]Well, I'm moving out of my dormitory this week,
but I just realized I received two room fines. I
want to know if I have to pay them.

M: [5]Can you give me a little more information, like
your name and which dormitory you're in?

W: Sure. I'm Sienna Parsons, and I'm in Brown Hall.

M: Hmm... I don't see anything here... So these
fines... Uh...

W: I'll explain. Um, the first one has to do with a stain
on the carpet. But I know this isn't my fault. My
roommate spilled a cup of coffee at the start of
the semester and didn't clean it up.

M: Well... The rules state that it doesn't matter if it
was you or your roommate who made the mess.
It's impossible for us to check whose fault it is, so
each roommate has to pay part of the fine.

W: I know that's the rule, but it doesn't seem fair.
Why should I have to pay when I didn't do
anything wrong?

M: Have you tried talking to your roommate? If she is
the one who made the stain, she might agree to
pay the fine herself, right?

W: [2]Uh... You don't know my roommate... I tried
talking to her, but she says she doesn't remember
who made the stain! And it's not the first time
she's been careless this way. Anyway, I guess
there's no way for me to prove my case. So I
have no choice but to accept the decision.

M: Yes, unfortunately, rules are rules. There's

nothing I can do... Now, um, can I help you with anything else?

W: Actually, there's still the other fine... Um, the notice I received says that my closet door was broken. But I'm not the one responsible for that, either. You see, it was already broken when I first came here... I even asked the maintenance manager to fix it earlier...

M: You made a request?

W: Yeah... But she never fixed the problem. I didn't think it was that serious, so I just forgot about it eventually.

M: Did she ask you to submit a form to report the problem?

W: [3]Oh, no. I never submitted a form... She didn't say anything about that.

M: We don't do repairs without that form, so that's probably why it never got fixed... But you can go talk to the maintenance manager now. Maybe she can confirm that you reported the broken closet door. And once we hear from her, we can cancel your fine.

W: It's going to be hard to contact her... She's really busy since it's the end of the semester. Everyone is moving out of their dormitories.

M: OK... [4]Then, I'll talk to the maintenance manager, so you don't have to do it yourself. That will save us both some time, actually.

W: Wow, that's so kind of you... Thanks a lot! I really appreciate all your help.

학생과 대학 기숙사 사무실 직원 사이의 대화를 들으시오.

W: 안녕하세요. 제게 뭔가 설명해 주실 수 있는지 궁금해요... 음, 혹시, 여기가 기숙사 사무실이죠, 그렇지 않나요?

M: 네, 맞아요. 문제가 무엇인지 말씀해 주시면, 제가 도와드릴 수 있는지 볼게요.

W: 음, 저는 이번 주에 기숙사에서 이사해 나가는데, 방 벌금 두 개를 받은 걸 방금 깨달았어요. 제가 그것들을 내야 하는지 알고 싶어요.

M: 학생의 이름과 어떤 기숙사에 계신 지와 같은 정보를 좀 더 주실 수 있나요?

W: 물론이죠. 전 Sienna Parsons이고, Brown Hall에 있어요.

M: 흠... 여기에는 아무것도 없네요... 그러니까 이 벌금들이... 어...

W: 제가 설명할게요. 음, 첫 번째 것은 카펫에 있는 얼룩과 관계가 있어요. 그런데 저는 이게 제 잘못이 아니라는 걸 알아요. 제 룸메이트가 학기 초에 커피 한잔을 쏟았고 그걸 청소하지 않았어요.

M: 음... 규정에는 실수를 저지른 게 학생인지 학생의 룸메이트인지는 상관이 없다고 명시되어 있어요. 저희가 그게 누구의 잘못인지 확인하는 게 불가능하기 때문에, 각 룸메이트가 벌금의 일부를 내야 해요.

W: 그게 규정이라는 건 알지만, 공평한 것 같지 않아요. 잘못한 게 없는데 제가 왜 돈을 내야 하나요?

M: 룸메이트와는 얘기해 보셨어요? 얼룩을 만든 게 그녀라면, 자신이 벌금을 내는 것에 동의할지도 몰라요, 그렇죠?

W: 어... 제 룸메이트를 모르시죠... 그녀에게 얘기해 봤는데, 그녀는 누가 그 얼룩을 만들었는지 기억하지 못한대요! 그리고 그녀가 이런 식으로 부주의한 것은 처음이 아니에요. 어쨌든, 제 주장을 증명할 방법이 없을 것 같네요. 그러니까 제가 그 결정을 받아들일 수밖에 없네요.

M: 맞아요, 안타깝지만, 규정은 규정이니까요. 제가 해드릴 수 있는 게 없어요... 자, 음, 제가 더 도와 드릴 건 없을까요?

W: 사실, 아직 다른 벌금이 남아있어요... 음, 제가 받은 통지서에 제 옷장 문이 망가졌다고 되어있어요. 하지만 저는 그것에도 책임이 없어요. 있잖아요, 제가 처음 여기에 왔을 때 그건 이미 망가져 있었어요... 저는 심지어 예전에 보수 관리 담당자께 그것을 고쳐 달라고 요청했어요...

M: 요청하셨다고요?

W: 네... 그런데 그녀는 그 문제를 고쳐 주시지 않았어요. 저는 그게 그렇게 심각하다고 생각하지 않아서, 결국 그것을 잊어버렸어요.

M: 그녀가 그 문제를 신고하기 위해 신청서를 제출하라고 요청했나요?

W: 오, 아뇨. 저는 신청서를 제출한 적이 없어요... 그녀는 그것에 대해 아무것도 말씀하시지 않았거든요.

M: 저희는 그 신청서 없이는 수리를 하지 않아서, 아마 그게 그것이 고쳐지지 않은 이유일 거예요... 그런데 지금 가서 보수 관리 담당자에게 얘기하실 수 있어요. 아마 그녀는 학생이 망가진 옷장 문을 신고했다고 확인해 줄 수 있을 거예요. 그리고 저희가 그녀에게서 연락을 받으면, 학생의 벌금을 취소할 수 있어요.

W: 그녀에게 연락하는 건 어려울 거예요... 학기 말이라 그녀는 정말 바빠요. 모두가 기숙사에서 이사해 나가고 있잖아요.

M: 네... 그럼, 제가 보수 관리 담당자에게 얘기할게요, 그럼 학생이 직접 그렇게 하실 필요가 없어요. 사실, 그게 우리 둘 다의 시간을 절약해 주겠네요.

W: 와, 정말 친절하시네요... 정말 감사해요! 도와주신 것 모두 정말 감사해요.

---

realize (동) 깨닫다, 알아채다   fine (명) 벌금   stain (명) 얼룩
fault (명) 잘못   spill (동) 쏟다   careless (형) 부주의한
prove (동) 증명하다   responsible for ~에 책임이 있는
maintenance (명) 보수 관리   eventually (부) 결국
confirm (동) 확인해 주다

1 학생은 왜 대학 기숙사 사무실을 찾아가는가?

(A) 그녀의 기숙사 벌금 납부 기한이 언제인지 알아보기 위해

(B) 그녀의 룸메이트가 이사해 나간 이유를 설명하기 위해

(C) 그녀가 몇몇 벌금을 내야 하는지 확인하기 위해

(D) 그녀가 청구서를 미리 지불할 수 있는지 문의하기 위해

2 학생은 그녀의 룸메이트에 관해 무엇을 암시하는가?

(A) 그녀는 조심성 있는 사람이 아니다.

(B) 그녀는 이미 기숙사를 떠났다.

(C) 그녀는 학생과 이야기하기를 거부하고 있다.

(D) 그녀는 벌금을 낼 돈이 없다.

3 학생의 옷장 문은 왜 수리되지 않았는가?

(A) 학생이 담당자에게 알리는 것을 잊었다.

(B) 필요한 신청서가 제출되지 않았다.

(C) 학생이 문제를 너무 늦게 신고했다.

(D) 요청이 시스템에 기록되지 않았다.

4 직원은 학생에게 무엇을 해주기로 하는가?

(A) 그는 그녀가 새 기숙사로 이사하는 것을 도와줄 것이다.

(B) 그는 그녀가 내야 하는 벌금의 액수를 줄여줄 것이다.

(C) 그는 기술자에게 그녀 방의 문을 수리해 달라고 지시할 것이다.

(D) 그는 담당자에게 그녀의 상황에 대해 물어볼 것이다.

대화의 일부를 다시 듣고 질문에 답하시오.

M: Can you give me a little more information, like your name and which dormitory you're in?

W: Sure. I'm Sienna Parsons, and I'm in Brown Hall.

M: Hmm… I don't see anything here… So these fines… Uh…

5 직원은 왜 이렇게 말하는가:

M: So these fines… Uh…

(A) 학생에게 지불해야 한다는 것을 상기시키기 위해

(B) 학생에게 세부 정보를 제공할 것을 독려하기 위해

(C) 그가 벌금에 관해 잊어버렸다는 것을 나타내기 위해

(D) 학생이 벌금을 받았다는 것에 놀라움을 표현하기 위해

PART 1. Passage 2   본문 p.156

6 (C)   7 (B)   8 (B)   9 (D)   10 (A)   11 (C)

Note-taking

Thomas Cole

- Cole = famous for landscape painting
- 1825, became portrait painter in NY
- Natural beauty inspired → 1st landscape paintings
- Painted in Romantic style
  - 1st in Am., wanted paintings to make feel emotions
- Represented America
  - Inspired by actual places in America
  - Telling story about America = new country
- Inspired other painters w/ style
- Early environmentalist = view against development

Listen to part of a lecture in an art history class.

P: Today, I'd like to continue our discussion of American art during the 1800s. In particular, I'd like to talk about an important painter called Thomas Cole. Um, Cole became famous for his landscape paintings. Landscape paintings, of course, are a very common type of painting. You know… They show scenes from nature, such as mountains, trees, clouds, and so on… Cole, however, became known for painting them in a Romantic style. This means that they looked very dramatic, almost like scenes from a movie. [6]Anyway, let's talk about what makes him an important American artist.

So Thomas Cole was actually born in England in 1801. But he moved to America in 1818. From a young age, he was interested in art and mostly taught himself how to draw. He also received some art training while in his teens. Then, in 1825, he became a professional portrait painter in New York City. So, um, he started his career painting pictures of people. [7]However, shortly after moving to New York City, he visited the town of Catskill for the first time. The natural beauty around Catskill inspired Cole to make many drawings. When he returned home, Cole used these drawings to create his first landscape paintings. The paintings were soon bought by some famous art collectors in New York City. They encouraged Cole to continue painting and helped him to become a successful artist.

S: [10]But, uh, what was so special about Cole's work? Didn't many artists paint landscapes?

P: I'm glad you asked that. Well, one of the reasons Cole was important is that he painted in the Romantic style. This style was popular in Europe at the time, but Cole was the first to use it in America. So what this means is that his landscape paintings were full of drama and mystery. You see, Cole didn't just paint nature. He used his imagination… Uh, he thought that a nice sunset or big storm clouds could provide an emotional experience. And he wanted his paintings to make the viewer feel these emotions.

OK. Now, another reason Cole is important is that his art also represented America itself in a way. Let me explain… First of all, Cole painted scenes that were inspired by actual places in America. So he was showing what America looked like, both to Europeans and even to Americans themselves. [8]Um, you see, many Americans during the 1800s spent most of their time working in the cities. They did not have many chances to go out and see America's natural lands. [9]Plus, through his paintings, Cole was also telling a story about America. Um, you have to remember that American Independence was just declared in 1776. So, during the early 1800s, America was still quite a new country. Cole's paintings captured that feeling by showing landscapes that were wild, open, and full of possibilities for the future.

[11]And lastly, Cole inspired other American painters with his style. Some of these painters formed a group and tried to paint in the same style as Cole. Even many landscape painters from the early 20th century showed Cole's lasting influence in their work. That's almost a hundred years later. That's quite a while. And, uh, Cole's significance even went beyond art… He was actually an early environmentalist. During his life, he expressed strong views against industrial and urban development, particularly the way that people were destroying natural lands to build railways and houses… In this sense, his interest in the environment and his art were closely connected… After Cole died in 1848, the people of Catskill named one of their mountains in his honor. It's called Thomas Cole Mountain.

미술사학 강의의 일부를 들으시오.

P: 오늘은, 1800년대 미국의 미술에 대한 논의를 계속할 거예요. 특히, 토머스 콜이라는 중요한 화가에 대해 얘기하고 싶네요. 음, 콜은 그의 풍경화로 유명해졌어요. 풍경화는, 물론, 매우 흔한 종류

의 그림이에요. 알다시피... 그것들은 산, 나무, 구름 등과 같은 자연의 풍경을 보여주죠... 하지만, 콜은 그것들을 낭만주의 화풍으로 그린 것으로 알려지게 됐어요. 이는 그것들이 거의 영화의 장면처럼 매우 극적으로 보였다는 것을 의미해요. 어쨌든, 무엇이 그를 중요한 미국 화가로 만들었는지에 대해 얘기해보죠.

자, 토머스 콜은 사실 1801년 영국에서 태어났어요. 하지만 그는 1818년에 미국으로 이주했죠. 어린 나이부터, 그는 미술에 관심이 있었고 그림 그리는 법을 대부분 독학했어요. 그는 10대 시절에 약간의 미술 훈련을 받기도 했어요. 그 후, 1825년에, 그는 뉴욕시에서 전문 초상화 화가가 되었습니다. 그러니까, 음, 그는 사람들의 그림을 그리는 것으로 그의 경력을 시작했죠. 하지만, 뉴욕시로 이사한 직후, 그는 처음으로 캐츠킬 마을을 방문했어요. 캐츠킬 주변의 자연적 아름다움은 콜이 많은 스케치를 하도록 영감을 주었어요. 집으로 돌아왔을 때, 콜은 이 스케치들을 이용하여 그의 첫 풍경화들을 제작했어요. 그 그림들은 곧 뉴욕시의 몇몇 유명한 미술품 수집가들에 의해 구입됐어요. 그들은 콜에게 계속 그림을 그리라고 독려했고 그가 성공적인 화가가 되는 데 도움을 주었죠.

S: 그런데, 어, 콜의 작품에서 무엇이 그렇게 특별했나요? 많은 화가들이 풍경을 그리지 않았나요?

P: 그걸 물어봐 줘서 기뻐요. 음, 콜이 중요했던 이유들 중 하나는 그가 낭만주의 화풍으로 그렸다는 거예요. 이 화풍은 당시에 유럽에서 인기가 있었지만, 미국에서 그것을 사용한 것은 콜이 최초였어요. 그러니까 이게 의미하는 건 그의 풍경화가 극적 요소와 신비로움으로 가득했다는 거예요. 그러니까, 콜은 그저 자연을 그린 게 아니에요. 그는 그의 상상력을 발휘했어요... 어, 그는 멋진 노을이나 큰 폭풍 구름이 감정적 경험을 제공할 수 있다고 생각했죠. 그리고 그는 그의 그림이 보는 이로 하여금 이 감정들을 느끼게 해주기를 원했어요.

좋아요. 자, 콜이 중요한 또 다른 이유는 그의 미술이 어떤 면에서 미국 자체를 대표하기도 했기 때문이에요. 설명할게요... 우선, 콜은 미국의 실제 장소들에서 영감을 받은 풍경들을 그렸어요. 그래서 그는 유럽인들과 심지어는 미국인 자신들에게 미국이 어떻게 보이는지를 보여주고 있었죠. 음, 그러니까, 1800년대의 많은 미국인들은 대부분의 시간을 도시에서 일하며 보냈어요. 그들은 미국의 자연적인 지역들을 보러 나갈 기회가 많지 않았어요. 게다가, 그의 그림을 통해, 콜은 미국에 대한 이야기를 해주고 있었어요. 음, 여러분은 미국의 독립이 1776년에 막 선언되었음을 기억해야 해요. 그래서, 1800년대 초반 동안, 미국은 여전히 꽤 새로운 국가였어요. 콜의 그림은 야생적이고, 개방적이며, 미래에 대한 가능성으로 가득 찬 풍경을 보여줌으로써 그 느낌을 담아냈어요.

그리고 마지막으로, 콜은 그의 화풍으로 다른 미국 화가들에게 영감을 주었습니다. 이 화가들 중 일부는 그룹을 형성했고 콜과 똑같은 화풍으로 그리려고 노력했어요. 심지어 20세기 초반의 많은 풍경화 화가들도 그들의 작품에 콜의 지속적인 영향을 보여주었어요. 그건 거의 100년이 지난 후죠. 그건 꽤나 오랜 시간이에요. 그리고, 어, 콜의 중요성은 심지어 미술을 넘어섰어요... 그는 사실 초기 환경운동가였어요. 일생 동안, 그는 산업과 도시 개발, 특히 사람들이 철도와 집을 건설하기 위해 자연적인 지역들을 파괴하고 있던 방식에 반대하는 강한 견해를 표명했어요... 이런 점에서, 환경에 대한 그의 관심과 그의 미술은 밀접하게 연결되어 있었죠... 1848년에 콜이 사망한 후에, 캐츠킬 사람들은 그를 기리기 위해 그들의 산들 중 하나에 이름을 붙였어요. 그것은 토머스 콜 산이라고 불려요.

landscape 명 풍경   Romantic 형 낭만주의의
teach oneself 독학하다   return 동 돌아오다   collector 명 수집가
mystery 명 신비로움   emotional 형 감정적인

represent 동 대표하다   capture 동 담아내다, 포착하다
lasting 형 지속적인   significance 명 중요성   particularly 부 특히

6 강의의 주된 주제는 무엇인가?

(A) 초기 미국 미술의 일반적인 역사

(B) 1800년대에 인기 있었던 미국식 화풍

(C) 한 화가가 중요하게 여겨지는 이유들

(D) 유명한 풍경화 화가에 의해 사용된 재료들

7 교수에 따르면, 콜은 왜 풍경화를 그렸는가?

(A) 그는 그의 그림 실력을 향상시키기를 희망했다.

(B) 그는 그가 방문한 장소에서 영감을 받았다.

(C) 그는 그의 미술 선생님들 중 한 명으로부터 격려를 받았다.

(D) 그는 다른 화가만큼 성공적이 되고 싶어 했다.

8 교수는 1800년대의 미국인들에 관해 무엇을 암시하는가?

(A) 그들은 유럽의 사상에 관심이 없었다.

(B) 그들은 도시 밖으로 자주 여행하지 않았다.

(C) 그들은 인기 있다고 여겨지는 작품을 좋아했다.

(D) 그들은 풍경화보다 초상화를 더 많이 구입했다.

9 교수는 왜 미국의 독립을 언급하는가?

(A) 콜이 미국으로 이주한 이유를 제시하기 위해

(B) 콜이 개인적인 화풍을 개발하려고 한 이유를 설명하기 위해

(C) 콜이 매우 독립적인 사람이었다는 것을 보여주기 위해

(D) 콜의 미술이 어떻게 미국의 이야기를 대표했는지 설명하기 위해

강의의 일부를 다시 듣고 질문에 답하시오.

S: But, uh, what was so special about Cole's work? Didn't many artists paint landscapes?

P: I'm glad you asked that. Well, one of the reasons Cole was important is that he painted in the Romantic style. This style was popular in Europe at the time, but Cole was the first to use it in America.

10 교수는 왜 이렇게 말하는가:
P: I'm glad you asked that.

(A) 그가 주제에 대해 설명하려 했다는 것을 나타내기 위해

(B) 미술에 대한 학생의 관심을 인정하기 위해

(C) 학생에게 더 자세히 들으라고 독려하기 위해

(D) 그가 콜의 작품에 감탄한다는 것을 보여주기 위해

강의의 일부를 다시 듣고 질문에 답하시오.

P: And lastly, Cole inspired other American painters with his style. Some of these painters formed a group and tried to paint in the same style as Cole. Even many landscape painters from the early 20th century showed Cole's lasting influence in their work. That's almost a hundred years later. That's quite a while.

11 교수는 이렇게 말함으로써 무엇을 의미하는가:
P: That's quite a while.

(A) 그는 미국 미술이 매우 느리게 발전했다고 생각한다.

(B) 그는 사람들이 수년 동안 콜의 미술의 진가를 알아보지 못했다고 생각한다.

(C) 그는 콜의 영향력이 그렇게 오래 지속되었다는 것에 감명을 받았다.

(D) 그는 콜의 그림의 가치가 어떻게 증가했는지를 보여주고 싶어 한다.

PART 2. Passage 1 본문 p. 158

1 (C)　　2 (A)　　3 (A)　　4 (A), (B)　　5 (D)

Note-taking

S: Struggling w/ asgmt. = topic & what you're expecting
P: Write a report about reducing univ. environ. impact
　 Focus on idea or strategy or discuss program
　 Huge campus = a lot of resources ∴ important topic
　 80% of impact = related to ppl. on campus
S: About plastic waste = install water fountains
P: School already has free tumbler program
S: Provide bikes for free & limit # of cars & scooters
　 Set up repair stations & air pumps
P: 2-part asgmt. = present report & written report

Listen to a conversation between a student and a professor.

S: Professor Grimley? I'm Robert Taylor. I'm taking your environmental science course.

P: Hi, Robert. What can I do for you?

S: [1]Well, I'm really struggling with the assignment you gave us last week. I would like some suggestions about it. Um, for instance, I don't know how to choose a topic. Also, I'm not sure what you're expecting from us.

P: [3]Well, I requested that everyone write a report about reducing the university's environmental impact. So I'm specifically interested in things that we can do on campus. You should focus on one idea or strategy. Or, um, discuss a program that would help accomplish this.

S: OK, that's helpful...

P: [3]And as you know, we have a huge campus that consumes a lot of resources. So this is an especially important topic for the university. [2]For instance, some of our buildings are extremely large and old, and it takes a lot of energy to heat and cool them. However, the university doesn't have any renewable energy sources.

S: And I assume that the student population has a big effect, too. There are just so many of us coming and going on the campus... All the cars and waste probably have negative consequences too, right?

P: You're right. About 80 percent of the university's environmental impact is related to the behavior of the people on campus. And now that we all know about climate change, we have to do something about it.

S: [5]Actually, that gives me an idea... It's about all of the plastic waste on campus. We could install more water fountains throughout the campus. Then, students won't have to buy bottled water.

P: [3/5]Hmm... I don't know about that. As you may know, the school already has a free tumbler program. The university gives free tumblers to students so they can fill them up at fountains.

S: Ah, I forgot about that! I have a tumbler, myself. I guess water fountains wouldn't make much of a difference then... Um, what about transportation on campus? I mean, our campus is extremely large and a lot of people use their cars to move around. All those cars release a lot of greenhouse gases, of course...

P: Uh-huh, keep going...

S: Well, I'm thinking the university could provide bikes for free. People could use the bikes to go between their classes and their dormitories or wherever else. And we could even limit the number of cars and scooters on campus. At the same time, for people who already own bikes, we could set up free repair stations and air pumps for them to use.

P: [3]That sounds great. Why don't you go ahead and start writing your report on this topic?

S: OK, I will. And, uh, when did you say the deadline is?

P: Keep in mind that it's a two-part assignment. [4A]At the end of the semester, everyone will present their reports to the class. [4B]Then, the written report will be due on the final day of class.

S: Got it. Thanks, Professor, and I'll see you next class.

학생과 교수 사이의 대화를 들으시오.

S: Grimley 교수님? 저는 Robert Taylor입니다. 저는 교수님의 환경 과학 강의를 수강하고 있어요.

P: 안녕, Robert. 무엇을 도와줄까?

S: 음, 저는 교수님이 지난주에 내주신 과제 때문에 정말 힘들어하고 있어요. 그것에 대한 의견을 좀 주셨으면 좋겠어요. 음, 예를 들어, 주제를 어떻게 선택할지 모르겠어요. 또, 교수님이 저희에게 기대하시는 게 무엇인지 잘 모르겠어요.

P: 음, 나는 모두에게 대학의 환경영향을 줄이는 것에 대한 보고서를 쓰라고 요청했어. 그러니까 나는 우리가 캠퍼스 내에서 할 수 있는 것들에 특히 관심이 있어. 너는 하나의 아이디어나 전략에 집중해야 해. 아니면, 음, 이것을 성취하는 데 도움을 줄 프로그램에 대해 논해보렴.

S: 좋아요, 도움이 되네요...

P: 그리고 너도 알다시피, 우리는 많은 자원을 소비하는 거대한 캠퍼스를 가지고 있어. 그래서 이것은 대학에 특히 중요한 주제야. 예를 들어, 우리 건물들 중 몇 개는 매우 크고 오래되었고, 그것들을 따뜻하게 하고 시원하게 하는 데 많은 에너지가 필요해. 하지만, 대학은 재생 가능한 에너지원을 가지고 있지 않지.

S: 그리고 학생 수도 큰 영향을 미치는 것 같아요. 캠퍼스를 드나드는 학생들이 너무 많아요... 모든 자동차들과 쓰레기도 아마 부정적인 결과를 가져오겠죠, 그렇죠?

P: 맞아. 대학의 환경영향 중 약 80퍼센트가 캠퍼스 내 사람들의 행동과 관련이 있어. 그리고 이제 우리 모두가 기후변화에 대해 알

고 있으니, 그것에 대해 무엇인가를 해야만 해.

S: 사실, 그게 저에게 아이디어를 떠올리게 하네요... 그건 캠퍼스의 모든 플라스틱 쓰레기에 관한 거예요. 우리는 캠퍼스 곳곳에 더 많은 식수대를 설치할 수 있을 거예요. 그러면, 학생들은 병에 든 물을 살 필요가 없을 거예요.

P: 흠... 그건 잘 모르겠구나. 아마 너도 알다시피, 학교는 이미 무료 텀블러 프로그램을 가지고 있어. 대학은 학생들에게 무료 텀블러를 줘서 그들이 식수대에서 그것들을 채울 수 있게 해.

S: 아, 그걸 깜빡했네요! 저도 텀블러를 가지고 있어요. 그럼 식수대는 큰 차이를 만들지 못하겠네요... 음, 캠퍼스 내 교통수단은 어떤가요? 그러니까, 저희 캠퍼스는 매우 크고 이동하기 위해 많은 사람들이 그들의 차를 이용하잖아요. 물론, 그 모든 차들은 많은 양의 온실가스를 배출하죠...

P: 그래, 계속하렴...

S: 음, 대학이 자전거를 무료로 제공할 수 있을 것 같아요. 사람들은 그들의 수업과 그들의 기숙사 사이, 아니면 어디든지 다른 곳을 오가기 위해 자전거를 이용할 수 있을 거예요. 그리고 우리는 심지어 캠퍼스 내의 자동차와 스쿠터의 수를 제한할 수 있을 거예요. 동시에, 이미 자신의 자전거를 가지고 있는 사람들을 위해, 무료 수리소와 그들이 사용하도록 공기 펌프를 설치할 수 있을 거예요.

P: 좋은 생각이구나. 이 주제에 대해 네 보고서를 작성하기 시작하는 게 어떠니?

S: 네, 그럴게요. 그리고, 어, 기한이 언제라고 하셨죠?

P: 그게 두 부분으로 된 과제라는 걸 명심하렴. 학기 말에, 모두가 수업에서 그들의 보고서를 발표할 거야. 그런 다음, 글로 된 보고서가 수업의 마지막 날까지 제출되어야 해.

S: 알겠습니다. 감사합니다, 교수님, 그리고 다음 수업 때 뵙겠습니다.

reduce 동 줄이다 specifically 부 특히 accomplish 동 성취하다
consume 동 소비하다 resource 명 자원
renewable 형 재생 가능한 consequence 명 결과
install 동 설치하다 water fountain 식수대
greenhouse gas 온실가스 present 동 발표하다

1 학생은 왜 교수를 찾아가는가?

(A) 수업에 결석한 이유를 대기 위해
(B) 다가오는 세미나를 위한 아이디어를 논의하기 위해
(C) 과제에 대한 조언을 구하기 위해
(D) 강의를 위한 글로 된 보고서를 제출하기 위해

2 교수는 캠퍼스에 있는 몇몇 건물들에 관해 무엇이라고 말하는가?

(A) 그것들은 크기와 나이 때문에 더 많은 자원을 사용한다.
(B) 그것들은 학교의 학생 수에 비해 너무 작다.
(C) 새 건물보다 오래된 건물이 더 많다.
(D) 그것들의 전등은 심지어 안에 아무도 없을 때에도 종종 켜져 있다.

3 교수는 어떻게 학생을 돕는가?

(A) 과제에 대해 설명한 다음 아이디어를 평가함으로써
(B) 좋은 보고서를 보여준 다음 질문에 답함으로써
(C) 이전의 과제들을 설명한 다음 방법을 설명함으로써
(D) 주제를 추천한 다음 의견을 제공함으로써

4 교수에 따르면, 학생들은 학기 말에 무엇을 해야 하는가? 2개의 답을 고르시오.

(A) 수업에서 발표하기
(B) 글로 된 보고서 제출하기
(C) 그들의 아이디어를 캠퍼스에 적용하기
(D) 다른 학생들과 공동 작업하기

대화의 일부를 다시 듣고 질문에 답하시오.

S: Actually, that gives me an idea... It's about all of the plastic waste on campus. We could install more water fountains throughout the campus. Then, students won't have to buy bottled water.

P: Hmm... I don't know about that. As you may know, the school already has a free tumbler program.

5 교수는 이렇게 말함으로써 무엇을 의미하는가:

P: Hmm... I don't know about that.

(A) 그녀는 대화의 주제에 대해 잘 알지 못한다.
(B) 그녀는 학생의 정보가 올바른지에 대해 확실히 알지 못한다.
(C) 그녀는 보고서의 품질에 만족하지 못한다.
(D) 그녀는 학생의 아이디어가 효과가 있을지 의심한다.

PART 2. Passage 2
본문 p. 160

6 (B)   7 (D)   8 (C)   9 (C)   10 (B), (D)   11 (A)

Note-taking

Removing Pollution from Soil Using Fungi

- Developing methods to remove pollution = use fungi
- Fungi = thousands of diff. kinds
  - Break down org. → new materials → used again
- Carbon = form of pollution
  - Fungi can easily break down → source of food
- Use fungi to remove metals = diff. process used
  - Fungi's branches attract metals ∵ diff. in atoms
  - Cheaper & use less energy & leave chemicals X
  - Perfect X ∵ too slow & need lots of fungi

Listen to part of a lecture in a biology class.

P: For the past week, we've been talking about the problem of soil pollution. It is mainly caused by industrial activity, oil spills, chemicals used in agriculture, and so on. And of course, pollution is harmful to human health. 6Well, recently, scientists have been developing new methods to remove pollution from the soil. Some of these methods use fungi.

So, uh, first, let's talk about the basics of fungi. There are thousands of different kinds. All of them help to maintain the health of the natural environment. 7They do this by breaking down organisms that have died. Thus, they turn them into new materials. And, uh, these can be used again by other living things. How does this happen? Well, to find out, we have to look underground... Uh, normally, we only see a small part of fungi above the ground, right? For example, we see this part when we see a mushroom… But this is just the part above. Most of the fungi is underground, and the underground part grows very big. They have branches that spread over a wide area. These branches are just like the roots of a plant. They absorb water and nutrients from the soil. But the branches also help fungi break down organisms that have died. You see, when plants die, they break down into smaller materials that enter the soil.

And to get nutrients from these materials, the fungi have to break them down further. This is where the branches come in. The branches release special chemicals that break down the plant materials into even smaller materials. Now, the fungi can use the materials as food. [11]And what's interesting is that the fungi's branches don't just absorb nutrients from plant materials. They also absorb nutrients from pollution…

S: Hold on a second, Professor… We're talking about pollution, right? I don't see how that works. How do the fungi get nutrients from pollution? Aren't pollutants dangerous chemicals?

P: Yes, but carbon is a form of pollution. [8]And the oil and the chemicals that farmers use to kill insects contain carbon. Carbon is also found in the materials left by plants after they die. So fungi can easily break down carbon pollutants. For the fungi, this type of pollution just becomes another source of food. That's the first method of using fungi to remove pollution.

Of course, there are pollutants other than carbon. These are metals, like lead and mercury. Metals usually come from factories and they are much more dangerous to humans. They can also last a very long time in the soil. [9]To use fungi to remove metals, a different process is used. The fungi don't absorb the metals. Instead, the fungi's branches attract the metals like a magnet. Um, this happens because of differences in the atoms of fungi and metals. The two kinds of atoms attract each other. So what happens is that the metals stick to the fungi's branches. Once the metals are stuck, the fungi can be removed from the ground and thrown away. In some cases, it's also possible to separate the metals from the fungi and use the metals again. This second process has many advantages. For instance, it's cheaper than other methods since you only have to plant fungi in the ground. Second, it uses less energy than other methods because the fungi do most of the work. And third, it does not leave behind harmful chemicals like some other methods do. However, this process isn't perfect yet. [10D]Um, for one thing, it's too slow… People are polluting the soil faster than fungi can remove it. [10B]Also, you need lots of fungi for it to work effectively. So scientists are still trying to find a way to make the process more useful.

___

생물학 강의의 일부를 들으시오.

P: 지난주 동안, 우리는 토양 오염 문제에 대해 이야기해 왔어요. 그

것은 주로 산업 활동, 기름 유출, 농업에 사용되는 화학 물질 등에 의해 발생해요. 그리고 물론, 오염은 사람의 건강에 해로워요. 음, 최근에, 과학자들은 토양에서 오염 물질을 제거하기 위한 새로운 방법들을 개발해 오고 있어요. 이 방법들 중 일부는 균류를 사용합니다.

그래서, 어, 우선, 균류에 대한 기본적인 것들에 관해 이야기해 봅시다. 수천 가지의 서로 다른 종이 있어요. 그것들은 모두 자연환경의 건강을 유지하는 데 도움을 줍니다. 그것들은 죽은 유기체들을 분해함으로써 이렇게 해요. 이렇게 하여, 그것들을 새로운 물질로 바꾸어 놓습니다. 그리고, 어, 이것들은 다른 생물체들에 의해 다시 사용될 수 있어요. 어떻게 이런 일이 일어날까요? 음, 알아내기 위해, 우리는 땅속을 살펴봐야 해요… 어, 보통, 우리는 땅 위에 있는 균류의 작은 부분만을 보죠, 그렇죠? 예를 들어, 우리가 버섯을 볼 때 이 부분을 보는 거예요… 하지만 이것은 단지 위에 있는 부분이에요. 균류의 대부분은 땅속에 있고, 땅속 부분은 매우 크게 자라요. 그것들은 넓은 지역에 퍼지는 가지들을 가지고 있어요. 이 가지들은 꼭 식물의 뿌리와 같아요. 그것들은 토양에서 물과 영양분을 흡수하죠. 하지만 그 가지들은 균류가 죽은 유기체를 분해하는 것을 도와주기도 해요. 그러니까, 식물이 죽을 때, 그것들은 토양으로 들어가는 더 작은 물질들로 분해돼요.

그리고 이 물질들로부터 영양분을 얻기 위해, 균류는 그것들을 더 분해해야 해요. 이것이 그 가지들이 관여하게 되는 부분이에요. 가지들은 식물 물질을 훨씬 더 작은 물질로 분해하는 특수한 화학 물질을 방출해요. 이제, 균류는 그 물질들을 양분으로 사용할 수 있어요. 그리고 흥미로운 것은 균류의 가지가 식물 물질에서 단지 영양분을 흡수하는 것만이 아니라는 거예요. 그것들은 또한 오염 물질로부터 영양분을 흡수합니다…

S: 잠깐만요, 교수님… 우리가 오염 물질에 대해 이야기하고 있는 거죠, 그렇죠? 그게 어떻게 되는 것인지 모르겠어요. 균류가 어떻게 오염 물질로부터 영양분을 얻나요? 오염 물질은 위험한 화학 물질 아닌가요?

P: 맞아요, 하지만 탄소는 오염 물질의 한 형태예요. 그리고 기름과 농부들이 곤충을 죽이기 위해 사용하는 화학 물질은 탄소를 포함하고 있어요. 탄소는 죽은 후에 식물들에 의해 남겨지는 물질들에서도 발견돼요. 그래서 균류는 탄소 오염 물질을 쉽게 분해할 수 있죠. 균류에게, 이런 종류의 오염 물질은 그저 양분의 또 다른 원천이 돼요. 그것이 오염 물질을 제거하기 위해 균류를 사용하는 첫 번째 방법이에요.

물론, 탄소 이외의 오염 물질들도 있어요. 이것들은 납과 수은 같은 금속들이죠. 금속은 보통 공장에서 나오며 인간에게 훨씬 더 위험해요. 그것들은 또한 토양 속에서 매우 오랫동안 지속될 수 있어요. 균류를 이용하여 금속을 제거하기 위해서는, 다른 방법이 사용돼요. 균류는 금속을 흡수하지 않습니다. 대신, 균류의 가지는 자석처럼 금속을 끌어당겨요. 음, 균류와 금속의 원자의 차이 때문에 이런 일이 일어나죠. 그 두 종류의 원자는 서로 끌어당겨요. 그래서 금속은 균류의 가지에 달라붙게 돼요. 일단 금속이 달라붙으면, 균류는 땅에서 제거되어 버려질 수 있어요. 어떤 경우에는, 금속을 균류에서 분리하여 그 금속을 다시 사용하는 것도 가능해요. 이 두 번째 방법에는 많은 이점들이 있습니다. 예를 들어, 균류를 땅에 심기만 하면 되기 때문에 다른 방법들보다 더 저렴해요. 두 번째로, 균류가 대부분의 일을 하기 때문에 다른 방법들보다 에너지를 덜 사용해요. 그리고 세 번째로, 그것은 일부 다른 방법들처럼 해로운 화학 물질들을 남기지 않아요. 하지만, 이 방법은 아직 완벽하지 않아요. 음, 우선, 그건 너무 느려요… 사람들은 균류가 제거할 수 있는 것보다 더 빠르게 토양을 오염시키고 있죠. 또한, 그것이 효과적으로 작동하게 하려면 많은 균류가 필요해요. 그래서 과학자들은 여전히 그 방법을 더 유용하게 만들 방법을 찾으려고 노력하고 있어요.

pollution 명 오염, 오염 물질   industrial 형 산업의   spill 명 유출
agriculture 명 농업   fungus 명 균류   break down 분해하다
branch 명 가지   absorb 동 흡수하다   nutrient 명 영양분
pollutant 명 오염 물질   carbon 명 탄소   contain 동 포함하다
lead 명 납   mercury 명 수은   magnet 명 자석
separate 동 분리하다

6 교수는 주로 무엇에 관해 논의하는가?

(A) 토양 오염에 의해 발생하는 문제들

(B) 토양을 깨끗하게 하기 위해 균류가 사용될 수 있는 방법

(C) 균류의 서로 다른 부분들과 그것들의 용도들

(D) 균류가 토양에서 영양분을 얻는 방법

7 교수는 균류에 관해 무엇이라고 말하는가?

(A) 그것들은 땅속에 많은 버섯을 생산한다.

(B) 그것들은 토양에 물과 영양분을 더한다.

(C) 그것들은 종종 식물의 뿌리 근처에서 발견된다.

(D) 그것들은 죽은 유기체들을 재사용 가능한 물질로 바꾼다.

8 교수에 따르면, 균류가 기름과 농장에서 사용되는 화학 물질에서
나오는 오염 물질을 분해할 수 있는 이유는 무엇인가?

(A) 오염 물질이 토양에 천천히 들어간다.

(B) 곤충들이 먼저 오염 물질을 분해한다.

(C) 식물 물질과 오염 물질은 비슷한 화학 물질들을 가지고 있다.

(D) 탄소 같은 오염 물질은 자연적으로 균류에 달라붙는다.

9 교수는 왜 자석을 언급하는가?

(A) 금속이 얼마나 오래 토양에 머물러 있는지를 강조하기 위해

(B) 흔한 금속의 종류를 소개하기 위해

(C) 균류의 가지가 금속을 끌어당기는 방법을 설명하기 위해

(D) 균류가 땅에서 제거되는 방법을 설명하기 위해

10 교수에 따르면, 토양에서 금속을 제거하기 위해 균류를 사용하는
것의 단점은 무엇인가?
2개의 답을 고르시오.

(A) 그것은 다른 방법들보다 더 많은 돈이 든다.

(B) 그것이 작동하기 위해서는 많은 양의 균류가 필요하다.

(C) 그것은 금속이 재사용되는 것을 허용하지 않는다.

(D) 그것은 금속을 제거하는 데 너무 오래 걸린다.

강의의 일부를 다시 듣고 질문에 답하시오.

P: And what's interesting is that the fungi's branches don't
just absorb nutrients from plant materials. They also absorb
nutrients from pollution…

S: Hold on a second, Professor… We're talking about pollution,
right? I don't see how that works. How do the fungi get
nutrients from pollution? Aren't pollutants dangerous
chemicals?

11 학생은 이렇게 말함으로써 무엇을 의미하는가:
S: We're talking about pollution, right?

(A) 그는 교수의 주장이 믿기 어렵다고 생각한다.

(B) 그는 용어의 의미를 확인하고 싶어 한다.

(C) 그는 교수가 말한 것을 반복해주기를 바란다.

(D) 그는 교수가 실수를 했다고 생각한다.

12 (B)   **13** (B)   **14** (C)   **15** Yes: (A), (B), (D) No: (C)
16 (D)   **17** (C)

Note-taking

Durand Line

- Durand Line = separates Afghanistan and Pakistan
- Created in 1893 = India was colony of British Empire
  - Afgh. wanted clear border ∵ Brit. influence X
  - Brit. secretary w/ Afgh. leaders created border
- Pakistan & India independent → increased opposition
  - Pashtuns = main ethnic group in Afgh.
  - Pashtuns in Pakistan = other options X ∴ unhappy
- 1947~, Afgh. has not accepted Durand Line
- Problem became international issue

Listen to part of a lecture in a sociology class.

P: ¹²Today, we're going to learn about a conflict
over a border between two countries. This is a
political dispute that has been going on for many
years and continues today… ¹⁵ᴬSpecifically, I'm
talking about the Durand Line, which separates
Afghanistan and Pakistan. This border is over
2,600 kilometers long and follows geographical
features like rivers and mountains…

¹⁵ᴮUh, the Durand Line was originally created
in 1893. At the time, India was a colony of the
British Empire. And what is Pakistan today
was still a part of India. ¹³But, uh, the leader of
Afghanistan wanted a clearer border between
his territory and that of India. He did not want
England to have any influence in Afghanistan.
So, uh, a British secretary named Mortimer
Durand worked with the leaders of Afghanistan
to create a border… Thus, the Durand Line
was formed. For a while, Afghanistan accepted
the line as its border. But after Pakistan and
India became independent in 1947, there
was increased opposition to the agreement in
Afghanistan. This was when the British left the
region.

S1: Uh, but why exactly? I mean, Afghanistan
accepted the Durand Line before, right? So what
changed their minds?

P: Well, actually, the agreement was never popular
in Afghanistan… The country's leaders simply
accepted it because the British had some power
and influence in the region… That power and
influence became weaker, of course, after the
British left. So, um, when the British left, people
in Afghanistan thought the Durand Line was no
longer valid.

And they also thought it was unfair for
other reasons. ¹⁴Uh, after Pakistan became
independent, there were problems between two
ethnic groups or tribes. You see, there were two
main tribes in the region: the Punjabis and the
Pashtuns. Both of these groups were Muslim.
But they had ethnic differences. And they
were like political rivals… Now, Pashtuns are

considered to be people of Afghanistan. They have been the main ethnic group in Afghanistan since the 1700s. In their view, the Pashtuns in Pakistan should have been given other options. Specifically, they should have been allowed to join Afghanistan. Or they should have been allowed to create their own independent state. Instead, their homeland became part of Pakistan. [16]So the Pashtuns were divided between Afghanistan and Pakistan. Those in Pakistan were especially unhappy about the situation. In Pakistan, they were not a majority group and had to be ruled by the Punjabis.

[15D]Anyway, since 1947, the Afghanistan government has not accepted the Durand Line at all. Um, this is interesting because the type of government in Afghanistan has changed many times over the years... It has had a republican government, a communist government, and a democratic government... It even had a monarchy... So the leaders of Afghanistan have disagreed about many things, but not the Durand Line. None of Afghanistan's governments has accepted it. This is probably one of the only things they have all agreed on...

S2: Um, I watch the news a lot. Maybe not much has changed there. Uh, the problems in that area seem just as serious today.

P: That's very true. The problem even became an international issue... [17]America's recent war in Afghanistan was the longest in all of American history... That certainly was a big deal... And the region around the Durand Line remains an extremely complex and dangerous place. You see, the Durand Line goes through very isolated areas, which makes the nearby region difficult to control. So people can easily cross the border without being noticed. Millions of refugees have passed through this border in recent decades. And it continues to have regular armed conflicts and violence among various groups in the area.

사회학 강의의 일부를 들으시오.

P: 오늘, 우리는 두 국가 사이의 국경을 둘러싼 갈등에 대해 알아볼 거예요. 이것은 오랜 세월 동안 지속되어 왔으며 오늘날에도 계속되고 있는 정치적 분쟁이에요... 구체적으로 말하면, 아프가니스탄과 파키스탄을 나누는 듀랜드선을 말하는 거예요. 이 국경은 2,600킬로미터가 넘으며 강과 산 같은 지형을 따라갑니다...

어, 듀랜드선은 원래 1893년에 만들어졌어요. 당시에, 인도는 대영제국의 식민지였어요. 그리고 오늘날 파키스탄인 것은 여전히 인도의 일부였습니다. 하지만, 어, 아프가니스탄의 지도자는 그의 영토와 인도의 그것 사이에 더 명확한 국경을 원했어요. 그는 영국이 아프가니스탄에서 어떠한 영향력도 갖지 않기를 원했어요. 그래서, 어, 모티머 듀랜드라는 영국 장관이 국경을 만들기 위해 아프가니스탄의 지도자들과 함께 작업했어요... 그리하여, 듀랜드선이 형성되었습니다. 얼마 동안, 아프가니스탄은 그 선을 그것의 국경으로 받아들였어요. 하지만 1947년에 파키스탄과 인도가 독립한 후에, 아프가니스탄에서는 이 협정에 대한 반대가 높아졌어요. 이것이 영국이 그 지역에서 떠날 때입니다.

S1: 어, 그런데 정확히 왜죠? 그러니까, 아프가니스탄은 이전에 듀랜드선을 받아들였잖아요, 그렇죠? 그러니까 무엇이 그들의 마음을

바꾼 거죠?

P: 음, 사실, 그 협정은 아프가니스탄에서 인기가 있었던 적이 없어요... 그 나라의 지도자들은 단지 영국이 그 지역에서 어느 정도의 힘과 영향력을 가지고 있었기 때문에 그것을 받아들였어요... 물론, 그 힘과 영향력은 영국이 떠난 후에 약해졌어요. 그래서, 음, 영국이 떠났을 때, 아프가니스탄 사람들은 듀랜드선이 더 이상 유효하지 않다고 생각했죠.

그리고 그들은 다른 이유들 때문에도 그것이 불공평하다고 생각했어요. 어, 파키스탄이 독립한 후에, 두 민족 집단 혹은 부족들 사이에 문제가 있었어요. 그러니까, 그 지역에는 펀자비족과 파슈툰족이라는 두 개의 주요 부족이 있었습니다. 이 집단은 둘 다 이슬람교도였어요. 하지만 그들에게는 민족적 차이점들이 있었어요. 그리고 그들은 정치적 라이벌과 같았어요. 자, 파슈툰족은 아프가니스탄의 민족으로 여겨져요. 그들은 1700년대부터 아프가니스탄의 주요 민족 집단이어왔어요. 그들의 관점에서, 파키스탄에 있는 파슈툰족은 다른 선택지들을 제시받았어야 해요. 구체적으로 말하면, 그들은 아프가니스탄에 합류하는 것이 허용되었어야 했어요. 혹은 그들은 자신의 독립적인 국가를 만들도록 허용되었어야 해요. 대신, 그들의 조국은 파키스탄의 일부가 되었죠. 그래서 파슈툰족은 아프가니스탄과 파키스탄으로 나뉘었어요. 파키스탄에 있는 사람들은 그 상황에 대해 특히 불만족스러워했어요. 파키스탄에서, 그들은 다수 집단이 아니었고 펀자비족의 지배를 받아야 했죠.

그건 그렇고, 1947년부터, 아프가니스탄 정부는 듀랜드선을 전혀 받아들이지 않아 왔어요. 음, 아프가니스탄 정부의 유형이 수년간 여러 번 바뀌어 왔기 때문에 이건 흥미로워요... 그것은 공화주의 정부, 공산주의 정부, 민주주의 정부를 가지고 있었어요... 심지어 군주제도 있었죠. 자, 아프가니스탄의 지도자들은 많은 것들에 대해 의견이 달랐지만, 듀랜드선에 관해서는 아니었어요. 아프가니스탄 정부들 중 어느 것도 그것을 받아들이지 않았어요. 이것은 아마 그들 모두가 동의했던 유일한 것 중 하나일 거예요...

S2: 음, 저는 뉴스를 많이 봐요. 아마 그곳에서는 많은 변화가 없었던 것 같아요. 어, 그 지역의 문제들은 오늘날에도 그만큼 심각해 보여요.

P: 아주 맞는 말이에요. 그 문제는 심지어 국제적인 문제가 되었어요... 미국의 아프가니스탄에서의 최근 전쟁은 미국 역사 전체에서 가장 긴 것이었어요... 그건 분명히 큰 일이었죠... 그리고 듀랜드선 주변의 지역은 극도로 복잡하고 위험한 곳으로 남아 있어요. 그러니까, 듀랜드선은 매우 고립된 지역을 통과하는데, 이것은 근처 지역을 통제하기 어렵게 만들어요. 그래서 사람들은 눈에 띄지 않고 쉽게 국경을 건널 수 있죠. 최근 수십 년 동안 수백만 명의 난민들이 이 국경을 건너갔어요. 그리고 그곳은 계속해서 그 지역의 다양한 집단들 사이의 정기적인 무력 충돌과 폭력을 겪고 있어요.

conflict 몡 갈등, 충돌   border 몡 국경   political 혱 정치적인
originally 閈 원래   colony 몡 식민지   territory 몡 영토
secretary 몡 장관   opposition 몡 반대   agreement 몡 협정
valid 혱 유효한   unfair 혱 불공평한   ethnic 혱 민족의
tribe 몡 부족   republican 혱 공화주의의
democratic 혱 민주주의의   monarchy 몡 군주제
isolated 혱 고립된

12 강의의 주된 주제는 무엇인가?

(A) 아프가니스탄의 정치사

(B) 진행 중인 국경 문제

(C) 아프가니스탄에서의 군사적 갈등들

(D) 파키스탄의 국제 관계

13 교수에 따르면, 아프가니스탄의 지도자는 왜 더 명확한 국경을 원했는가?

(A) 그는 파키스탄이 인도에서 분리되어야 한다고 생각했다.

(B) 그는 그의 국가에서 영국의 영향력을 원치 않았다.

(C) 그는 이전의 국경이 헷갈린다고 생각했다.

(D) 그는 파키스탄 영토의 일부를 원했다.

14 교수는 파키스탄의 독립 이후의 지역적 상황을 어떻게 설명하는가?

(A) 문화적 유사성을 강조함으로써

(B) 개인적인 예시를 듦으로써

(C) 두 개의 민족 집단을 비교함으로써

(D) 최신 연구에 대해 논의함으로써

15 강의에서, 교수는 듀랜드선의 몇 가지 특징들을 언급한다. 다음의 항목이 특징으로 언급된 것인지를 표시하시오.
각 항목에 적절한 칸을 클릭하시오.

	예	아니오
(A) 아프가니스탄과 파키스탄을 분리한다	V	
(B) 인도가 영국의 식민지였을 때 처음 만들어졌다	V	
(C) 영국 장관에 의해 거부되었다		V
(D) 1947년 이후 아프가니스탄에서 받아들여지지 않았다	V	

16 교수는 파슈툰족에 관해 무엇을 암시하는가?

(A) 그들은 1700년대부터 파키스탄을 통치해왔다.

(B) 그들은 편자비족의 정치적 파트너였다.

(C) 그들은 아프가니스탄의 정부에 반대한다.

(D) 그들은 파키스탄에서 소수 민족 집단이었다.

17 미국의 아프가니스탄에서의 최근 전쟁에 대한 교수의 태도는 무엇인가?

(A) 그는 그것이 다시 일어날까 봐 걱정한다.

(B) 그는 그것이 성공적이었다고 확신한다.

(C) 그는 그것이 중대했다고 확신한다.

(D) 그는 그것이 불공평했다고 걱정한다.

Actual Test 2

PART 1. Passage 1
본문 p. 164

1 (B)   2 (C)   3 (C)
4 Included: (A), (C), (D) Not Included: (B)   5 (A)

Note-taking

W: 3 exams scheduled for same day

M: Deadline to report schedule conflicts = last Fri.

W: Access the website X for a while
Contacted IT dept. → solution X
History 103 = Tue. @ noon = 2 other exams that day

M: Permission to reschedule = allowed for emergencies
Application = mention trouble accessing website
Get IT dept. to confirm → brief note
Write down name & job title of IT dept. person

Listen to a conversation between a student and a university employee at the registrar's office.

W: Hi. Uh, sorry to bother you. ¹But, um, I just found out that I have three exams scheduled for the same day. That's way too many. My friend told me I could report this here.

M: That's true, but the deadline to report schedule conflicts was last Friday. Also, as you know, it's been more than two weeks since the final schedule was uploaded on the school website. So you should have reported the problem earlier.

W: ⁵Right... Um, I was worried that something like this would happen, so I printed out a copy as soon as the schedule was posted. Everything was fine then...

M: Well, at that point, the schedule was not fixed. Um, this was clearly stated on the website as well. It was probably changed after you printed it.

W: Oh, I didn't know that the schedule could change.

M: Yes, that's why it's important to check for the final version of the schedule.

W: ²But actually, I haven't been able to access the school website for a while now...

M: Really? Have you contacted the IT department? They should be able to help you.

W: Yes, I have. They said that there have been problems lately and many students have reported similar issues. Um, they didn't have a solution, though. They just said that I should try again later.

M: ²Hmm... That's not good. Everything about university policies and schedule changes is posted online. What exam do you need to reschedule?

W: Uh, that would be the exam for History 103. It was originally scheduled for Monday at 10 in the morning. Now it is being held on Tuesday at noon. I already have two other exams scheduled for that day, and I'm afraid this will affect my scores.

M: ³Um, students that are unavailable at the scheduled exam time can request permission to reschedule the exam. Usually, this is only allowed for emergencies, such as a serious illness.

W: Um, but my situation is a little different... Do you have any other suggestions?

M: The best I can do is to give you an application form to fill out. ⁴ᴰMake sure you write down that you didn't know about the schedule change. You should also mention that you had trouble accessing the university's website. I can't make any promises, but they might agree to make an exception for you.

W: Um, OK. It doesn't seem like I have a better option, so that's what I'll do.

M: ⁴ᴬIt would also be very helpful if you could get someone from the IT department to confirm that the website could not be accessed. They should write a brief note about it. The person who reviews your application might be more likely to listen to another university employee than a student.

W: That's a great idea. Um, would you let me know where the IT department office is located?

M: Sure. It's on the first floor of the administration building. ⁴ᶜUh, by the way, don't forget to write down the full name and job title of the IT department person you talk to.

W: Thanks for all of your help!

학적과에서 학생과 교직원 사이의 대화를 들으시오.

W: 안녕하세요. 어, 방해해서 죄송합니다. 그런데, 음, 제가 같은 날에 예정된 시험이 3개 있다는 걸 방금 알았어요. 그건 너무 많아서요. 제 친구가 여기에서 이걸 신고할 수 있다고 말해줬어요.

M: 맞아요, 그런데 일정 충돌 신고 기한은 지난주 금요일이었어요. 또, 아시다시피, 학교 웹사이트에 최종 일정이 업로드 된지 2주가 넘었어요. 그러니까 학생은 그 문제를 더 일찍 신고하셨어야 해요.

W: 그렇군요... 음, 이런 일이 일어날까 봐 걱정돼서, 일정이 게시되자마자 한 부 인쇄했어요. 그때는 모든 게 괜찮았거든요...

M: 음, 그 당시에는, 일정이 확정되지 않았어요. 음, 이건 웹사이트에도 분명히 명시되어 있었어요. 아마 학생이 인쇄하신 후에 변경되었을 거예요.

W: 오, 일정이 변경될 수 있는지는 몰랐네요.

M: 네, 그게 일정 최종본을 확인하는 게 중요한 이유예요.

W: 그런데 사실, 지금까지 얼마 동안 학교 웹사이트에 접속할 수 없었어요...

M: 정말요? IT 부서에 연락해 보셨나요? 그들이 도와줄 수 있을 거예요.

W: 네, 해봤어요. 그들은 최근에 문제가 있어 왔고 많은 학생들이 비슷한 문제를 신고해오고 있다고 했어요. 음, 그런데, 그들은 해결책이 없었어요. 그냥 제가 나중에 다시 시도해야 한다고 했어요.

M: 흠... 그건 좋지 않네요. 대학 정책과 일정 변경에 대한 모든 것은 온라인에 게시돼요. 어떤 시험의 일정을 변경하셔야 하죠?

W: 어, 역사 103 시험일 거예요. 그건 원래 월요일 아침 10시로 예정되어 있었어요. 이제 그건 화요일 정오에 치러질 거예요. 저는 이미 그날로 예정된 두 개의 다른 시험이 있고, 이게 제 성적에 영향을 미칠까 봐 걱정돼요.

M: 음, 예정된 시험 시간에 참석할 수 없는 학생들은 시험 일정을 변경하기 위한 허가를 요청할 수 있어요. 보통, 이건 심각한 질병 같은 비상 상황에만 허용돼요.

W: 음, 근데 제 상황은 조금 다르네요... 다른 제안이 있으신가요?

M: 제가 해드릴 수 있는 최선은 작성할 신청서를 드리는 거예요. 학생이 일정 변경에 대해 모르셨다는 걸 꼭 적으세요. 대학 웹사이트에 접속하는 데 어려움이 있었다는 것도 언급하셔야 해요. 어떤 약속도 해드릴 수 없지만, 그들이 학생을 위해 예외를 두는 것에

동의할지도 몰라요.

W: 음, 알겠습니다. 제게 더 좋은 선택지가 있는 것 같지 않으니, 그렇게 할게요.

M: IT 부서의 누군가에게 웹사이트에 접속할 수 없었다는 것을 확인해 주도록 하면 매우 도움이 될 거예요. 그들은 그것에 대해 간단한 메모를 작성해야 해요. 학생의 신청서를 검토하는 사람이 학생보다는 다른 교직원의 말을 더 잘 들을지도 몰라요.

W: 좋은 생각이네요. 음, IT 부서 사무실이 어디에 있는지 알려주시겠어요?

M: 물론이죠. 그건 행정동 1층에 있어요. 어, 그런데, 학생과 이야기하는 IT 부서 사람의 성명과 직함을 적는 걸 잊지 마세요.

W: 도와주셔서 감사합니다!

---

conflict 명 충돌 fixed 형 확정된 clearly 부 분명히
lately 부 최근에 reschedule 동 일정을 변경하다
originally 부 원래 emergency 명 비상 상황 illness 명 질병
exception 명 예외

1 학생은 왜 학적과를 찾아가는가?

(A) 그녀의 일정의 최종 복사본을 얻기 위해

(B) 그녀가 하루에 너무 많은 시험을 본다고 설명하기 위해

(C) 온라인 시스템의 문제에 대해 불평하기 위해

(D) 대학 정책을 확인하기 위해

2 직원은 학교 웹사이트에 관해 무엇을 암시하는가?

(A) 그것은 접속하기 위해 비밀번호를 필요로 한다.

(B) 그것은 더 자주 업데이트되어야 한다.

(C) 그것은 많은 유용한 정보를 포함하고 있다.

(D) 그것은 최근 학교에 의해 다시 디자인되었다.

3 직원은 왜 심각한 질병을 언급하는가?

(A) 학생들이 시험을 잘 못 보는 이유의 예시를 제공하기 위해

(B) 일정을 변경하는 게 불가능한 이유를 설명하기 위해

(C) 시험 날짜를 변경하는 데 허용되는 이유를 제시하기 위해

(D) 학생에게 신청서에 작성해야 하는 것을 상기시키기 위해

4 학생은 신청서에 어떤 정보를 포함할 것인가? 다음의 항목이 포함되는 것인지를 표시하시오.
각 항목에 적절한 칸을 클릭하시오.

	포함됨	포함 안 됨
(A) IT 부서에서 받은 메모	V	
(B) 시험 일정 사본		V
(C) IT 부서 직원의 성명과 직함	V	
(D) 변경 요청 사유들	V	

대화의 일부를 다시 듣고 질문에 답하시오.

W: Right... Um, I was worried that something like this would happen, so I printed out a copy as soon as the schedule was posted. Everything was fine then...

5 학생은 이렇게 말함으로써 무엇을 암시하는가:

W: Everything was fine then...

(A) 상황이 더 이상 같지 않다.

(B) 직원이 문제를 오해했다.

(C) 그녀는 시험이 언제 치러지는지 잊어버렸다.

(D) 일정이 한 달째 그대로이다.

PART 1. Passage 2

본문 p. 166

6 (D)   7 (C)   8 (B)   9 (C)   10 (B)   11 (C)

Note-taking

How Scientists Have Determined the Age of Earth

- Bf. geology, ideas about Earth's age ← Bible = 6,000
- Scientific attempts to find age of Earth = Kelvin
  - Calculated time for Earth to cool & become solid
  - Mistakes = temp. diff. fixed & inner part = solid rock
  - Concluded that Earth = 20~400 mil. years old
- Geologists = studying layers → Earth = billions of years
- 20c. a new method = radiometric dating
  - Finding age of object by measuring radiation inside
- Carbon dating = used to find age of sth. alive in past
  - Most effective when used together w/ others
- Scientists now believe Earth = 4.5 bil. years old

Listen to part of a lecture in a geology class.

P: [6]In the 17th century, scientists studying Earth's rocks realized that the planet must have gone through many changes in its history. This caused them to think about the planet's age. Uh, and they have tried different methods to determine it. Today. We're going to discuss some of these…

Um, before the science of geology was developed, many Europeans got their ideas about Earth's age from the Christian Bible. They thought Earth was around 6,000 years old. But by the 17th century, people increasingly used scientific methods to study the planet.

One of the first scientific attempts to find the age of Earth was done by Lord Kelvin in the 19th century. Lord Kelvin knew that Earth was hotter under the surface. Because of this, he thought that Earth began as an extremely hot liquid… [7]Um, he believed that Earth was originally about 4,000 degrees Celsius. And, uh, he also believed that the planet had been cooling at a constant rate ever since it was formed… So Lord Kelvin tried to calculate the time it would take for Earth to cool and become solid. To do this, he measured Earth's temperature. His calculations were based on the change in temperature every 15 meters. But Kelvin made some mistakes. First, he assumed that temperature differences were fixed. And he thought that the inner part of Earth was made of solid rock. [8]Still, he calculated an age that was older than most people believed. He concluded that Earth was between 20 million and 400 million years old. Today, we know that Earth is much older. But considering Kelvin worked in a much earlier time period, this is quite impressive. Although Kelvin was not correct, he used modern scientific methods. So his work inspired later scientists…

Since then, finding the age of Earth has become more precise. So let's look at a couple of other methods… [9]Geologists know that some rocks occur in layers. These rocks are called sedimentary rocks. Naturally, layers of sedimentary rocks that are beneath other layers are older. And layers that are closer to the surface are younger. By studying these layers, scientists learned that Earth was not just millions of years old. It was actually billions of years old. Still, studying layers did not produce exact results about Earth's age.

Then, in the early 20th century, a new method was discovered. This method is known as radiometric dating. Um, the word radiometric comes from two words that mean radiation and the process of measuring. So radiometric dating is a method for finding the age of an object by measuring amounts of radiation inside it. You see, many rocks on Earth are made of materials that contain radiation. These are radioactive elements, uh, like radium and thorium. If a material has radiation in it, it will break down over time. And, uh, scientists know exactly how fast each radioactive element breaks down. So, um, by measuring the radiation of materials in a rock, scientists can guess how long ago the rock was formed.

S: Um, I've heard of carbon dating. How is that different from radiometric dating?

P: Well, carbon dating is a type of radiometric dating. It is mainly used to find the age of something that was alive in the past. This is because carbon is left behind by living things, like plants and animals. It is most effective when it is used together with other forms of radiometric dating because it is not enough on its own. [10]One reason is that carbon breaks down more quickly than other materials. It only lasts about 10,000 years. Other materials, like uranium, however, take millions of years. That's why other materials are more useful.

[11]Anyway, using radiometric dating, scientists now believe Earth is around 4.5 billion years old. This is much older than Kelvin predicted. However, it is still a mere guess. And we probably will never know the exact age of Earth.

지질학 강의의 일부를 들으시오.

P: 17세기에, 지구의 암석을 연구하는 과학자들은 지구가 그것의 역사에서 많은 변화를 겪었음이 틀림없다는 것을 깨달았습니다. 이는 그들이 지구의 나이에 대해 생각해보게 했어요. 어, 그리고 그들은 그것을 알아내기 위해 여러 방법들을 시도해 왔죠. 오늘, 우리는 이것들 중 몇몇에 대해 논의할 거예요…

음, 지질학이 발전하기 전에, 많은 유럽인들은 지구의 나이에 대한 그들의 생각을 기독교 성경에서 얻었습니다. 그들은 지구가 6,000년 정도 되었다고 생각했어요. 하지만 17세기에 이르러, 사람들은 지구를 연구하기 위해 과학적인 방법들을 점점 더 많이 사용했어요.

지구의 나이를 알아내기 위한 최초의 과학적인 시도들 중 하나는 19세기에 켈빈 경에 의해 행해졌습니다. 켈빈 경은 지구가 표면 아래에서 더 뜨겁다는 것을 알고 있었어요. 이 때문에, 그는 지구가 극도로 뜨거운 액체로 시작되었다고 생각했죠... 음, 그는 지구가 원래 섭씨 약 4,000도 정도였다고 생각했어요. 그리고, 어, 그는 또한 지구가 형성된 이후로 계속 일정한 속도로 냉각되고 있다고 믿었어요... 그래서 켈빈 경은 지구가 냉각되고 고체가 되는 데 걸릴 시간을 계산하려 노력했어요. 이것을 하기 위해, 그는 지구의 온도를 측정했어요. 그의 계산은 15미터마다의 온도 변화에 기초하고 있었어요. 하지만 켈빈은 몇 가지 실수를 했어요. 첫째로, 그는 온도 차이가 고정되어 있다고 가정했어요. 그리고 그는 지구의 내부가 고체 암석으로 만들어져 있다고 생각했어요. 그럼에도, 그는 대부분의 사람들이 믿었던 것보다 더 오래된 나이를 계산해냈어요. 그는 지구의 나이가 2천만 년에서 4억 년 사이라고 결론지었어요. 오늘날, 우리는 지구가 훨씬 더 오래되었다는 것을 알고 있어요. 하지만 켈빈이 훨씬 이전의 시대에 작업했다는 걸 고려하면, 이건 꽤 인상적이에요. 비록 켈빈은 틀렸지만, 그는 현대의 과학적 방법들을 사용했어요. 그래서 그의 연구는 이후의 과학자들에게 영감을 주었죠...

그 이후로, 지구의 나이를 알아내는 것은 더 정확해졌어요. 자, 두어 개의 다른 방법들을 살펴봅시다... 지질학자들은 일부 암석들이 층으로 존재한다는 것을 알고 있어요. 이 암석들은 퇴적암이라고 불리죠. 당연히, 다른 층들의 아래에 있는 퇴적암들은 더 오래되었어요. 그리고 지면에 더 가까운 층들은 더 최근에 만들어졌죠. 이 층들을 연구함으로써, 과학자들은 지구가 단지 수백만 년 된 것이 아니라는 것을 알게 되었습니다. 그것은 사실 수십억 년이 되었어요. 그럼에도 불구하고, 층들을 연구하는 것은 지구의 나이에 대한 정확한 결과를 산출하지 못했어요.

그 후, 20세기 초반에, 새로운 방법이 발견되었어요. 이 방법은 방사성 연대 측정이라고 알려져 있어요. 음, 방사성 측정이라는 단어는 방사선과 측정하는 과정이라는 두 단어에서 유래했어요. 그래서 방사성 연대 측정은 물체의 안에 있는 방사선의 양을 측정함으로써 그것의 나이를 알아내는 방법이에요. 그러니까, 지구의 많은 암석은 방사선을 포함하고 있는 물질로 만들어져요. 이것들은 라듐과 토륨 같은 방사성 원소들이에요. 어떤 물질이 안에 방사선을 가지고 있으면, 그것은 시간이 지남에 따라 분해될 거예요. 그리고, 어, 과학자들은 각 방사성 원소가 얼마나 빨리 분해되는지 정확히 알고 있어요. 그래서, 음, 암석에 있는 물질의 방사선을 측정함으로써, 과학자들은 그 암석이 얼마나 오래전에 형성되었는지 추측할 수 있죠.

S: 음, 방사성 탄소 연대 측정에 대해 들어본 적이 있어요. 그건 방사성 연대 측정과 어떻게 다른가요?

P: 음, 방사성 탄소 연대 측정은 방사성 연대 측정의 일종이에요. 그것은 주로 과거에 살아있었던 것의 나이를 알아내기 위해 사용돼요. 이것은 탄소가 식물과 동물 같은 생물들에 의해 남겨지기 때문이에요. 그 자체로는 충분하지 않기 때문에 그것은 다른 종류의 방사성 연대 측정과 함께 사용될 때 가장 효과적이죠. 한 가지 이유는 탄소가 다른 물질들보다 더 빠르게 분해되기 때문이에요. 그것은 겨우 약 1만 년 정도밖에 지속되지 않아요. 하지만, 우라늄 같은 다른 물질들은 수백만 년이 걸려요. 그게 다른 물질들이 더 유용한 이유예요.

어쨌든, 방사성 연대 측정을 사용하여, 과학자들은 이제 지구가 약 45억 년이 되었다고 믿습니다. 이것은 켈빈이 예상했던 것보다 훨씬 더 오래되었죠. 하지만, 그것은 여전히 단지 추측이에요. 그리고 우리는 아마 지구의 정확한 나이를 영원히 알 수 없을 거예요.

method 몡 방법   determine 동 알아내다
increasingly 부 점점 더   attempt 동 시도   liquid 몡 액체
constant 혱 일정한   rate 몡 속도   solid 혱 고체의
measure 동 측정하다   assume 동 가정하다   fixed 혱 고정된

conclude 동 결론짓다   impressive 혱 인상적인
precise 혱 정확한   sedimentary rock 퇴적암
radiometric 혱 방사성 측정의   radiation 몡 방사선
predict 동 예상하다

6 강의의 주된 주제는 무엇인가?

(A) 17세기에 지구에 대한 연구가 발전한 방식
(B) 우주의 기원에 관한 이론
(C) 지구의 층들을 측정하는 방법들
(D) 과학자들이 지구의 나이를 알아냈던 방법

7 교수는 켈빈 경의 지구에 대한 관점에 대해 무엇이라고 말하는가?

(A) 그는 그것의 중심이 그것의 표면보다 더 최근에 만들어졌다고 믿었다.
(B) 그는 그것이 다른 행성들보다 더 오래되었다고 생각했다.
(C) 그는 그것이 일정한 속도로 냉각되었다고 믿었다.
(D) 그는 그것의 안쪽이 뜨거운 액체로 만들어졌다고 추측했다.

8 지구의 나이에 대한 켈빈 경의 결론에 대한 교수의 태도는 무엇인가?

(A) 그녀는 날짜의 범주가 그렇게 큰 이유에 대해 확신하지 못한다.
(B) 그녀는 그것이 그 당시 다른 사람들의 것보다 더 정확했기 때문에 인상을 받았다.
(C) 그녀는 그것이 과학적 방법들에 기초하지 않았다고 우려한다.
(D) 그녀는 과학자들이 그것을 빠르게 받아들인 것에 놀랐다.

9 교수에 따르면, 과학자들은 지구가 수십억 년이 되었다는 것을 어떻게 알게 되었는가?

(A) 그들은 식물들과 동물들의 변화를 관찰했다.
(B) 그들은 물질들을 방사선에 노출시켰다.
(C) 그들은 암석들의 층을 연구했다.
(D) 그들은 수학적 공식들을 사용했다.

10 교수는 왜 우라늄을 언급하는가?

(A) 방사성 연대 측정에 사용된 첫 번째 물질을 설명하기 위해
(B) 천천히 분해되는 원소의 예시를 제공하기 위해
(C) 일부 화학 원소가 매우 희귀하다는 것을 설명하기 위해
(D) 탄소가 다른 물질들과 결합할 수 있는 방법을 보여주기 위해

11 교수는 방사성 연대 측정에 관해 무엇을 암시하는가?

(A) 그것은 탄소를 포함하고 있는 물체들에만 작동할 수 있다.
(B) 그것은 대부분의 과학자들에 따르면 매우 신뢰할 수 있다.
(C) 그것은 아마 결코 지구의 정확한 나이를 예측할 수 없을 것이다.
(D) 그것은 1만 년 이내의 나이를 정확히 예측할 수 없다.

PART 2. Passage 1
본문 p. 168

1 (B)   2 (B)   3 (B)   4 (C)   5 (A)

Note-taking
S: Struggled w/ concept = opportunity cost

P: Opp. cost = what you lose when choose one
  E.g. factory = limited materials = choose what we make
  6 violins & 2 guitars, 3 guitars & 4 violins
  1 guitar = 2 violins, opp. cost of 1 guitar = 2 violins
S: Opp. cost of going to the movies?
  Movies X → stayed at home & study
P: Every time choose one thing = give up something

Listen to a conversation between a student and a professor.

S: Hi, Professor Jennings. ¹Um, I have a few questions about the lecture this morning.

P: You're, uh, Billy, right? From my economics class? I've still got some time left. What did you want to ask me about?

S: ¹To be honest, I really struggled with one of the concepts you discussed... Uh, opportunity cost.

P: OK, let me try and explain it some more. At the beginning of the class, I provided an explanation of this concept. ²Basically, opportunity cost is what you lose when you choose to do one thing over another.

S: Hmm... I'm not sure I understand.

P: All right. ²Let me give you an example. Let's imagine that we own a factory that makes musical instruments. ⁵And our factory only has a limited amount of materials. That means we can't just make whatever we want. We have to choose what we make.

S: I see where you're going... If we make a certain number of violins, then that changes how many guitars we can make, right?

P: Exactly. If we make six violins, for example, then we can only make two guitars. And if we want to make three guitars, then we can only make four violins.

S: That makes sense. If we make more of one thing, then we have to make less of another thing. Um... But what does this have to do with opportunity cost?

P: Well, in our example, when we wanted to make one additional guitar, we had to make two less violins. So the opportunity cost of one guitar is two violins.

S: So we lose two violins for every guitar we make...

P: Right. The opportunity cost is the value of the two violins. If we can make $100 from selling two violins, then our opportunity cost is $100. That is the value that we lose to make one more guitar.

S: OK. That example helps... ³Um, but what about other choices that aren't quite as simple? How do I calculate the opportunity cost of going to the movies, for example?

P: Well, what you're talking about is an opportunity cost that cannot be seen. Um, you brought up a good example, so go ahead and tell me more about that.

S: OK... If I buy a movie ticket, the opportunity cost is the value of everything else that I could have bought for the price of a movie ticket. But I think money isn't the only thing that I lose...

P: Yes, keep going...

S: Uh, for example, if I hadn't gone to the movies, then I could have stayed at home and studied. What's the value of that? I guess studying can help me get good grades and a good job after graduation. Those things would be very valuable in the future.

P: Yes, those are also examples of opportunity costs. Every time you choose to do one thing, you have to give up something else that has value. ⁴Uh, there's a good chapter on this subject in the book, *Introductory Economics*, by Michelle Waldman. It's in the library if you'd like to read it.

S: That's a good idea. I'll head over there right now. Um, thanks for taking the time to go over this with me.

학생과 교수 사이의 대화를 들으시오.

S: 안녕하세요, Jennings 교수님. 음, 오늘 아침 강의에 대해 몇 가지 질문이 있습니다.

P: 너는, 어, Billy구나, 맞지? 내 경제학 수업의? 아직 시간이 좀 남아 있단다. 무엇에 대해 물어보고 싶었니?

S: 솔직히 말씀드리면, 교수님께서 논하신 개념 중 하나가 정말 어려웠어요... 어, 기회비용이요.

P: 그래, 좀 더 설명해보마. 수업이 시작할 때, 나는 이 개념의 설명을 제공했지. 기본적으로, 기회비용은 네가 한 가지 일을 다른 일 대신 하기로 선택할 때 잃어버리게 되는 거야.

S: 흠... 제가 이해했는지 잘 모르겠어요.

P: 알겠다. 내가 예를 들어보마. 우리가 악기를 만드는 공장을 소유하고 있다고 상상해 보자. 그리고 우리 공장은 제한된 양의 재료만을 가지고 있지. 그건 우리가 원하는 것은 무엇이든지 그냥 만들 수는 없다는 걸 의미해. 우리는 우리가 무엇을 만들지 선택해야 하지.

S: 무슨 말씀인지 알겠어요... 우리가 특정 개수의 바이올린을 만들면, 그게 우리가 만들 수 있는 기타의 수가 달라지게 한다는 말씀이시죠, 맞나요?

P: 정확해. 예를 들어, 우리가 바이올린을 6대 만들면, 그럼 우리는 기타를 2대만 만들 수 있어. 그리고 우리가 기타를 3대 만들고 싶으면, 우리는 바이올린을 4대만 만들 수 있지.

S: 이해가 되네요. 우리가 한 가지를 더 많이 만들면, 다른 것을 더 적게 만들어야 한다는 거네요. 음... 그런데 이게 기회비용과 무슨 상관이 있죠?

P: 음, 우리의 예시에서, 우리가 1대의 추가적인 기타를 만들고 싶으면, 우리는 바이올린을 2대 더 적게 만들어야 했어. 그러니까 기타 1대의 기회비용은 바이올린 2대야.

S: 그러니까 우리가 만드는 기타 1대마다 2대의 바이올린을 잃게 되는 거군요...

P: 맞아. 기회비용은 바이올린 2대의 가치야. 우리가 2대의 바이올린을 판매해서 100달러를 벌 수 있다면, 우리의 기회비용은 100달러지. 그게 기타 1대를 더 만들면서 우리가 잃게 되는 가치야.

S: 알겠어요. 그 예시가 도움이 되네요... 음, 그런데 그렇게 간단하지 않은 다른 선택들은 어떤가요? 예를 들어, 영화관에 가는 것의 기회비용은 어떻게 계산하나요?

P: 음, 네가 얘기하고 있는 건 눈으로 볼 수 없는 기회비용이야. 음,

네가 좋은 예를 들었으니, 그것에 대해 더 말해보렴.

S: 네... 제가 영화표를 사면, 기회비용은 제가 영화표의 가격으로 살 수 있었던 다른 모든 것의 가치가 되죠. 그런데 제가 돈만 잃어버리는 게 아닌 것 같아요...

P: 그래, 계속하렴...

S: 어, 예를 들어, 제가 영화관에 가지 않았더라면, 집에 머물며 공부할 수 있었을 거예요. 그것의 가치는 무엇인가요? 공부하는 건 제가 좋은 성적을 받고 졸업 후에 좋은 직장을 얻는 데 도움이 될 수 있을 것 같아요. 그런 것들은 미래에 매우 가치가 있을 거예요.

P: 그래, 그런 것들도 기회비용의 예시란다. 네가 한 가지 일을 하기로 선택할 때마다, 너는 가치를 지니고 있는 다른 무언가를 포기해야 해. 어, Michelle Waldman의 '경제학 입문' 교재에 이 주제에 대한 좋은 장이 있어. 네가 읽고 싶으면 그건 도서관에 있단다.

S: 좋은 생각이에요. 지금 바로 거기로 갈게요. 음, 시간 내서 설명해주셔서 감사합니다.

economics 명 경제학   concept 명 개념
opportunity cost 기회비용   imagine 동 상상하다
musical instrument 악기   additional 형 추가적인
valuable 형 가치 있는

1 학생의 문제는 무엇인가?

(A) 그는 연구 논문 몇 개를 찾는 데 어려움을 겪고 있다.

(B) 그는 수업에서 논의된 주제를 이해하는 데 어려움을 겪고 있다.

(C) 그는 다가오는 시험을 어떻게 준비해야 하는지에 대해 확신하지 못한다.

(D) 그는 그의 경제학 과제를 바꾸는 것에 대해 생각하고 있다.

2 교수는 어떻게 학생을 도와주는가?

(A) 문제를 언급한 다음 해결책을 제공함으로써

(B) 개념을 설명한 다음 상황을 묘사함으로써

(C) 기회비용의 단점을 강조함으로써

(D) 공장과 영화관을 비교하고 대조함으로써

3 학생은 왜 영화관에 가는 것을 언급하는가?

(A) 그가 주제에 대해 잘 알고 있음을 보여주기 위해

(B) 개념에 대한 그의 이해를 명확히 하기 위해

(C) 다른 경제학 개념의 예를 들기 위해

(D) 영화표의 가격 상승을 강조하기 위해

4 학생은 다음에 무엇을 할 것인가?

(A) 다른 교수의 연락처 정보 얻기

(B) 교과서를 구입하기 위해 캠퍼스 서점에 가기

(C) 주제에 관해 더 읽기 위해 도서관 방문하기

(D) 교수에게 경제학책 빌리기

대화의 일부를 다시 듣고 질문에 답하시오.

P: And our factory only has a limited amount of materials. That means we can't just make whatever we want. We have to choose what we make.

S: I see where you're going...

5 학생은 이렇게 말함으로써 무엇을 의미하는가:

S: I see where you're going...

(A) 그는 교수가 말하려는 것을 이해한다.

(B) 그는 교수가 다음에 무엇에 대해 얘기할지 확신하지 못한다.

(C) 그는 더 이상 주제에 대한 설명을 들을 필요가 없다.

(D) 그는 개념의 다른 예시를 생각하고 있다.

PART 2. Passage 2
본문 p. 170

6 (D)   7 (B)   8 (C)   9 (C)   10 (C)
11 Yes: (A), (C), (D) No: (B)

Note-taking
Great Pacific Garbage Patch

- GPGP = island of garbage in Pacific Ocean
- Started w/ ppl. throwing away garbage wrong way
  - Plastic floats & break down X → stay on water
- Currents = water moves in circle ∴ patch can't break
- Animals think plastic = food → eat = deadly
- Blocks sunlight from entering water
- Solving problem = challenge
  - Work together & more recycling
  - Manufacture plastic that break down quicker
  - Clean up garbage patch

Listen to part of a lecture in an environmental science class.

P: OK... [6]Let's continue our discussion of pollution in the ocean... Today, I want to focus on a specific example. This is the Great Pacific Garbage Patch. This area of the Pacific is a huge floating island of garbage. It is located in the northern Pacific Ocean... Uh, it's about halfway between California and Hawaii...

So, uh, how did a large island of trash get in the middle of the ocean? Well, it started with people throwing away garbage the wrong way. [7]Instead of using a garbage site, some people throw their garbage in the water. Many times, these people are just careless individuals who throw their garbage wherever they like. But, unfortunately, some companies do this as well. Either way, most of the garbage is plastic... This includes fishing equipment, water bottles, and other things like that... And, naturally, plastic materials float rather than sink. Moreover, they do not break down fast. So, uh, the plastic just stays on top of the water and piles up...

Um, this garbage was not thrown away in the middle of the ocean, though. It came from many different areas. In some cases, it traveled 1,000 kilometers or more. Then, what brought it here? [8]It's mainly ocean currents. Various currents in the Pacific Ocean come together in the region. They cause the water to move in a circle. Because the water moves in a circle, the garbage patch cannot break apart. And as new garbage arrives, the pile keeps getting bigger...

Now, the garbage patch is far from where humans live. So it doesn't harm us directly. However, it can be harmful to marine life...

Some of the plastic eventually breaks into smaller pieces. Because plastic is often clear, it can look like small prey, such as plankton and shrimp. [9]As a result, many animals think the plastic is food. When animals eat lots of plastic, it can be deadly… Uh, the United Nations has an environmental program, and its researchers estimated the number of deaths. They believe that plastic garbage has killed more than a million seabirds and over 100,000 marine mammals. Um, and another harmful effect of the garbage patch is that it blocks sunlight from entering the water. Many important organisms, like plankton, depend on sunlight to survive. The dark shadow below the garbage patch does not support these creatures. So the fish and other organisms that eat plankton cannot find enough food…

[10]Well, then… What can we do about the garbage problem in the Pacific? Unfortunately, solving the problem will be a challenge. This is because it requires international cooperation. Everyone must do their part to help. But, at the same time, no country wants to take responsibility. Still, we must take steps to protect the Pacific. [11A]To start with, all countries should be encouraged to work together. [11D]Second, we have to stop throwing garbage into the water and put more resources toward recycling. This is a form of prevention, and it is the most sustainable solution. [11C]Third, we must manufacture plastic that will break down much quicker. This would help a little, but only if we also limit the amount of garbage that people throw away as well… Finally, we must clean up the garbage patch. This is challenging because of the extreme cost. However, it is not impossible. [11B]One option is to build large ships with machines that can turn plastic into oil. The oil can then be used to pay for cleaning costs. In summary, we can get rid of the Great Pacific Garbage Patch if we use different methods. We have to stop garbage from entering the water, find better ways of making products, and clean up the garbage patch itself.

환경 과학 강의의 일부를 들으시오.

P: 자... 바다 오염에 대한 논의를 계속해 보죠... 오늘은, 구체적인 예시에 초점을 맞추고 싶어요. 이것은 태평양 거대 쓰레기 지대입니다. 태평양의 이 지역은 쓰레기가 떠다니는 거대한 섬입니다. 그것은 북태평양에 위치해 있어요... 어, 그것은 캘리포니아와 하와이 중간쯤에 있어요...

자, 어, 어떻게 거대한 쓰레기 섬이 바다 한가운데로 들어왔을까요? 음, 그것은 사람들이 잘못된 방법으로 쓰레기를 버리는 것으로부터 시작됐어요. 쓰레기장을 이용하는 대신, 일부 사람들은 그들의 쓰레기를 물속에 버려요. 많은 경우, 이 사람들은 쓰레기를 아무 데나 원하는 곳에 버리는 그저 부주의한 개인들이에요. 하지만, 불행하게도, 일부 기업들도 이렇게 하죠. 어느 쪽이든, 쓰레기의 대부분은 플라스틱이에요... 이것은 낚시 도구, 물병, 그리고 비슷한 다른 것들을 포함합니다... 그리고, 자연스럽게, 플라스틱 물질들은 가라앉기보다는 떠다녀요. 게다가, 그것들은 빠르게 분해되지 않아요. 그래서, 어, 플라스틱은 그냥 물 위에 머무르며 쌓여가요...

음, 하지만, 이 쓰레기는 바다 한가운데에 버려지지 않았어요. 그것은 많은 서로 다른 지역들에서 왔어요. 어떤 경우에는, 그것은 1,000킬로미터나 그 이상을 이동했어요. 그렇다면, 무엇이 그것을 여기로 가져올까요? 그것은 주로 해류예요. 태평양의 다양한 해류들은 그 지역에 모여들어요. 그것들은 물이 원으로 움직이게 하죠. 물이 원으로 움직이기 때문에, 쓰레기 지대는 분해될 수 없죠. 그리고 새로운 쓰레기가 도착하면서, 그 더미는 점점 더 커지고 있어요...

자, 쓰레기 지대는 사람들이 사는 곳에서 멀리 떨어져 있어요. 그래서 그것은 우리에게 직접적으로 해를 끼치지 않아요. 하지만, 그것은 해양 생물에게 해로울 수 있어요... 플라스틱 중 일부는 결국 더 작은 조각들로 분해돼요. 플라스틱이 종종 투명하기 때문에, 그것은 플랑크톤과 새우 같은 작은 먹이같이 보일 수 있어요. 그 결과, 많은 동물들은 플라스틱을 먹이로 생각해요. 동물들이 많은 플라스틱을 먹으면, 치명적일 수 있어요... 어, UN은 환경 보호 프로그램을 가지고 있고, 그것의 연구자들은 죽음의 수를 추정했어요. 그들은 플라스틱 쓰레기가 백만 마리 이상의 바닷새와 십만 마리 이상의 해양 포유동물을 죽였다고 믿고 있어요. 음, 그리고 쓰레기 지대의 또 다른 해로운 영향은 그것이 햇빛이 물에 들어가는 것을 막는다는 거예요. 플랑크톤 같은 많은 중요한 유기체들은 생존하기 위해 햇빛에 의존해요. 쓰레기 지대 아래의 어두운 그림자는 이 생물들을 부양하지 않아요. 그래서 플랑크톤을 먹는 물고기와 다른 유기체들은 충분한 먹이를 찾을 수 없죠...

음, 그럼... 태평양의 쓰레기 문제에 대해 무엇을 할 수 있을까요? 불행하게도, 그 문제를 해결하는 것은 도전이 될 거예요. 이는 그것에 국제적인 협조가 필요하기 때문이에요. 돕기 위해 모두가 그들의 역할을 해야만 해요. 하지만, 동시에, 어떤 국가도 책임을 지고 싶어 하지 않아요. 그럼에도, 우리는 태평양을 보호하기 위해 조치를 취해야만 해요. 우선, 모든 국가들은 협력하도록 장려되어야 해요. 둘째로, 우리는 물속으로 쓰레기를 버리는 것을 멈추고 재활용에 더 많은 자원을 투입해야 해요. 이것은 예방의 한 형태이고, 가장 지속 가능한 해결책이에요. 세 번째로, 우리는 훨씬 더 빠르게 분해될 플라스틱을 만들어야 합니다. 이것은 약간 도움이 되겠지만, 또한 우리가 사람들이 버리는 쓰레기의 양을 제한할 때만 그럴 거예요... 마지막으로, 우리는 반드시 쓰레기 지대를 청소해야 해요. 엄청난 비용 때문에 이것은 어려워요. 하지만, 불가능하지는 않아요. 한 가지 선택지는 플라스틱을 기름으로 바꿀 수 있는 기계를 가지고 있는 큰 배를 만드는 거예요. 기름은 그 후에 청소 비용을 지불하는 데 사용될 수 있어요. 요약하자면, 우리가 여러 방법들을 이용한다면 태평양 거대 쓰레기 지대를 제거할 수 있어요. 우리는 쓰레기가 물에 들어가는 것을 막고, 제품을 만들 더 좋은 방법을 찾고, 쓰레기 지대 자체를 청소해야만 해요.

---

pollution 몡 오염   floating 혱 떠다니는   careless 혱 부주의한
pile up 쌓이다   ocean current 해류   harm 통 해를 끼치다
clear 혱 투명한   deadly 혱 치명적인   estimate 통 추정하다
cooperation 몡 협조   resource 몡 자원   prevention 몡 예방
sustainable 혱 지속 가능한   manufacture 통 만들다

6 강의의 주된 주제는 무엇인가?

(A) 바다를 청소하는 새로운 방법들

(B) 최근 플라스틱 기술의 발전

(C) 태평양의 다양한 종류의 생태계들

(D) 바다 오염의 구체적인 예시

7 교수는 기업들과 개인들의 쓰레기에 대해 무엇이라고 말하는가?

(A) 그것은 고도로 통제된다.

(B) 그것은 주로 플라스틱이다.

(C) 그것은 보통 재활용된다.

(D) 그것은 때때로 무해하다.

8 교수는 그 지역의 해류에 관해 무엇을 암시하는가?

(A) 그 지대는 그것들이 없으면 더 커질 것이다.

(B) 그것들은 항상 동쪽에서 서쪽으로 이동한다.

(C) 그 지대는 그것들이 없으면 분해될 것이다.

(D) 그것들은 쓰레기를 캘리포니아에서 하와이로 운반한다.

9 교수는 동물들이 플라스틱을 먹는 것의 치명적인 영향에 대한 정보를 어떻게 구성하는가?

(A) 그는 한 이론을 언급한 다음 반대되는 것에 대해 논의한다.

(B) 그는 가장 위험한 플라스틱 종류들을 나열한다.

(C) 그는 문제를 소개한 다음 그것을 연구로 뒷받침한다.

(D) 그는 다양한 해양 종들에 대한 영향을 비교한다.

10 태평양의 쓰레기 문제에 대한 교수의 의견은 무엇인가?

(A) 그는 그것이 해류에 의해 줄어들기를 희망한다.

(B) 그는 그것을 고치기 위해 기술이 요구된다고 생각한다.

(C) 그는 그것이 해결하기 어려울 것이라고 생각한다.

(D) 그는 몇몇 국가들만 그것에 책임이 있다고 생각한다.

11 강의에서, 교수는 태평양을 보호하기 위해 취해질 수 있는 조치들을 제안한다. 다음의 항목이 제안된 조치인지를 표시하시오.
각 항목에 적절한 칸을 클릭하시오.

	예	아니오
(A) 국가들에게 협력할 것을 장려하기	V	
(B) 쓰레기를 옮기기 위해 배 사용하기		V
(C) 새로운 종류의 플라스틱 생산하기	V	
(D) 재활용하는 양 늘리기	V	

PART 2. Passage 3

본문 p.172

12 (B) **13** (C)-(D)-(B)-(A) **14** (C) **15** (A) **16** (B)
17 (B)

Note-taking

Classical Conditioning

- Psychological conditioning = associative learning
  - Learns to associate two ideas, event, or actions
- Pavlov used dogs in exp.
  - Introduced sound → gave food → dogs learned
  - Sound → food X → dogs responded → lost interest
- Conclusions about conditioning
  - Dogs had interest in food, no interest in sound
  - Developed response to sound & food
  - After conditioning → response to sound itself
- Experiment 2nd time → dogs learned faster
- Used other signals → produced same result

Listen to part of a lecture in a psychology class.

P: [12]Today, we'll talk about a famous idea in psychology. It was developed through the experiments of Ivan Pavlov, a Russian scientist, in the early 20th century. [12]Specifically, I'm referring to classical conditioning.

But first, what is psychological conditioning in general? Uh, it is a psychological term for a process called associative learning. Associative learning is when a person or an animal learns to associate or connect two ideas, events, or actions. So, for example, a person who has learned that exams are stressful can feel stress simply by thinking of exams. Or a wild animal that finds food in garbage cans will learn to associate all garbage cans with food. Classical conditioning is similar, but it is based on controlled experiments.

Now, going back to Pavlov, he used dogs in his experiments. In his first experiment, he taught dogs to respond to a signal. [13C]First, Pavlov introduced a sound, which was the sound of a whistle. [13D]After making the sound, he gave the dogs the food. He did this several times. Soon, the dogs learned to associate the sound with food. [13B]So whenever Pavlov made the sound, the dogs responded because they expected to receive food. They responded to the sound even when there was no food. Next, Pavlov tried something else… Uh, he continued to make the sound, but he did not provide the dogs with food. At first, the dogs responded to the sound. But they lost interest in the sound because there was no food. [13A]Eventually, the dogs did not respond to the sound at all. This clearly proved that the dogs had learned to associate the sound with food. And Pavlov realized that the sound was not really important. The dogs were only interested in the sound because they associated it with food.

This led Pavlov to make several conclusions about conditioning. First, before conditioning, the dogs had an interest in food. At the same time, they had no interest in the sound. Second, during conditioning, the dogs developed an automatic response to the combination of a sound and food. Third, after conditioning, the dogs had an automatic response to the sound itself. [17]However, when the food was taken away, the automatic response to the sound gradually disappeared. His conclusions make sense, no? I mean, they are very convincing…

Still, Pavlov continued his research. And he found out something else. [14]When he repeated the experiment a second time, the dogs learned to associate the sound with food much faster. This suggested that the original conditioning was not completely gone. Somehow, the dogs "remembered" the original experiments.

Later, Pavlov used other signals besides sound. And, in each case, the experiments produced the same result. So Pavlov concluded that dogs could learn to associate any signal at all with an item that they wanted, such as food.

Now, imagine doing a simple experiment. Let's say that you give people the option to choose between two colors: green or orange. Whenever people choose green, they receive money. And whenever they choose orange, they receive nothing. According to classical conditioning, most people will learn to choose green because they associate the color green with the money. [15]And the color that you use isn't important. Just like in Pavlov's experiments, the signal is less important than what it's associated with. Therefore, if you use the color blue instead of green, people will choose blue because they associate it with the money.

S: Yes, I get it. But this conditioning seems like common sense. Why does this kind of learning have a special term? And why is it called classical?

P: [16]Actually, I think it only seems like common sense now because Pavlov's experiments proved it first... It wasn't so obvious before... And there's a good reason we call Pavlov's work classical. Since then, other forms of conditioning have been discovered. But we'll discuss those next time...

심리학 강의의 일부를 들으시오.

P: 오늘, 우리는 심리학에서 유명한 개념에 관해 이야기할 거예요. 그것은 20세기 초에 러시아 과학자인 이반 파블로프의 실험을 통해 개발되었죠. 구체적으로, 고전적 조건 형성을 말하는 거예요.

하지만 먼저, 일반적으로 심리적 조건 형성이란 무엇일까요? 어, 그것은 연상 학습이라고 불리는 과정을 위한 심리학 용어예요. 연상 학습은 사람이나 동물이 두 개의 생각, 사건, 혹은 행동을 연관시키거나 연결하는 것을 배울 때입니다. 자, 예를 들어, 시험이 스트레스가 많다는 것을 알게 된 사람은 시험에 대해 생각하는 것만으로 스트레스를 느낄 수 있어요. 혹은 쓰레기통에서 먹이를 찾는 야생 동물은 모든 쓰레기통을 먹이와 연관시키도록 학습할 거예요. 고전적 조건 형성은 이와 비슷하지만, 그것은 통제된 실험에 기반해요.

자, 파블로프로 돌아가서, 그는 그의 실험에 개를 이용했어요. 그의 첫 번째 실험에서, 그는 개들에게 신호에 반응하도록 가르쳤어요. 먼저, 파블로프는 휘파람 소리였던 소리를 접하게 했어요. 그 소리를 낸 후에, 그는 개들에게 먹이를 주었어요. 그는 이것을 여러 번 했죠. 곧, 개들은 그 소리를 먹이와 연관시키도록 학습했어요. 그래서 파블로프가 그 소리를 낼 때마다, 개들은 먹이를 받기를 기대했기 때문에 반응했어요. 그것들은 먹이가 없을 때조차 그 소리에 반응했어요. 다음으로, 파블로프는 다른 것을 시도했습니다... 어, 그는 계속해서 그 소리를 냈지만, 개들에게 먹이를 주지 않았어요. 처음에, 개들은 그 소리에 반응했어요. 하지만 먹이가 없었기 때문에 그것들은 소리에 관심을 잃었어요. 결국, 개들은 그 소리에 전혀 반응하지 않았어요. 이것은 개들이 그 소리를 먹이에 연관시키도록 학습했다는 것을 분명히 증명했어요. 그리고 파블로프는 그 소리가 그렇게 중요하지 않다는 것을 깨달았어요. 개들은 오직 그 소리를 먹이와 연관시켰기 때문에 그것에 관심이 있었어요.

이것은 파블로프가 조건 형성에 관한 몇 가지의 결론을 내리도록 했습니다. 첫 번째로, 조건 형성 전에, 개들은 먹이에 관심이 있었죠. 동시에, 그것들은 그 소리에 관심이 없었어요. 두 번째로, 조건 형성 동안, 개들은 소리와 먹이의 조합에 자동적인 반응을 발달시켰어요. 세 번째로, 조건 형성 이후에, 개들은 소리 자체에 자동적인 반응을 보였어요. 하지만, 먹이가 치워지자, 소리에 대한 자동적인 반응은 점차 사라졌죠. 그의 결론은 말이 돼요, 그렇지 않나요? 그러니까, 그것들은 매우 설득력 있어요...

하지만, 파블로프는 그의 연구를 계속했어요. 그리고 그는 다른 것을 알아냈죠. 그가 그 실험을 두 번째로 반복했을 때, 개들은 그 소리를 훨씬 더 빨리 먹이와 연관시키도록 학습했어요. 이것은 원래의 조건 형성이 완전히 없어진 것이 아니라는 것을 시사했어요. 어떻게든, 개들은 원래 실험을 "기억"했어요.

나중에, 파블로프는 소리 이외에도 다른 신호들을 이용했어요. 그리고, 각각의 경우에, 실험은 동일한 결과를 낳았죠. 그래서 파블로프는 개들이 어떠한 신호라도 먹이 같이 그것들이 원하는 물건과 연관시키도록 학습할 수 있다고 결론 내렸어요.

이제, 간단한 실험을 한다고 상상해 보세요. 여러분이 사람들에게 녹색과 주황색 두 가지 색 중에 선택할 수 있는 선택지를 준다고 가정해 보죠. 사람들이 녹색을 고를 때마다, 그들은 돈을 받아요. 그리고 그들이 주황색을 고를 때마다, 그들은 아무것도 받지 않아요. 고전적 조건 형성에 따르면, 대부분의 사람들은 그들이 녹색을 돈과 연관시키기 때문에 녹색을 선택하도록 학습할 거예요. 그리고 여러분이 사용하는 색은 중요하지 않아요. 파블로프의 실험에서와 동일하게, 신호는 그것이 연관되는 것보다 덜 중요해요. 그래서, 여러분이 녹색 대신 파란색을 이용하면, 사람들은 그들이 그것을 돈과 연관시키기 때문에 파란색을 선택할 거예요.

S: 네, 이해했어요. 하지만 이 조건 형성은 상식처럼 보이는데요. 이런 종류의 학습이 왜 특수한 용어를 가지고 있나요? 그리고 그것이 왜 고전적이라고 불리나요?

P: 사실, 파블로프의 실험이 그것을 먼저 증명했기 때문에 이제 그것이 그저 상식처럼 보인다고 생각해요... 전에는 그것이 그렇게 분명하지 않았어요... 그리고 우리가 파블로프의 연구를 고전적이라고 부르는 데는 그만한 이유가 있어요. 그 이후로, 다른 형태의 조건 형성이 발견되었어요. 하지만 그것들은 다음 시간에 논의할 거예요.

conditioning 뗑 조건 형성   associative 휑 연상의
controlled 휑 통제된   respond 됨 반응하다   conclusion 뗑 결론
automatic 휑 자동적인   combination 뗑 조합
gradually 뮈 점차   convincing 휑 설득력 있는
completely 뮈 완전히   common sense 상식
obvious 휑 분명한

12 강의의 주된 목적은 무엇인가?

(A) 서로 다른 실험 방법들을 비교하기 위해

(B) 심리학에서 유명한 개념을 논의하기 위해

(C) 러시아 심리학의 기원을 설명하기 위해

(D) 최초의 심리학 실험들을 조사하기 위해

13 교수는 파블로프의 첫 번째 실험의 단계들을 설명한다. 아래의 단계들을 올바른 순서대로 나열하시오.
각 답변을 해당하는 곳으로 끌어다 놓으시오.

단계 1	(C) 파블로프가 소리를 접하게 했다.
단계 2	(D) 파블로프가 개에게 먹이를 주었다.
단계 3	(B) 개들이 먹이가 있거나 있지 않을 때 반응했다.
단계 4	(A) 개들이 소리에 반응하지 않았다.

14 교수에 따르면, 파블로프가 그의 실험을 반복했을 때 어떤 일이 일어났는가?

(A) 결과가 그대로였다.

(B) 개들이 처음에 먹이를 거부했다.

(C) 개들이 전보다 빠르게 학습했다.

(D) 조건 형성이 그만큼 오래 지속되지 않았다.

15 교수는 왜 파란색을 언급하는가?

    (A) 어떠한 신호라도 조건 형성에 사용될 수 있음을 강조하기 위해

    (B) 사람들이 특정 색을 선호하도록 조건 형성된다는 것을
         보여주기 위해

    (C) 실험이 보이는 것보다 덜 간단하다는 것을 시사하기 위해

    (D) 실험의 결과가 정확한지 시험하기 위해

16 파블로프의 실험에 대한 교수의 태도는 무엇인가?

    (A) 그녀는 그것들이 창의적인 방식으로 행해졌다고 생각한다.

    (B) 그녀는 그것들이 학습에 대해 새로운 것을 밝혀냈다고
         생각한다.

    (C) 그녀는 그것들이 다른 실험들과 비교되어야 한다고 생각한다.

    (D) 그녀는 파블로프가 그것들을 수행한 최초의 사람인지
         확신하지 못한다.

강의의 일부를 다시 듣고 질문에 답하시오.

P: However, when the food was taken away, the automatic response to the sound gradually disappeared. His conclusions make sense, no? I mean, they are very convincing...

17 교수는 왜 이렇게 말하는가:

P: His conclusions make sense, no?

    (A) 심리학자에 의해 사용된 방법을 비판하기 위해

    (B) 실험의 결과가 논리적이라는 것을 강조하기 위해

    (C) 결론의 정확성에 의문을 제기하기 위해

    (D) 실험에 더 많은 연구가 필요하다는 것을 시사하기 위해

MEMO

MEMO

HACKERS

APEX
LISTENING
for the
TOEFL iBT® Expert

Answer Book